Yamada-kun and the Seven Witches

7

Miki Yoshikawa

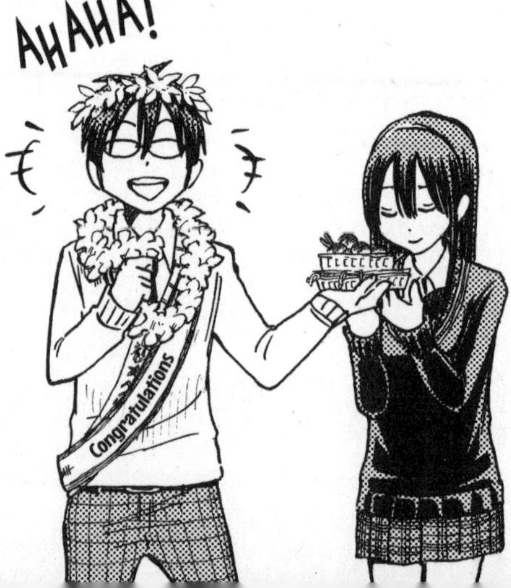
AHAHA!
Congratulations

CONTENTS

CHAPTER 52: Its ingredients are different!!

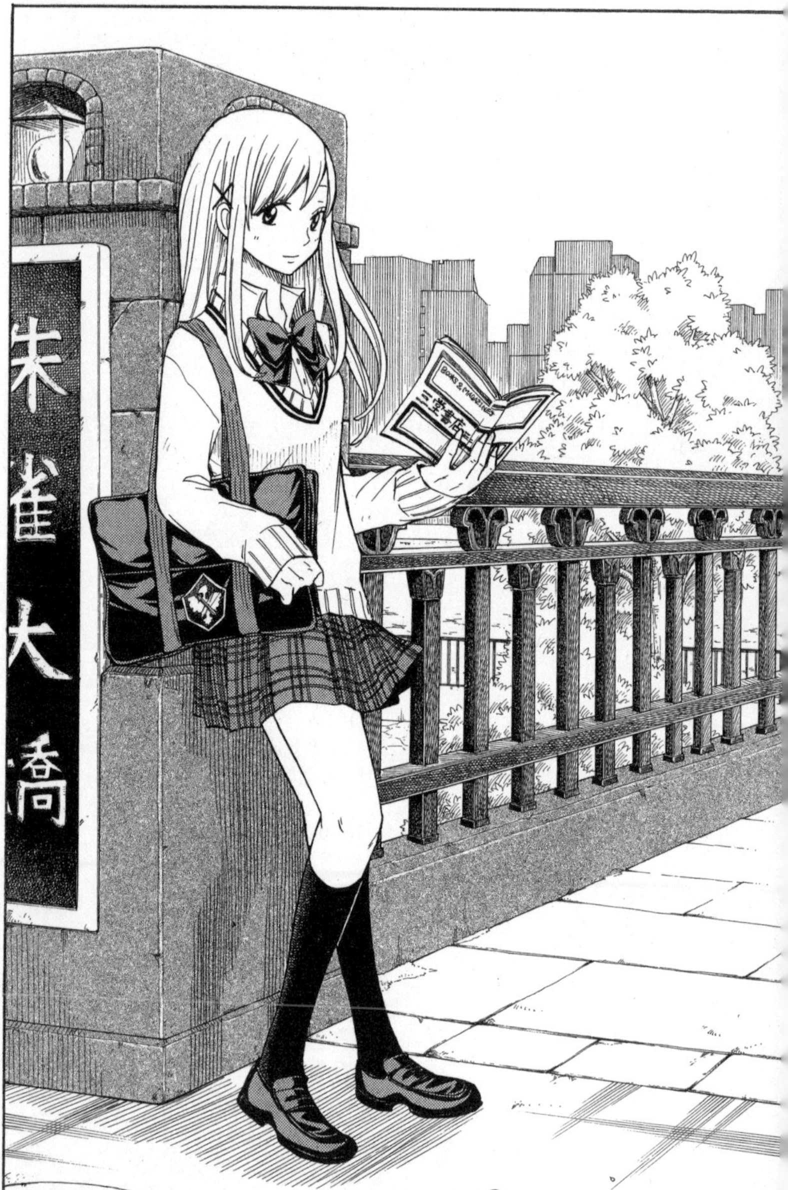

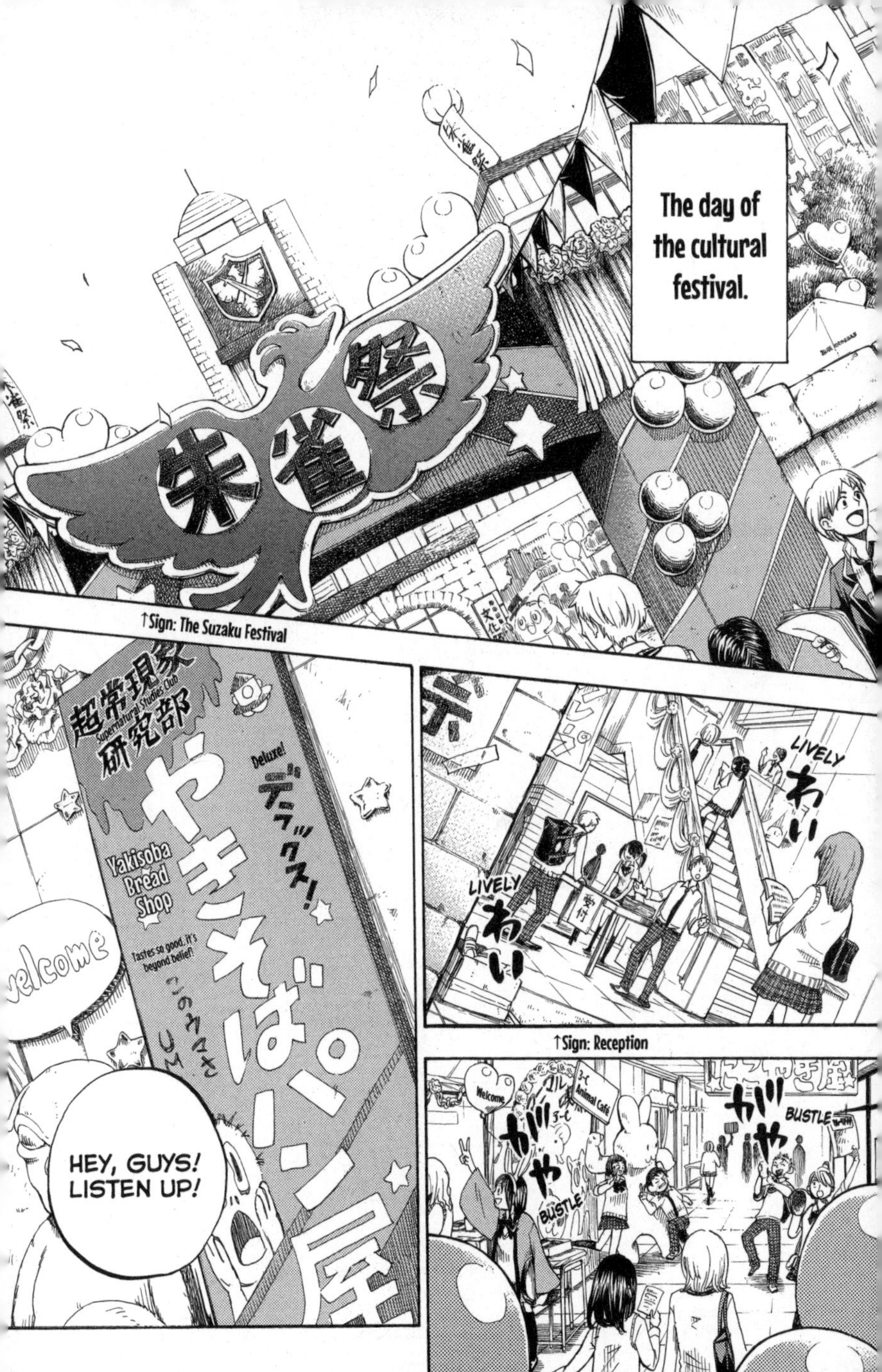
The day of the cultural festival.
↑Sign: The Suzaku Festival
LIVELY
LIVELY
↑Sign: Reception
Welcome
Animal Café
BUSTLE
BUSTLE
Supernatural Studies Club
Deluxe!
Yakisoba Bread Shop
Tastes so good, it's beyond belief!
welcome
HEY, GUYS! LISTEN UP!

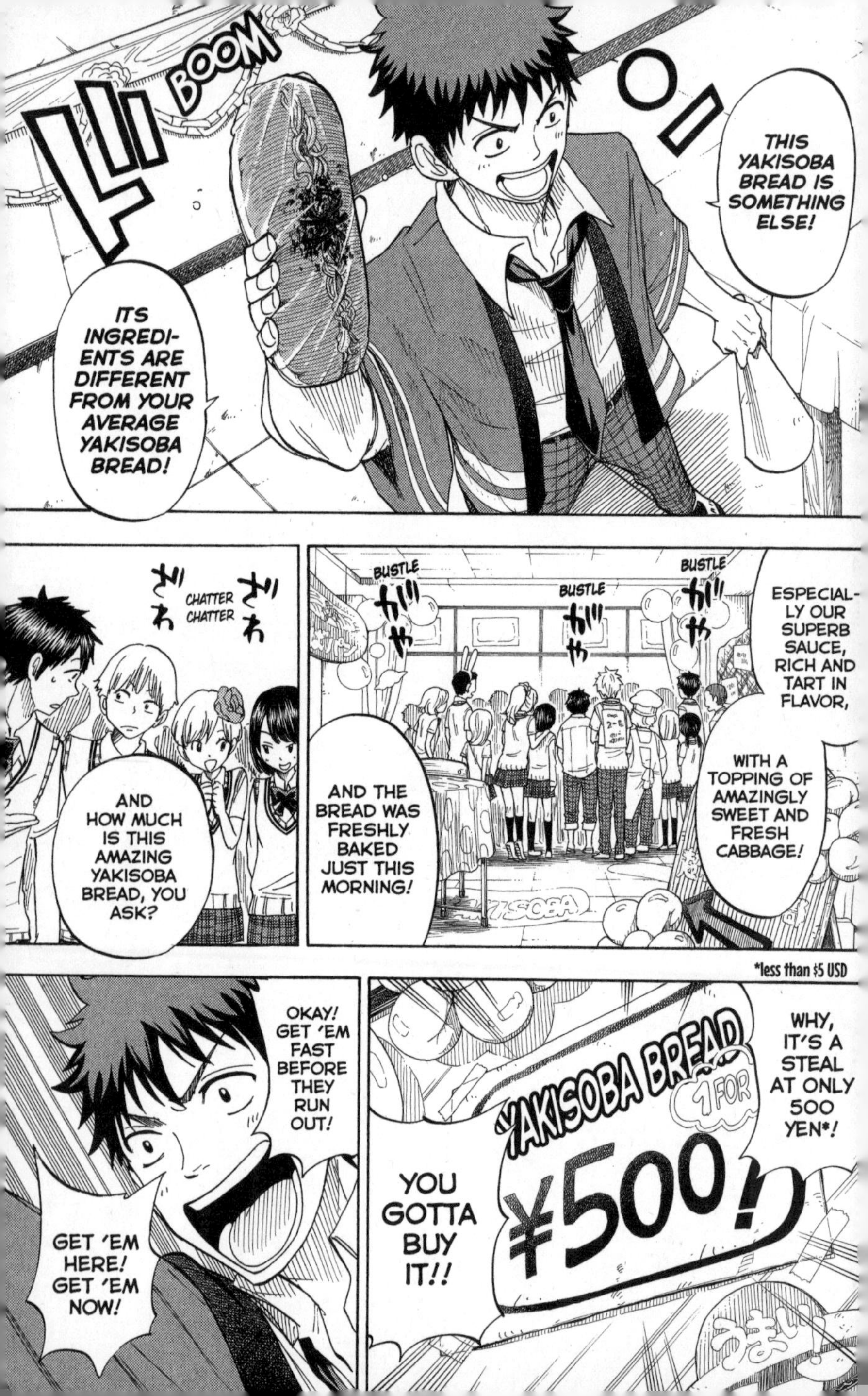
THIS YAKISOBA BREAD IS SOMETHING ELSE!
BOOM
ITS INGREDIENTS ARE DIFFERENT FROM YOUR AVERAGE YAKISOBA BREAD!
BUSTLE
ガヤ
ESPECIALLY OUR SUPERB SAUCE, RICH AND TART IN FLAVOR,
WITH A TOPPING OF AMAZINGLY SWEET AND FRESH CABBAGE!
BUSTLE
ガヤ
BUSTLE
ガヤ
AND THE BREAD WAS FRESHLY BAKED JUST THIS MORNING!
ざわ ざわ
CHATTER CHATTER
AND HOW MUCH IS THIS AMAZING YAKISOBA BREAD, YOU ASK?
*less than $5 USD
WHY, IT'S A STEAL AT ONLY 500 YEN*!
YAKISOBA BREAD
1 FOR
¥500!
YOU GOTTA BUY IT!!
うまい!
OKAY! GET 'EM FAST BEFORE THEY RUN OUT!
GET 'EM HERE! GET 'EM NOW!

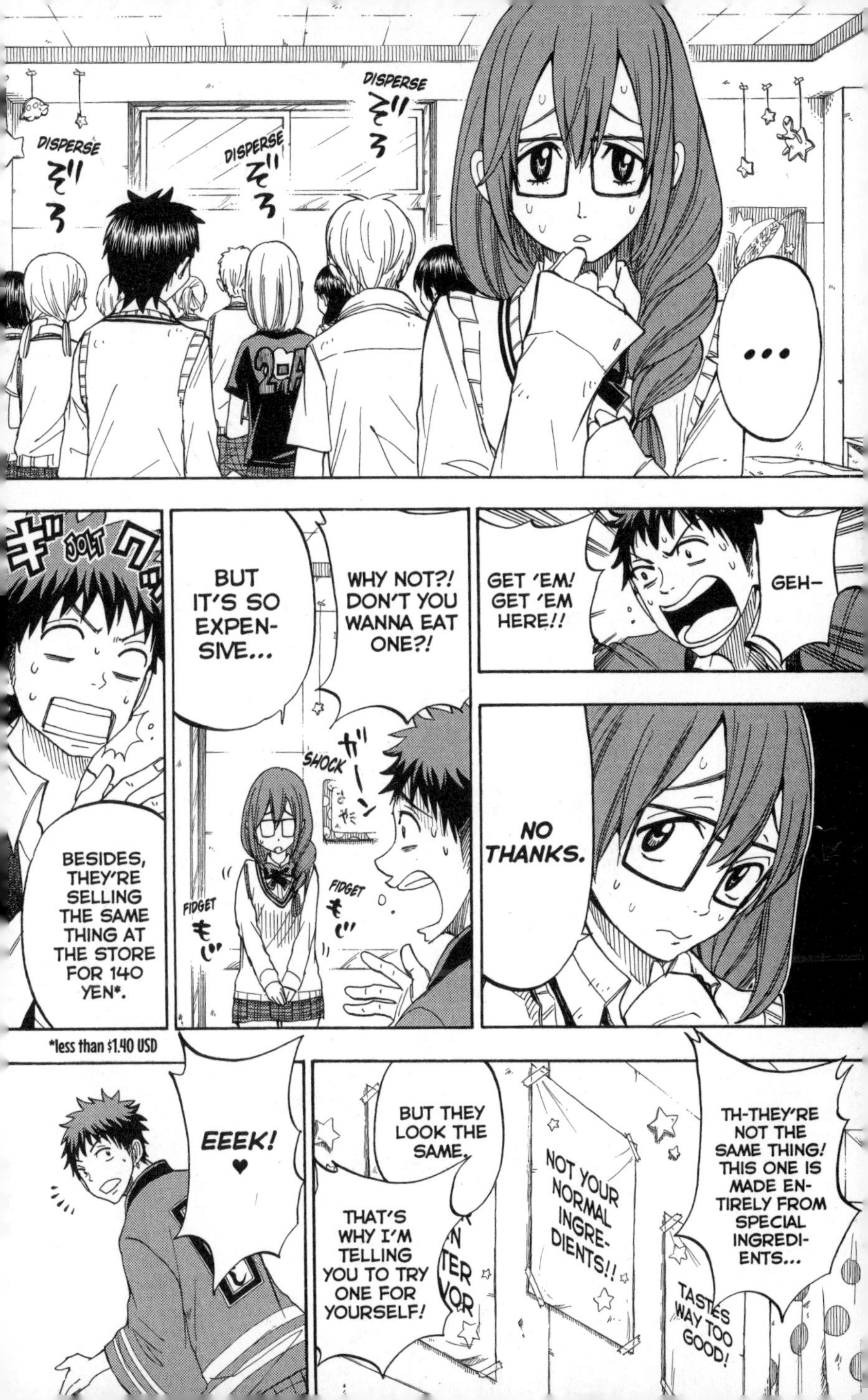
DISPERSE
ぞろ
DISPERSE
ぞろ
DISPERSE
ぞろ
...
GEH—
GET 'EM! GET 'EM HERE!!
NO THANKS.
WHY NOT?! DON'T YOU WANNA EAT ONE?!
BUT IT'S SO EXPEN-SIVE...
SHOCK
ガーン
FIDGET
もじ
FIDGET
もじ
ギクッ
JOLT
BESIDES, THEY'RE SELLING THE SAME THING AT THE STORE FOR 140 YEN*.
*less than $1.40 USD
TH-THEY'RE NOT THE SAME THING! THIS ONE IS MADE EN-TIRELY FROM SPECIAL INGREDI-ENTS...
TASTES WAY TOO GOOD!
NOT YOUR NORMAL INGRE-DIENTS!!
BUT THEY LOOK THE SAME.
THAT'S WHY I'M TELLING YOU TO TRY ONE FOR YOURSELF!
EEEK! ♥

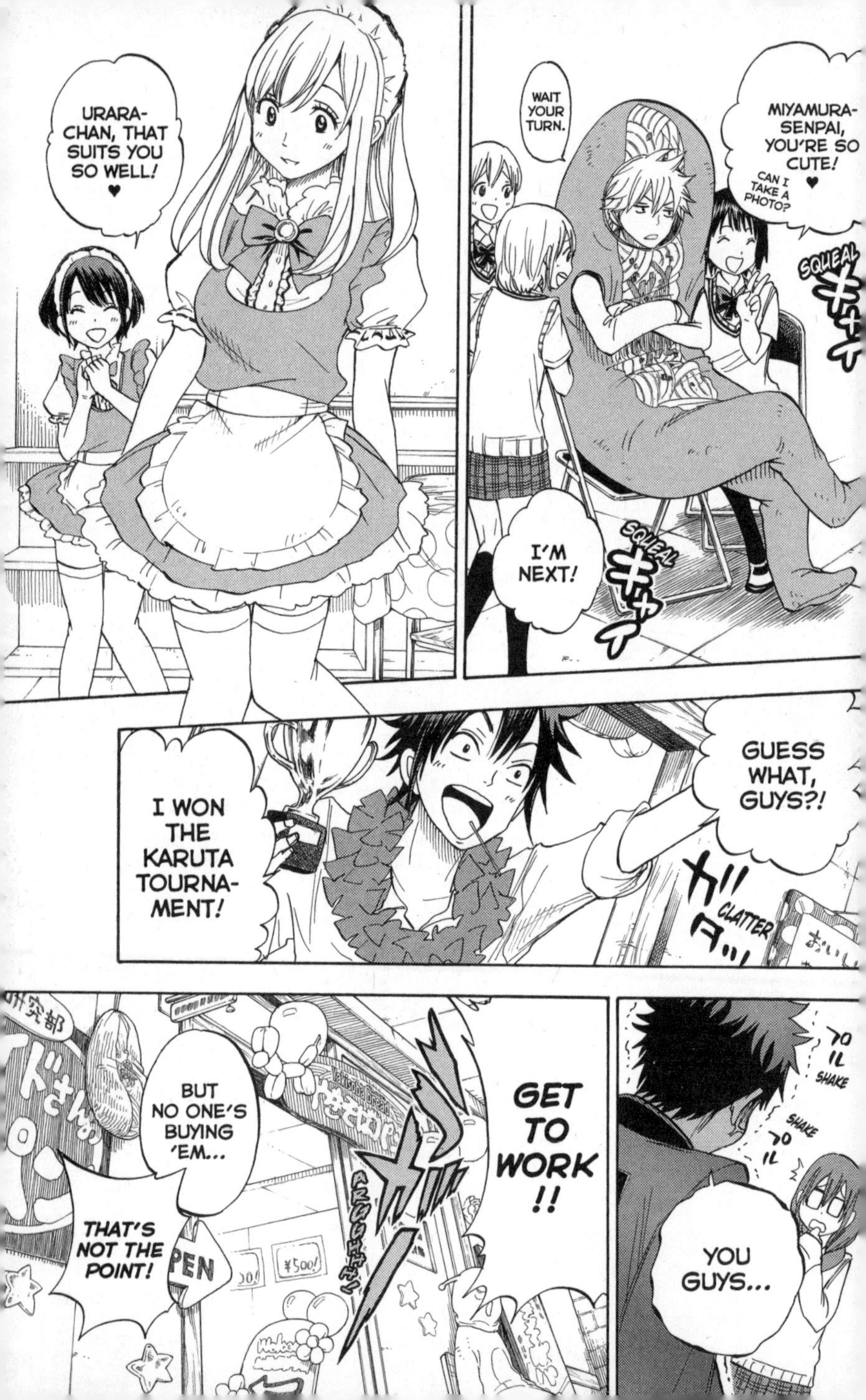
MIYAMURA-SENPAI, YOU'RE SO CUTE! ♥
CAN I TAKE A PHOTO?
SQUEAL
WAIT YOUR TURN.
SQUEAL
I'M NEXT!
URARA-CHAN, THAT SUITS YOU SO WELL! ♥
GUESS WHAT, GUYS?!
CLATTER
I WON THE KARUTA TOURNAMENT!
SHAKE
SHAKE
YOU GUYS...
GET TO WORK!!
Yakisoba Bread
BUT NO ONE'S BUYING 'EM...
THAT'S NOT THE POINT!
PEN
¥500!

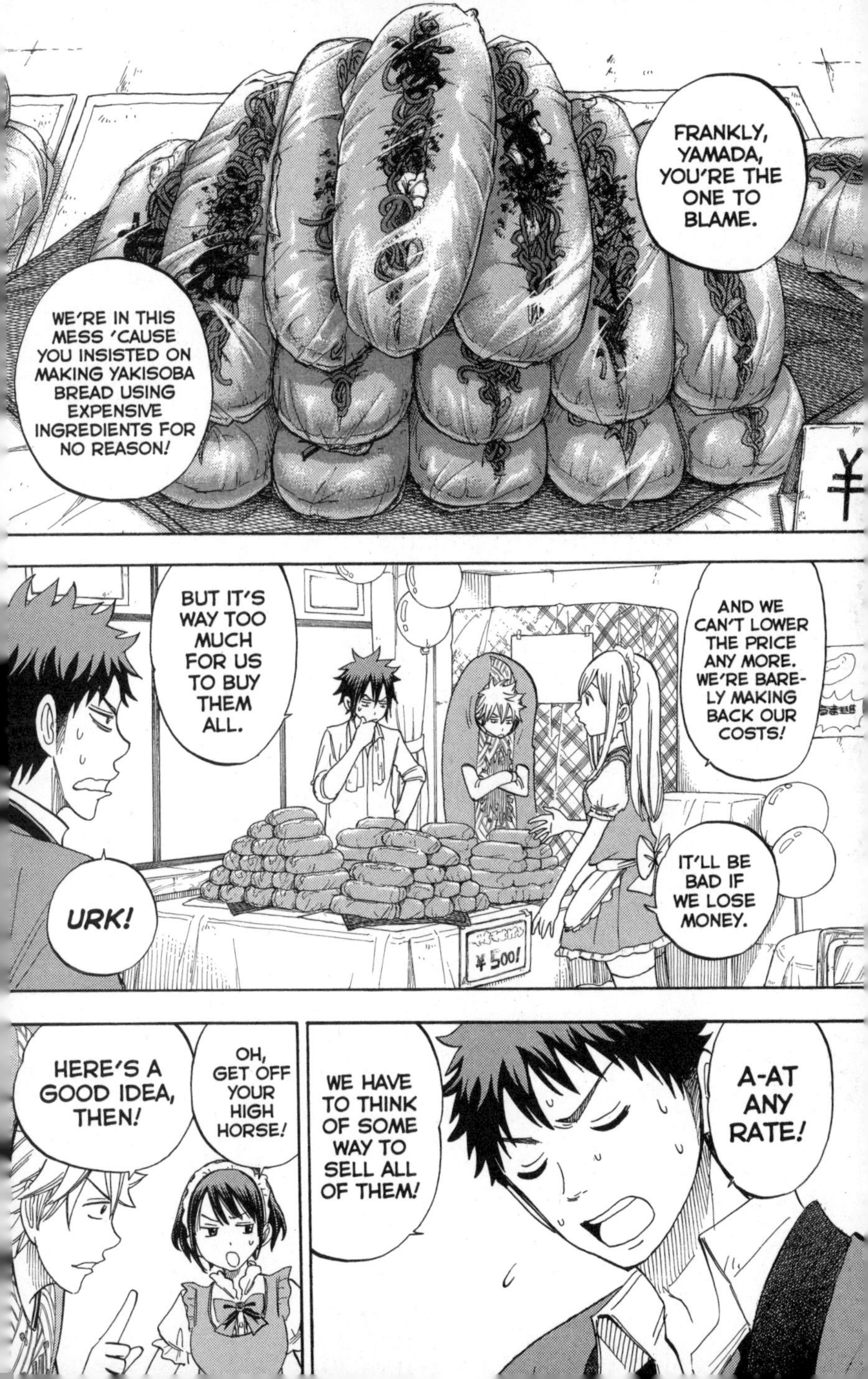
FRANKLY, YAMADA, YOU'RE THE ONE TO BLAME.
WE'RE IN THIS MESS 'CAUSE YOU INSISTED ON MAKING YAKISOBA BREAD USING EXPENSIVE INGREDIENTS FOR NO REASON!
AND WE CAN'T LOWER THE PRICE ANY MORE. WE'RE BARELY MAKING BACK OUR COSTS!
IT'LL BE BAD IF WE LOSE MONEY.
¥500!
BUT IT'S WAY TOO MUCH FOR US TO BUY THEM ALL.
URK!
A-AT ANY RATE!
WE HAVE TO THINK OF SOME WAY TO SELL ALL OF THEM!
OH, GET OFF YOUR HIGH HORSE!
HERE'S A GOOD IDEA, THEN!

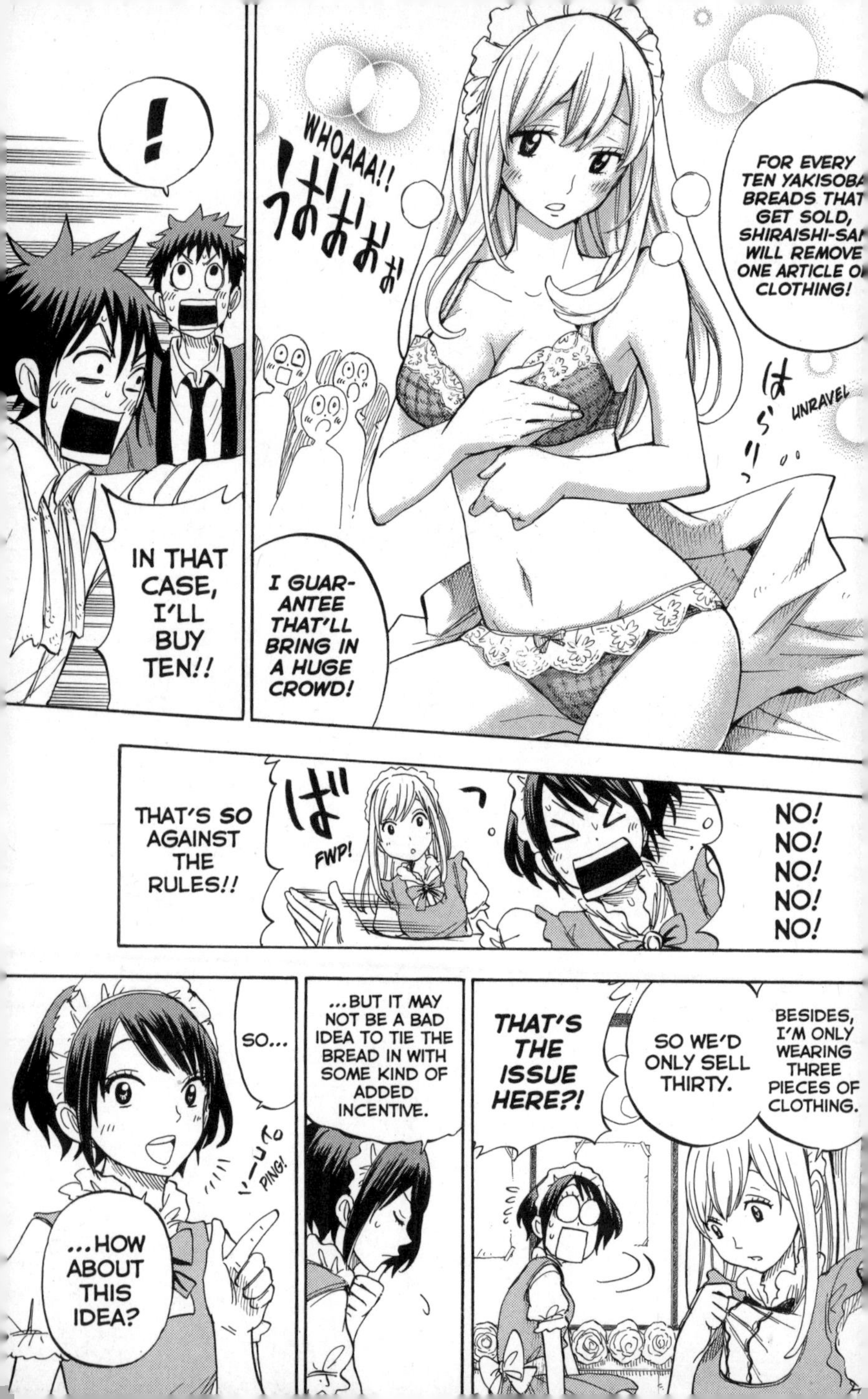
FOR EVERY TEN YAKISOBA BREADS THAT GET SOLD, SHIRAISHI-SAN WILL REMOVE ONE ARTICLE OF CLOTHING!
はらりっ
UNRAVEL
うおおおぉぉ
WHOAAA!!
I GUARANTEE THAT'LL BRING IN A HUGE CROWD!
!
IN THAT CASE, I'LL BUY TEN!!
NO! NO! NO! NO! NO!
ばっ
FWP!
THAT'S SO AGAINST THE RULES!!
BESIDES, I'M ONLY WEARING THREE PIECES OF CLOTHING.
SO WE'D ONLY SELL THIRTY.
THAT'S THE ISSUE HERE?!
...BUT IT MAY NOT BE A BAD IDEA TO TIE THE BREAD IN WITH SOME KIND OF ADDED INCENTIVE.
SO...
ピコーン
PING!
...HOW ABOUT THIS IDEA?

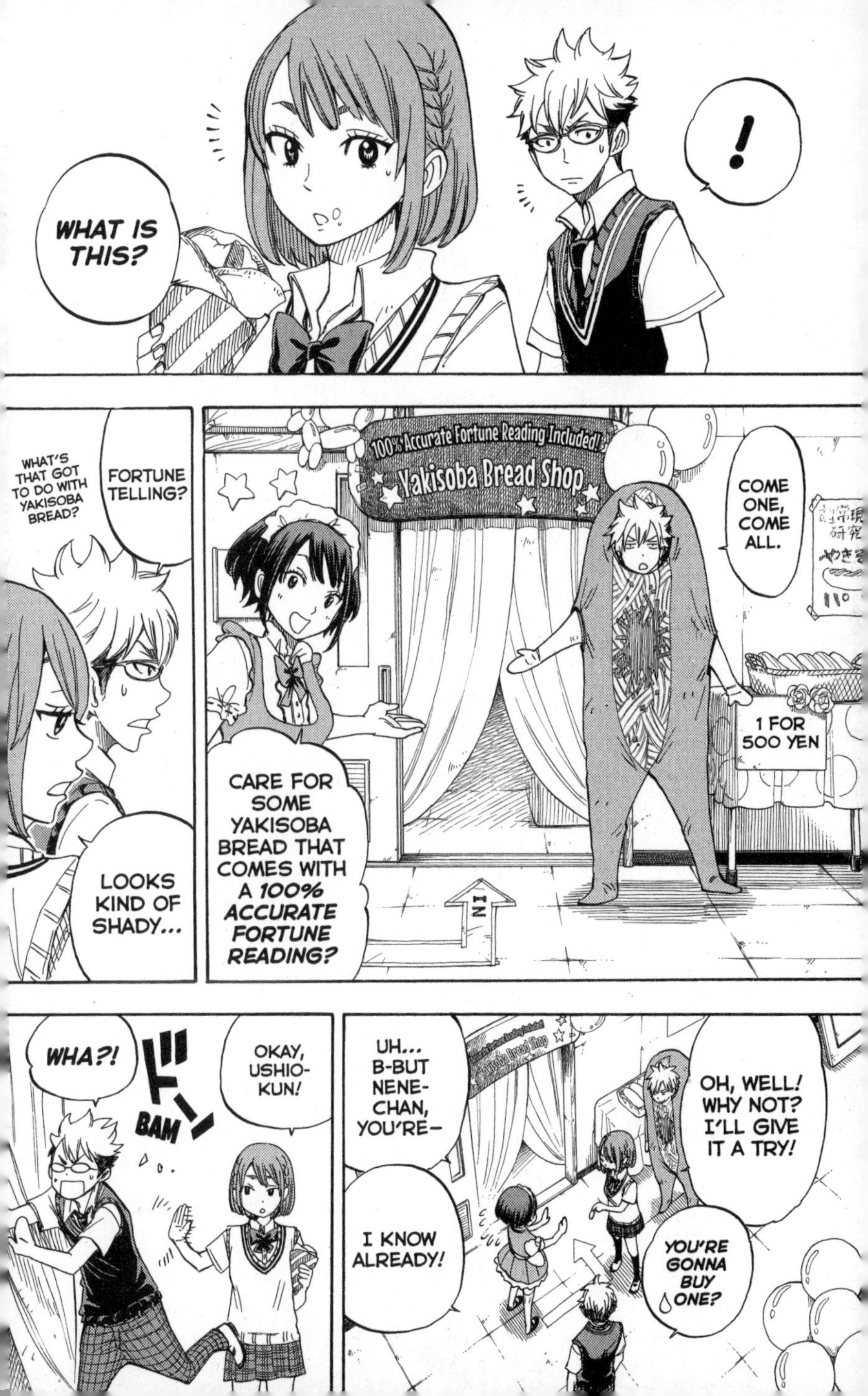

!
WHAT IS THIS?
100% Accurate Fortune Reading Included!
Yakisoba Bread Shop
COME ONE, COME ALL.
1 FOR 500 YEN
CARE FOR SOME YAKISOBA BREAD THAT COMES WITH A 100% ACCURATE FORTUNE READING?
IN
FORTUNE TELLING?
WHAT'S THAT GOT TO DO WITH YAKISOBA BREAD?
LOOKS KIND OF SHADY...
Yakisoba Bread Shop
OH, WELL! WHY NOT? I'LL GIVE IT A TRY!
UH... B-BUT NENE-CHAN, YOU'RE–
YOU'RE GONNA BUY ONE?
I KNOW ALREADY!
OKAY, USHIO-KUN!
ド
BAM
WHA?!

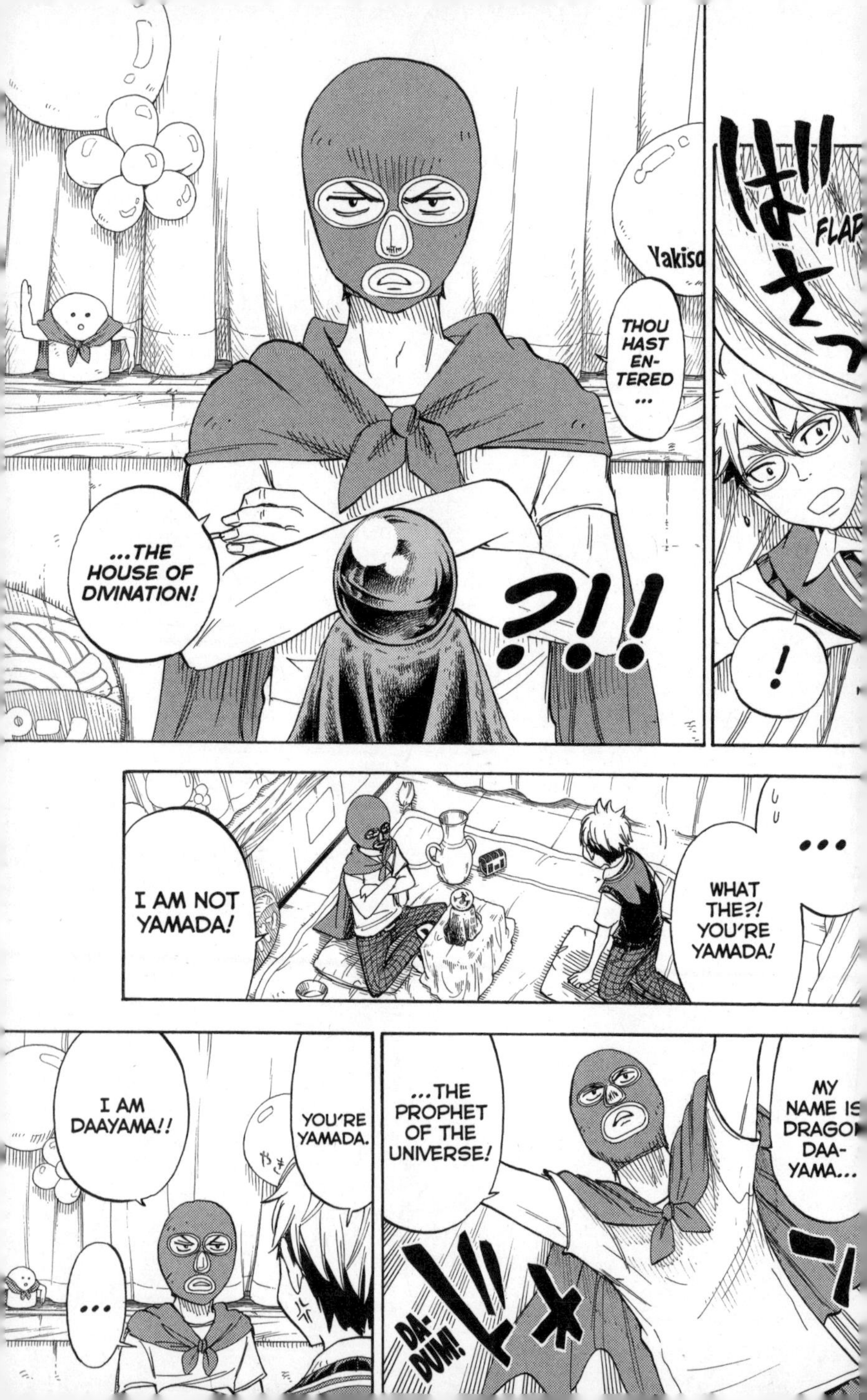
ばさっ
FLAP
!
Yakiso
THOU HAST EN-TERED...
...THE HOUSE OF DIVINATION!
?!!
...
WHAT THE?! YOU'RE YAMADA!
I AM NOT YAMADA!
MY NAME IS DRAGO DAA-YAMA...
...THE PROPHET OF THE UNIVERSE!
DA-DUM!
YOU'RE YAMADA.
I AM DAAYAMA!!
...

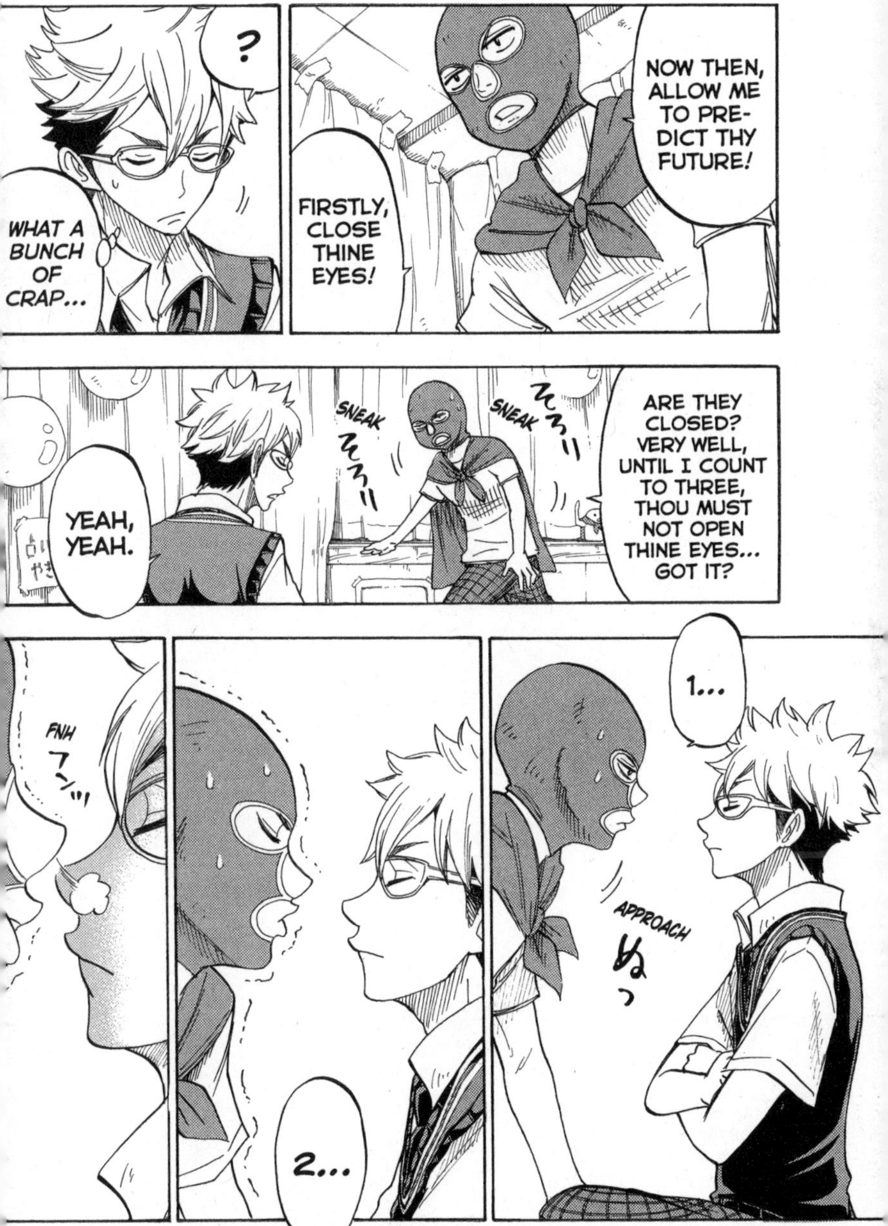
NOW THEN, ALLOW ME TO PRE-DICT THY FUTURE!
FIRSTLY, CLOSE THINE EYES!
?
WHAT A BUNCH OF CRAP...
ARE THEY CLOSED? VERY WELL, UNTIL I COUNT TO THREE, THOU MUST NOT OPEN THINE EYES... GOT IT?
SNEAK
SNEAK
YEAH, YEAH.
1...
APPROACH
ぬっ
2...
FNH
フンッ

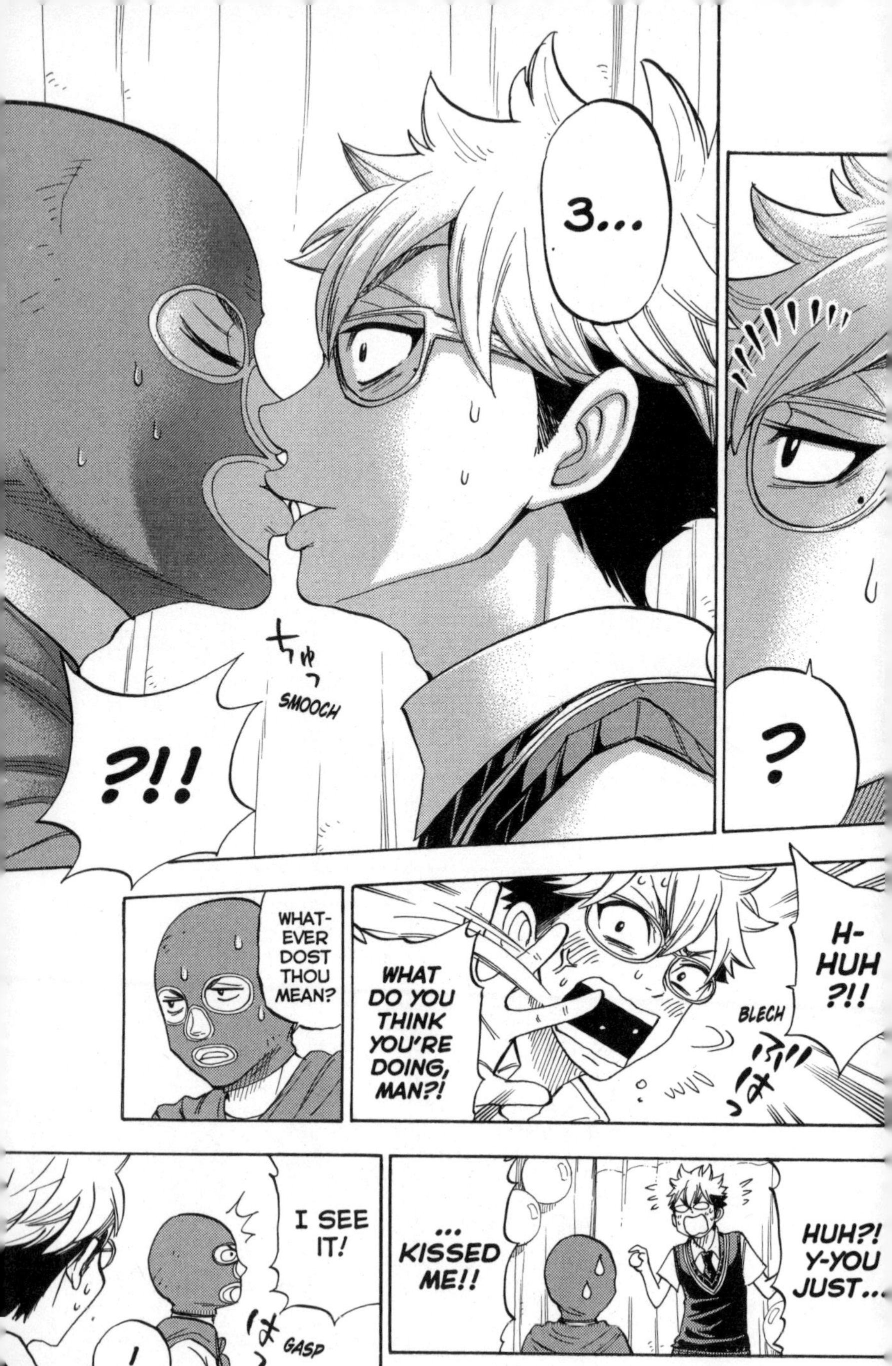
?
3...
ちゅっ
SMOOCH
?!!
H-HUH?!!
WHAT DO YOU THINK YOU'RE DOING, MAN?!
BLECH
ぷはっ
WHAT-EVER DOST THOU MEAN?
HUH?! Y-YOU JUST...
...KISSED ME!!
I SEE IT!
はっ
GASP
!

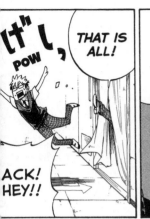

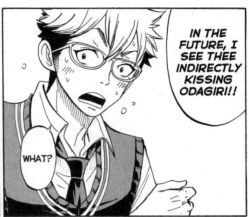

IN THE FUTURE, I SEE THEE INDIRECTLY KISSING ODAGIRI!!
WHAT?
THAT IS ALL!
げし
POW
ACK! HEY!!
...OF COURSE! SO YOU GUYS USED SARUSHIMA-SAN'S POWER!
CHEW CHEW
ムグムグ
GEEZ! YOU GUYS SURE THINK UP SOME LAME STUFF!
AHEM!
YOU KNOW IT'S A GOOD IDEA!
STILL... THAT BOY... HOW MANY PEOPLE IS HE PLANNING ON KISSING, EXACTLY?
LICK
ペロッ
LET'S GO, USHIO-KUN!
OH, AND HAVE THE REST! I DON'T NEED IT.
すた
STEP
すた
STEP
HUH?
...

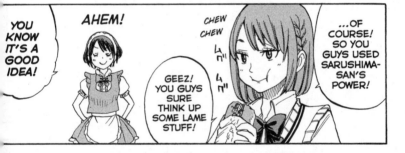

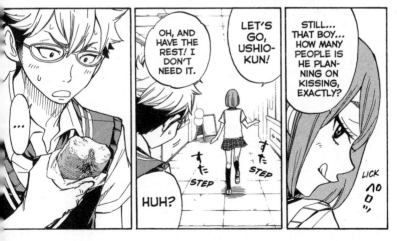

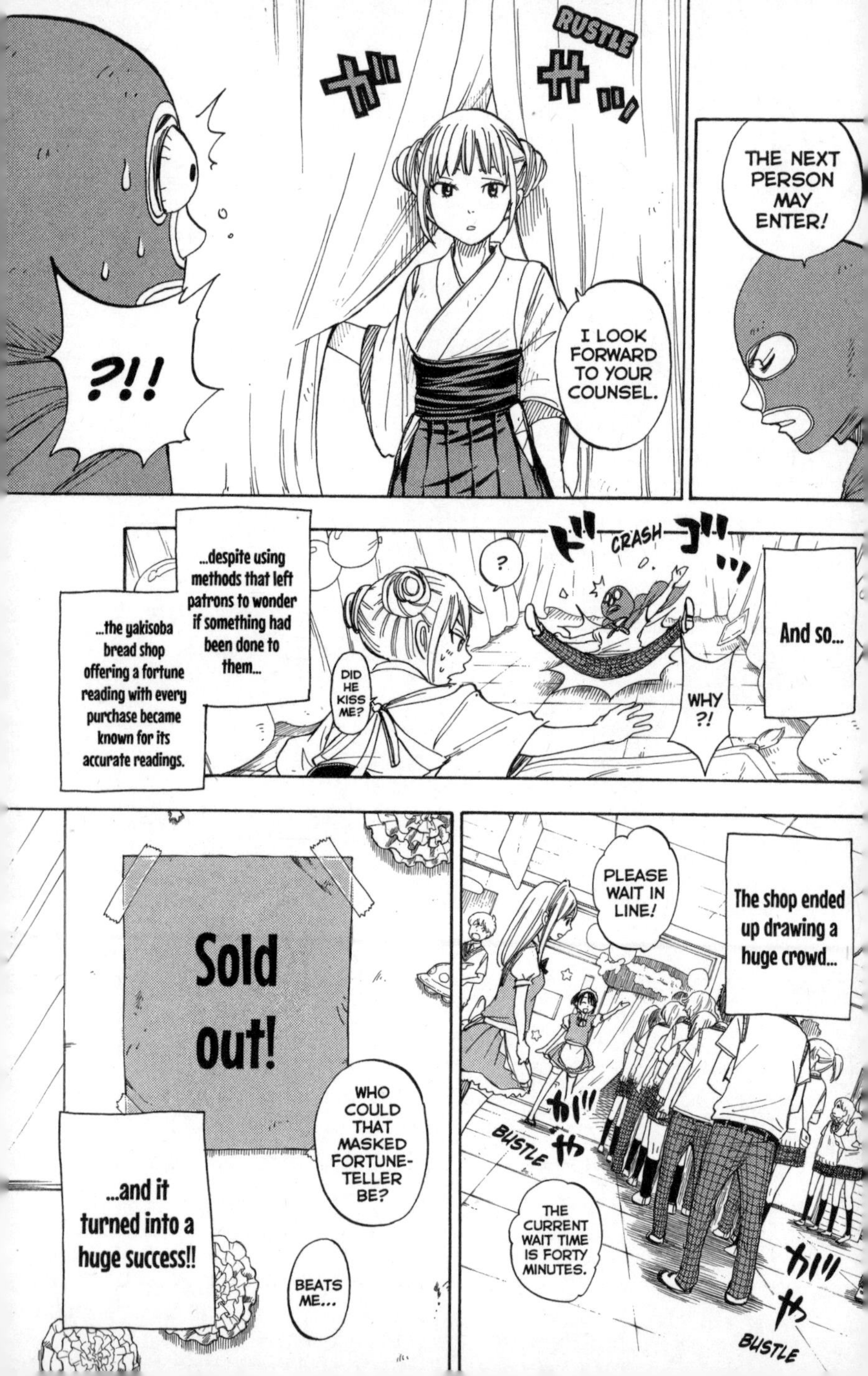
THE NEXT PERSON MAY ENTER!
RUSTLE
I LOOK FORWARD TO YOUR COUNSEL.
?!!
And so...
CRASH
WHY?!
?
DID HE KISS ME?
...despite using methods that left patrons to wonder if something had been done to them...
...the yakisoba bread shop offering a fortune reading with every purchase became known for its accurate readings.
The shop ended up drawing a huge crowd...
PLEASE WAIT IN LINE!
BUSTLE
THE CURRENT WAIT TIME IS FORTY MINUTES.
BUSTLE
Sold out!
WHO COULD THAT MASKED FORTUNE-TELLER BE?
...and it turned into a huge success!!
BEATS ME...

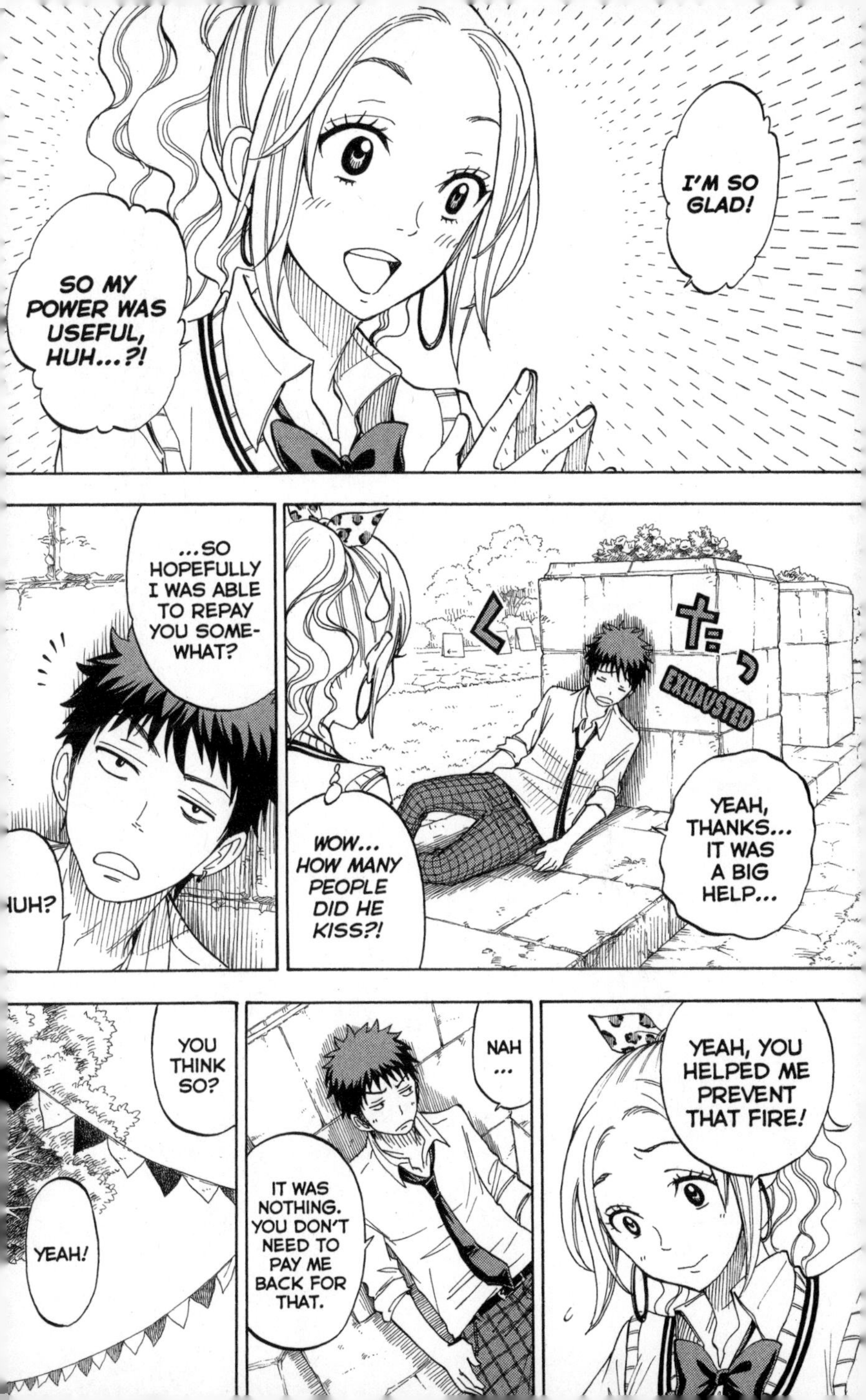
I'M SO GLAD!
SO MY POWER WAS USEFUL, HUH...?!
YEAH, THANKS... IT WAS A BIG HELP...
EXHAUSTED
WOW... HOW MANY PEOPLE DID HE KISS?!
...SO HOPEFULLY I WAS ABLE TO REPAY YOU SOME-WHAT?
YEAH, YOU HELPED ME PREVENT THAT FIRE!
NAH...
IT WAS NOTHING. YOU DON'T NEED TO PAY ME BACK FOR THAT.
YOU THINK SO?
YEAH!

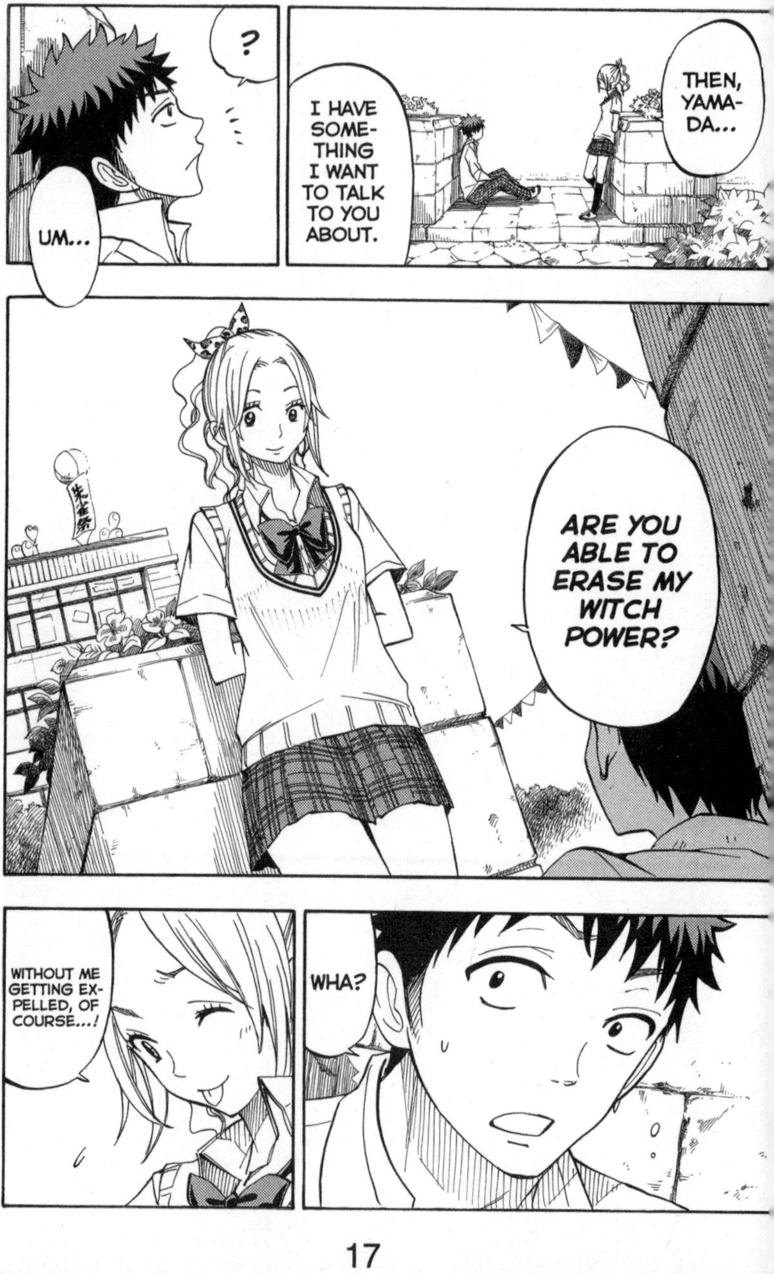
THEN, YAMADA...
I HAVE SOMETHING I WANT TO TALK TO YOU ABOUT.
?
UM...
ARE YOU ABLE TO ERASE MY WITCH POWER?
WHA?
WITHOUT ME GETTING EXPELLED, OF COURSE...!

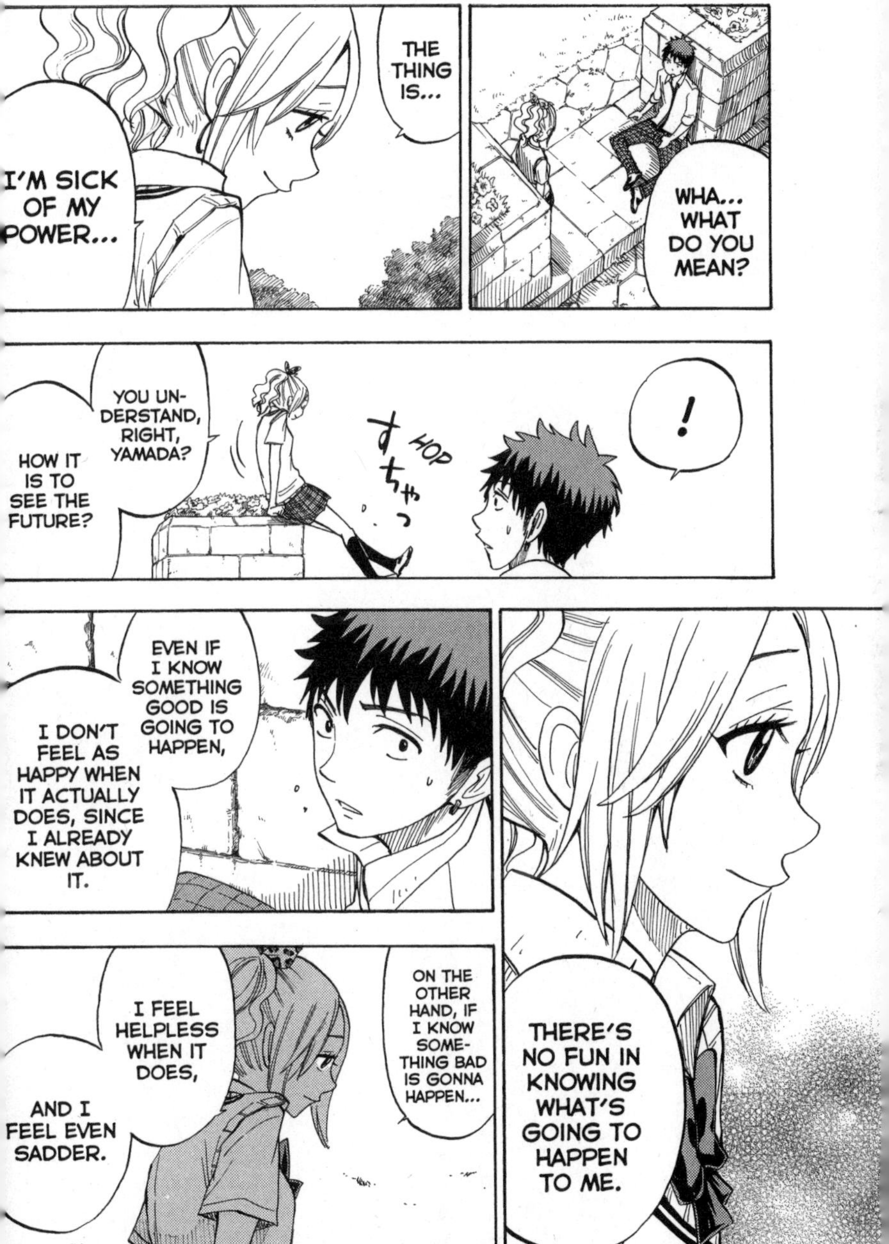
WHA... WHAT DO YOU MEAN?
THE THING IS...
I'M SICK OF MY POWER...
!
すちゃっ
HOP
YOU UNDERSTAND, RIGHT, YAMADA?
HOW IT IS TO SEE THE FUTURE?
THERE'S NO FUN IN KNOWING WHAT'S GOING TO HAPPEN TO ME.
EVEN IF I KNOW SOMETHING GOOD IS GOING TO HAPPEN,
I DON'T FEEL AS HAPPY WHEN IT ACTUALLY DOES, SINCE I ALREADY KNEW ABOUT IT.
ON THE OTHER HAND, IF I KNOW SOMETHING BAD IS GONNA HAPPEN...
I FEEL HELPLESS WHEN IT DOES,
AND I FEEL EVEN SADDER.

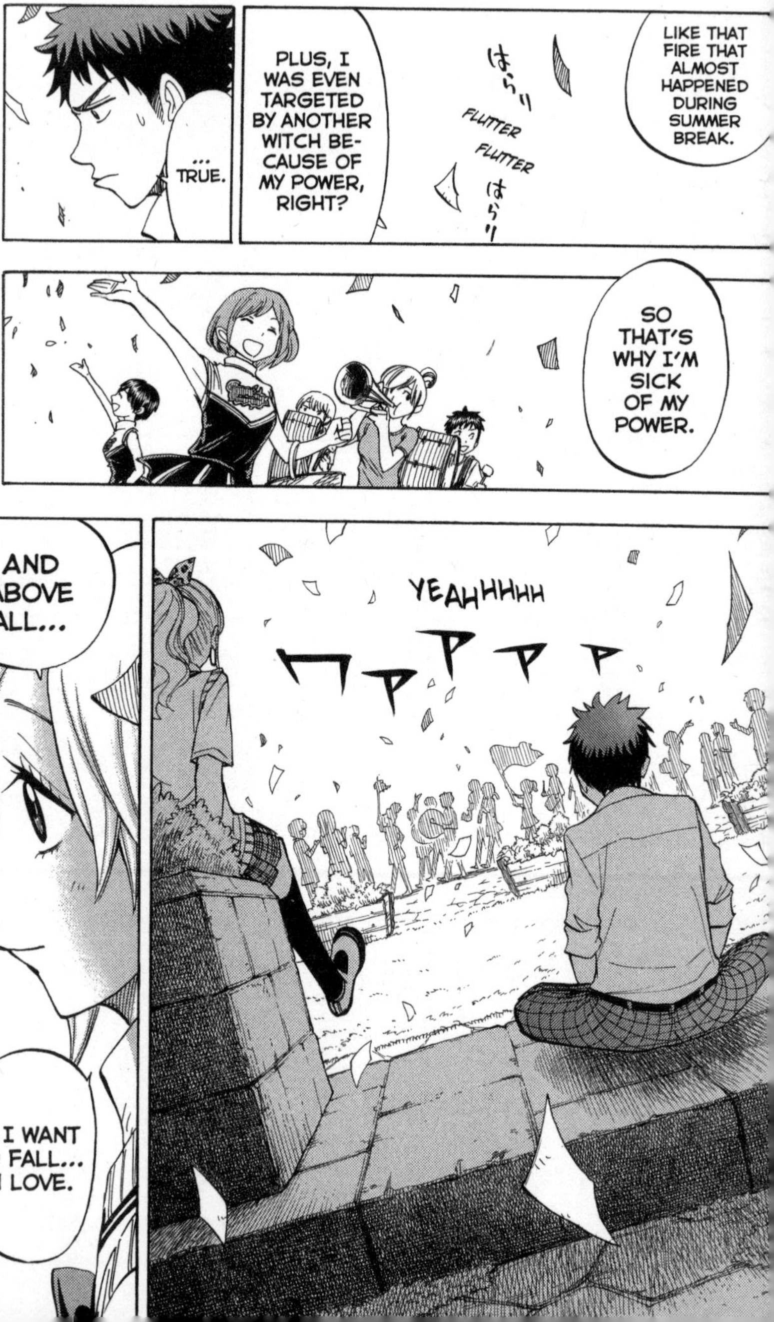
LIKE THAT FIRE THAT ALMOST HAPPENED DURING SUMMER BREAK.
はらり
FLUTTER
FLUTTER
はらり
PLUS, I WAS EVEN TARGETED BY ANOTHER WITCH BE-CAUSE OF MY POWER, RIGHT?
... TRUE.
SO THAT'S WHY I'M SICK OF MY POWER.
YEAHHHHH
ワァァァァ
AND ABOVE ALL...
...I WANT TO FALL... IN LOVE.

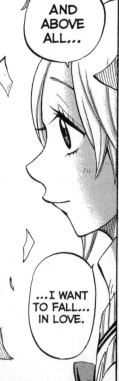

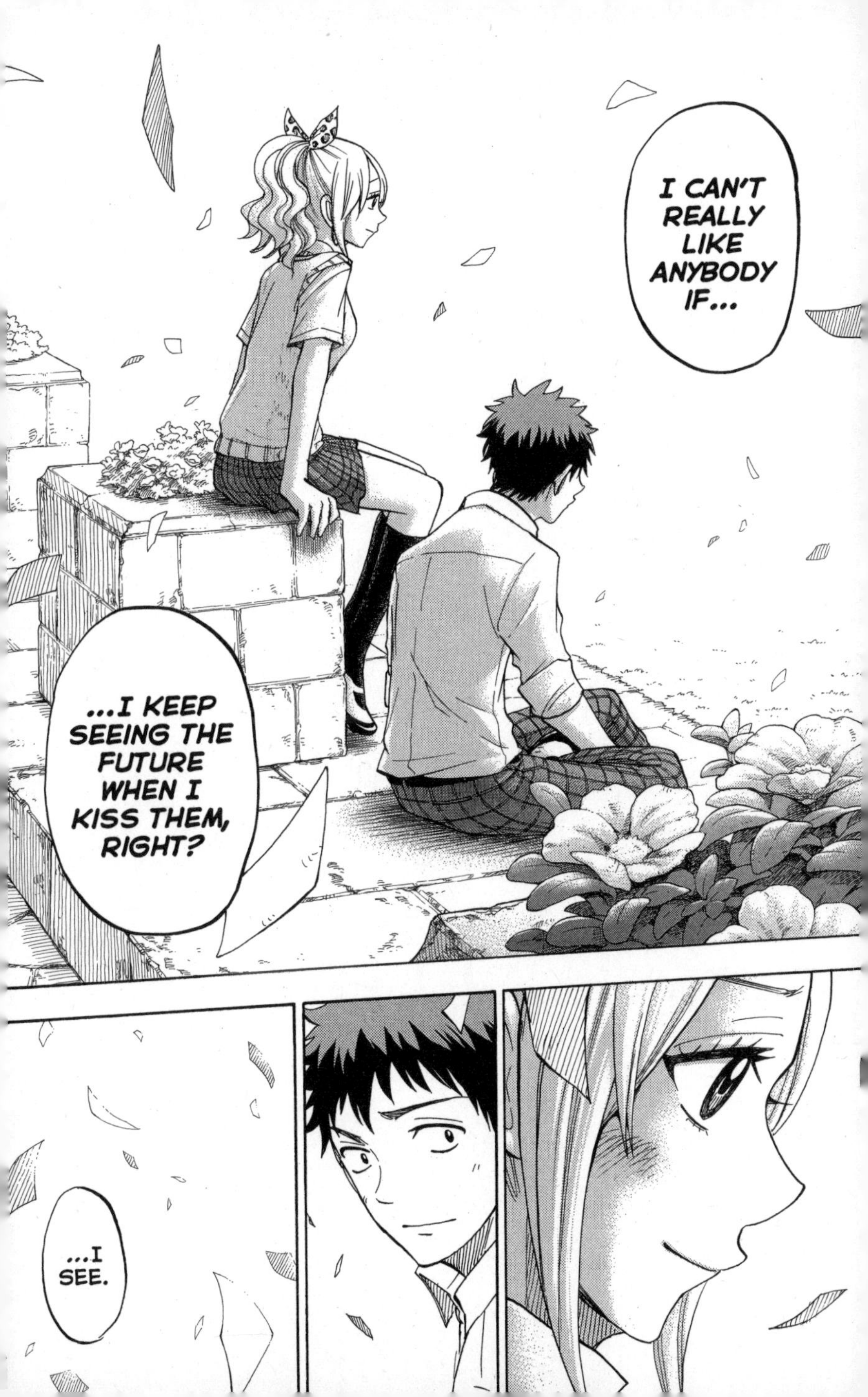
I CAN'T REALLY LIKE ANYBODY IF...
...I KEEP SEEING THE FUTURE WHEN I KISS THEM, RIGHT?
...I SEE.

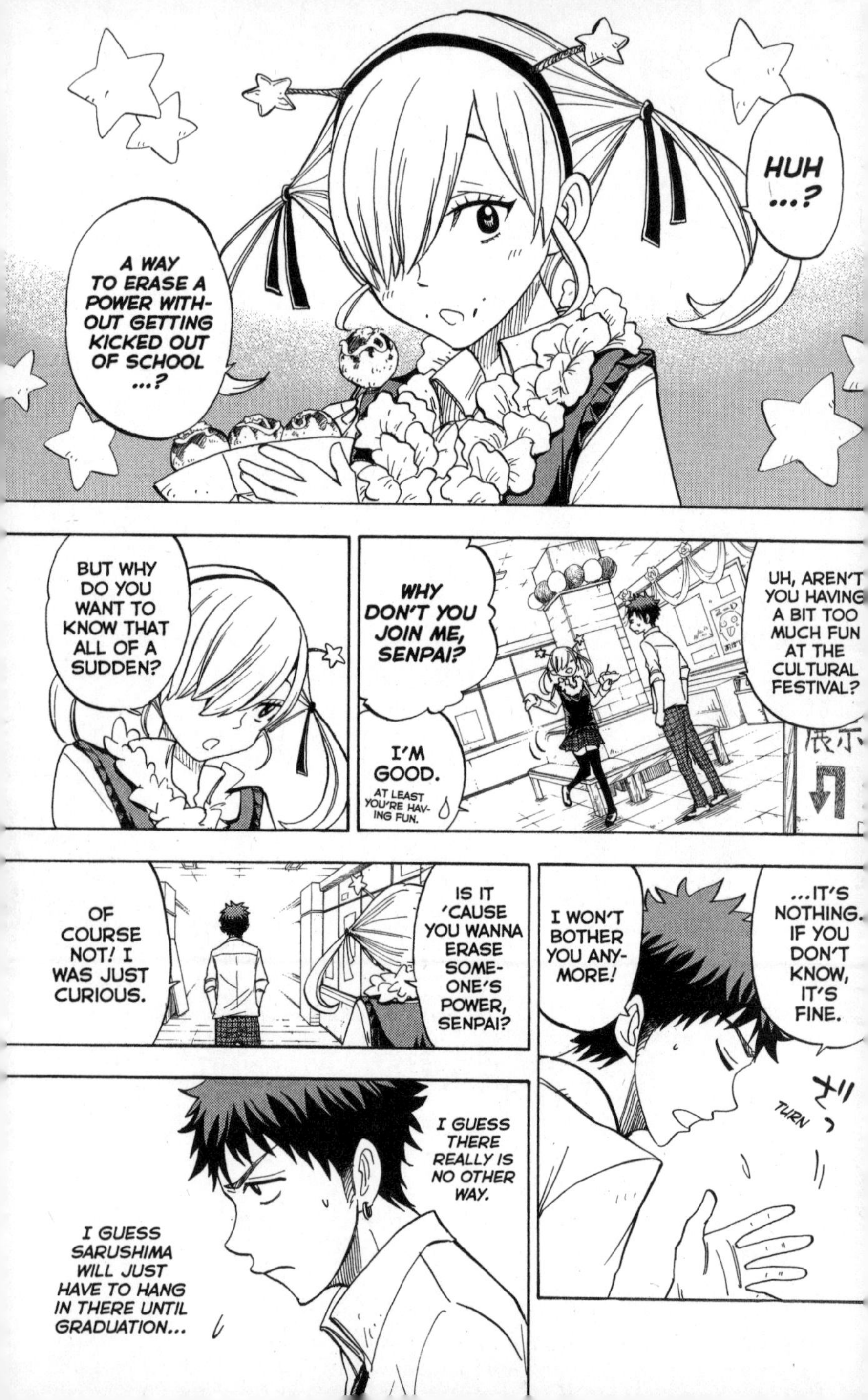
HUH ...?
A WAY TO ERASE A POWER WITHOUT GETTING KICKED OUT OF SCHOOL ...?
UH, AREN'T YOU HAVING A BIT TOO MUCH FUN AT THE CULTURAL FESTIVAL?
WHY DON'T YOU JOIN ME, SENPAI?
I'M GOOD.
AT LEAST YOU'RE HAVING FUN.
BUT WHY DO YOU WANT TO KNOW THAT ALL OF A SUDDEN?
...IT'S NOTHING. IF YOU DON'T KNOW, IT'S FINE.
I WON'T BOTHER YOU ANYMORE!
TURN
IS IT 'CAUSE YOU WANNA ERASE SOMEONE'S POWER, SENPAI?
OF COURSE NOT! I WAS JUST CURIOUS.
I GUESS THERE REALLY IS NO OTHER WAY.
I GUESS SARUSHIMA WILL JUST HAVE TO HANG IN THERE UNTIL GRADUATION...

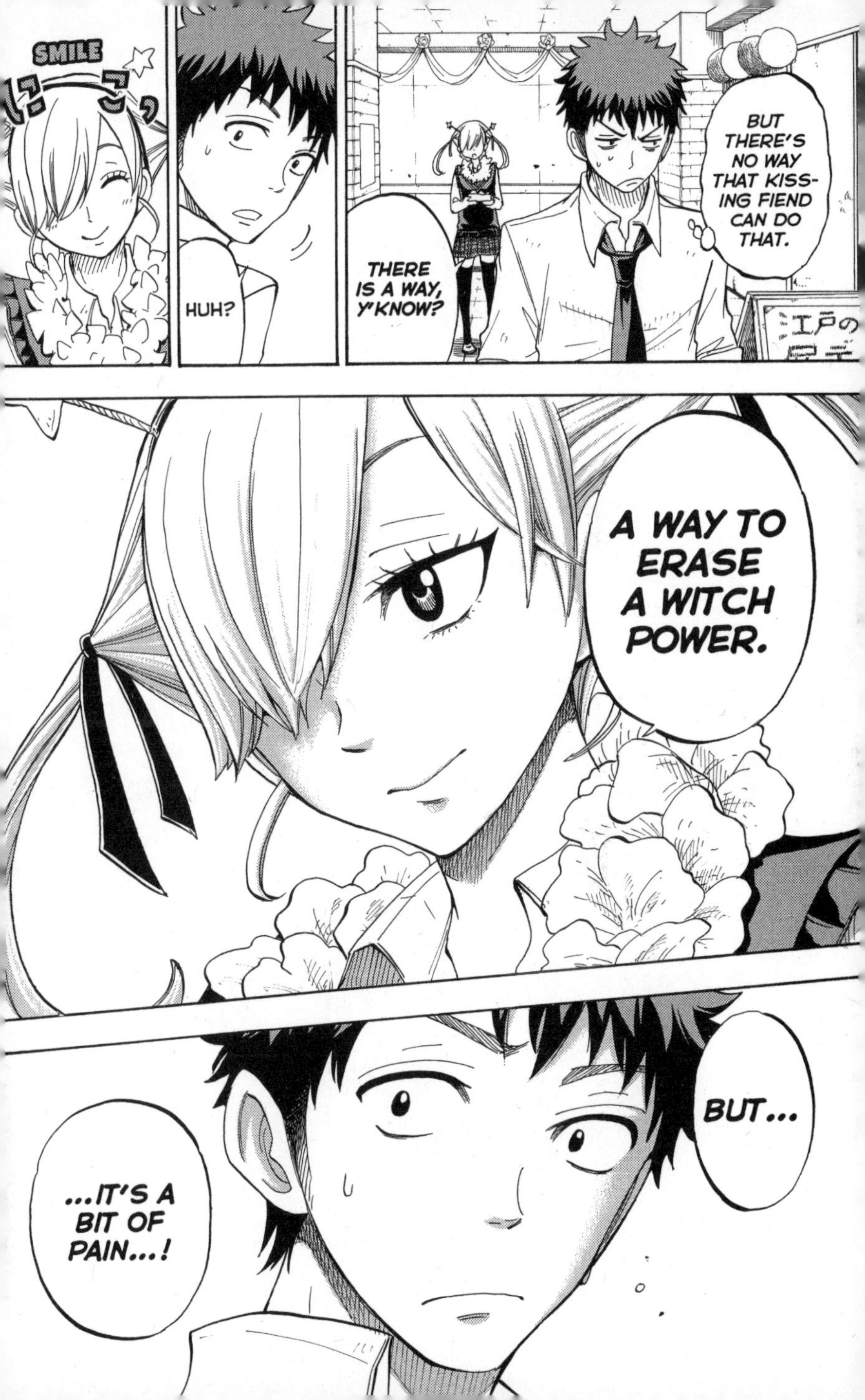
BUT THERE'S NO WAY THAT KISSING FIEND CAN DO THAT.
THERE IS A WAY, Y'KNOW?
HUH?
SMILE
A WAY TO ERASE A WITCH POWER.
BUT...
...IT'S A BIT OF PAIN...!

CHAPTER 53: Ugh, what a pain.

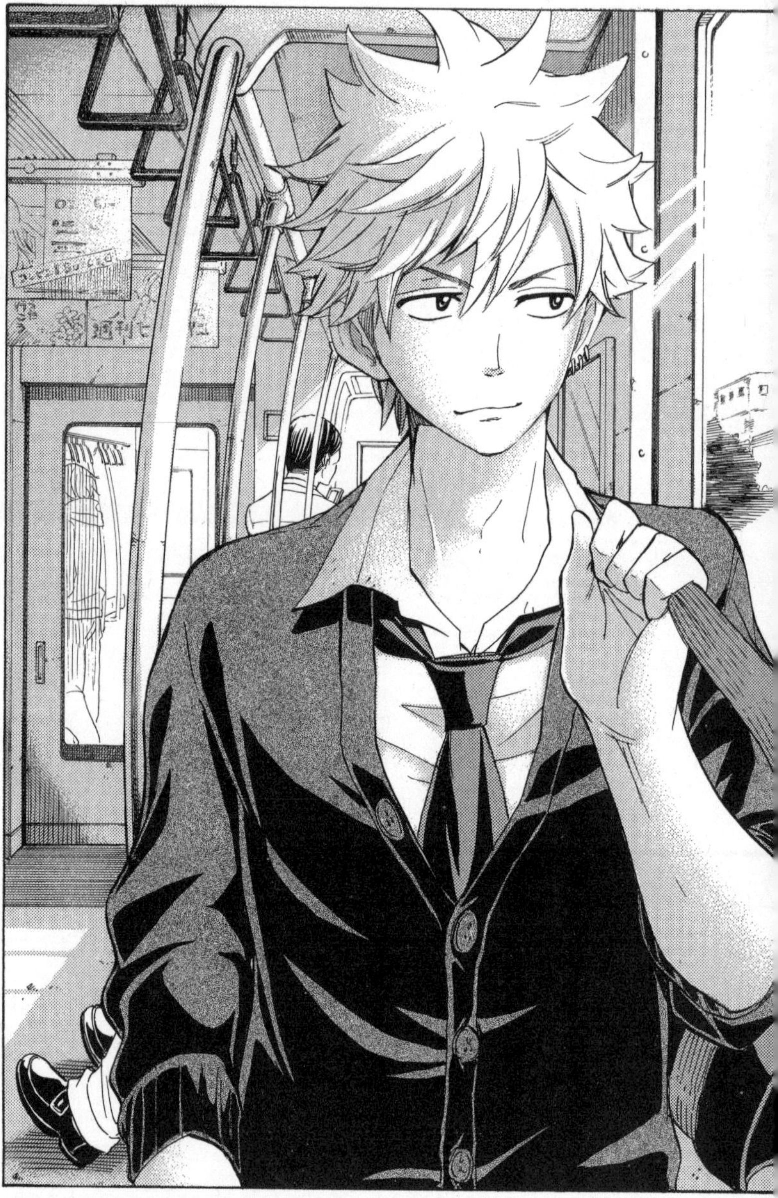

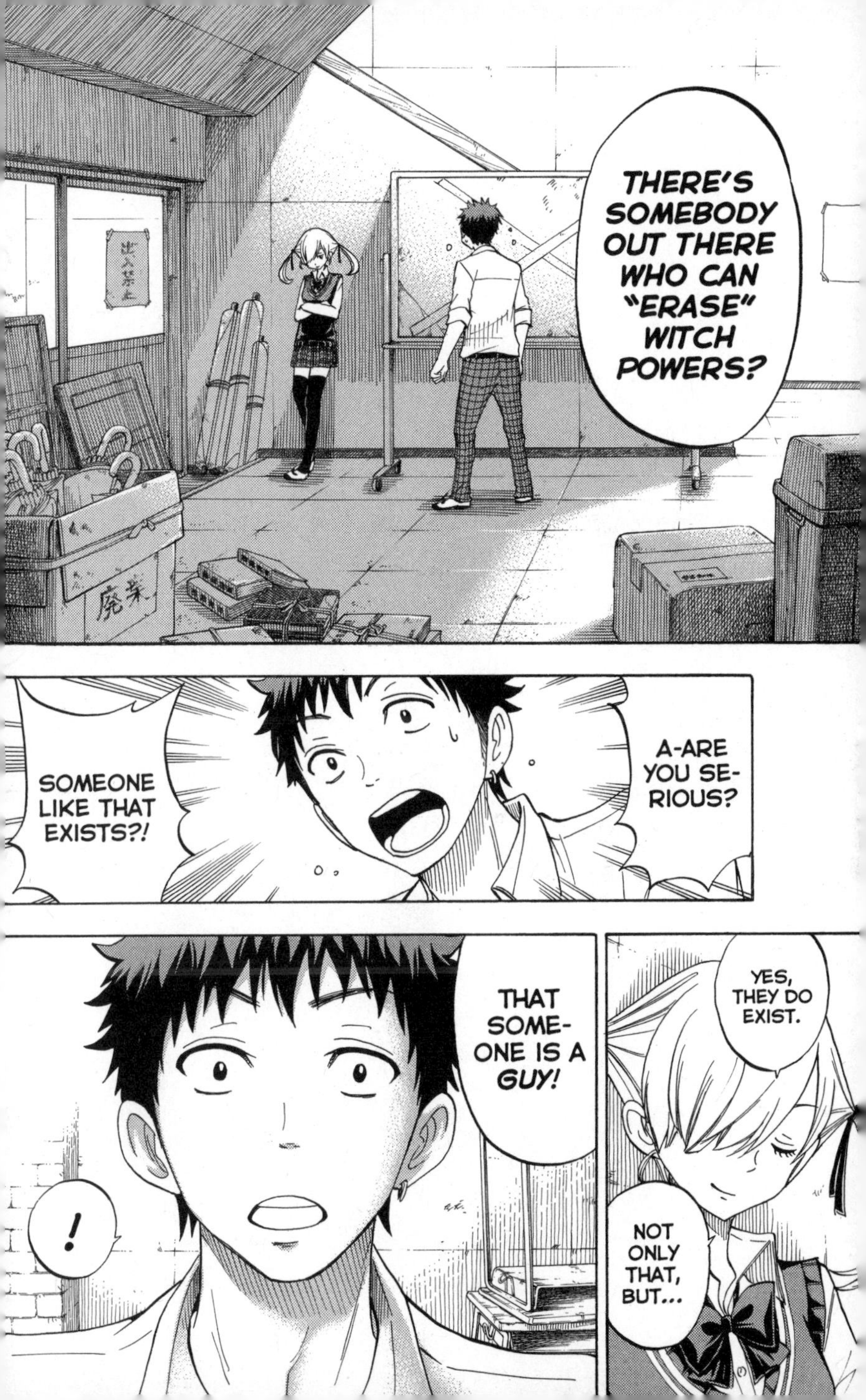
THERE'S SOMEBODY OUT THERE WHO CAN "ERASE" WITCH POWERS?
A-ARE YOU SE-RIOUS?
SOMEONE LIKE THAT EXISTS?!
YES, THEY DO EXIST.
NOT ONLY THAT, BUT...
THAT SOME-ONE IS A *GUY*!
!

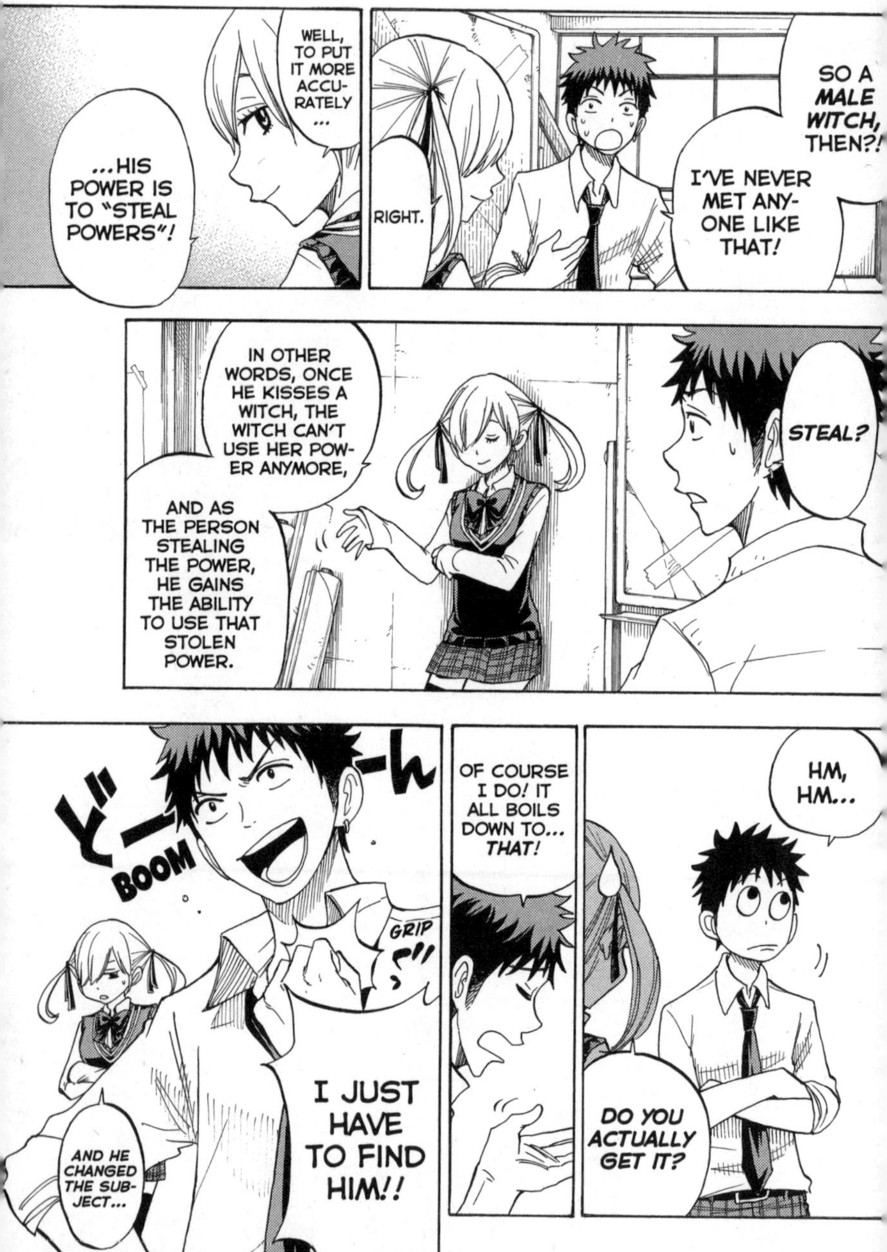
SO A MALE WITCH, THEN?!
I'VE NEVER MET ANYONE LIKE THAT!
RIGHT.
WELL, TO PUT IT MORE ACCURATELY...
...HIS POWER IS TO "STEAL POWERS"!
STEAL?
IN OTHER WORDS, ONCE HE KISSES A WITCH, THE WITCH CAN'T USE HER POWER ANYMORE,
AND AS THE PERSON STEALING THE POWER, HE GAINS THE ABILITY TO USE THAT STOLEN POWER.
HM, HM...
DO YOU ACTUALLY GET IT?
OF COURSE I DO! IT ALL BOILS DOWN TO... THAT!
BOOM
GRIP
I JUST HAVE TO FIND HIM!!
AND HE CHANGED THE SUBJECT...

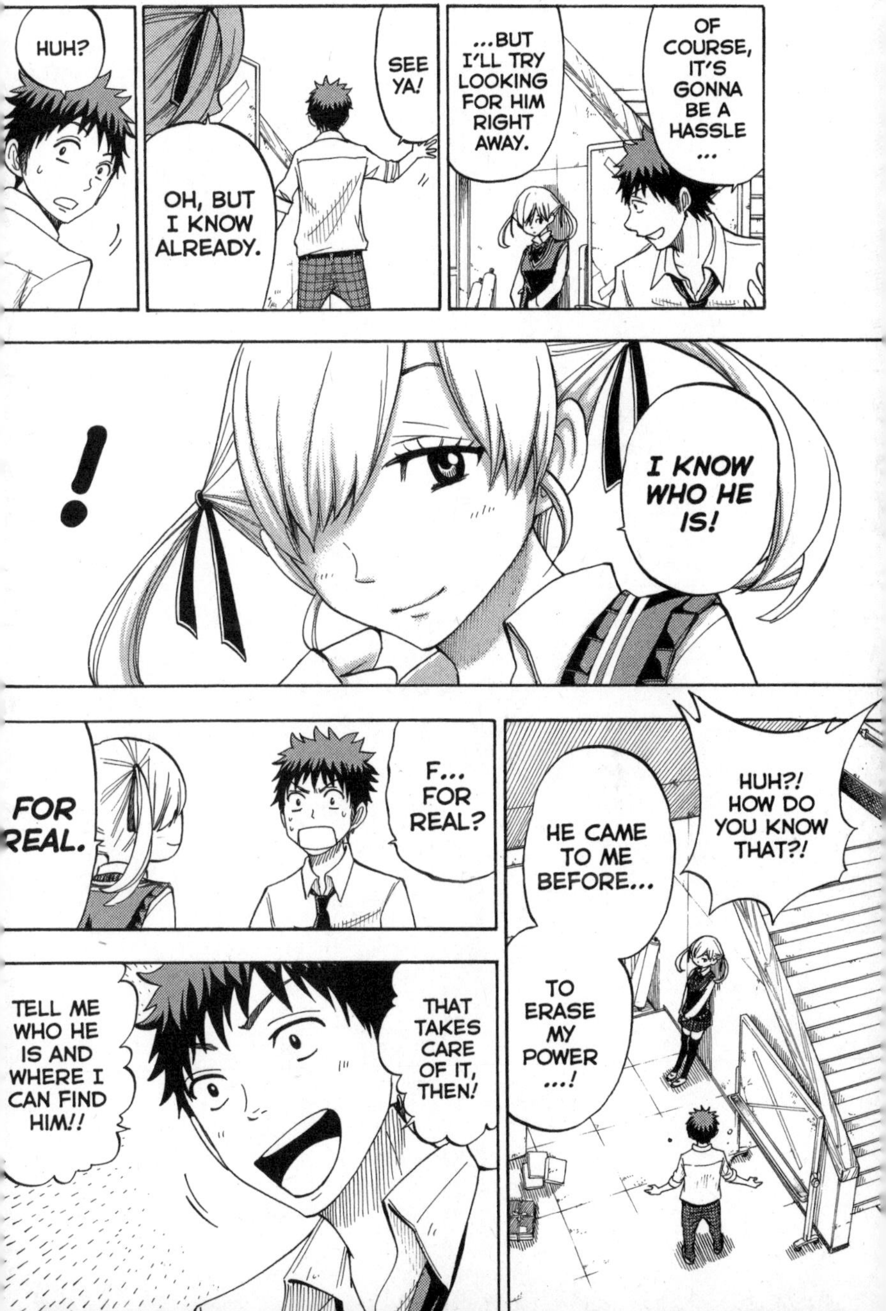
OF COURSE, IT'S GONNA BE A HASSLE ...
...BUT I'LL TRY LOOKING FOR HIM RIGHT AWAY.
SEE YA!
OH, BUT I KNOW ALREADY.
HUH?
I KNOW WHO HE IS!
!
HUH?! HOW DO YOU KNOW THAT?!
HE CAME TO ME BEFORE...
TO ERASE MY POWER ...!
F... FOR REAL?
FOR REAL.
THAT TAKES CARE OF IT, THEN!
TELL ME WHO HE IS AND WHERE I CAN FIND HIM!!

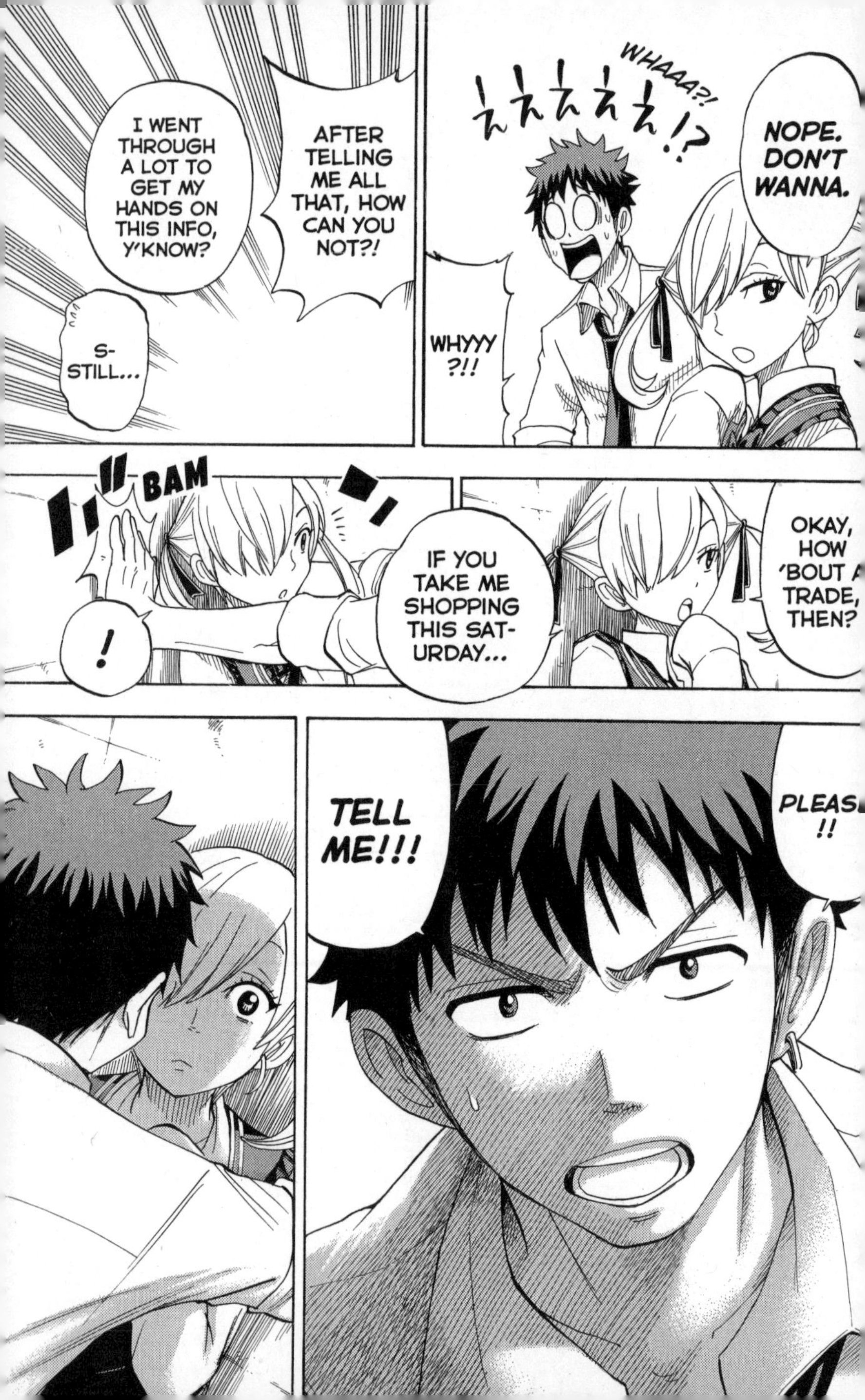
NOPE. DON'T WANNA.
えええええ!?
WHAAA?!
WHYYY ?!!
AFTER TELLING ME ALL THAT, HOW CAN YOU NOT?!
I WENT THROUGH A LOT TO GET MY HANDS ON THIS INFO, Y'KNOW?
S-STILL...
OKAY, HOW 'BOUT A TRADE, THEN?
IF YOU TAKE ME SHOPPING THIS SAT-URDAY...
BAM
!
PLEAS
!!
TELL ME!!!

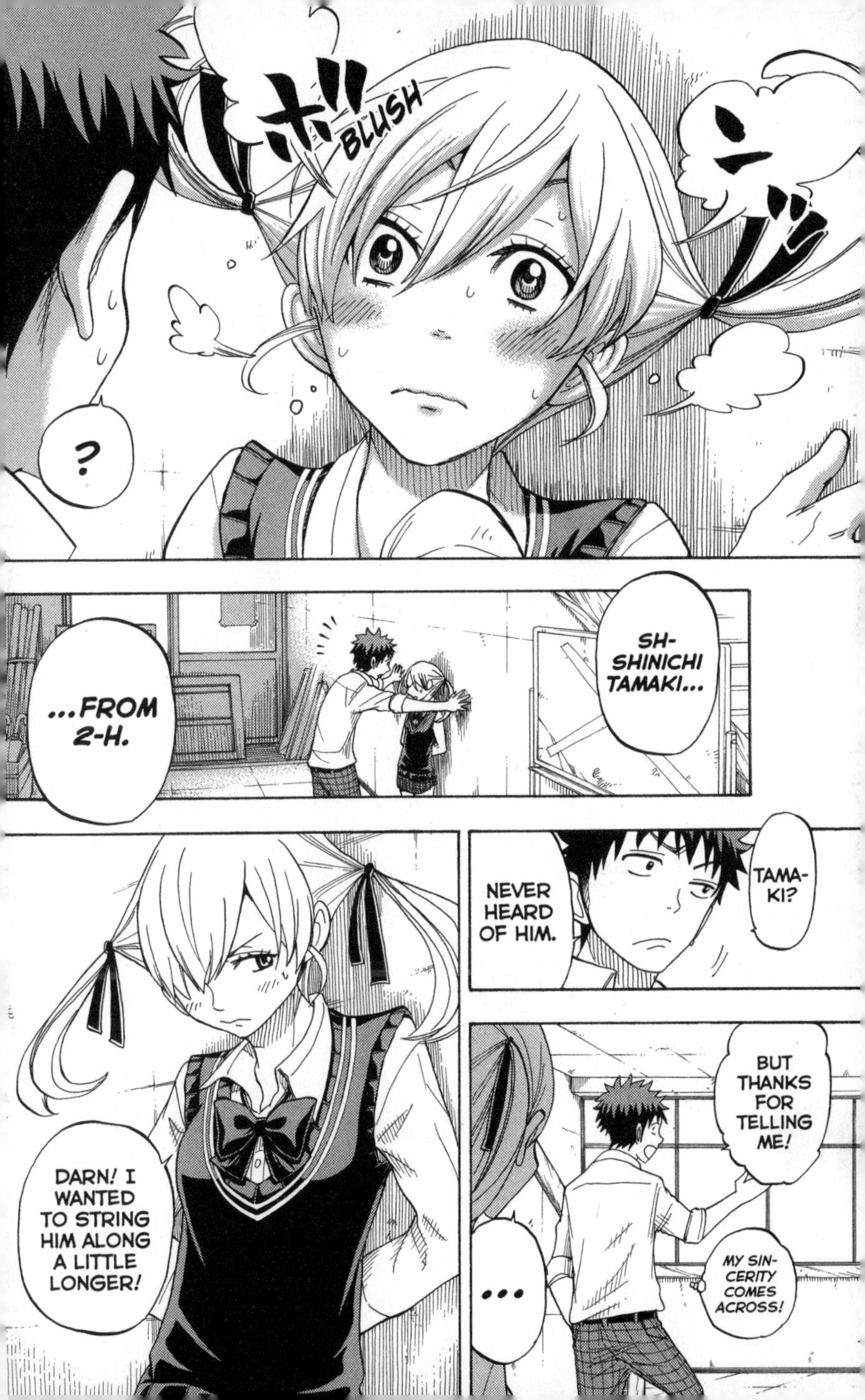
BLUSH
?
SH-SHINICHI TAMAKI...
...FROM 2-H.
TAMA-KI?
NEVER HEARD OF HIM.
BUT THANKS FOR TELLING ME!
MY SIN-CERITY COMES ACROSS!
...
DARN! I WANTED TO STRING HIM ALONG A LITTLE LONGER!

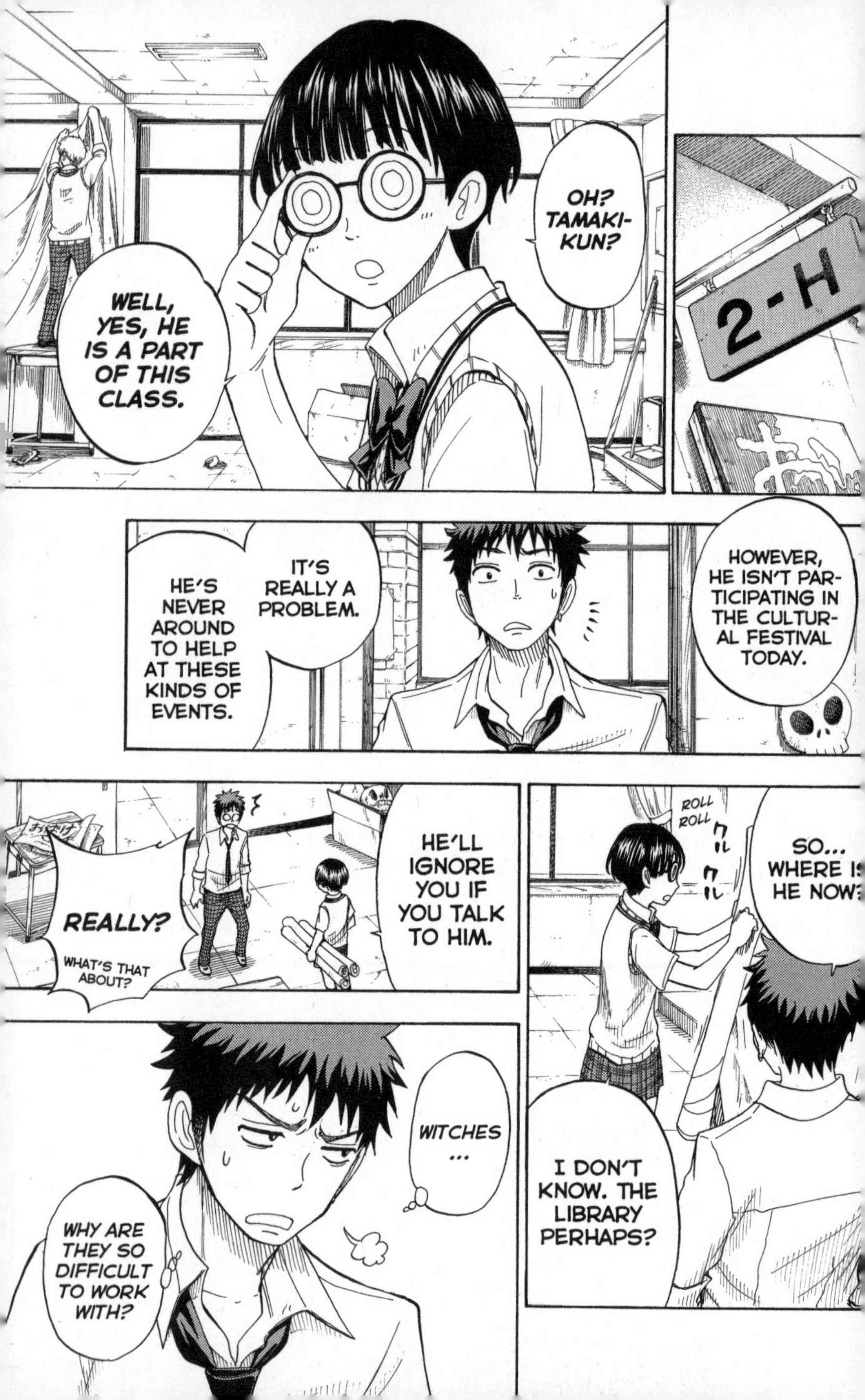
2-H
OH? TAMAKI-KUN?
WELL, YES, HE IS A PART OF THIS CLASS.
HOWEVER, HE ISN'T PARTICIPATING IN THE CULTURAL FESTIVAL TODAY.
IT'S REALLY A PROBLEM.
HE'S NEVER AROUND TO HELP AT THESE KINDS OF EVENTS.
SO... WHERE IS HE NOW?
ROLL ROLL
HE'LL IGNORE YOU IF YOU TALK TO HIM.
REALLY?
WHAT'S THAT ABOUT?
I DON'T KNOW. THE LIBRARY PERHAPS?
WITCHES...
WHY ARE THEY SO DIFFICULT TO WORK WITH?

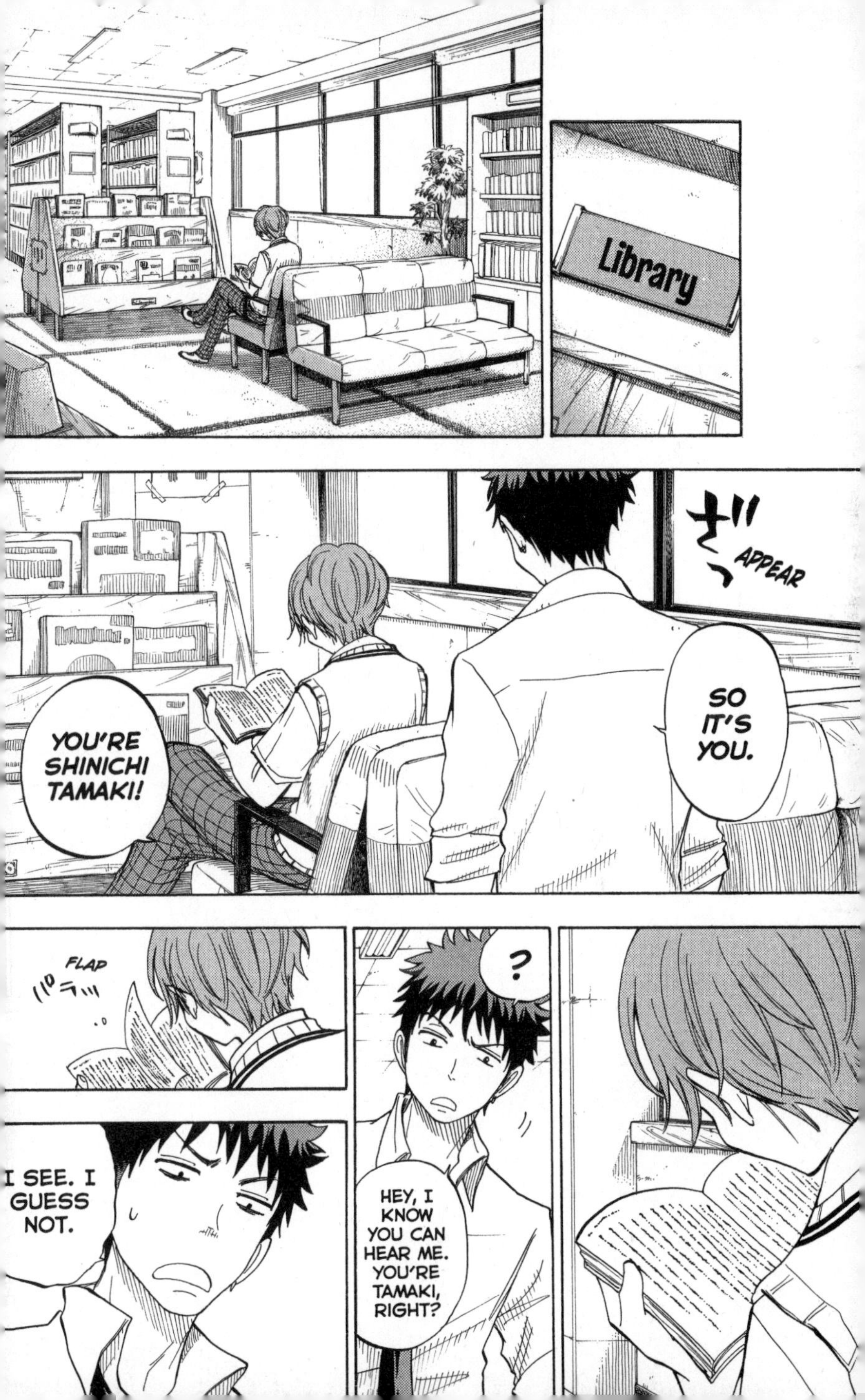
Library
ざッ
APPEAR
SO IT'S YOU.
YOU'RE SHINICHI TAMAKI!
?
HEY, I KNOW YOU CAN HEAR ME. YOU'RE TAMAKI, RIGHT?
パラッ
FLAP
I SEE. I GUESS NOT.

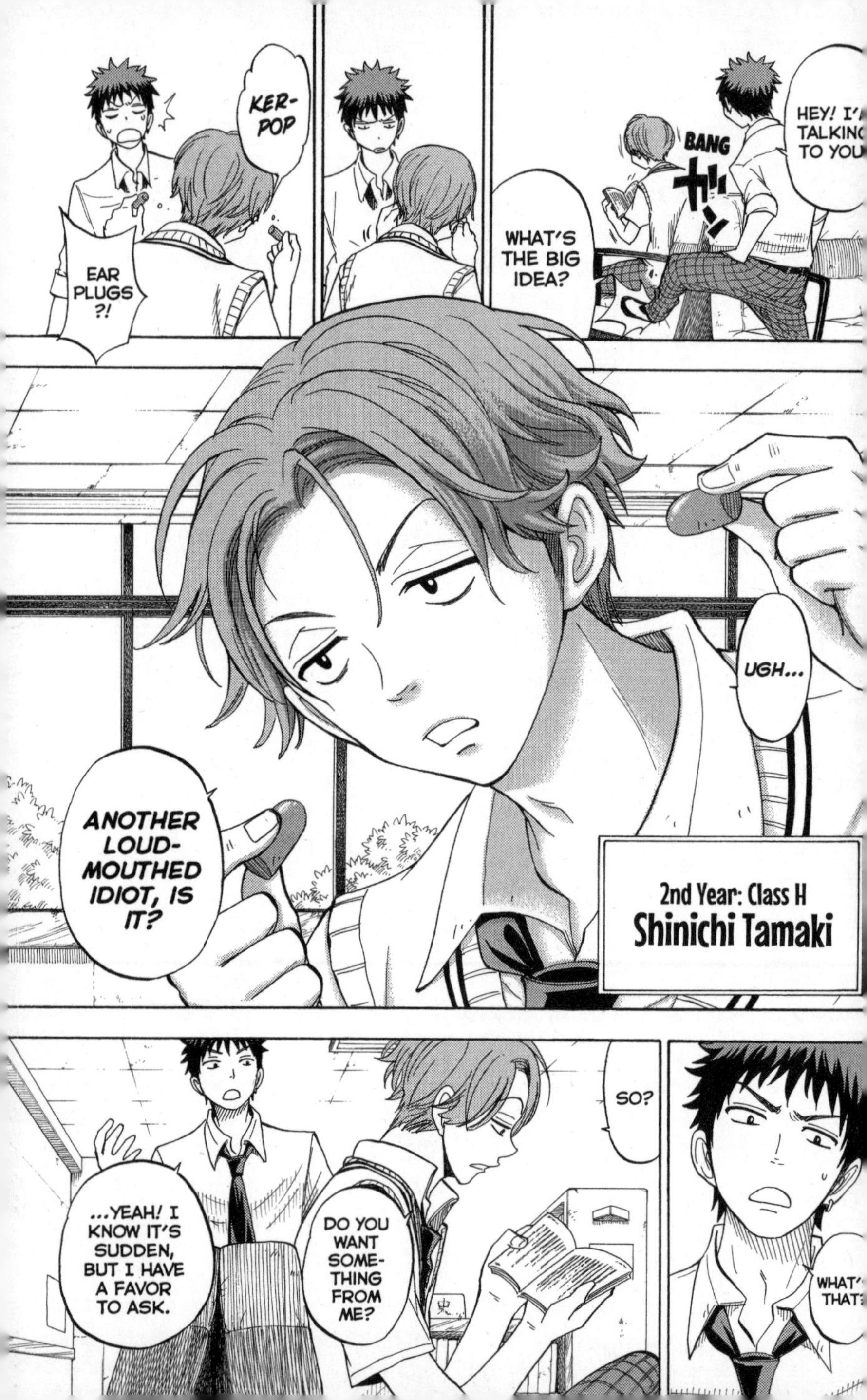
HEY! I' TALKIN TO YOU
BANG
WHAT'S THE BIG IDEA?
KER-POP
EAR PLUGS ?!
UGH...
ANOTHER LOUD-MOUTHED IDIOT, IS IT?
2nd Year: Class H
Shinichi Tamaki
WHAT' THAT
SO?
DO YOU WANT SOME-THING FROM ME?
...YEAH! I KNOW IT'S SUDDEN, BUT I HAVE A FAVOR TO ASK.

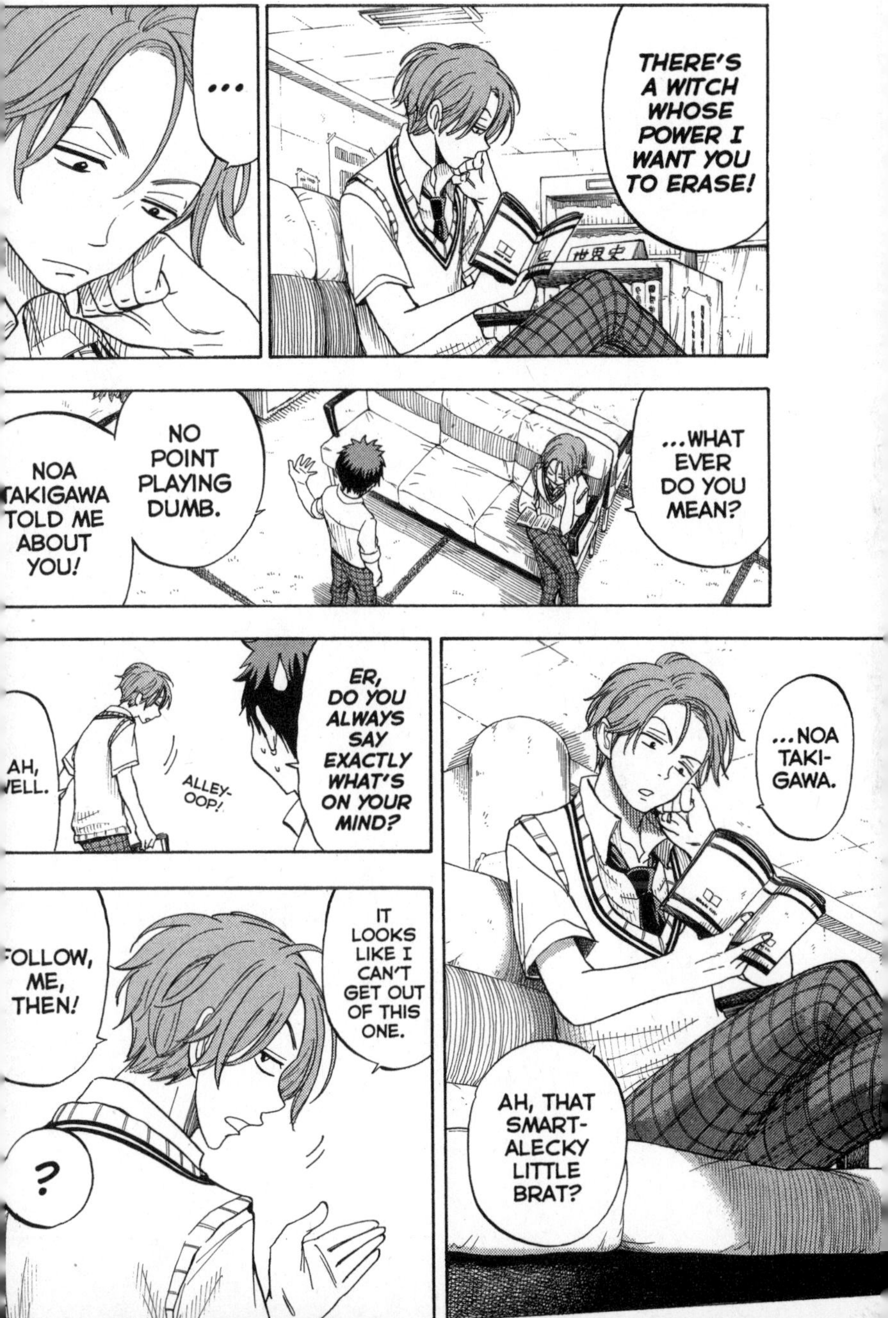
THERE'S A WITCH WHOSE POWER I WANT YOU TO ERASE!
...
...WHAT EVER DO YOU MEAN?
NO POINT PLAYING DUMB.
NOA TAKIGAWA TOLD ME ABOUT YOU!
...NOA TAKI-GAWA.
AH, THAT SMART-ALECKY LITTLE BRAT?
ER, DO YOU ALWAYS SAY EXACTLY WHAT'S ON YOUR MIND?
ALLEY-OOP!
AH, WELL.
IT LOOKS LIKE I CAN'T GET OUT OF THIS ONE.
FOLLOW, ME, THEN!
?

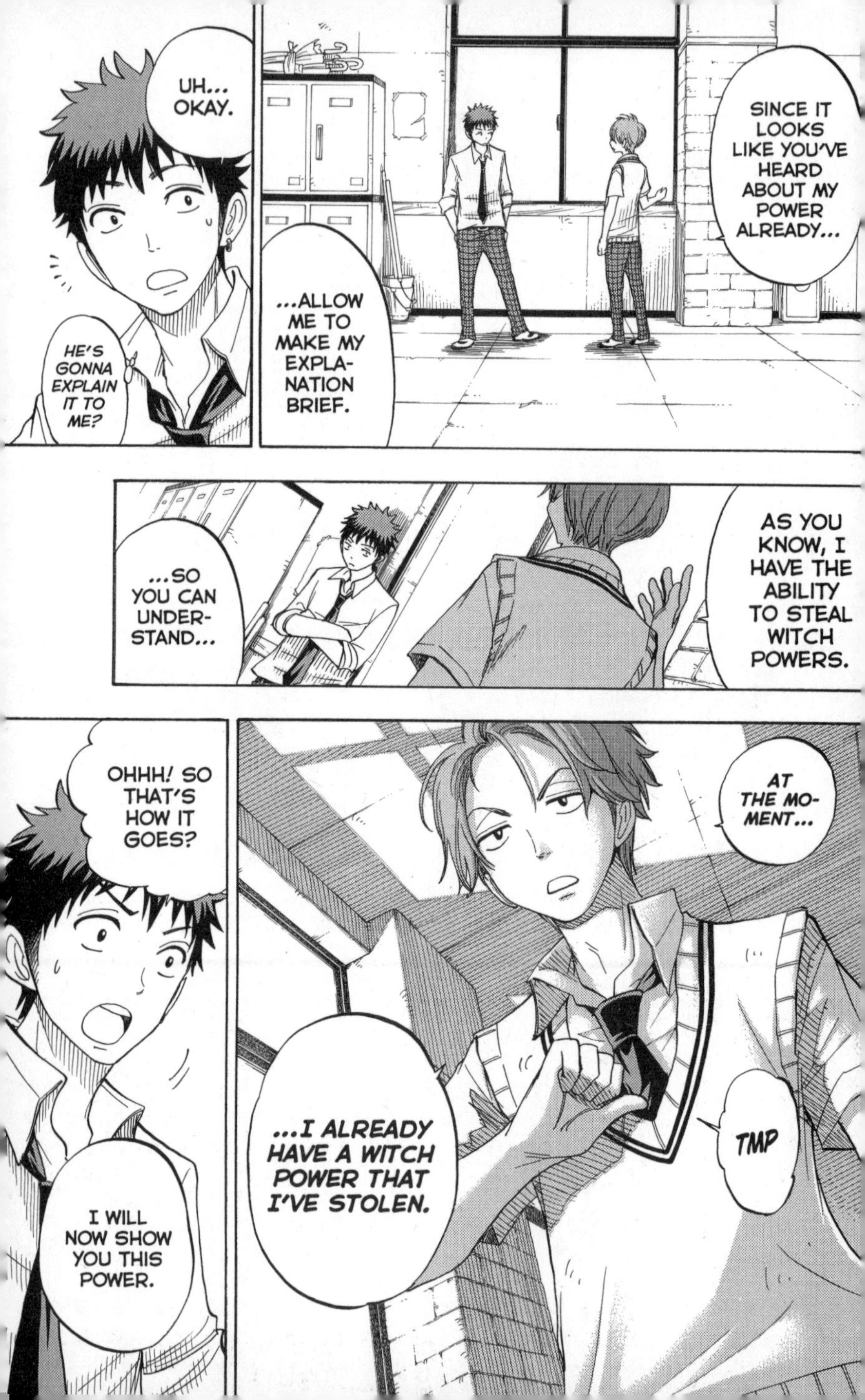
SINCE IT LOOKS LIKE YOU'VE HEARD ABOUT MY POWER ALREADY...
...ALLOW ME TO MAKE MY EXPLA-NATION BRIEF.
UH... OKAY.
HE'S GONNA EXPLAIN IT TO ME?
AS YOU KNOW, I HAVE THE ABILITY TO STEAL WITCH POWERS.
...SO YOU CAN UNDER-STAND...
AT THE MO-MENT...
TMP
...I ALREADY HAVE A WITCH POWER THAT I'VE STOLEN.
OHHH! SO THAT'S HOW IT GOES?
I WILL NOW SHOW YOU THIS POWER.

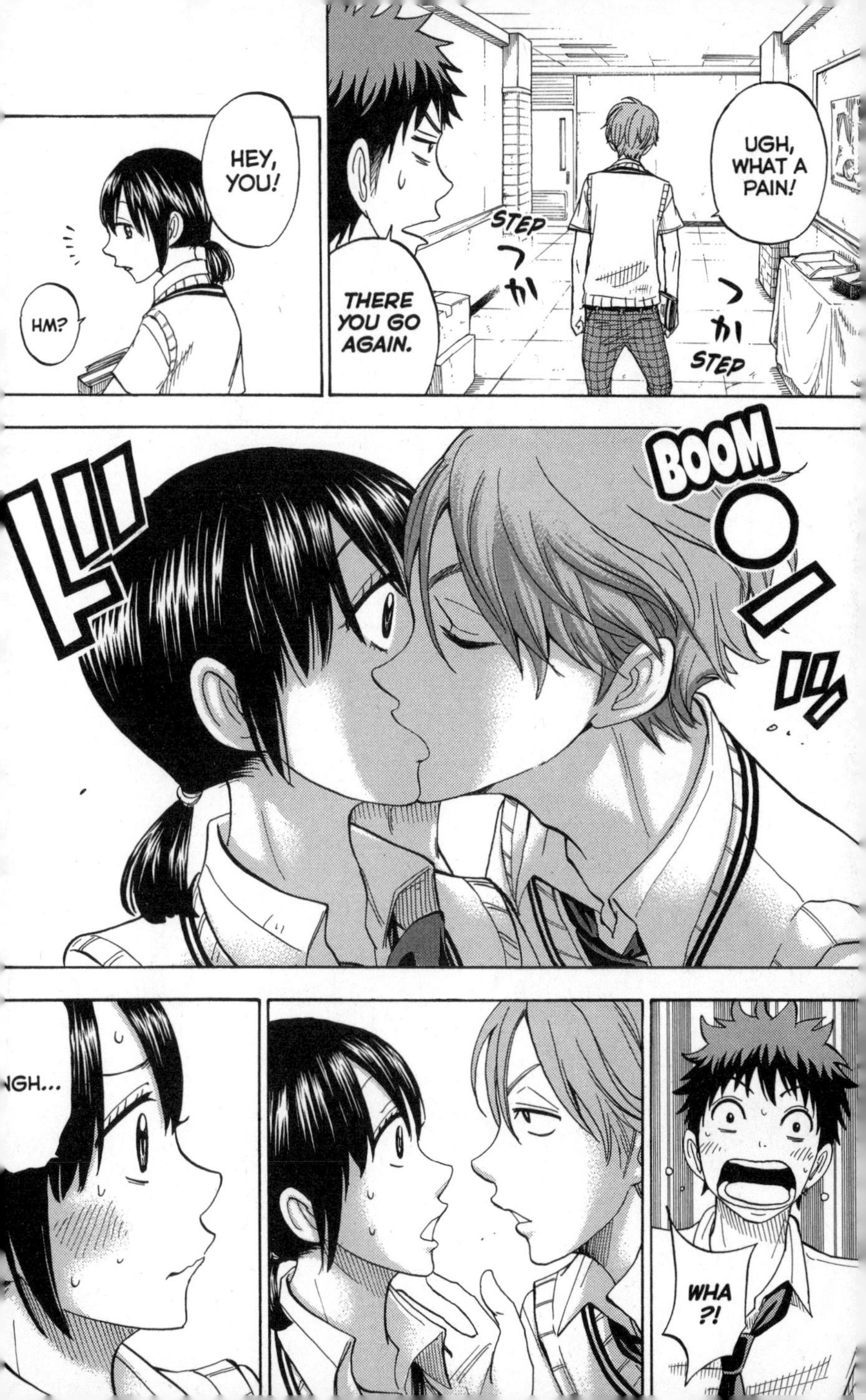

UGH, WHAT A PAIN!
STEP
つか
つか
STEP
THERE YOU GO AGAIN.
HEY, YOU!
HM?
BOOM
WHA ?!
NGH...

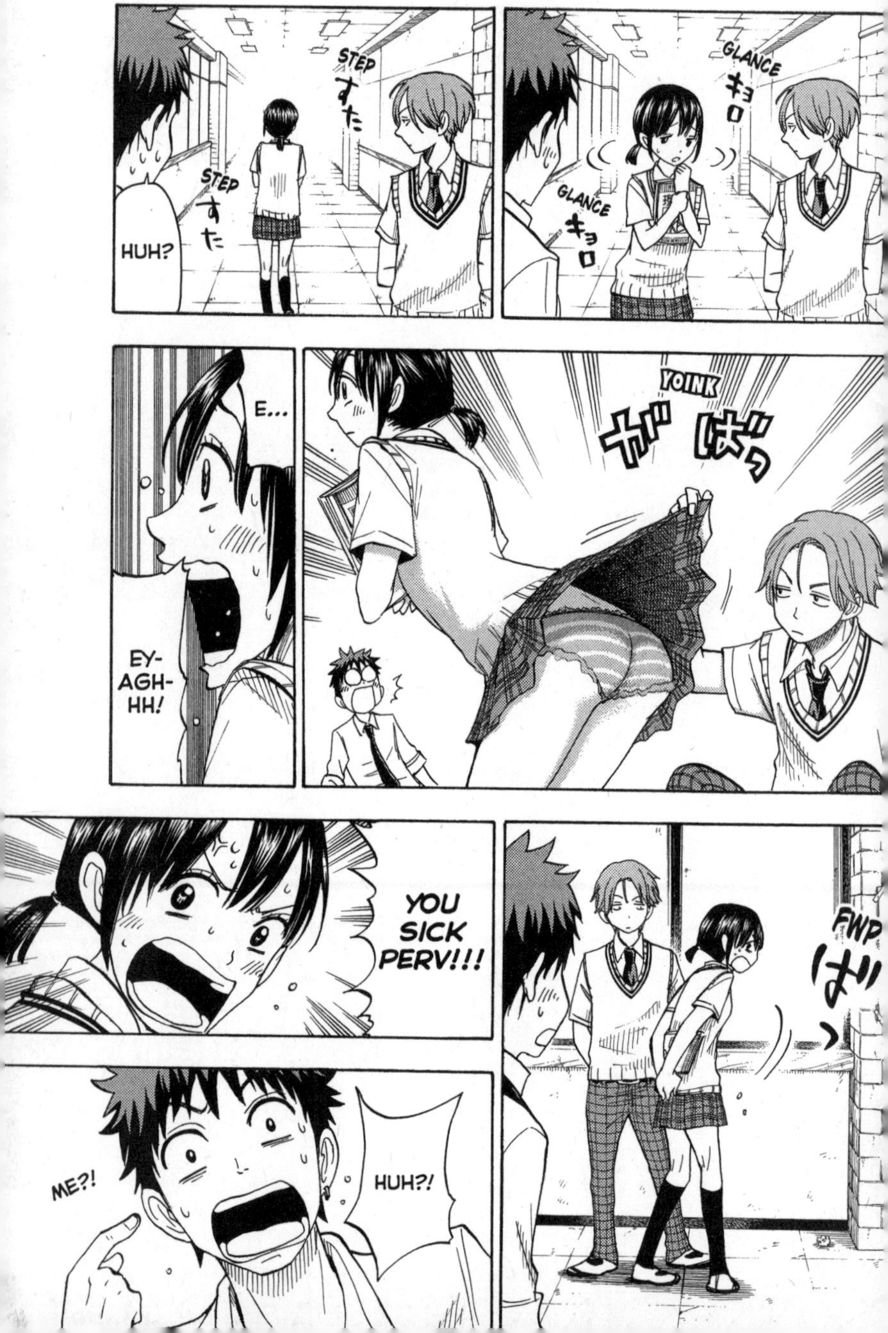
GLANCE
キョロ
GLANCE
キョロ
STEP
すた
STEP
すた
HUH?
YOINK
ガばっ
E...
EY-AGH-HH!
FWP
ぱっ
YOU SICK PERV!!!
HUH?!
ME?!

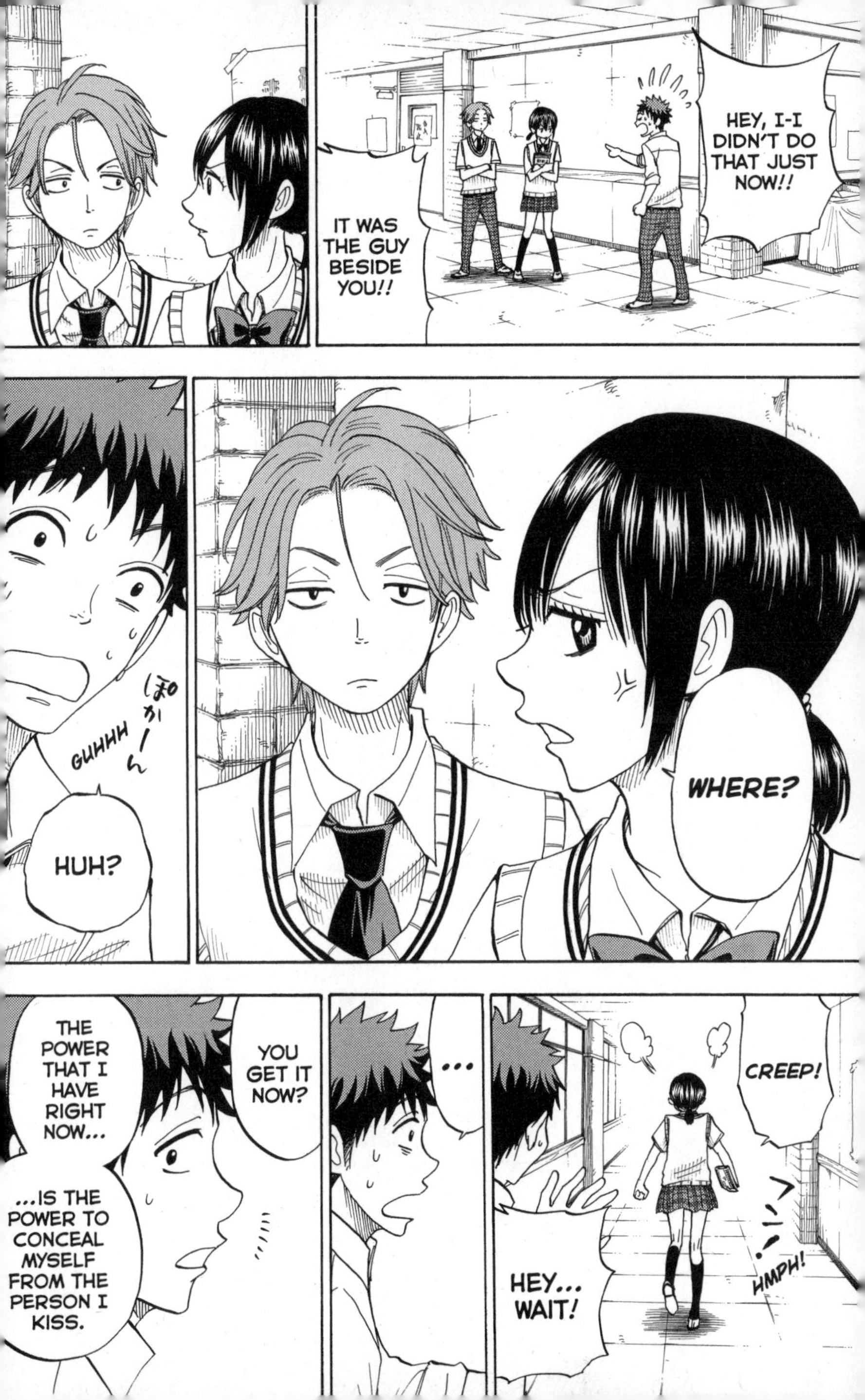
HEY, I-I DIDN'T DO THAT JUST NOW!!
IT WAS THE GUY BESIDE YOU!!
WHERE?
ぽかーん
GUHHH
HUH?
CREEP!
HMPH!
HEY... WAIT!
...
YOU GET IT NOW?
THE POWER THAT I HAVE RIGHT NOW...
...IS THE POWER TO CONCEAL MYSELF FROM THE PERSON I KISS.

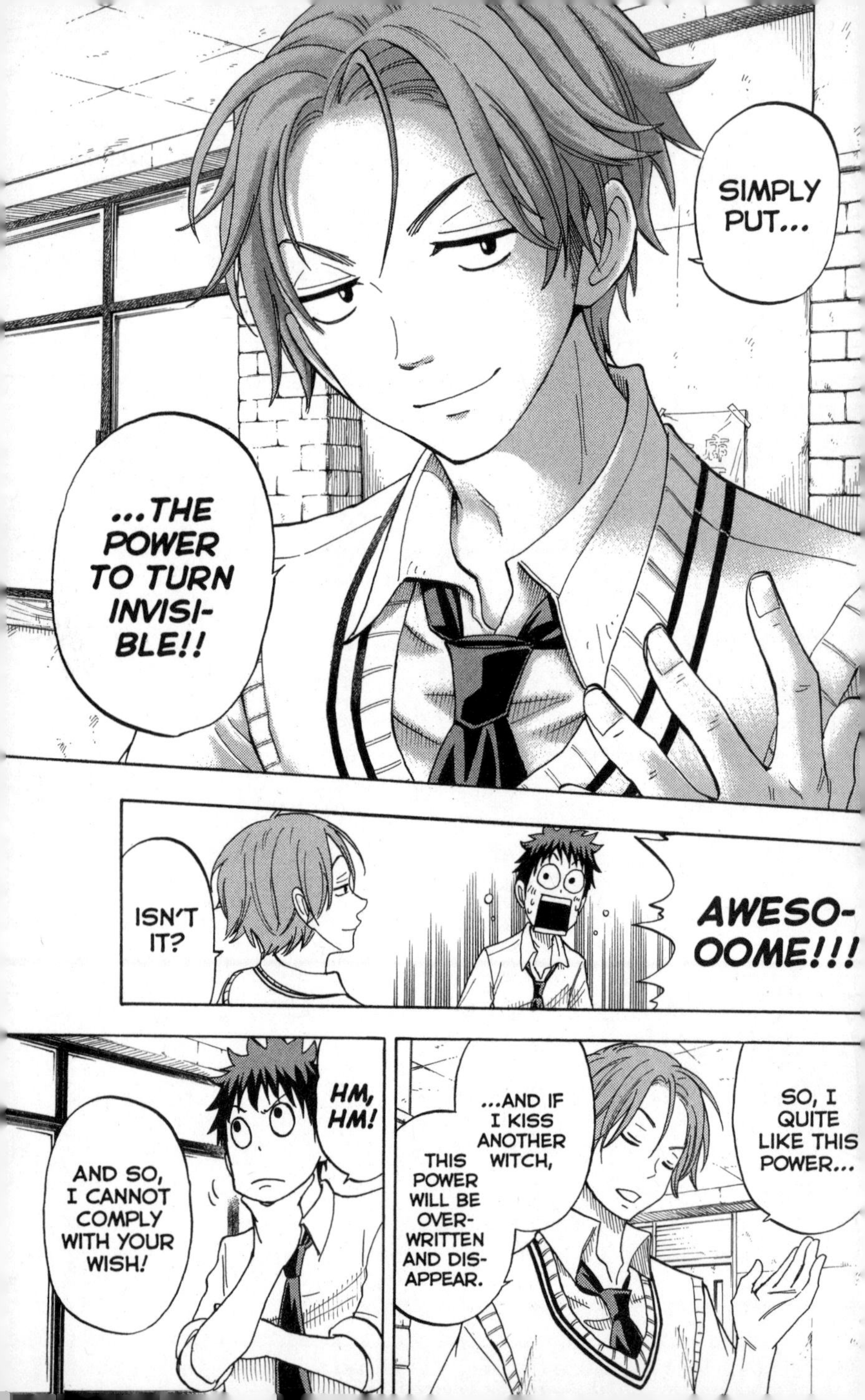
SIMPLY PUT...
...THE POWER TO TURN INVISI-BLE!!
AWESO-OOME!!!
ISN'T IT?
SO, I QUITE LIKE THIS POWER...
...AND IF I KISS ANOTHER WITCH,
THIS POWER WILL BE OVER-WRITTEN AND DIS-APPEAR.
HM, HM!
AND SO, I CANNOT COMPLY WITH YOUR WISH!

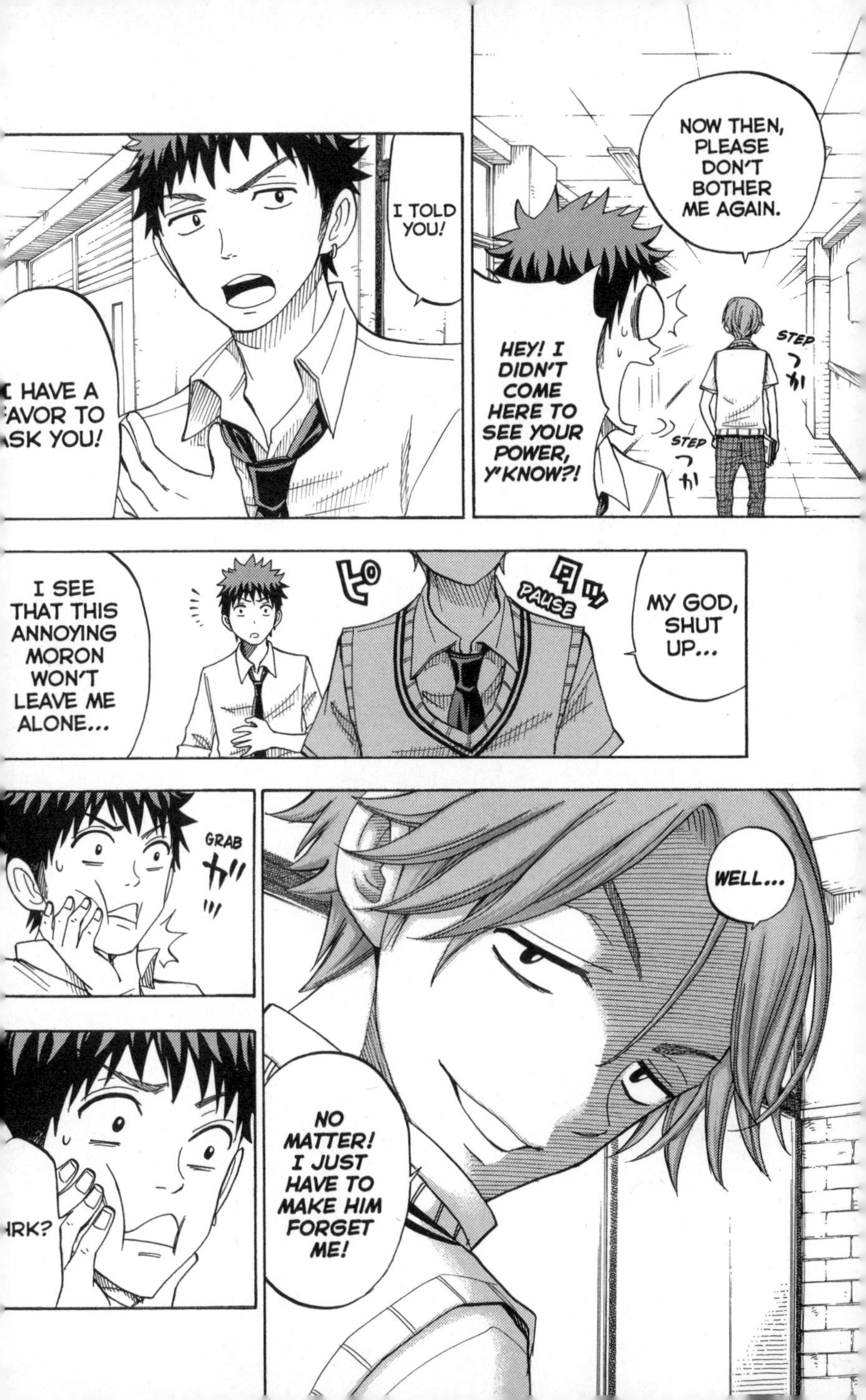
NOW THEN, PLEASE DON'T BOTHER ME AGAIN.
STEP
STEP
HEY! I DIDN'T COME HERE TO SEE YOUR POWER, Y'KNOW?!
I TOLD YOU!
I HAVE A FAVOR TO ASK YOU!
MY GOD, SHUT UP...
PAUSE
I SEE THAT THIS ANNOYING MORON WON'T LEAVE ME ALONE...
WELL...
NO MATTER! I JUST HAVE TO MAKE HIM FORGET ME!
GRAB
RK?

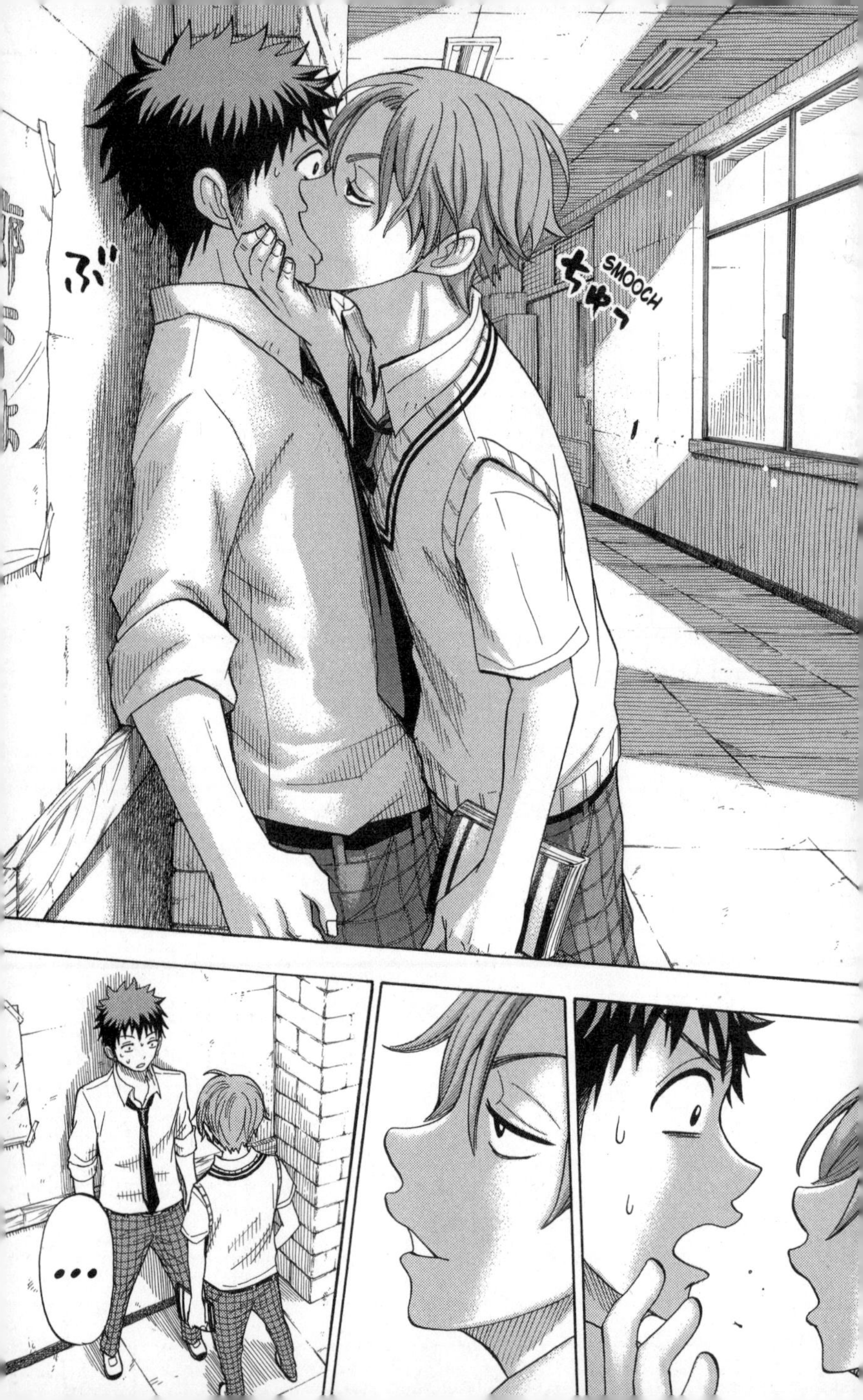
ちゅっ
SMOOCH
ぶ
...
...

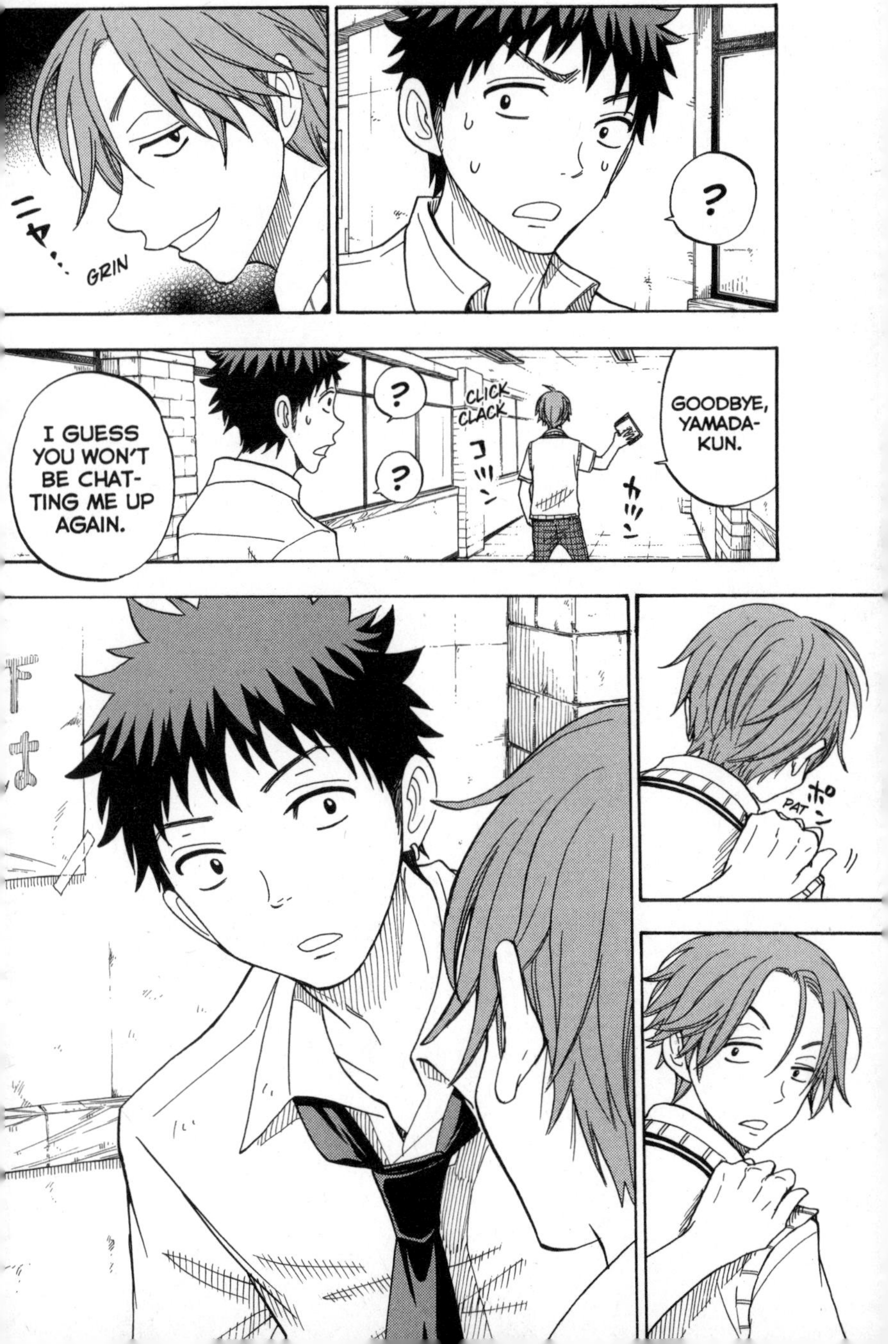
?
ニヤ…
GRIN
GOODBYE, YAMADA-KUN.
カツン
CLICK CLACK
コツン
?
?
I GUESS YOU WON'T BE CHAT-TING ME UP AGAIN.
ポン
PAT

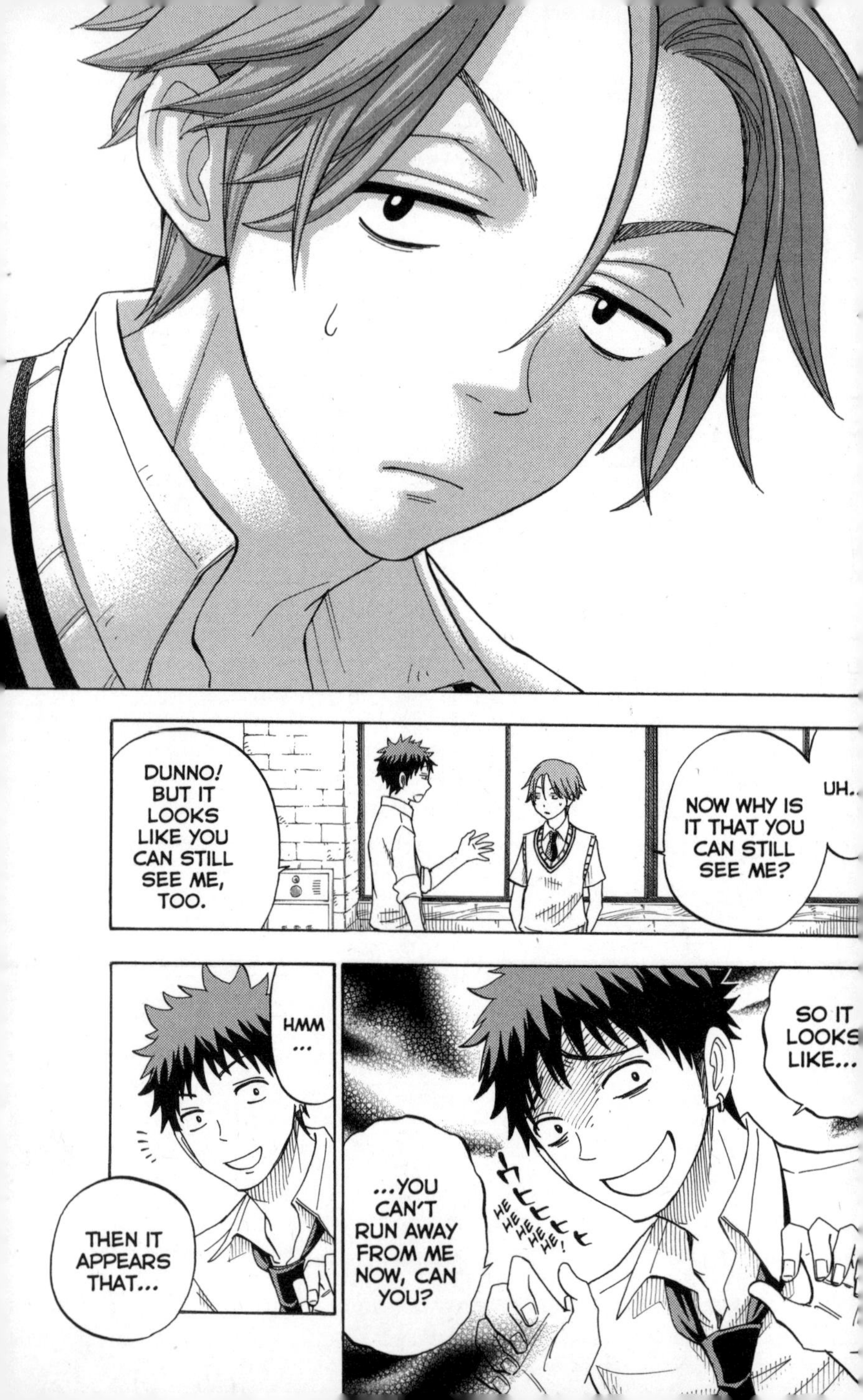
UH..
NOW WHY IS IT THAT YOU CAN STILL SEE ME?
DUNNO! BUT IT LOOKS LIKE YOU CAN STILL SEE ME, TOO.
SO IT LOOKS LIKE...
...YOU CAN'T RUN AWAY FROM ME NOW, CAN YOU?
HE HE HE HE HE!
HMM ...
THEN IT APPEARS THAT...

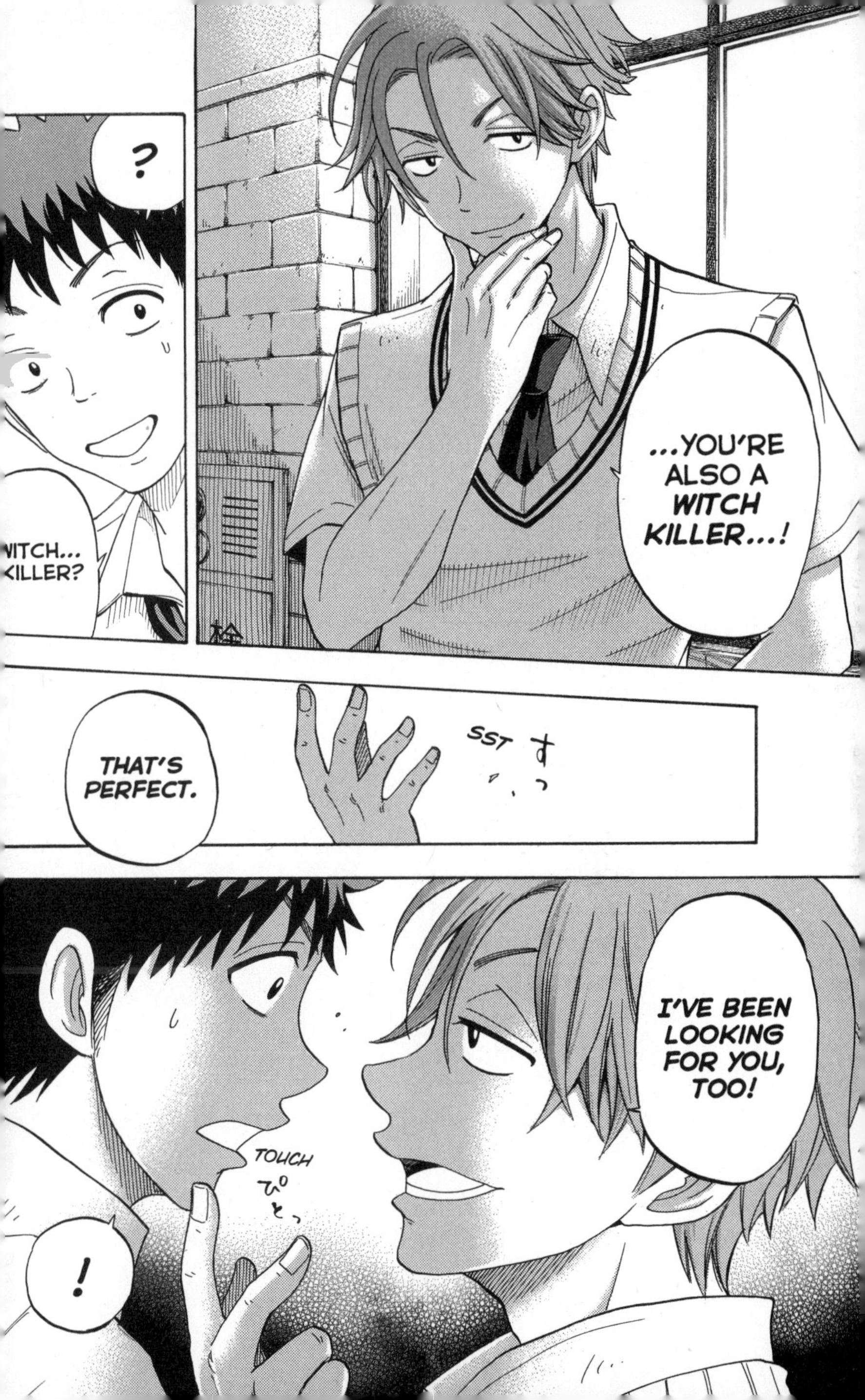
...YOU'RE ALSO A WITCH KILLER...!
?
WITCH... KILLER?
SST すっ
THAT'S PERFECT.
I'VE BEEN LOOKING FOR YOU, TOO!
TOUCH ぴとっ
!

CHAPTER 54: Why, Yamada-san!

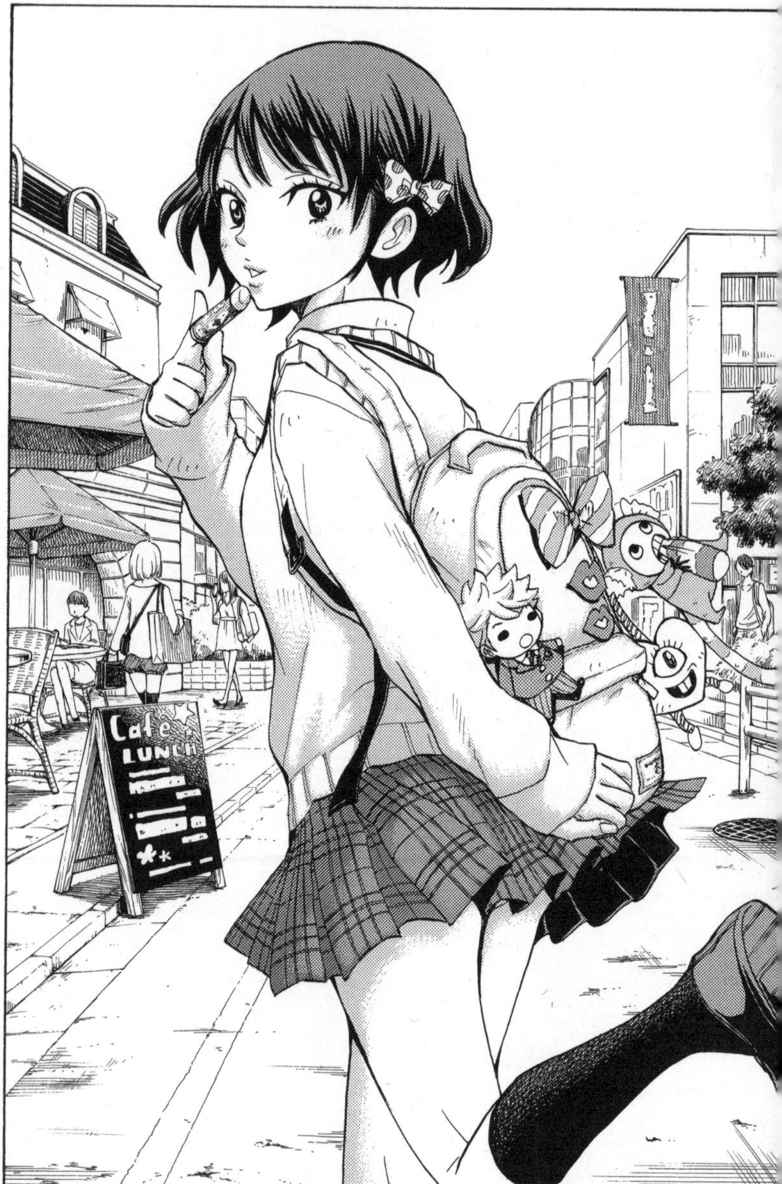
Café
LUNCH

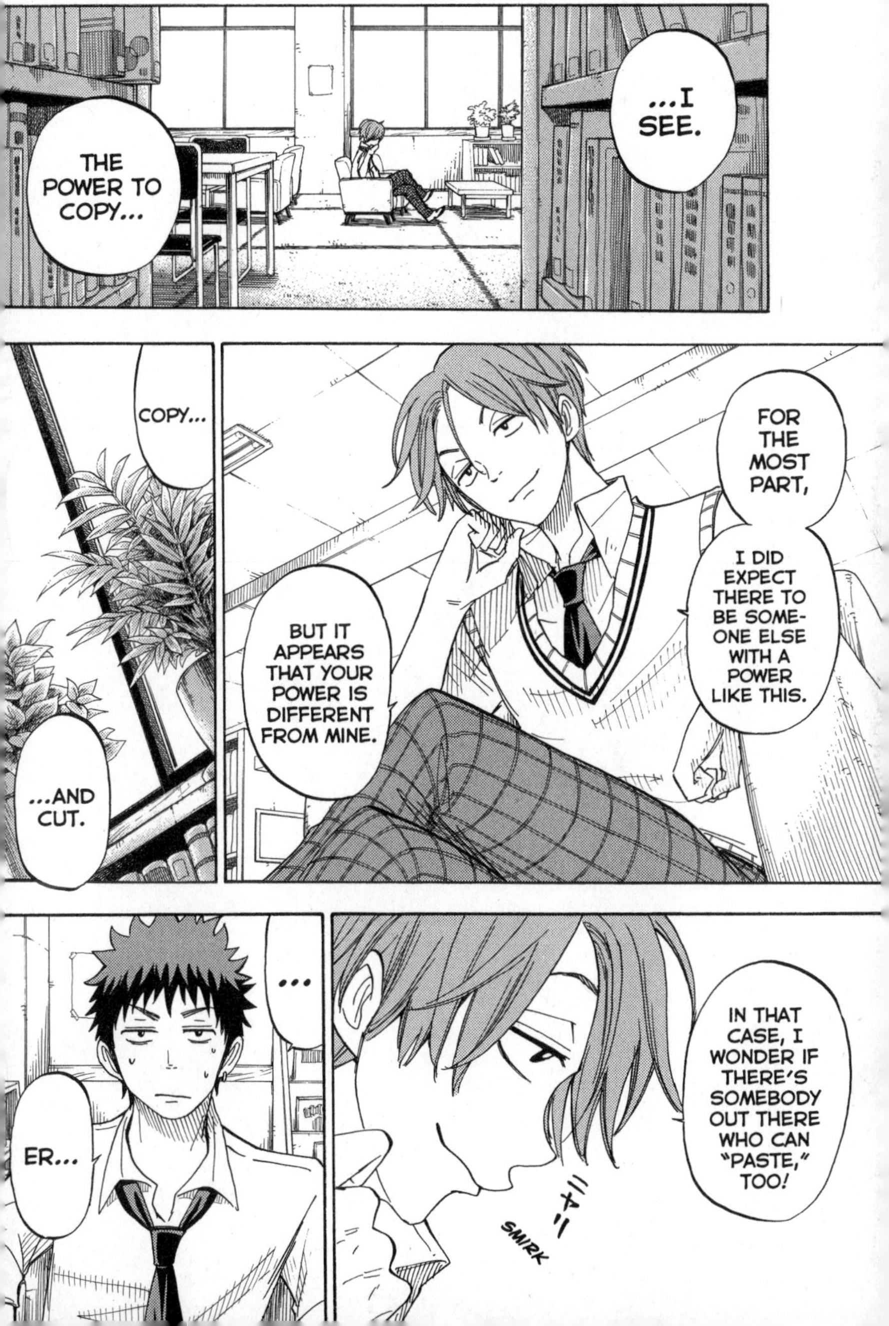
...I SEE.
THE POWER TO COPY...
FOR THE MOST PART,
I DID EXPECT THERE TO BE SOME-ONE ELSE WITH A POWER LIKE THIS.
BUT IT APPEARS THAT YOUR POWER IS DIFFERENT FROM MINE.
COPY...
...AND CUT.
IN THAT CASE, I WONDER IF THERE'S SOMEBODY OUT THERE WHO CAN "PASTE," TOO!
SMIRK
...
ER...

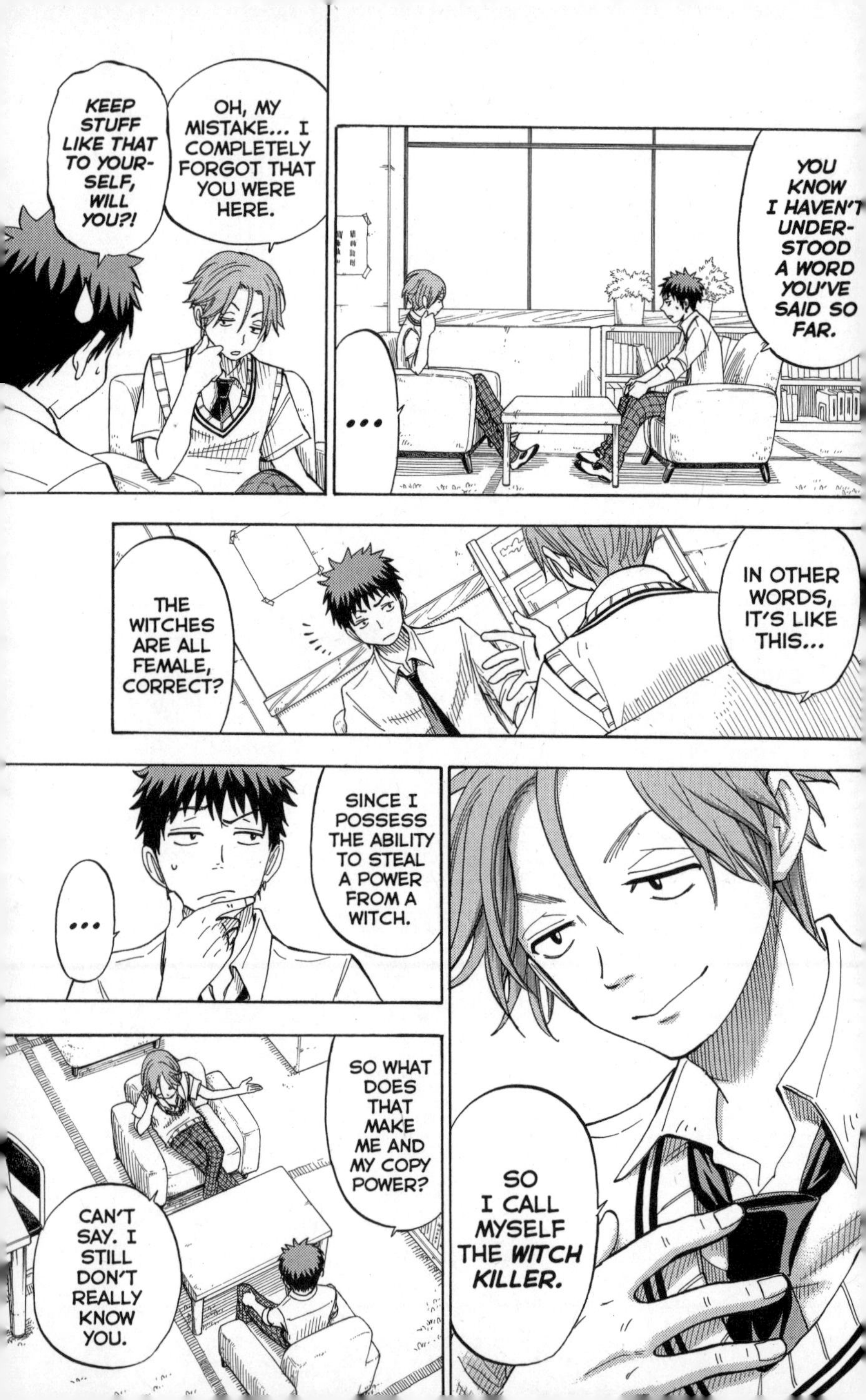
YOU KNOW I HAVEN'T UNDERSTOOD A WORD YOU'VE SAID SO FAR.
...
OH, MY MISTAKE... I COMPLETELY FORGOT THAT YOU WERE HERE.
KEEP STUFF LIKE THAT TO YOURSELF, WILL YOU?!
IN OTHER WORDS, IT'S LIKE THIS...
THE WITCHES ARE ALL FEMALE, CORRECT?
SO I CALL MYSELF THE *WITCH KILLER.*
SINCE I POSSESS THE ABILITY TO STEAL A POWER FROM A WITCH.
...
SO WHAT DOES THAT MAKE ME AND MY COPY POWER?
CAN'T SAY. I STILL DON'T REALLY KNOW YOU.

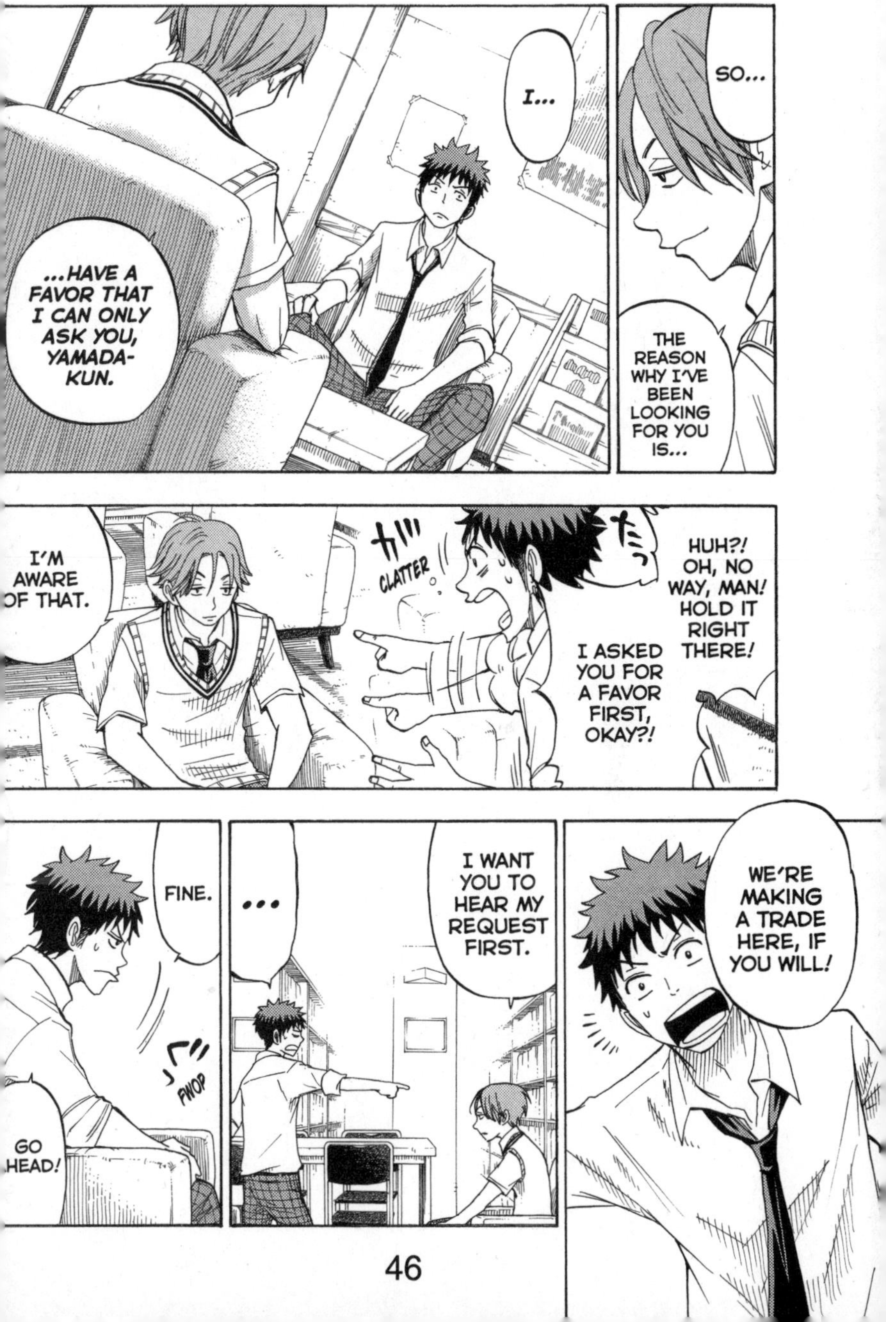
SO...
THE REASON WHY I'VE BEEN LOOKING FOR YOU IS...
I...
...HAVE A FAVOR THAT I CAN ONLY ASK YOU, YAMADA-KUN.
HUH?! OH, NO WAY, MAN! HOLD IT RIGHT THERE!
I ASKED YOU FOR A FAVOR FIRST, OKAY?!
CLATTER
I'M AWARE OF THAT.
WE'RE MAKING A TRADE HERE, IF YOU WILL!
I WANT YOU TO HEAR MY REQUEST FIRST.
...
FINE.
FWOP
GO HEAD!

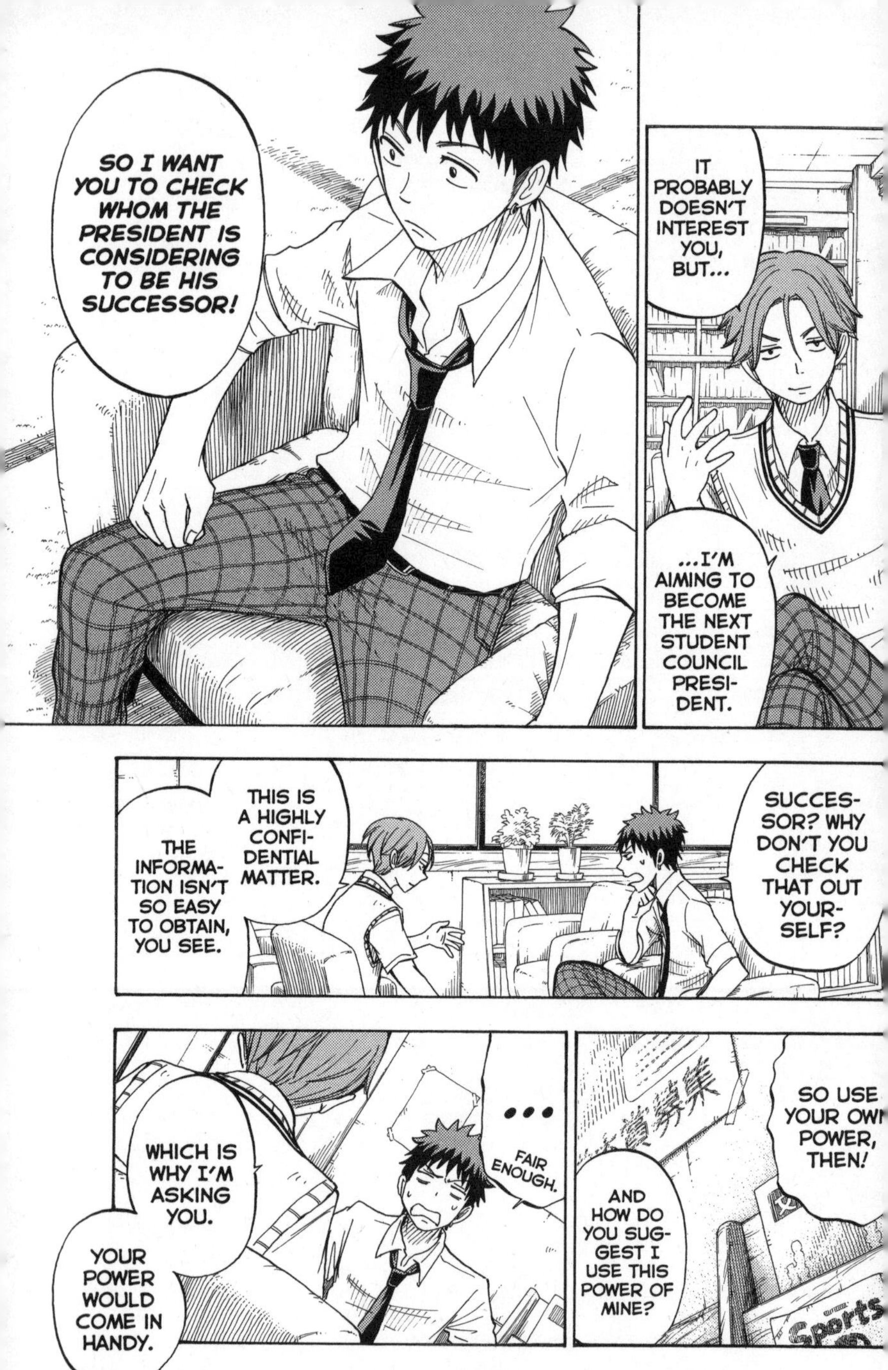
IT PROBABLY DOESN'T INTEREST YOU, BUT...
...I'M AIMING TO BECOME THE NEXT STUDENT COUNCIL PRESI-DENT.
SO I WANT YOU TO CHECK WHOM THE PRESIDENT IS CONSIDERING TO BE HIS SUCCESSOR!
SUCCES-SOR? WHY DON'T YOU CHECK THAT OUT YOUR-SELF?
THIS IS A HIGHLY CONFI-DENTIAL MATTER.
THE INFORMA-TION ISN'T SO EASY TO OBTAIN, YOU SEE.
SO USE YOUR OWN POWER, THEN!
AND HOW DO YOU SUG-GEST I USE THIS POWER OF MINE?
...
FAIR ENOUGH.
WHICH IS WHY I'M ASKING YOU.
YOUR POWER WOULD COME IN HANDY.

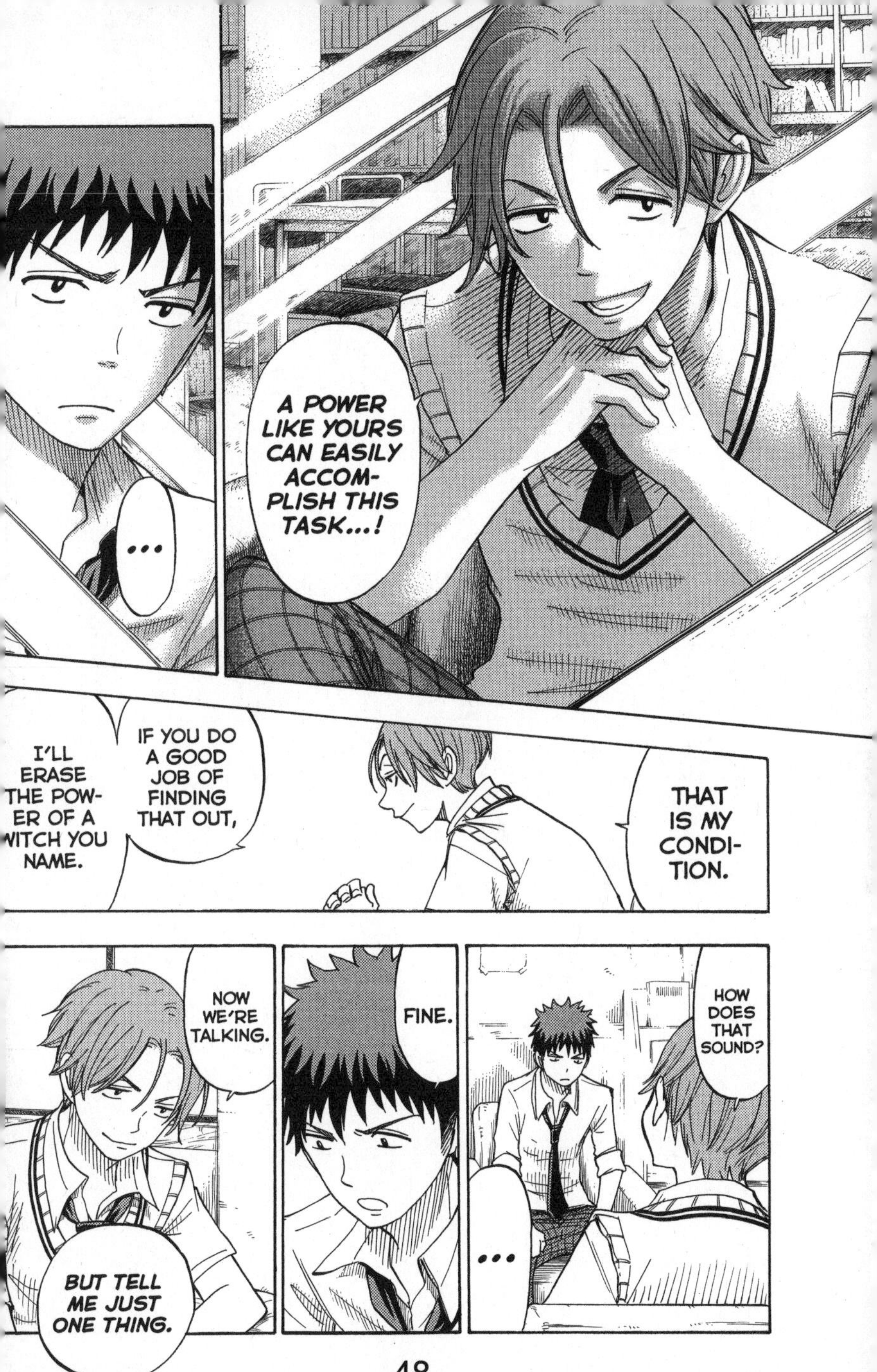
A POWER LIKE YOURS CAN EASILY ACCOMPLISH THIS TASK...!
...
THAT IS MY CONDITION.
IF YOU DO A GOOD JOB OF FINDING THAT OUT,
I'LL ERASE THE POWER OF A WITCH YOU NAME.
HOW DOES THAT SOUND?
...
FINE.
NOW WE'RE TALKING.
BUT TELL ME JUST ONE THING.

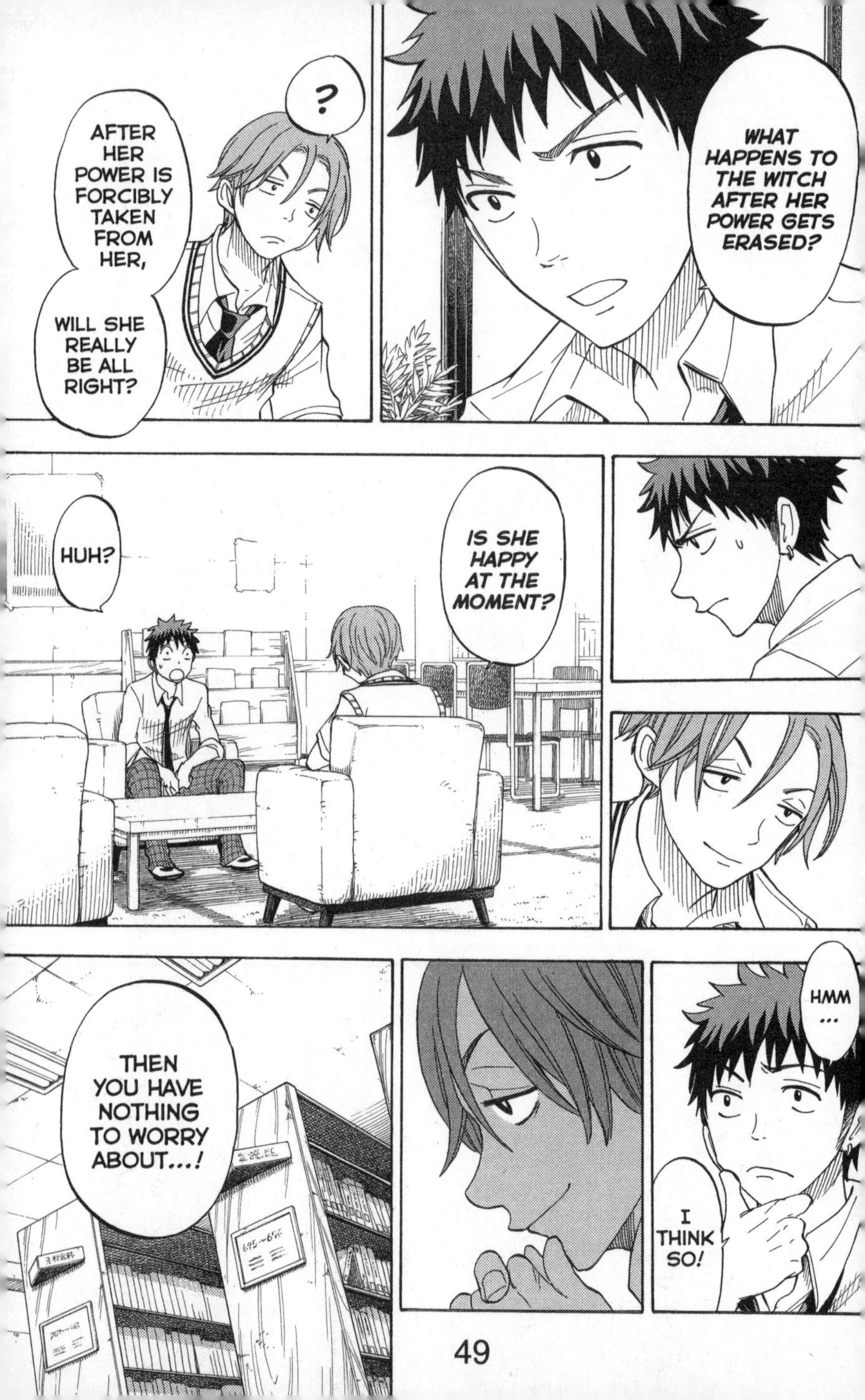
WHAT HAPPENS TO THE WITCH AFTER HER POWER GETS ERASED?
?
AFTER HER POWER IS FORCIBLY TAKEN FROM HER,
WILL SHE REALLY BE ALL RIGHT?
IS SHE HAPPY AT THE MOMENT?
HUH?
HMM...
I THINK SO!
THEN YOU HAVE NOTHING TO WORRY ABOUT...!

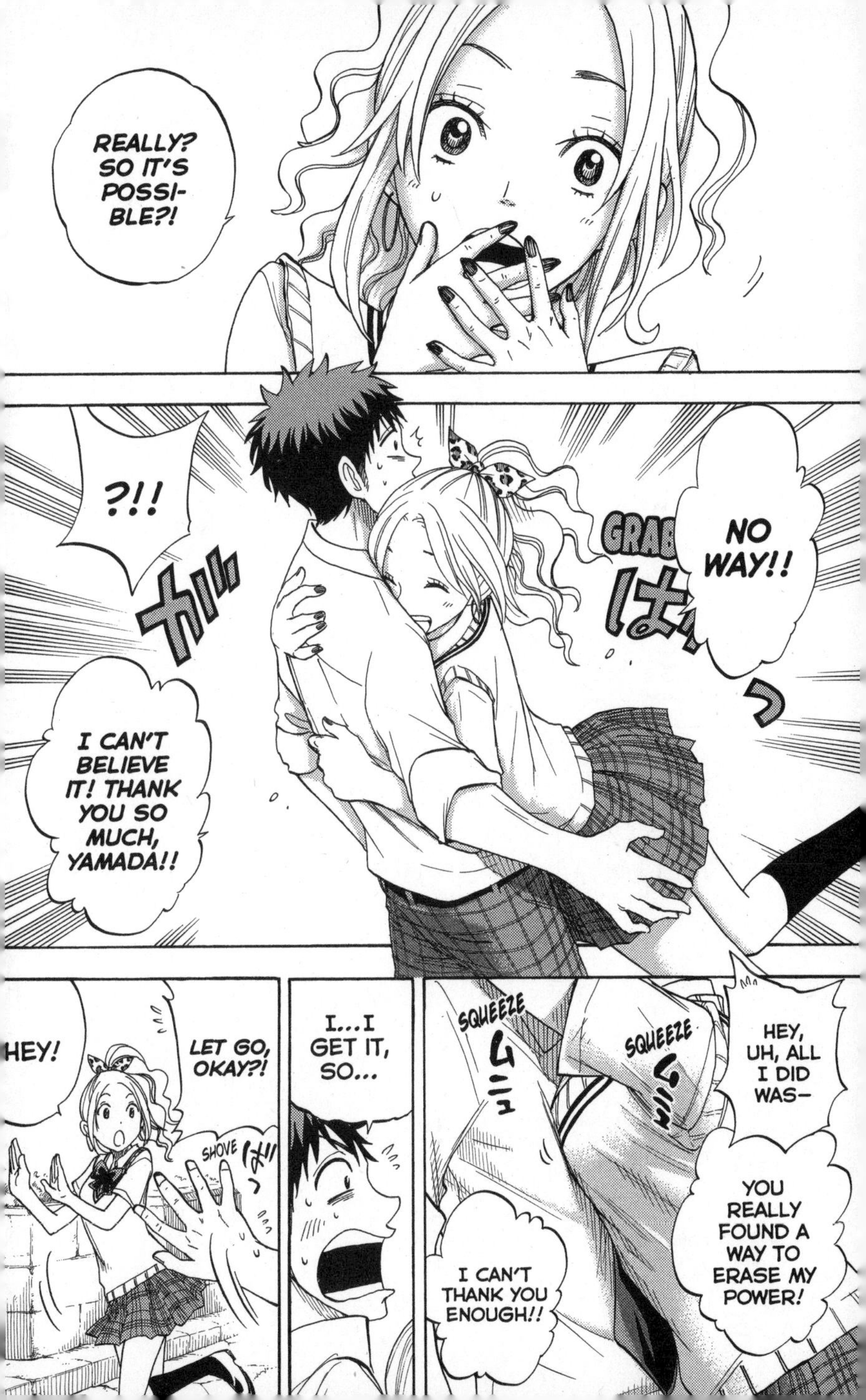
REALLY? SO IT'S POSSI- BLE?!
NO WAY!!
GRAB
?!!
カッ
I CAN'T BELIEVE IT! THANK YOU SO MUCH, YAMADA!!
HEY, UH, ALL I DID WAS—
SQUEEZE
ムニュ
YOU REALLY FOUND A WAY TO ERASE MY POWER!
SQUEEZE
ムニュ
I CAN'T THANK YOU ENOUGH!!
I...I GET IT, SO...
LET GO, OKAY?!
HEY!
SHOVE

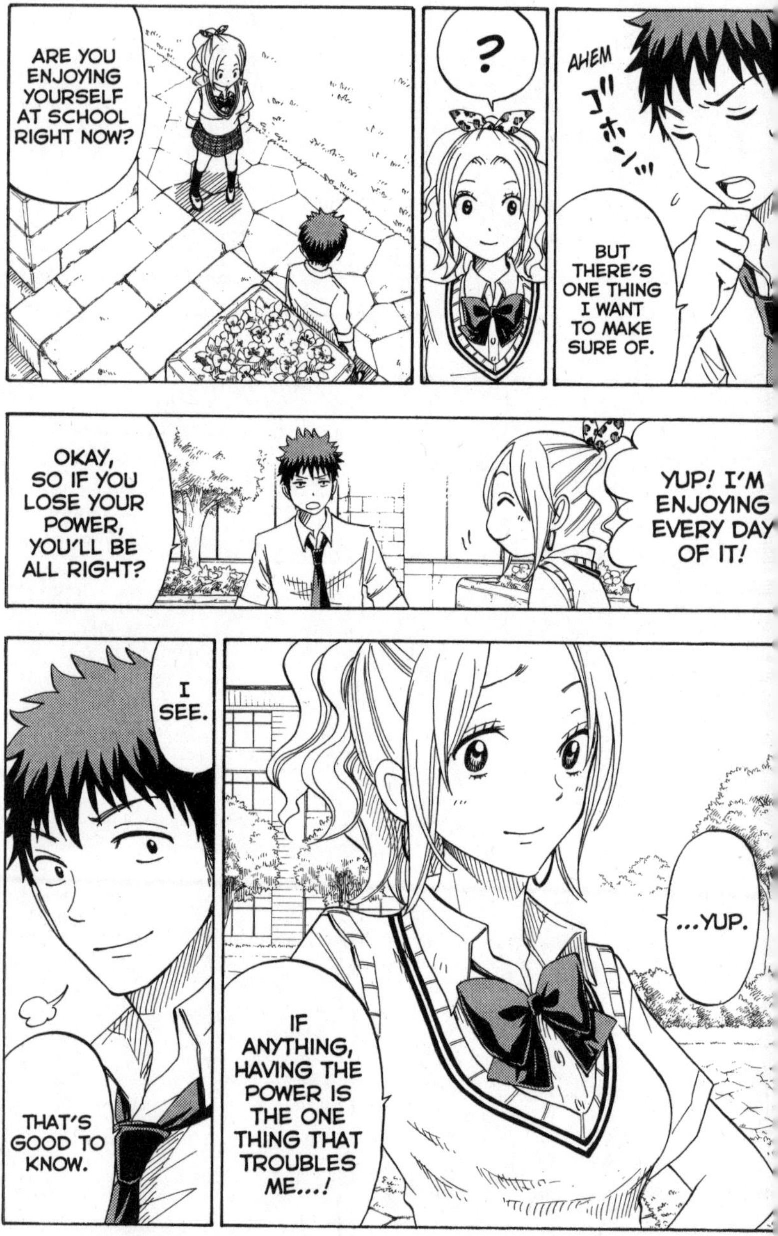
AHEM
ゴホンッ
BUT THERE'S ONE THING I WANT TO MAKE SURE OF.
?
ARE YOU ENJOYING YOURSELF AT SCHOOL RIGHT NOW?
YUP! I'M ENJOYING EVERY DAY OF IT!
OKAY, SO IF YOU LOSE YOUR POWER, YOU'LL BE ALL RIGHT?
...YUP.
IF ANYTHING, HAVING THE POWER IS THE ONE THING THAT TROUBLES ME...!
I SEE.
THAT'S GOOD TO KNOW.

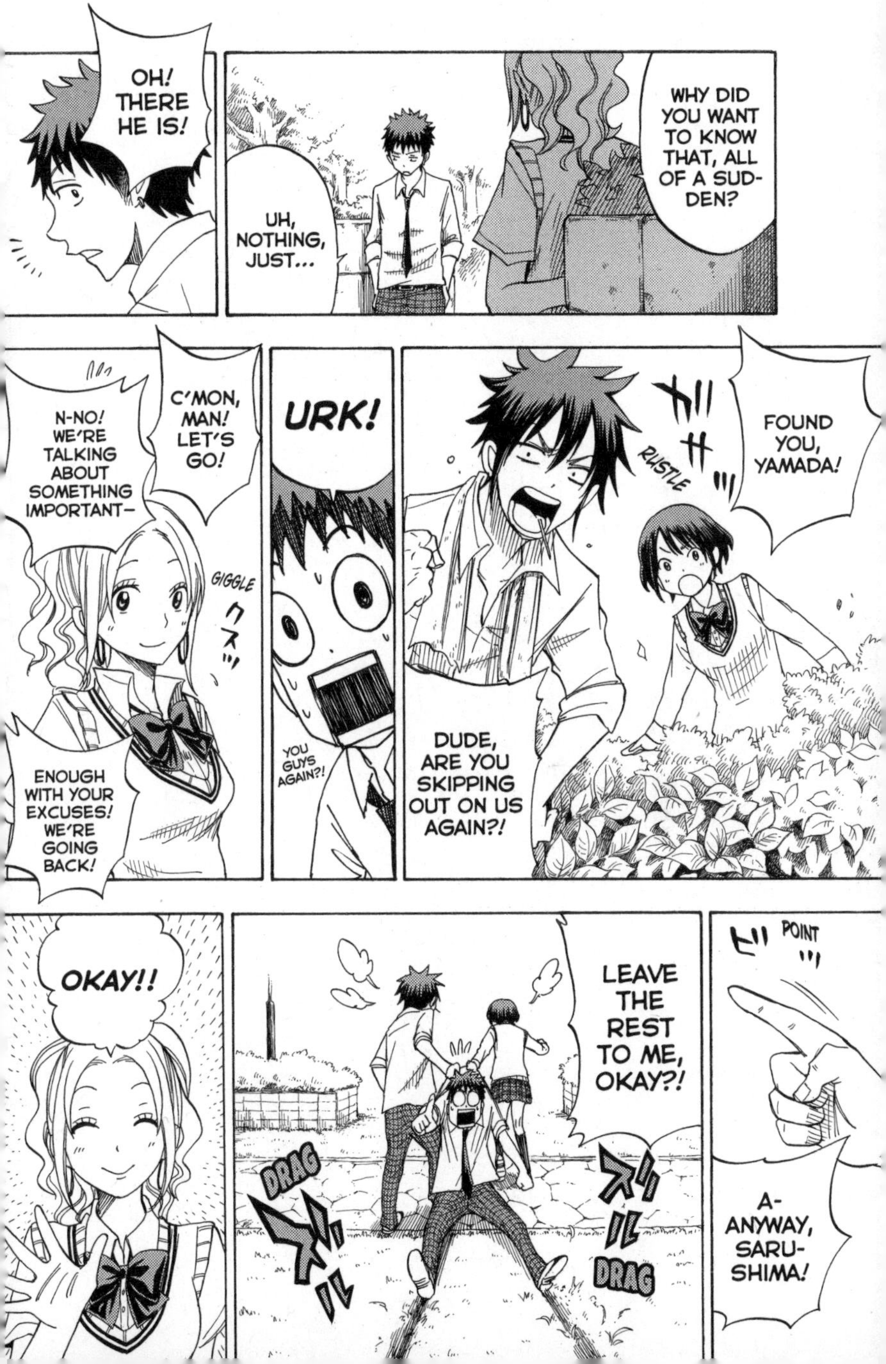
WHY DID YOU WANT TO KNOW THAT, ALL OF A SUDDEN?
UH, NOTHING, JUST...
OH! THERE HE IS!
FOUND YOU, YAMADA!
RUSTLE
DUDE, ARE YOU SKIPPING OUT ON US AGAIN?!
URK!
YOU GUYS AGAIN?!
C'MON, MAN! LET'S GO!
N-NO! WE'RE TALKING ABOUT SOMETHING IMPORTANT—
GIGGLE
ENOUGH WITH YOUR EXCUSES! WE'RE GOING BACK!
POINT
A-ANYWAY, SARUSHIMA!
LEAVE THE REST TO ME, OKAY?!
DRAG
DRAG
OKAY!!

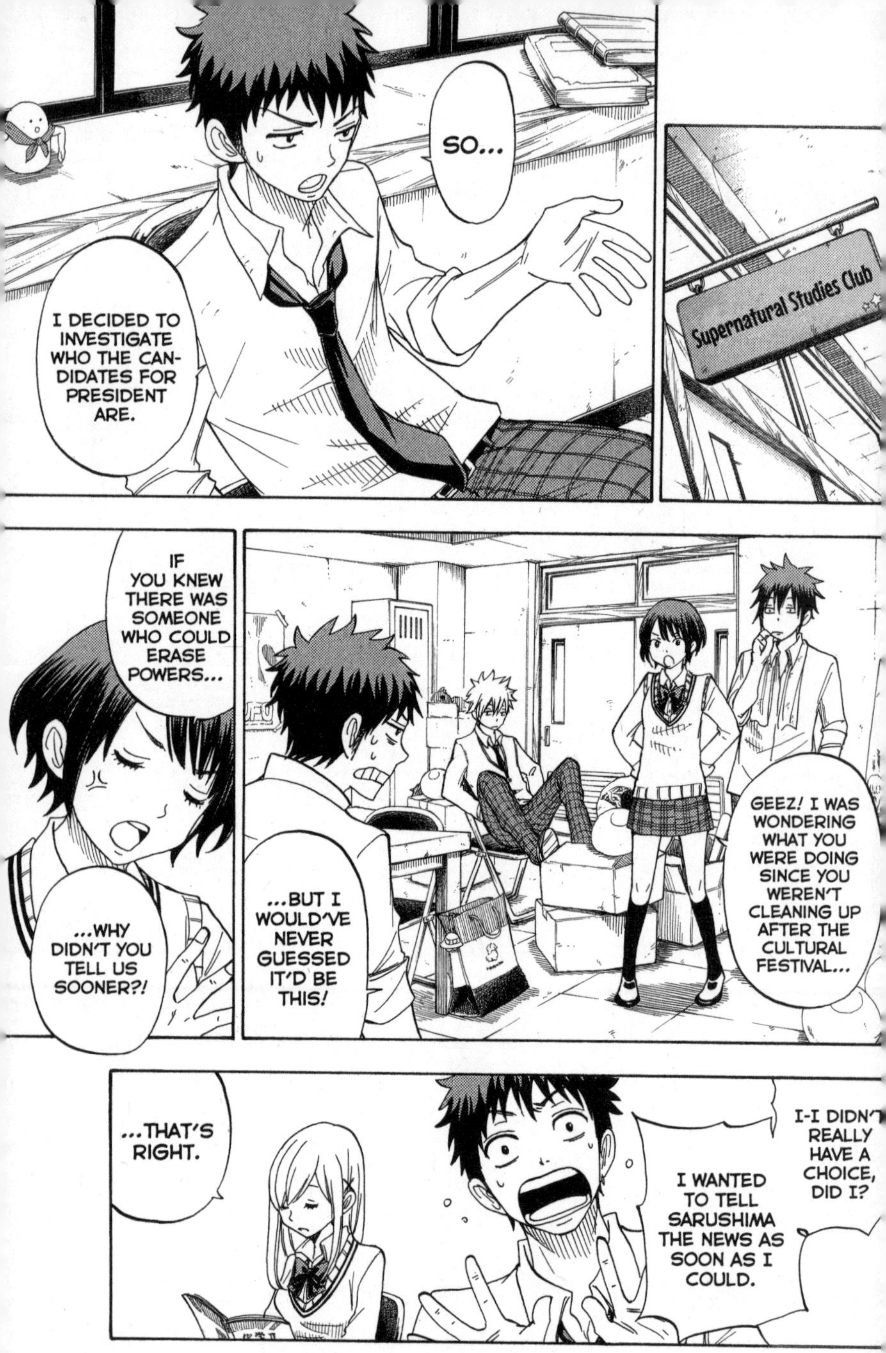
Supernatural Studies Club
SO...
I DECIDED TO INVESTIGATE WHO THE CAN-DIDATES FOR PRESIDENT ARE.
GEEZ! I WAS WONDERING WHAT YOU WERE DOING SINCE YOU WEREN'T CLEANING UP AFTER THE CULTURAL FESTIVAL...
...BUT I WOULD'VE NEVER GUESSED IT'D BE THIS!
IF YOU KNEW THERE WAS SOMEONE WHO COULD ERASE POWERS...
...WHY DIDN'T YOU TELL US SOONER?!
I-I DIDN'T REALLY HAVE A CHOICE, DID I?
I WANTED TO TELL SARUSHIMA THE NEWS AS SOON AS I COULD.
...THAT'S RIGHT.

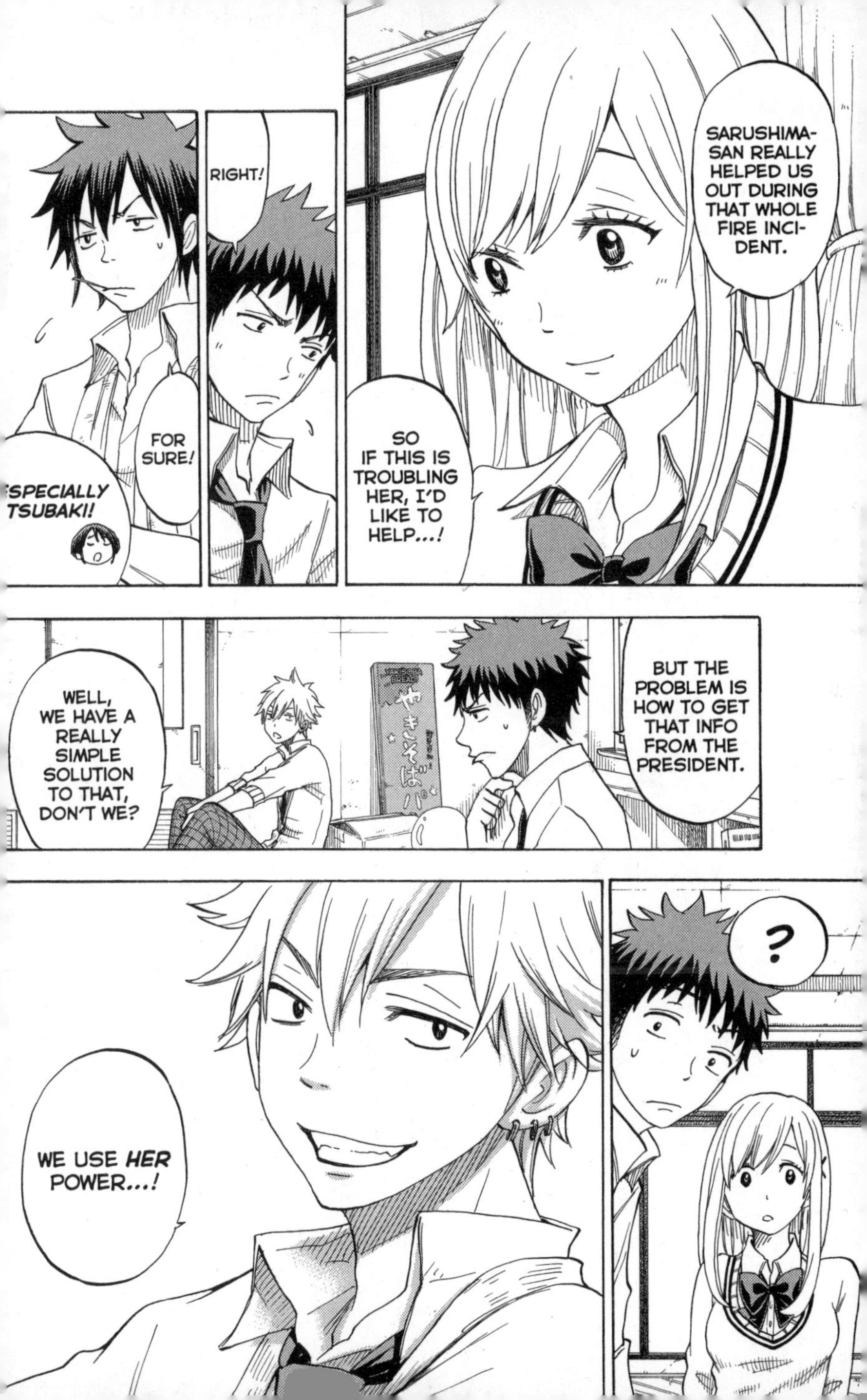
SARUSHIMA-SAN REALLY HELPED US OUT DURING THAT WHOLE FIRE INCIDENT.
SO IF THIS IS TROUBLING HER, I'D LIKE TO HELP...!
RIGHT!
FOR SURE!
SPECIALLY TSUBAKI!
BUT THE PROBLEM IS HOW TO GET THAT INFO FROM THE PRESIDENT.
YAKISOBA BREAD!
WELL, WE HAVE A REALLY SIMPLE SOLUTION TO THAT, DON'T WE?
?
WE USE *HER* POWER...!

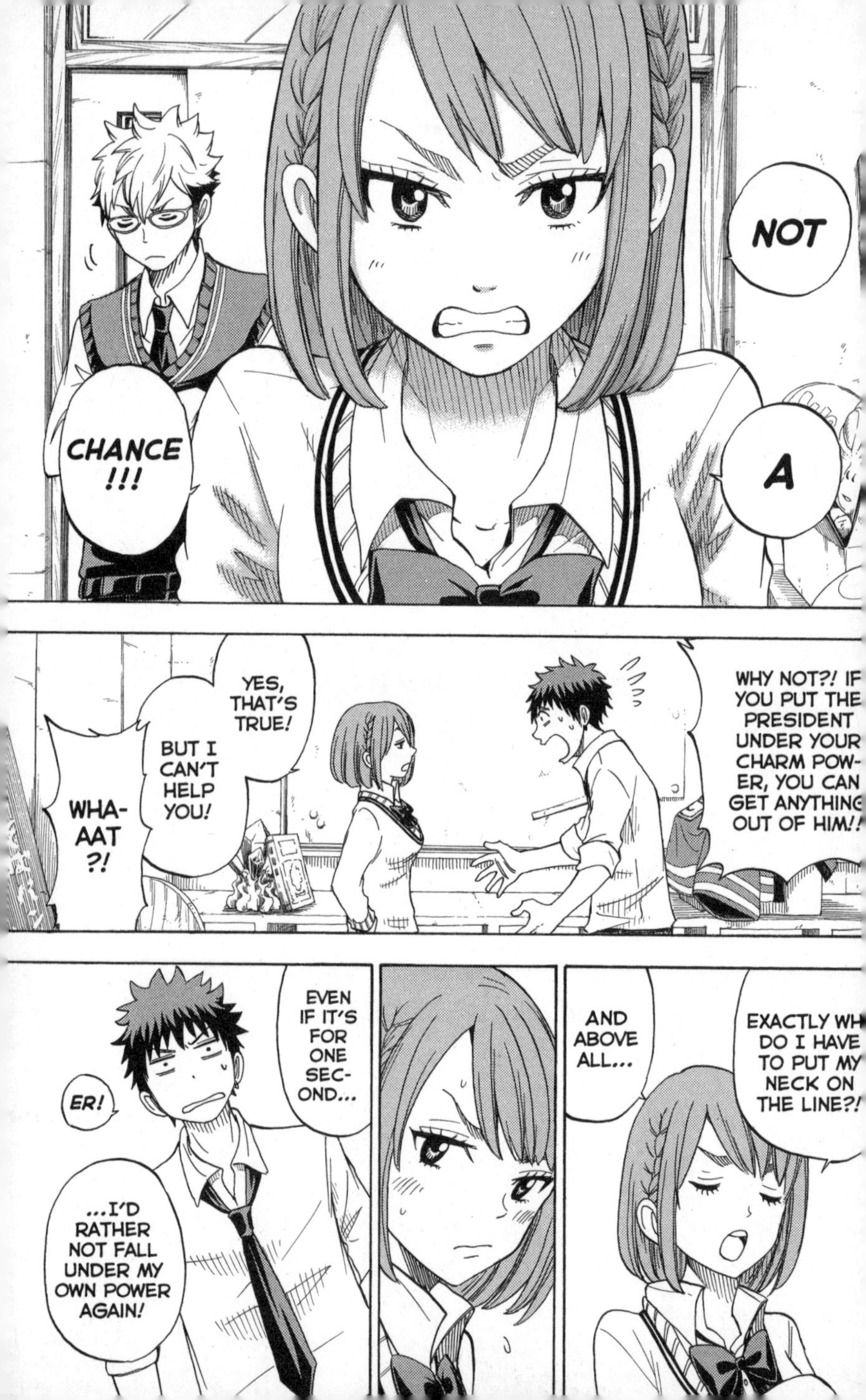
NOT
A
CHANCE !!!
WHY NOT?! IF YOU PUT THE PRESIDENT UNDER YOUR CHARM POW-ER, YOU CAN GET ANYTHING OUT OF HIM!!
YES, THAT'S TRUE!
BUT I CAN'T HELP YOU!
WHA-AAT ?!
EXACTLY WH DO I HAVE TO PUT MY NECK ON THE LINE?!
AND ABOVE ALL...
EVEN IF IT'S FOR ONE SEC-OND...
ER!
...I'D RATHER NOT FALL UNDER MY OWN POWER AGAIN!

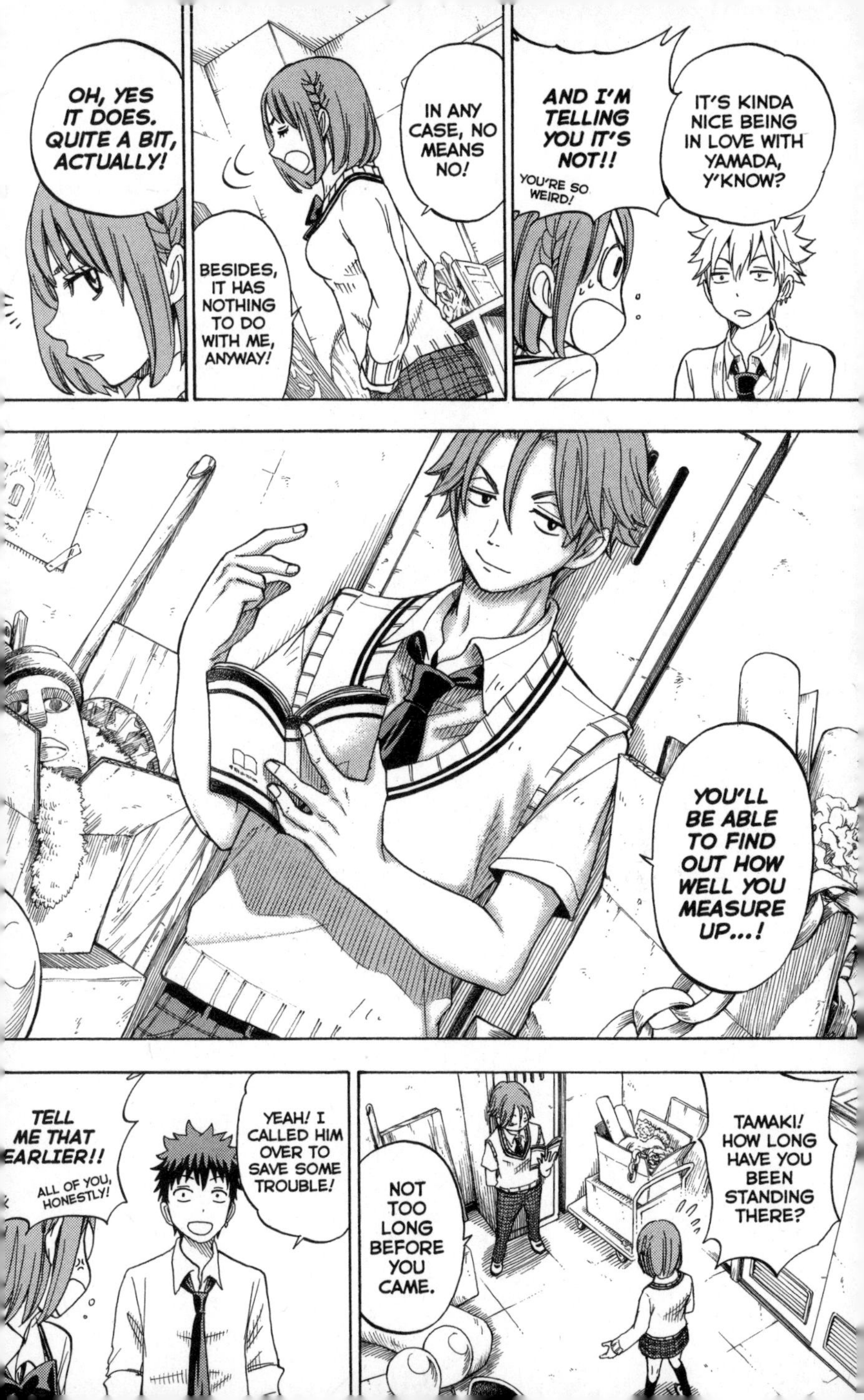
IT'S KINDA NICE BEING IN LOVE WITH YAMADA, Y'KNOW?
AND I'M TELLING YOU IT'S NOT!!
YOU'RE SO WEIRD!
IN ANY CASE, NO MEANS NO!
BESIDES, IT HAS NOTHING TO DO WITH ME, ANYWAY!
OH, YES IT DOES. QUITE A BIT, ACTUALLY!
YOU'LL BE ABLE TO FIND OUT HOW WELL YOU MEASURE UP...!
TAMAKI! HOW LONG HAVE YOU BEEN STANDING THERE?
NOT TOO LONG BEFORE YOU CAME.
YEAH! I CALLED HIM OVER TO SAVE SOME TROUBLE!
TELL ME THAT EARLIER!!
ALL OF YOU, HONESTLY!

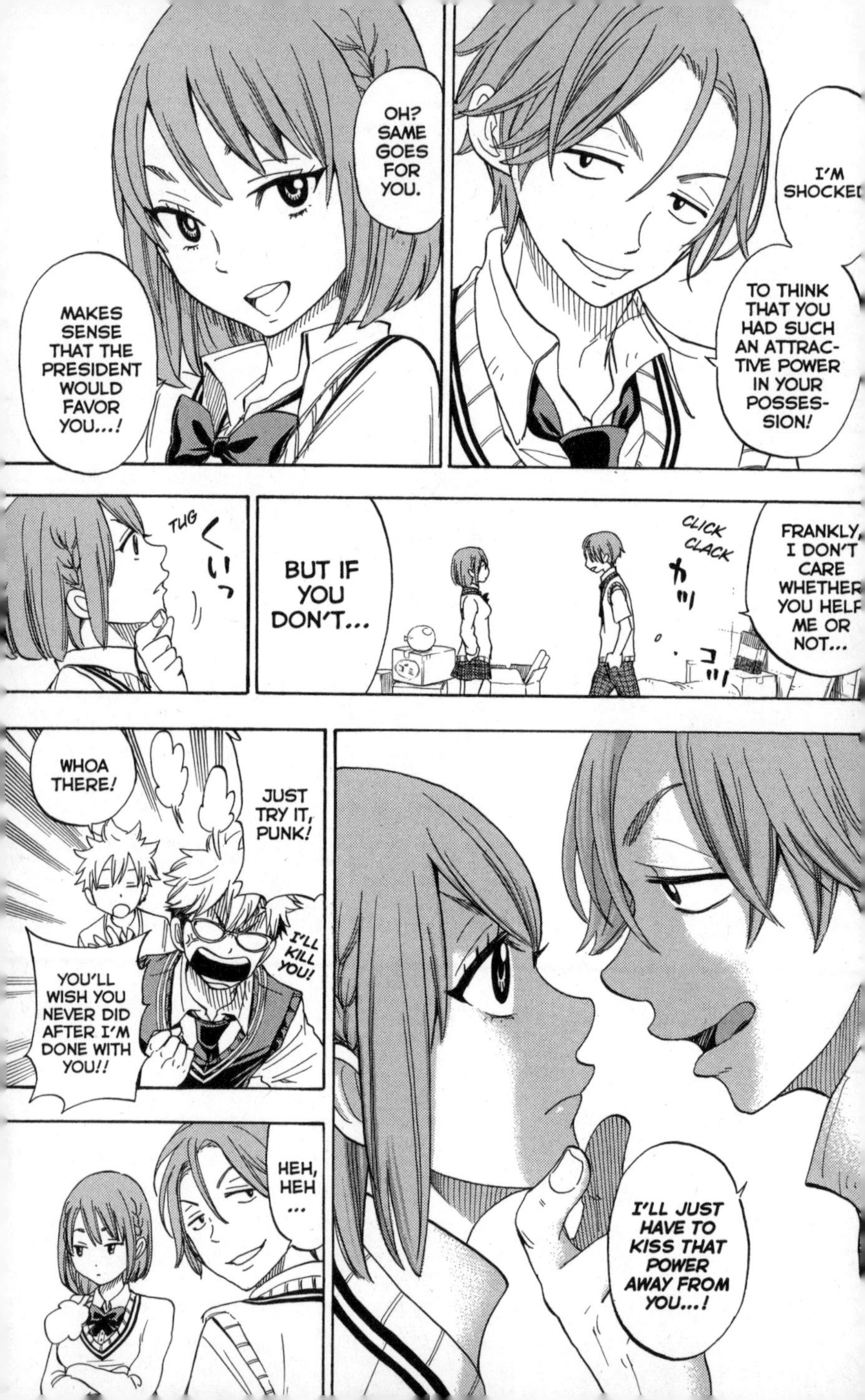
I'M SHOCKED
TO THINK THAT YOU HAD SUCH AN ATTRAC-TIVE POWER IN YOUR POSSES-SION!
OH? SAME GOES FOR YOU.
MAKES SENSE THAT THE PRESIDENT WOULD FAVOR YOU...!
FRANKLY, I DON'T CARE WHETHER YOU HELP ME OR NOT...
CLICK CLACK
BUT IF YOU DON'T...
TUG
I'LL JUST HAVE TO KISS THAT POWER AWAY FROM YOU...!
JUST TRY IT, PUNK!
WHOA THERE!
I'LL KILL YOU!
YOU'LL WISH YOU NEVER DID AFTER I'M DONE WITH YOU!!
HEH, HEH ...

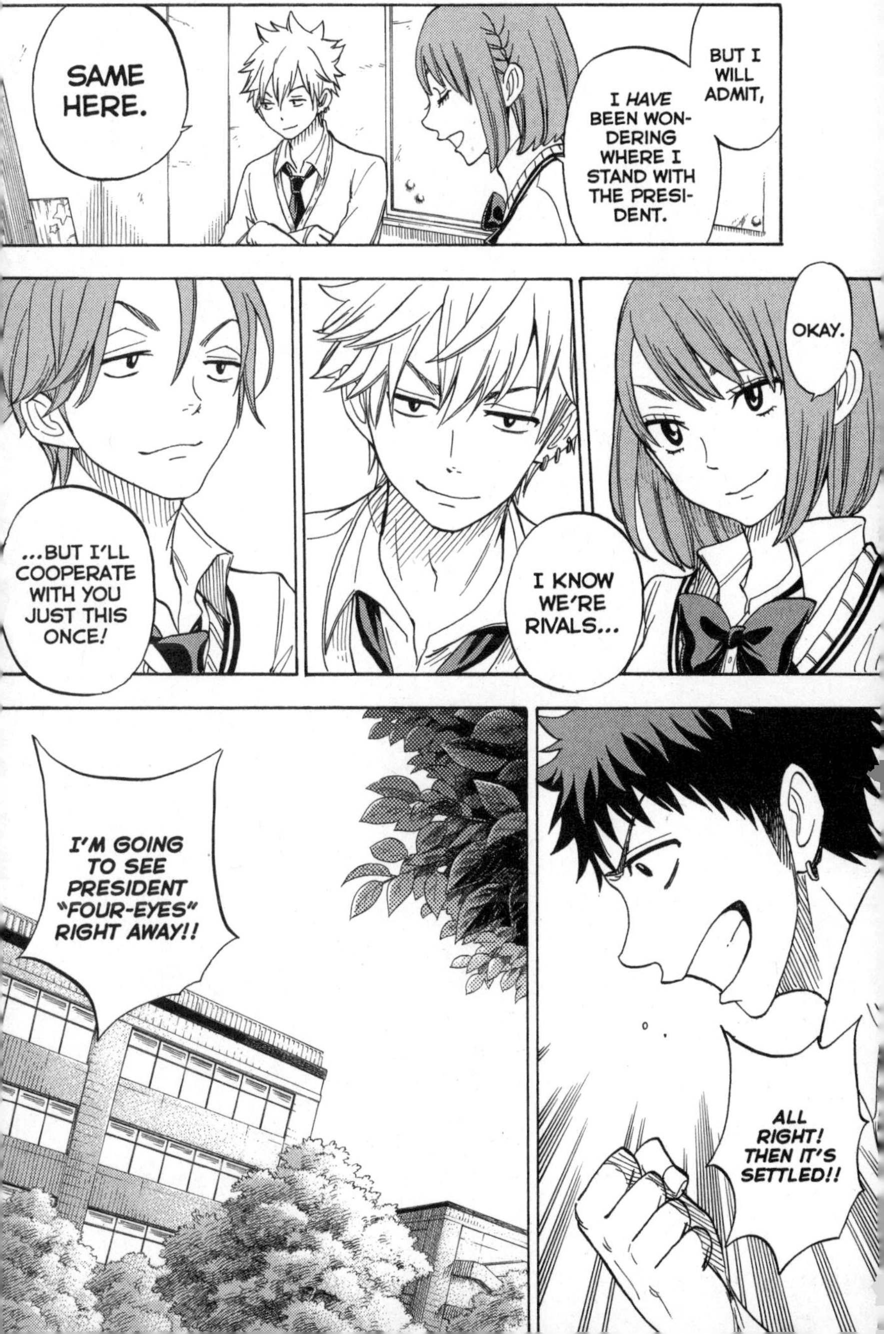
BUT I WILL ADMIT,
I *HAVE* BEEN WONDERING WHERE I STAND WITH THE PRESIDENT.
SAME HERE.
OKAY.
I KNOW WE'RE RIVALS...
...BUT I'LL COOPERATE WITH YOU JUST THIS ONCE!
ALL RIGHT! THEN IT'S SETTLED!!
I'M GOING TO SEE PRESIDENT "FOUR-EYES" RIGHT AWAY!!

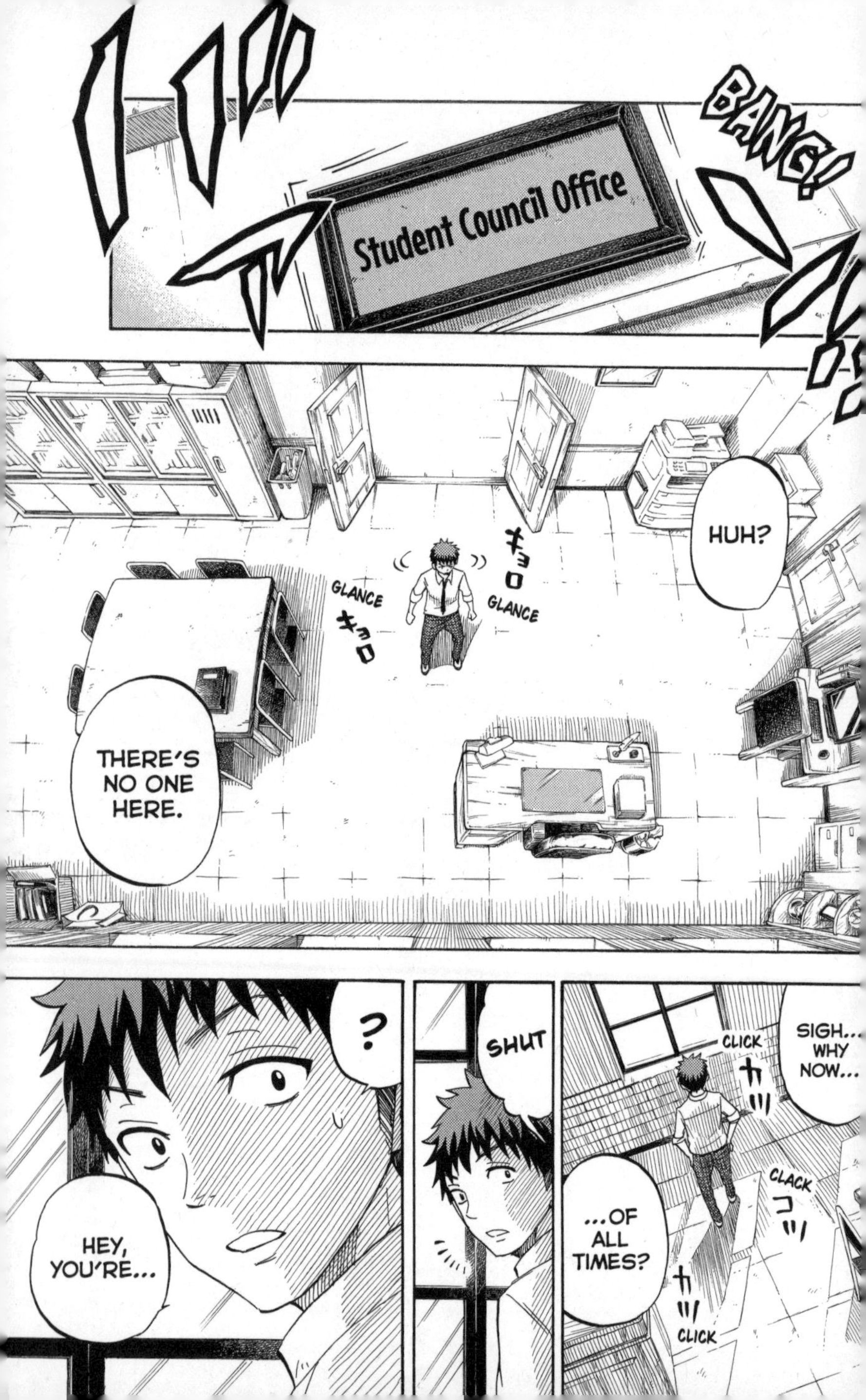
BANG!
Student Council Office
HUH?
キョロ
GLANCE
GLANCE
キョロ
THERE'S NO ONE HERE.
SIGH... WHY NOW...
CLICK
カツ
CLACK
コツ
カツ
CLICK
...OF ALL TIMES?
SHUT
?
HEY, YOU'RE...

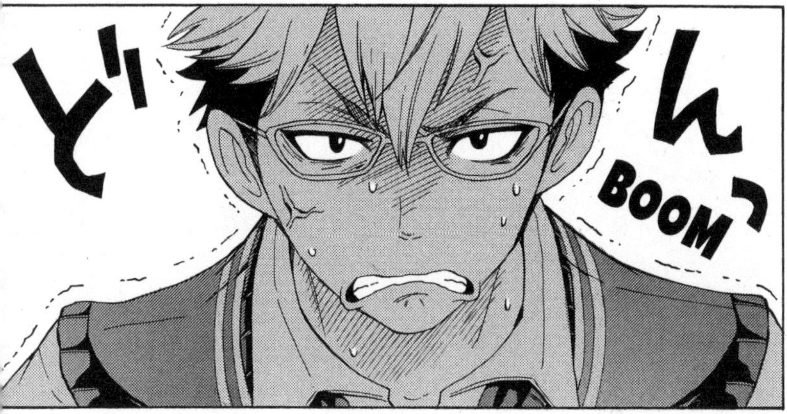

BOOM

↓Shirt: "Big Sale"

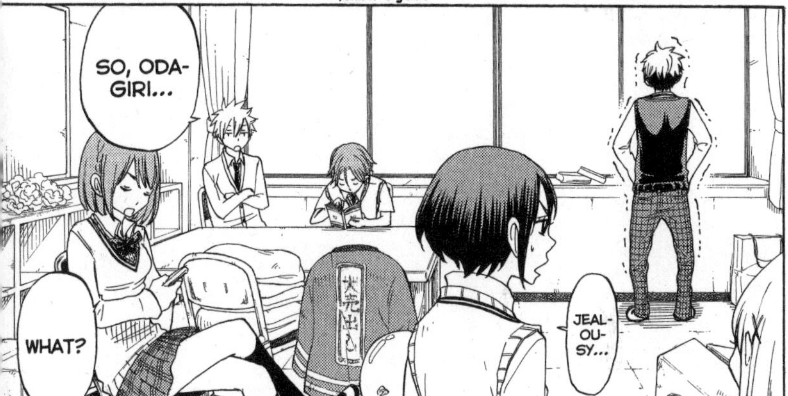

JEAL-OU-SY...
SO, ODA-GIRI...
WHAT?

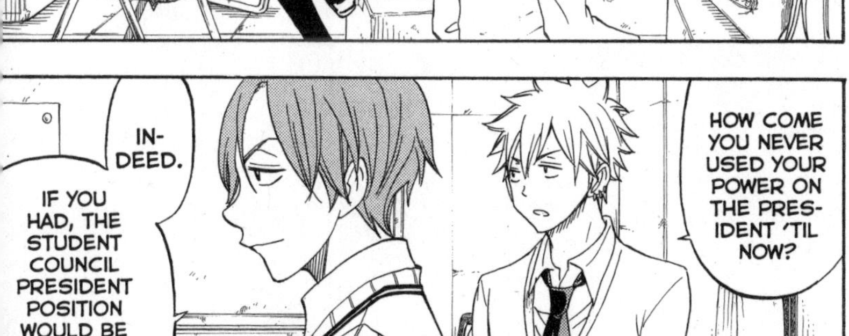

HOW COME YOU NEVER USED YOUR POWER ON THE PRES-IDENT 'TIL NOW?
IN-DEED.
IF YOU HAD, THE STUDENT COUNCIL PRESIDENT POSITION WOULD BE AS GOOD AS YOURS.

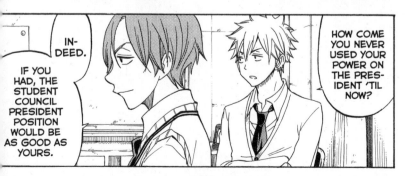

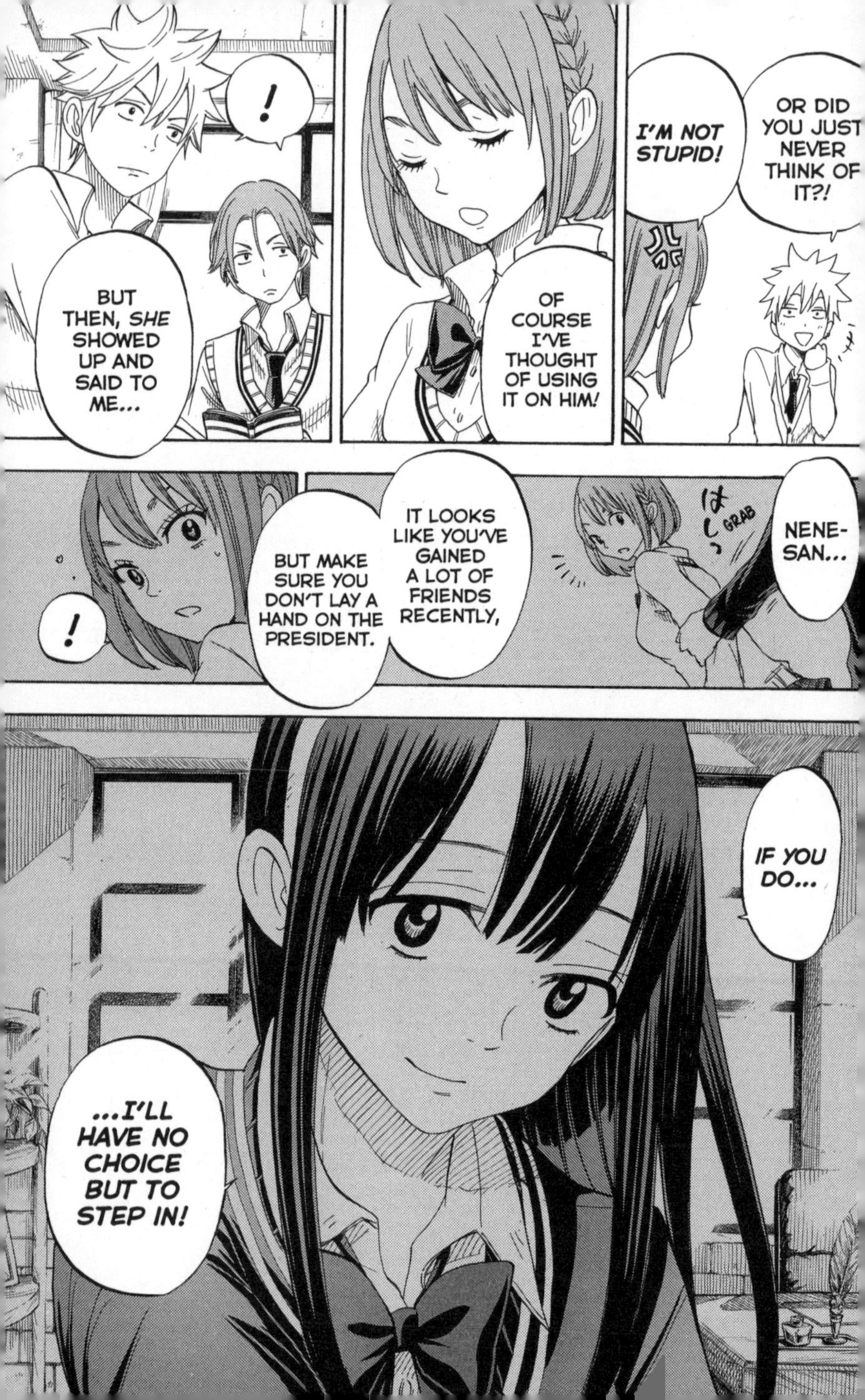
OR DID YOU JUST NEVER THINK OF IT?!
I'M NOT STUPID!
OF COURSE I'VE THOUGHT OF USING IT ON HIM!
!
BUT THEN, *SHE* SHOWED UP AND SAID TO ME...
NENE-SAN...
GRAB
IT LOOKS LIKE YOU'VE GAINED A LOT OF FRIENDS RECENTLY,
BUT MAKE SURE YOU DON'T LAY A HAND ON THE PRESIDENT.
!
IF YOU DO...
...I'LL HAVE NO CHOICE BUT TO STEP IN!

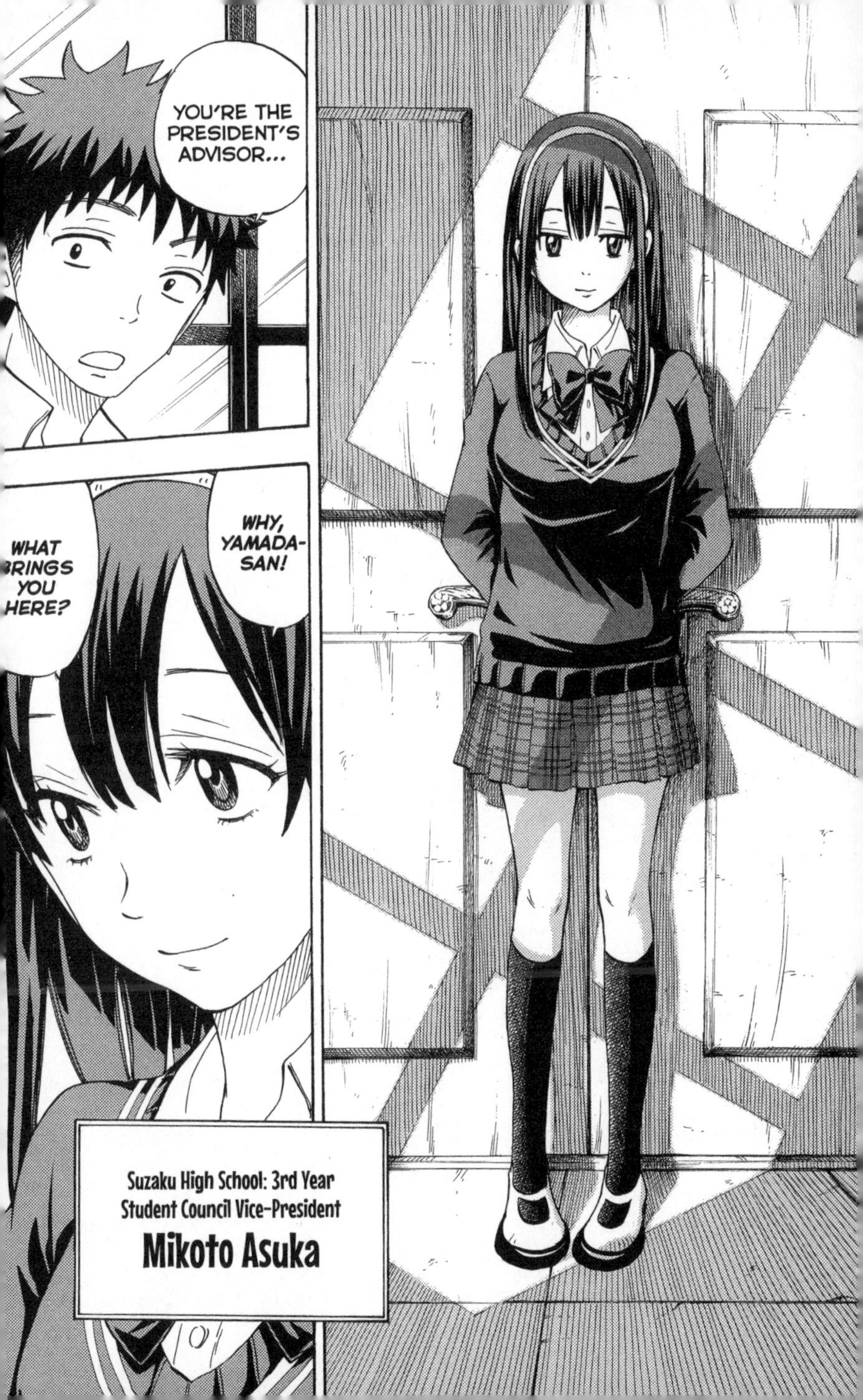
YOU'RE THE PRESIDENT'S ADVISOR...
WHY, YAMADA-SAN!
WHAT BRINGS YOU HERE?
Suzaku High School: 3rd Year
Student Council Vice-President
Mikoto Asuka

CHAPTER 55: Here we go!

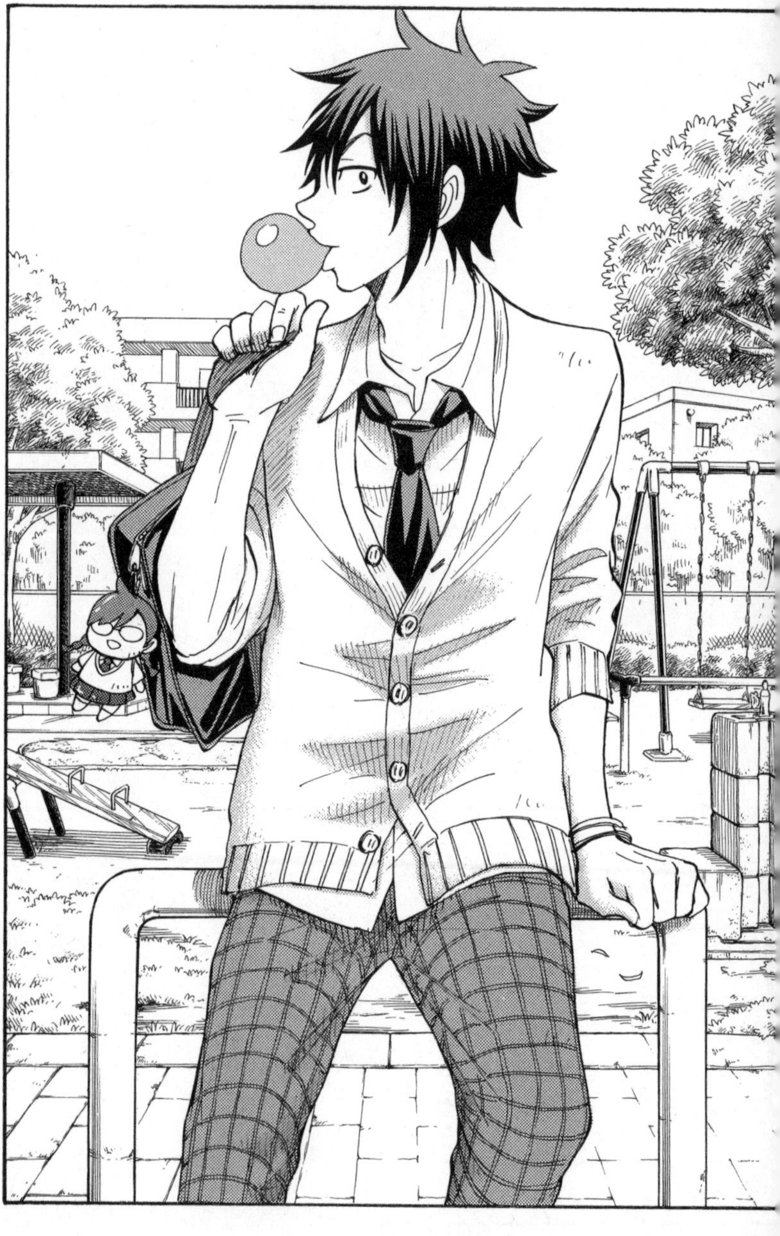

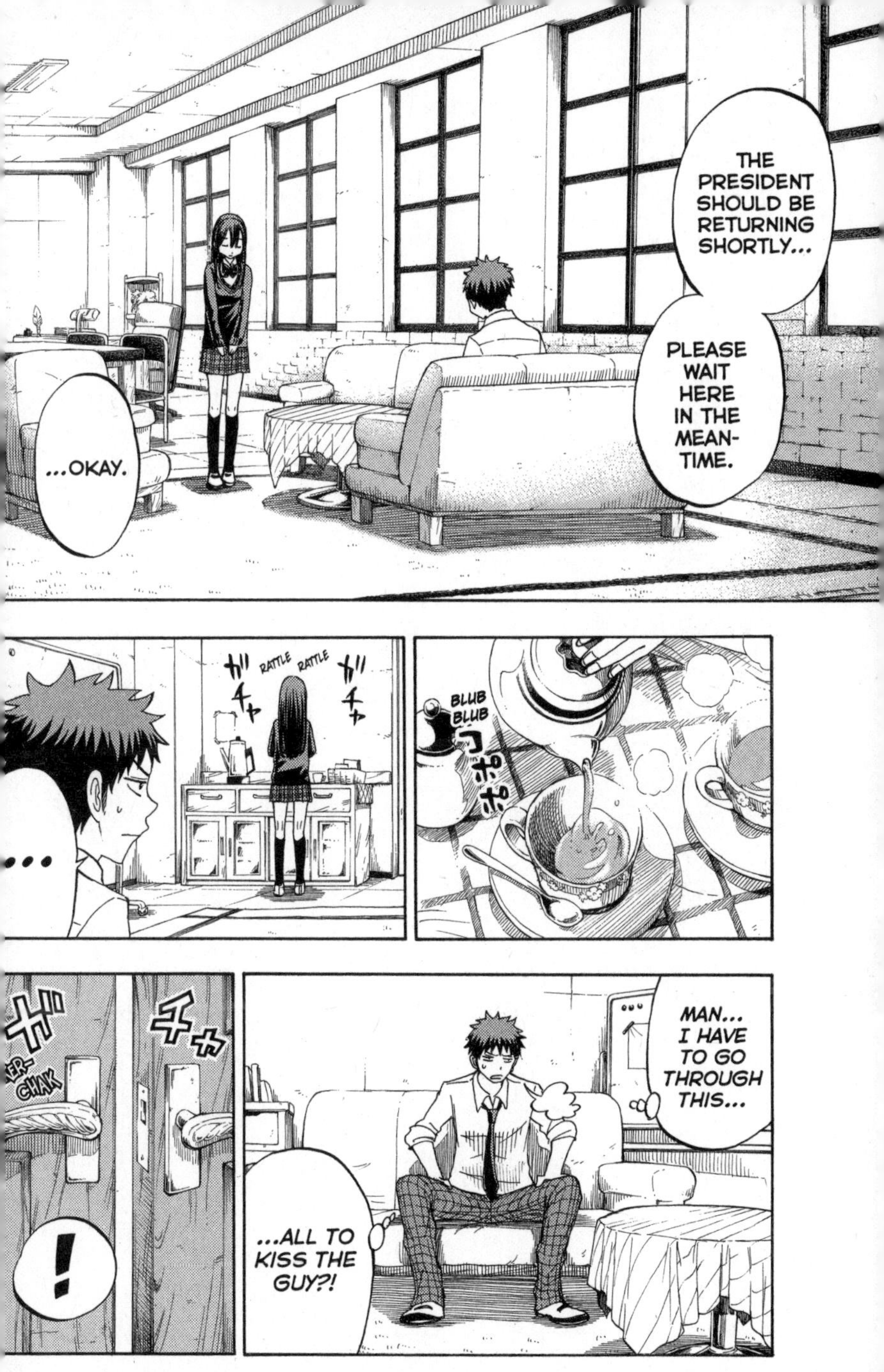
THE PRESIDENT SHOULD BE RETURNING SHORTLY...
PLEASE WAIT HERE IN THE MEAN-TIME.
...OKAY.
コポポ
BLUB BLUB
ガチャ
RATTLE
ガチャ
RATTLE
...
MAN... I HAVE TO GO THROUGH THIS...
...ALL TO KISS THE GUY?!
ガチャ
ER-CHAK
!

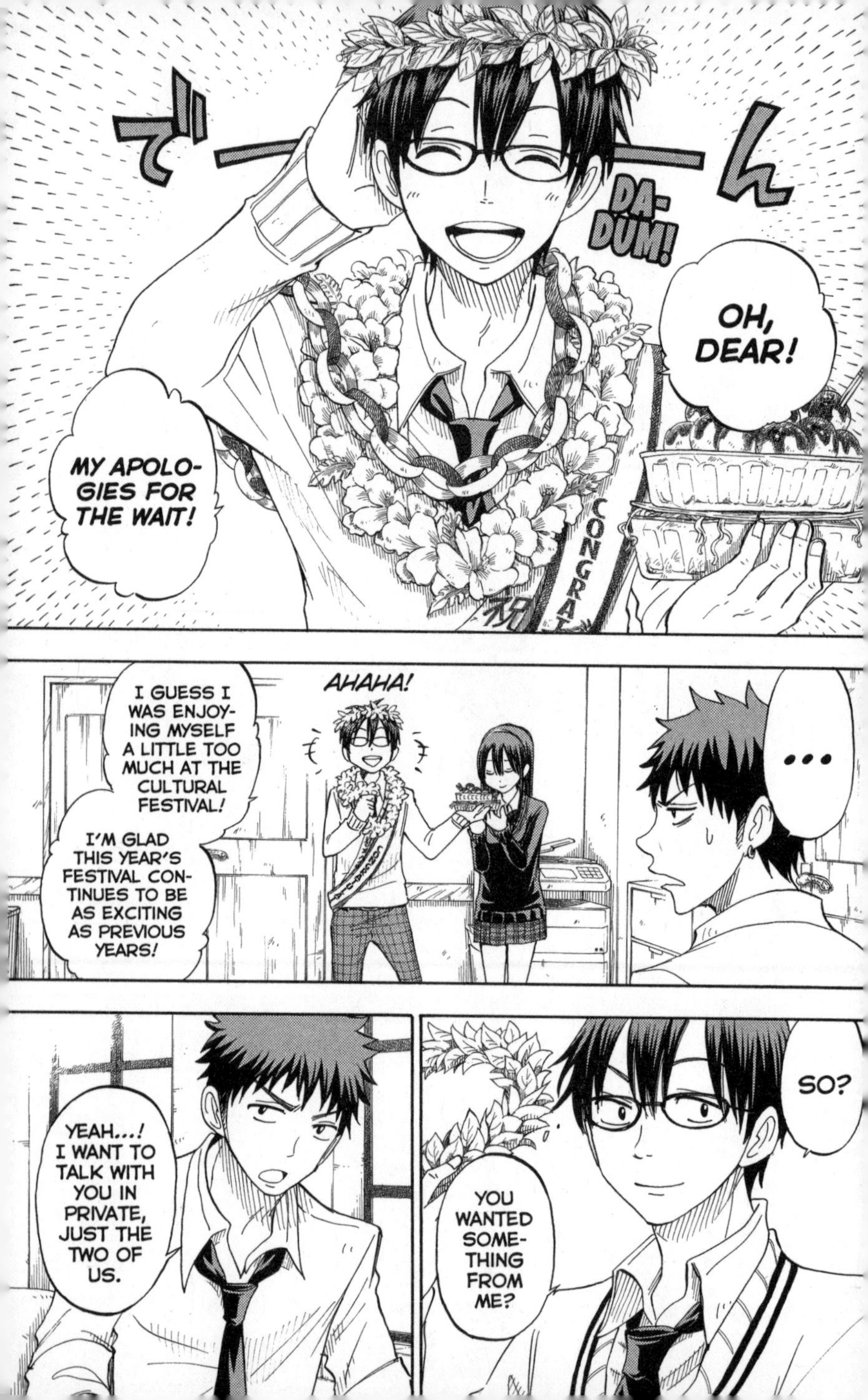
でーーん
DA-DUM!
OH, DEAR!
CONGRAT
MY APOLOGIES FOR THE WAIT!
...
AHAHA!
I GUESS I WAS ENJOYING MYSELF A LITTLE TOO MUCH AT THE CULTURAL FESTIVAL!
I'M GLAD THIS YEAR'S FESTIVAL CONTINUES TO BE AS EXCITING AS PREVIOUS YEARS!
SO?
YOU WANTED SOMETHING FROM ME?
YEAH...! I WANT TO TALK WITH YOU IN PRIVATE, JUST THE TWO OF US.

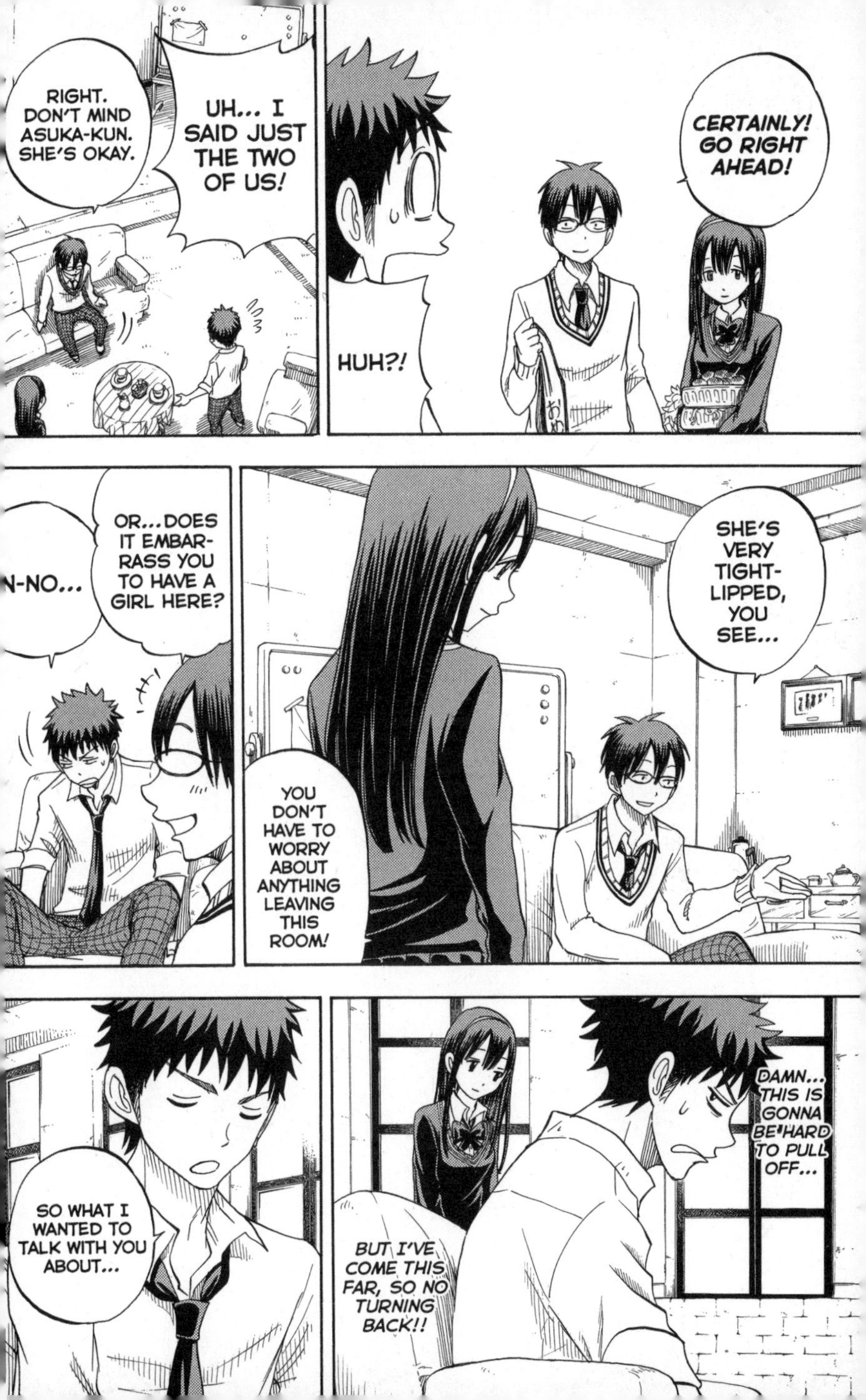
CERTAINLY! GO RIGHT AHEAD!
HUH?!
UH... I SAID JUST THE TWO OF US!
RIGHT. DON'T MIND ASUKA-KUN. SHE'S OKAY.
SHE'S VERY TIGHT-LIPPED, YOU SEE...
YOU DON'T HAVE TO WORRY ABOUT ANYTHING LEAVING THIS ROOM!
OR...DOES IT EMBARRASS YOU TO HAVE A GIRL HERE?
N-NO...
DAMN... THIS IS GONNA BE HARD TO PULL OFF...
BUT I'VE COME THIS FAR, SO NO TURNING BACK!!
SO WHAT I WANTED TO TALK WITH YOU ABOUT...

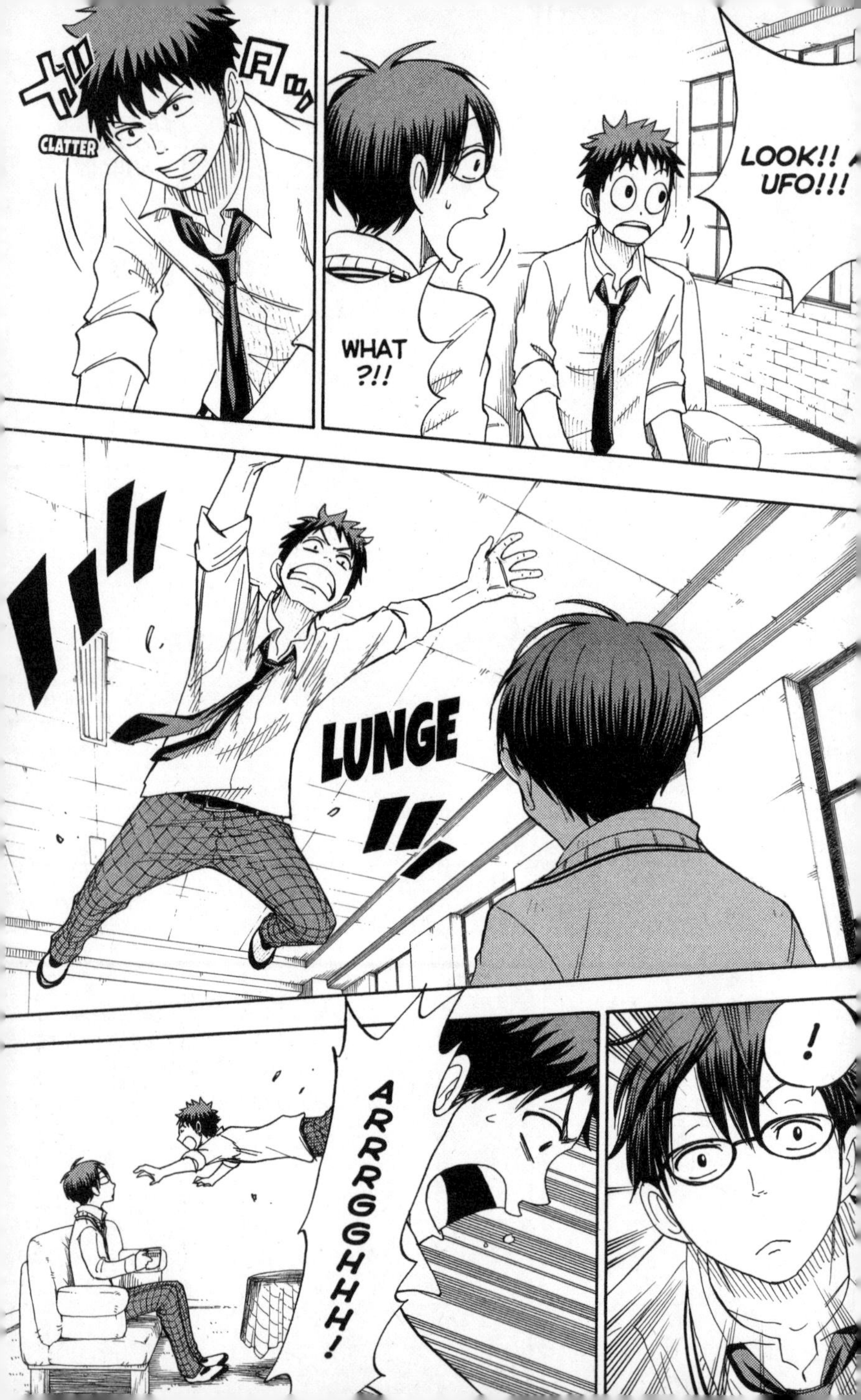
LOOK!! A UFO!!!
WHAT ?!!
CLATTER
LUNGE
!
ARRRGGHHH!

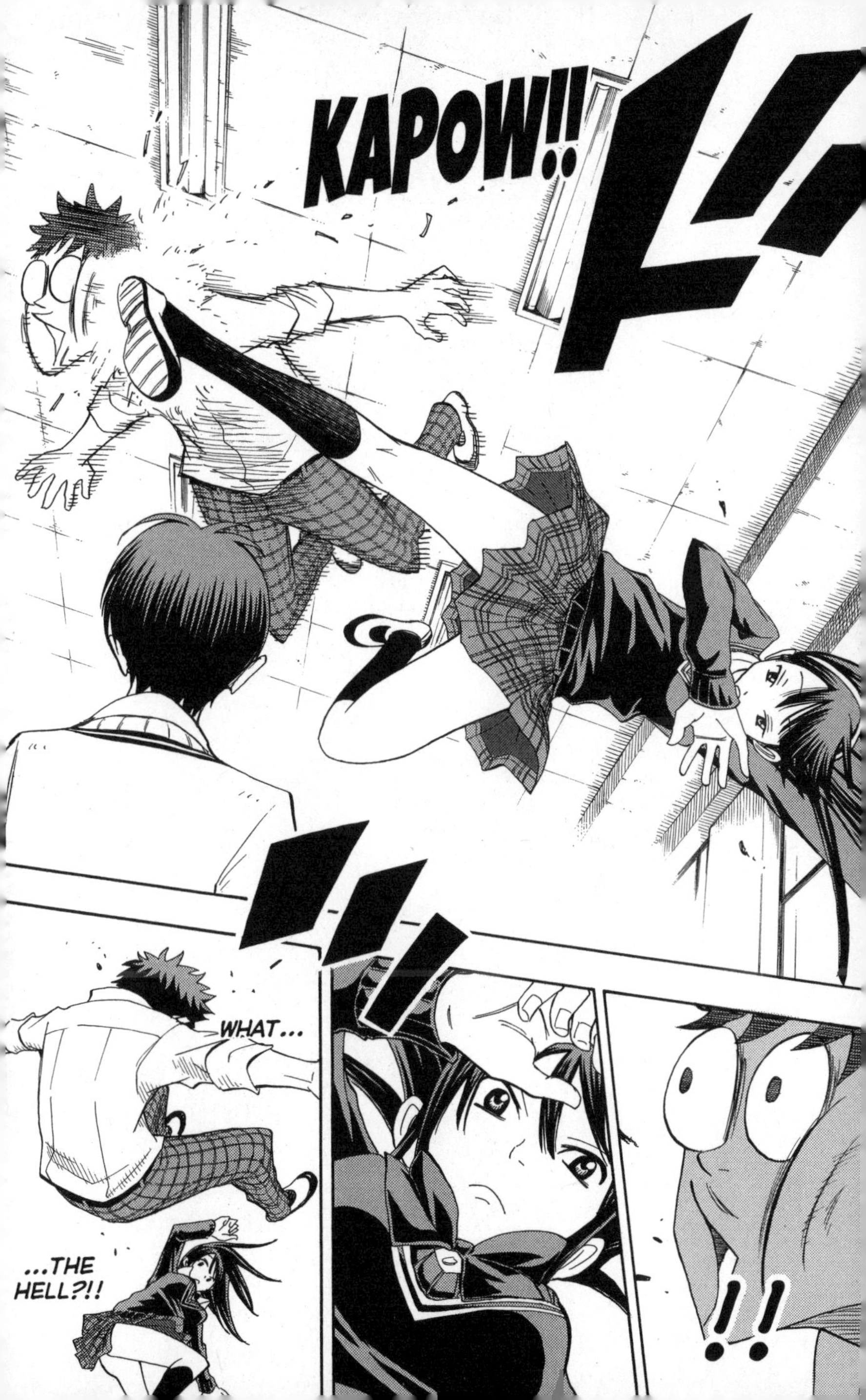
KAPOW!!
!!
WHAT...
...THE HELL?!!

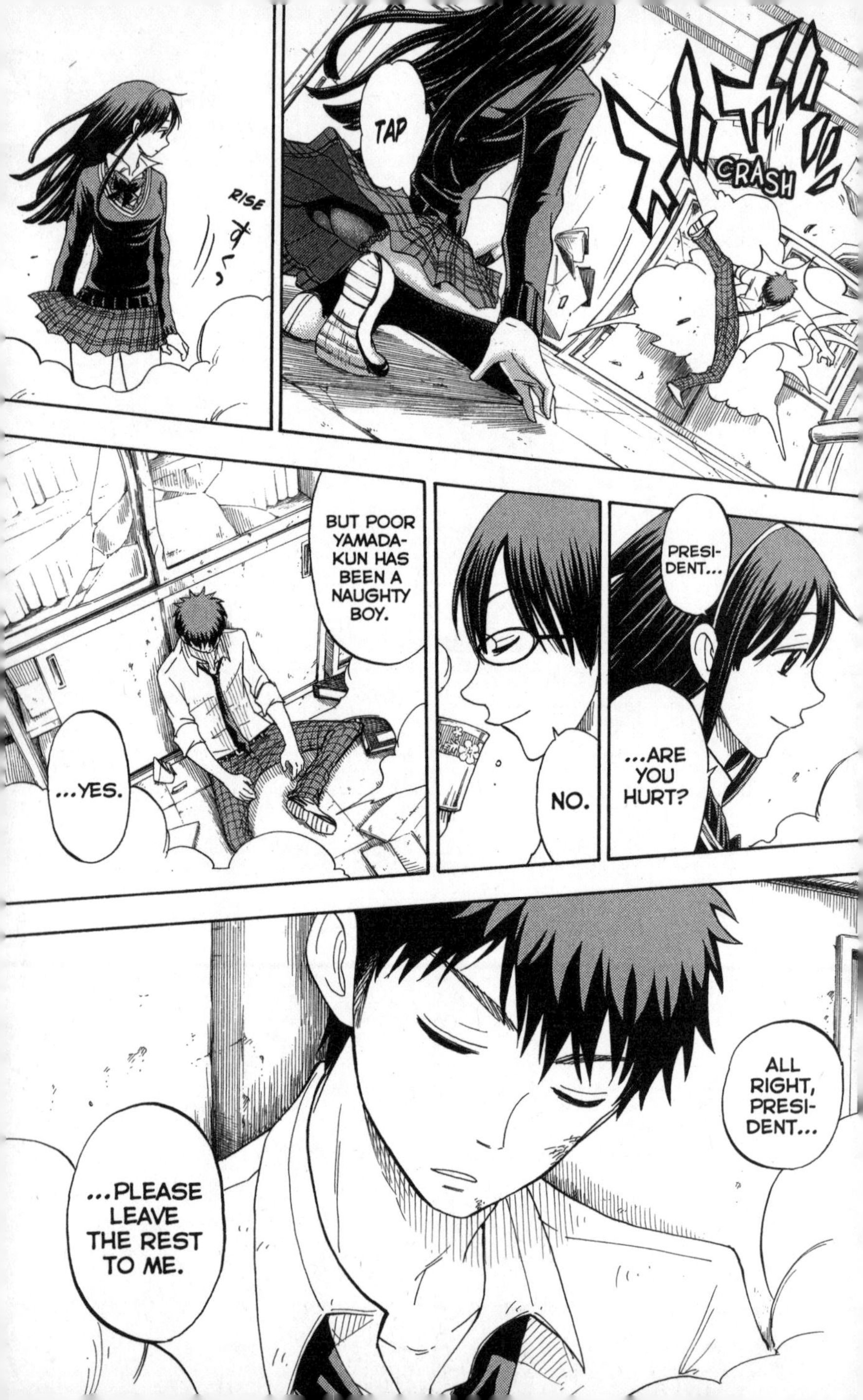
CRASH
TAP
RISE
すくっ
PRESI-DENT...
...ARE YOU HURT?
NO.
BUT POOR YAMADA-KUN HAS BEEN A NAUGHTY BOY.
...YES.
ALL RIGHT, PRESI-DENT...
...PLEASE LEAVE THE REST TO ME.

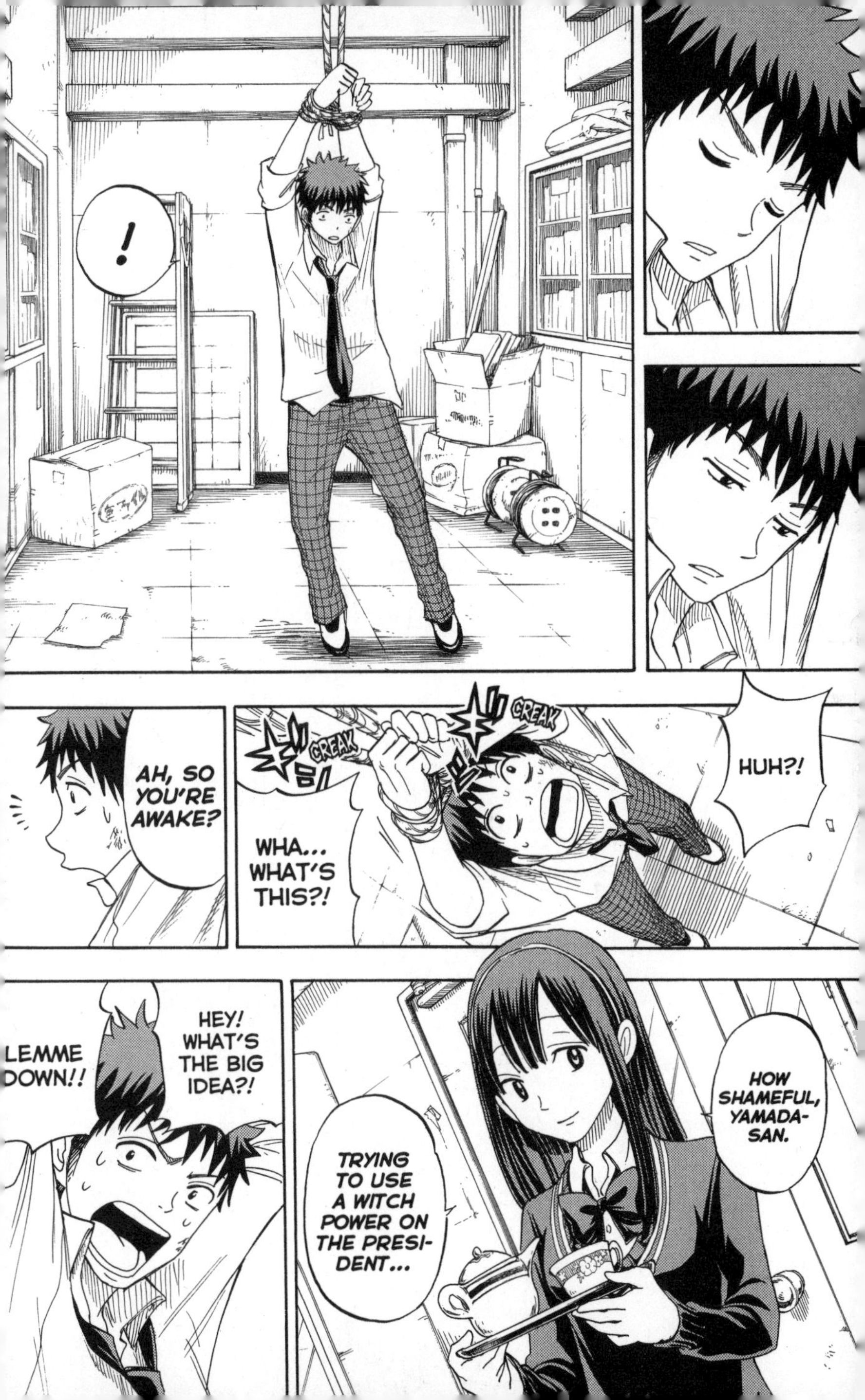
!
HUH?!
CREAK
CREAK
WHA... WHAT'S THIS?!
AH, SO YOU'RE AWAKE?
HOW SHAMEFUL, YAMADA-SAN.
TRYING TO USE A WITCH POWER ON THE PRESIDENT...
HEY! WHAT'S THE BIG IDEA?!
LEMME DOWN!!

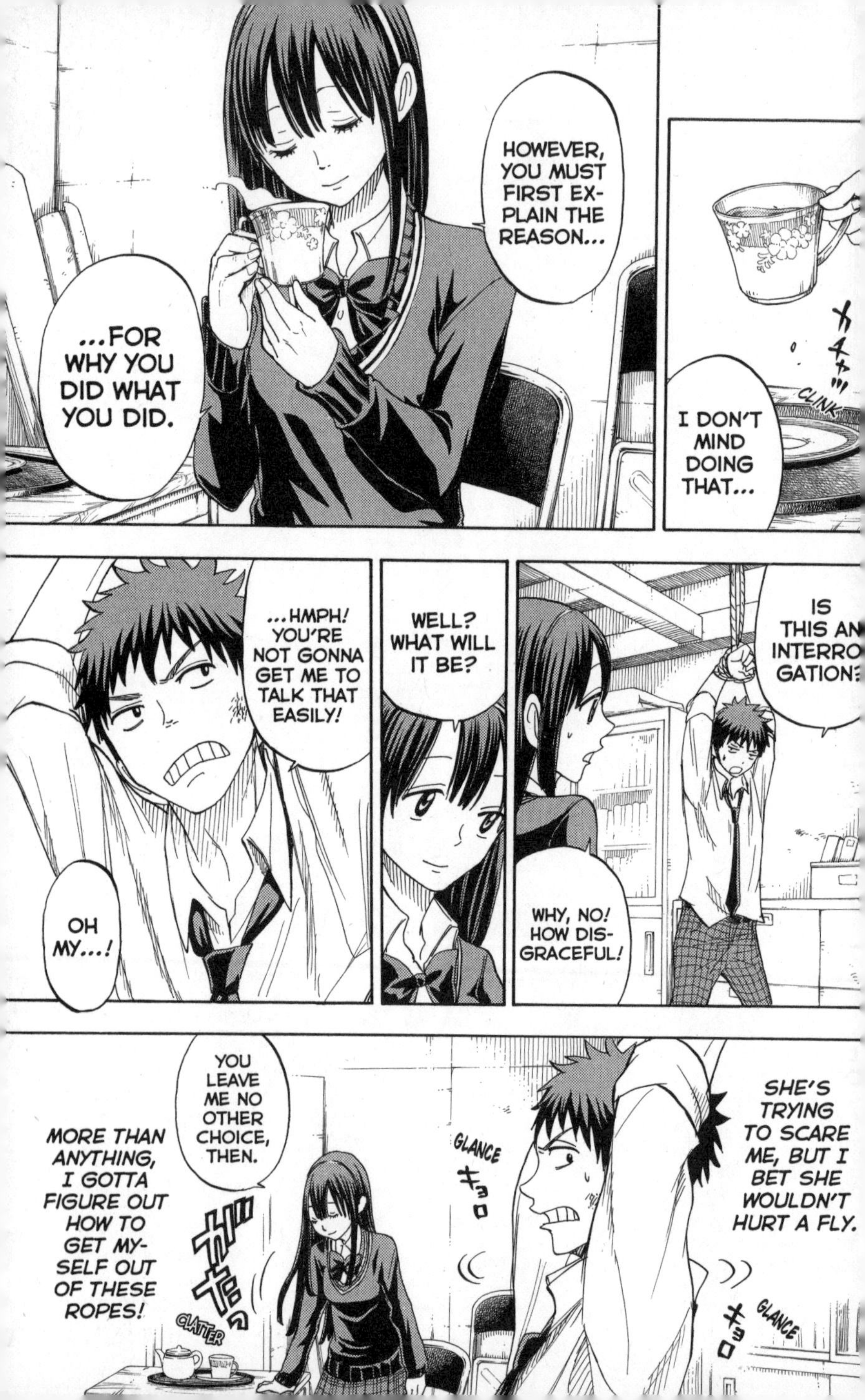
I DON'T MIND DOING THAT...
CLINK
HOWEVER, YOU MUST FIRST EX-PLAIN THE REASON...
...FOR WHY YOU DID WHAT YOU DID.
IS THIS AN INTERRO GATION?
WHY, NO! HOW DIS-GRACEFUL!
WELL? WHAT WILL IT BE?
...HMPH! YOU'RE NOT GONNA GET ME TO TALK THAT EASILY!
OH MY...!
SHE'S TRYING TO SCARE ME, BUT I BET SHE WOULDN'T HURT A FLY.
GLANCE
GLANCE
YOU LEAVE ME NO OTHER CHOICE, THEN.
MORE THAN ANYTHING, I GOTTA FIGURE OUT HOW TO GET MY-SELF OUT OF THESE ROPES!
CLATTER

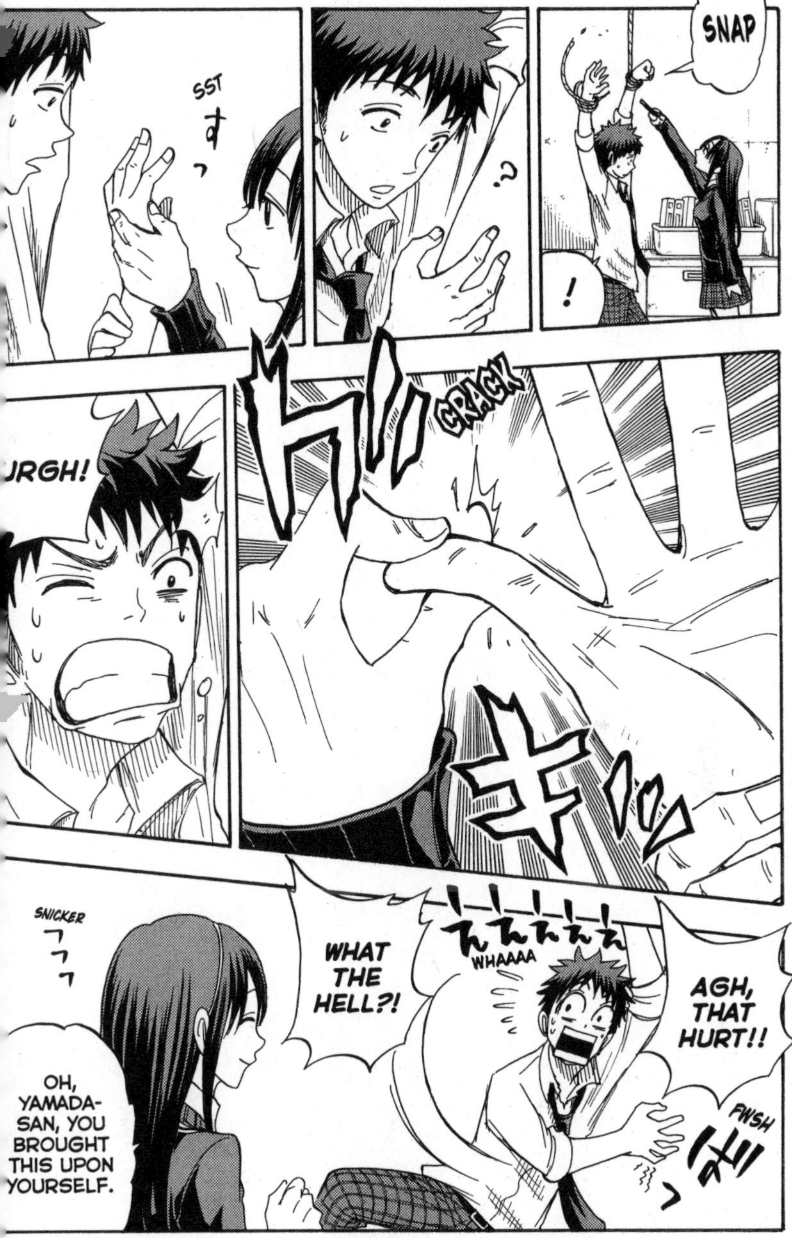
SNAP
!
?
SST
す
CRACK
URGH!
AGH, THAT HURT!!
FWSH
WHAAAA
WHAT THE HELL?!
SNICKER
OH, YAMADA-SAN, YOU BROUGHT THIS UPON YOURSELF.

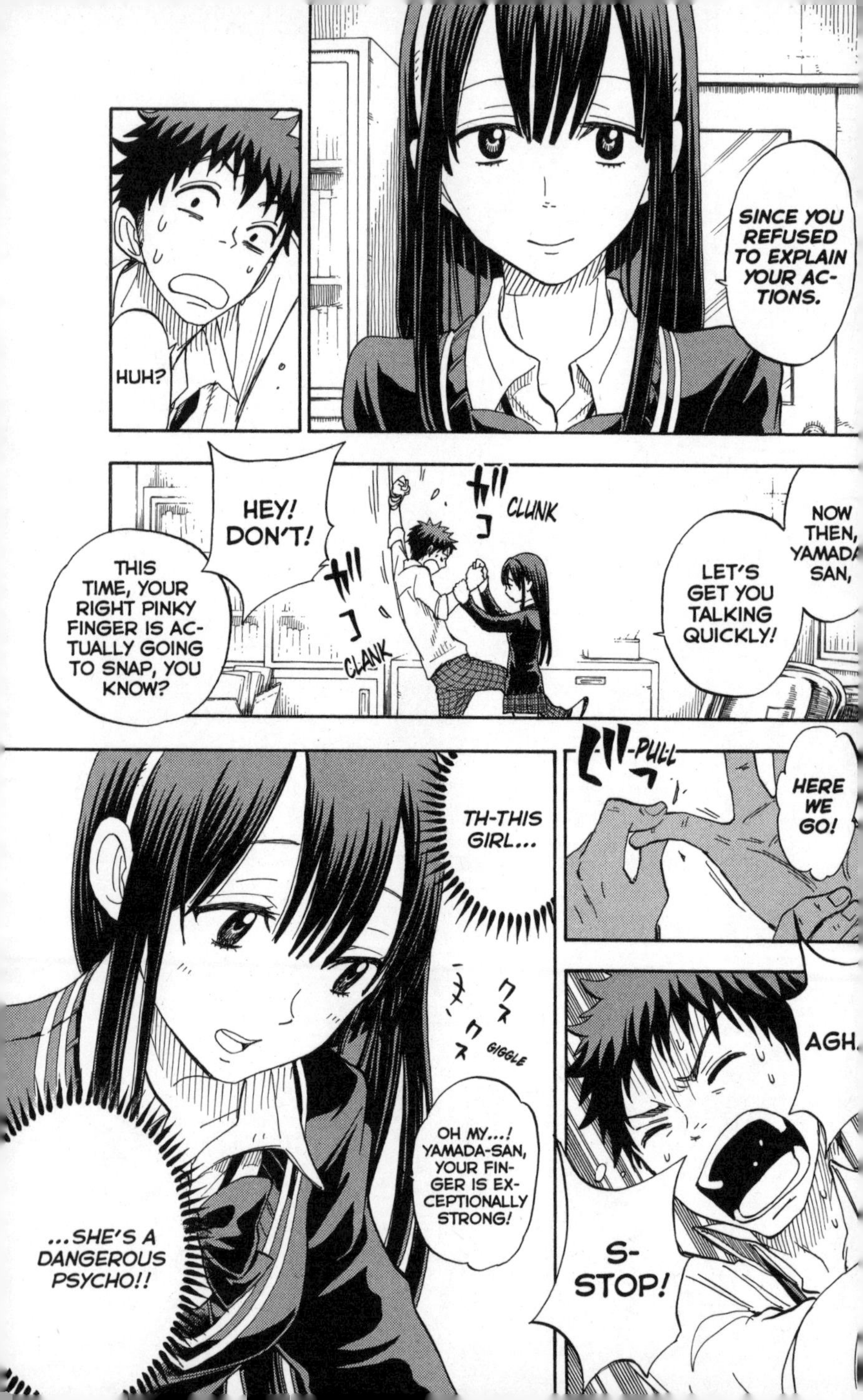
SINCE YOU REFUSED TO EXPLAIN YOUR ACTIONS.
HUH?
NOW THEN, YAMADA-SAN,
LET'S GET YOU TALKING QUICKLY!
CLUNK
HEY! DON'T!
THIS TIME, YOUR RIGHT PINKY FINGER IS ACTUALLY GOING TO SNAP, YOU KNOW?
CLANK
HERE WE GO!
PULL
AGH.
S-STOP!
TH-THIS GIRL...
GIGGLE
OH MY...! YAMADA-SAN, YOUR FINGER IS EXCEPTIONALLY STRONG!
...SHE'S A DANGEROUS PSYCHO!!

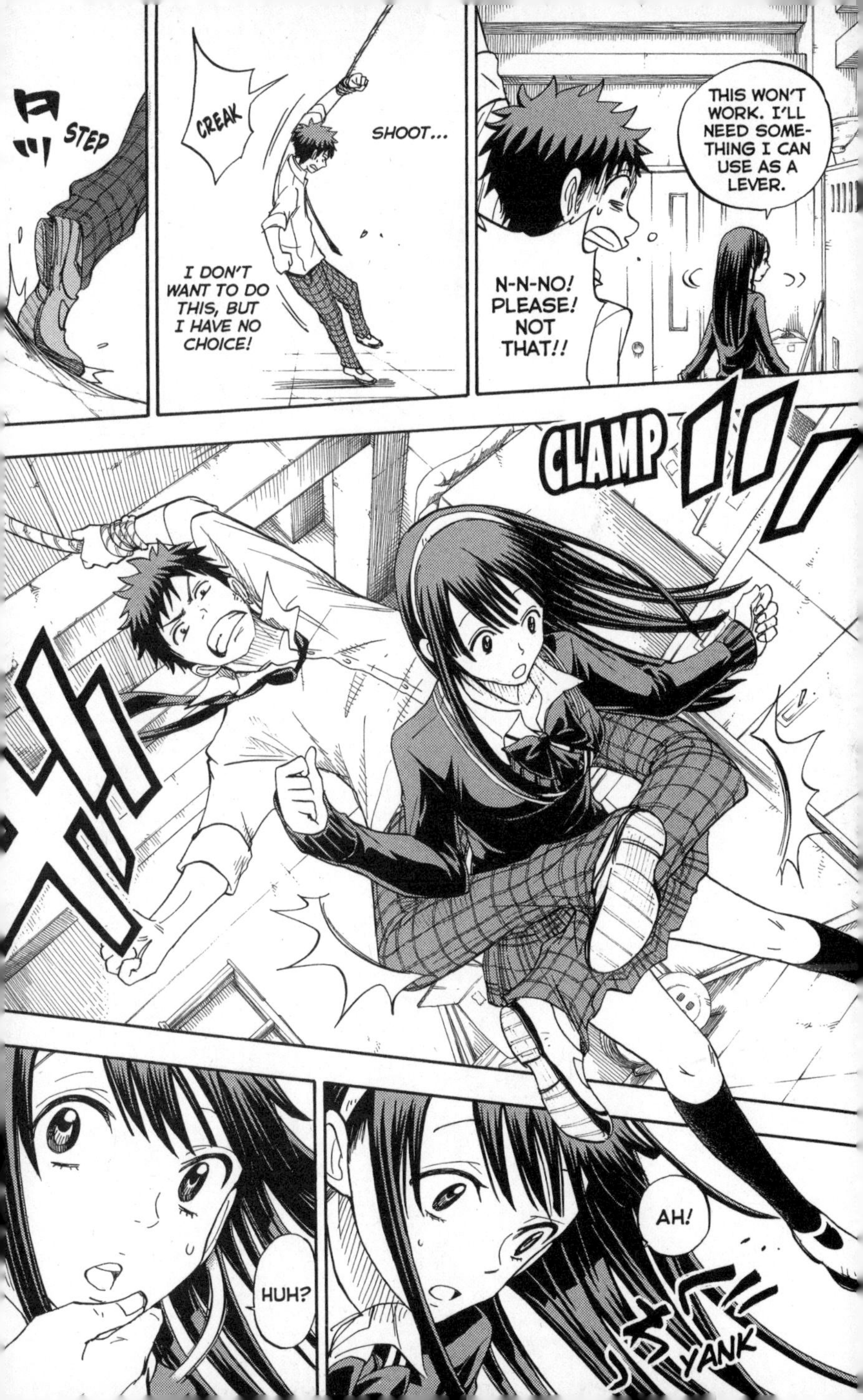
THIS WON'T WORK. I'LL NEED SOME-THING I CAN USE AS A LEVER.
N-N-NO! PLEASE! NOT THAT!!
CREAK
SHOOT...
I DON'T WANT TO DO THIS, BUT I HAVE NO CHOICE!
STEP
CLAMP
AH!
YANK
HUH?

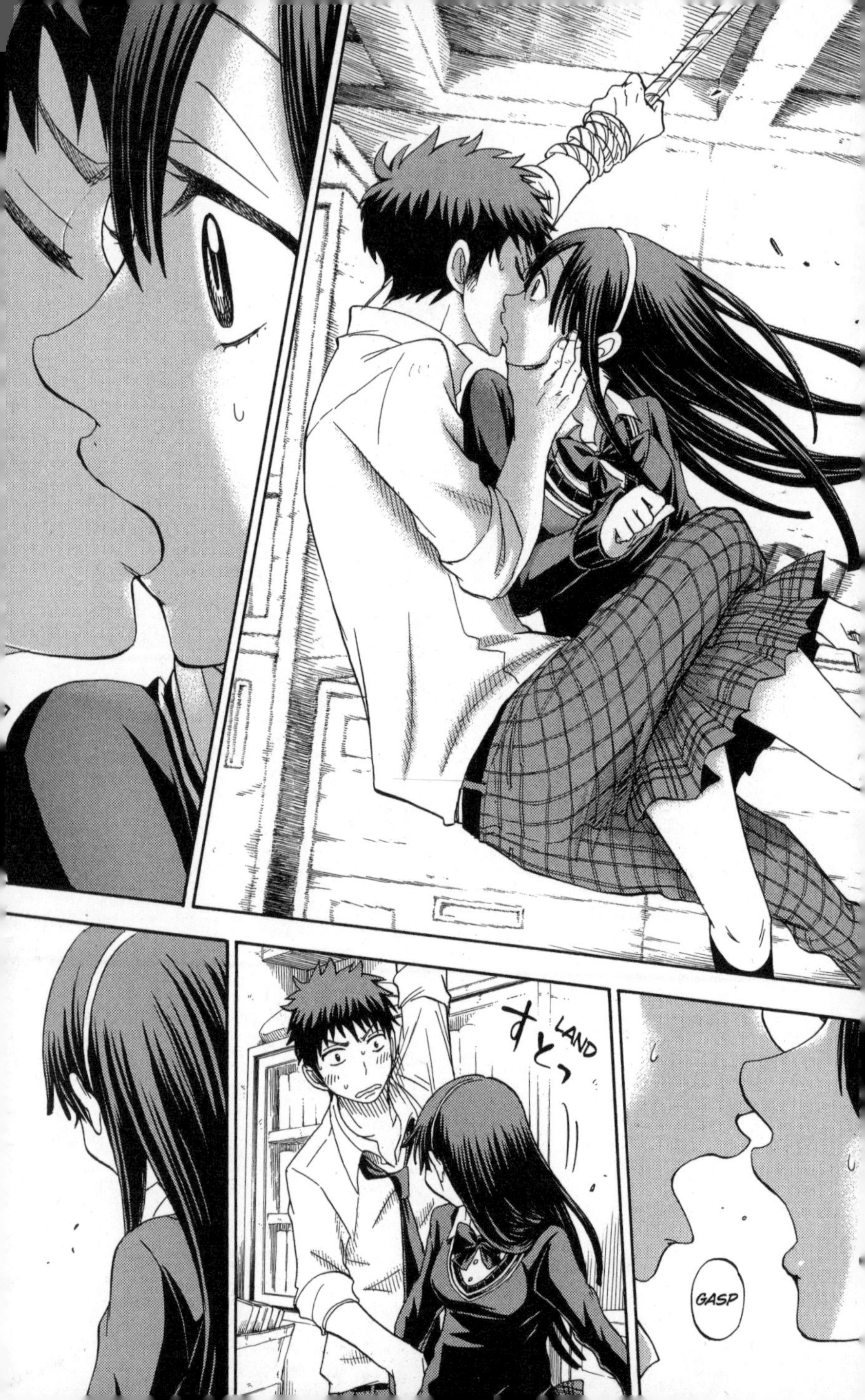
すとっ
LAND
GASP

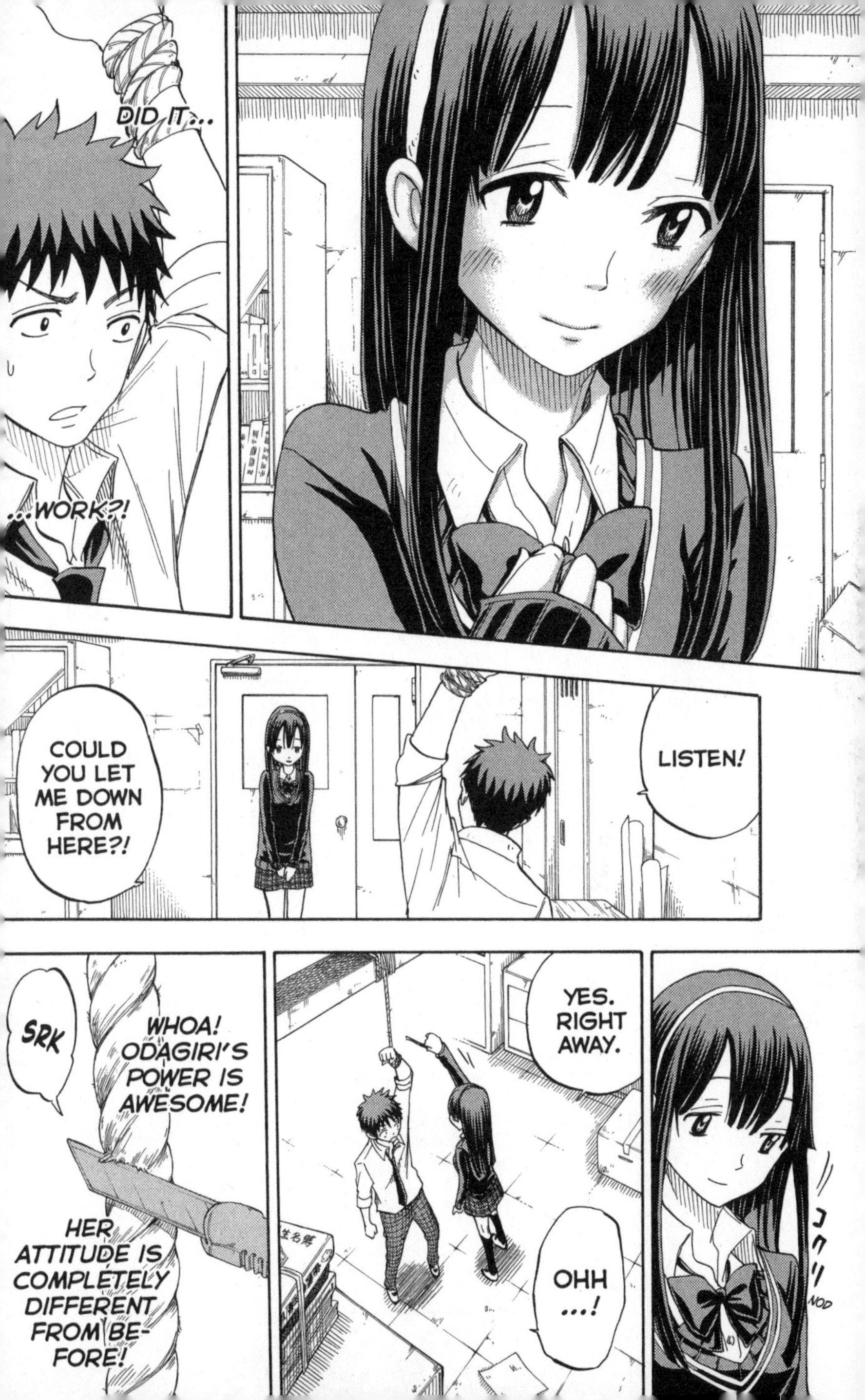
DID IT...
...WORK?!
LISTEN!
COULD YOU LET ME DOWN FROM HERE?!
コクリ
NOD
YES. RIGHT AWAY.
OHH ...!
WHOA! ODAGIRI'S POWER IS AWESOME!
SRK
HER ATTITUDE IS COMPLETELY DIFFERENT FROM BE-FORE!

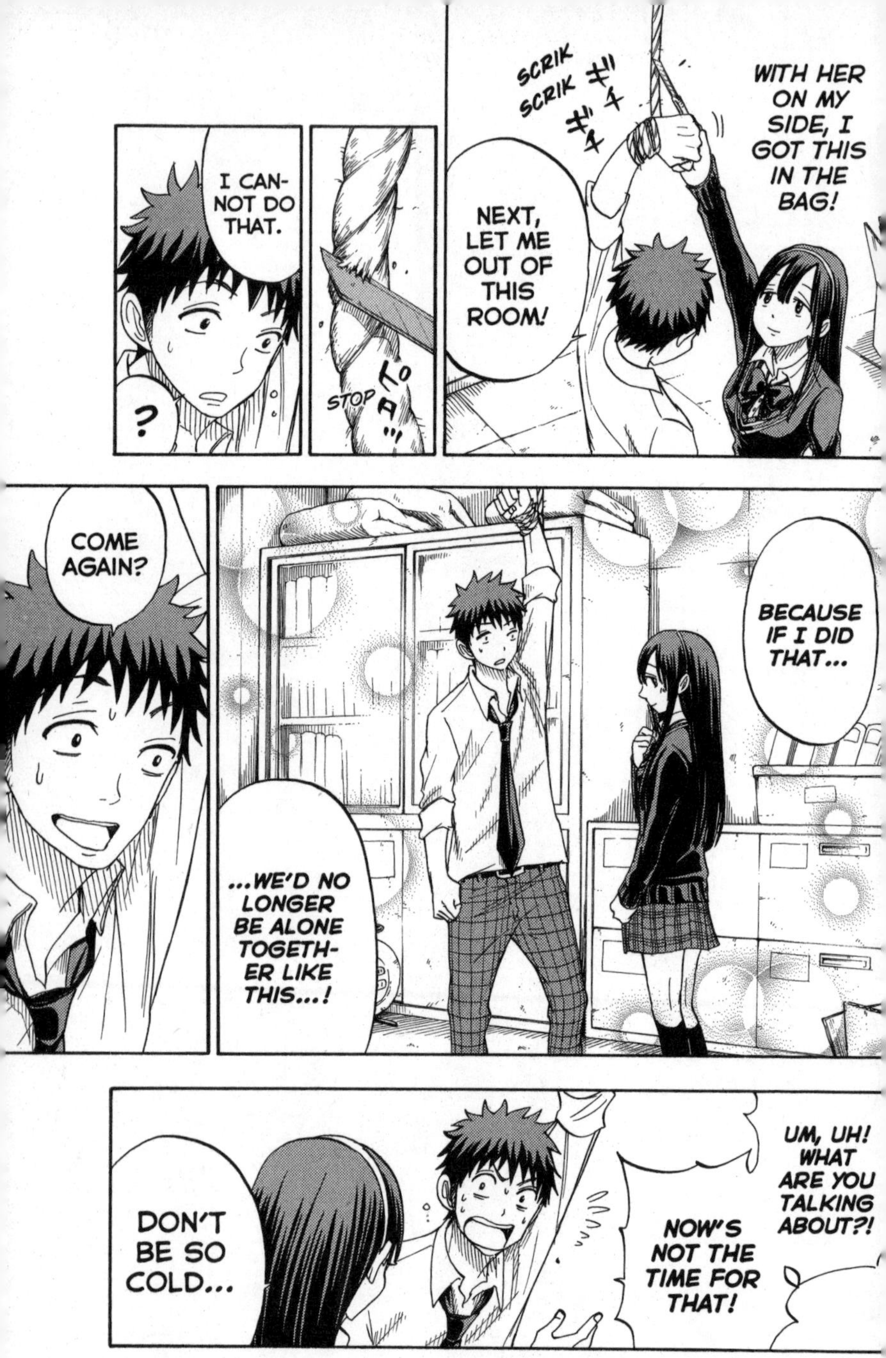
WITH HER ON MY SIDE, I GOT THIS IN THE BAG!
SCRIK SCRIK
ギチギチ
NEXT, LET ME OUT OF THIS ROOM!
STOP
ピタ
I CAN-NOT DO THAT.
?
BECAUSE IF I DID THAT...
...WE'D NO LONGER BE ALONE TOGETH-ER LIKE THIS...!
COME AGAIN?
UM, UH! WHAT ARE YOU TALKING ABOUT?!
NOW'S NOT THE TIME FOR THAT!
DON'T BE SO COLD...

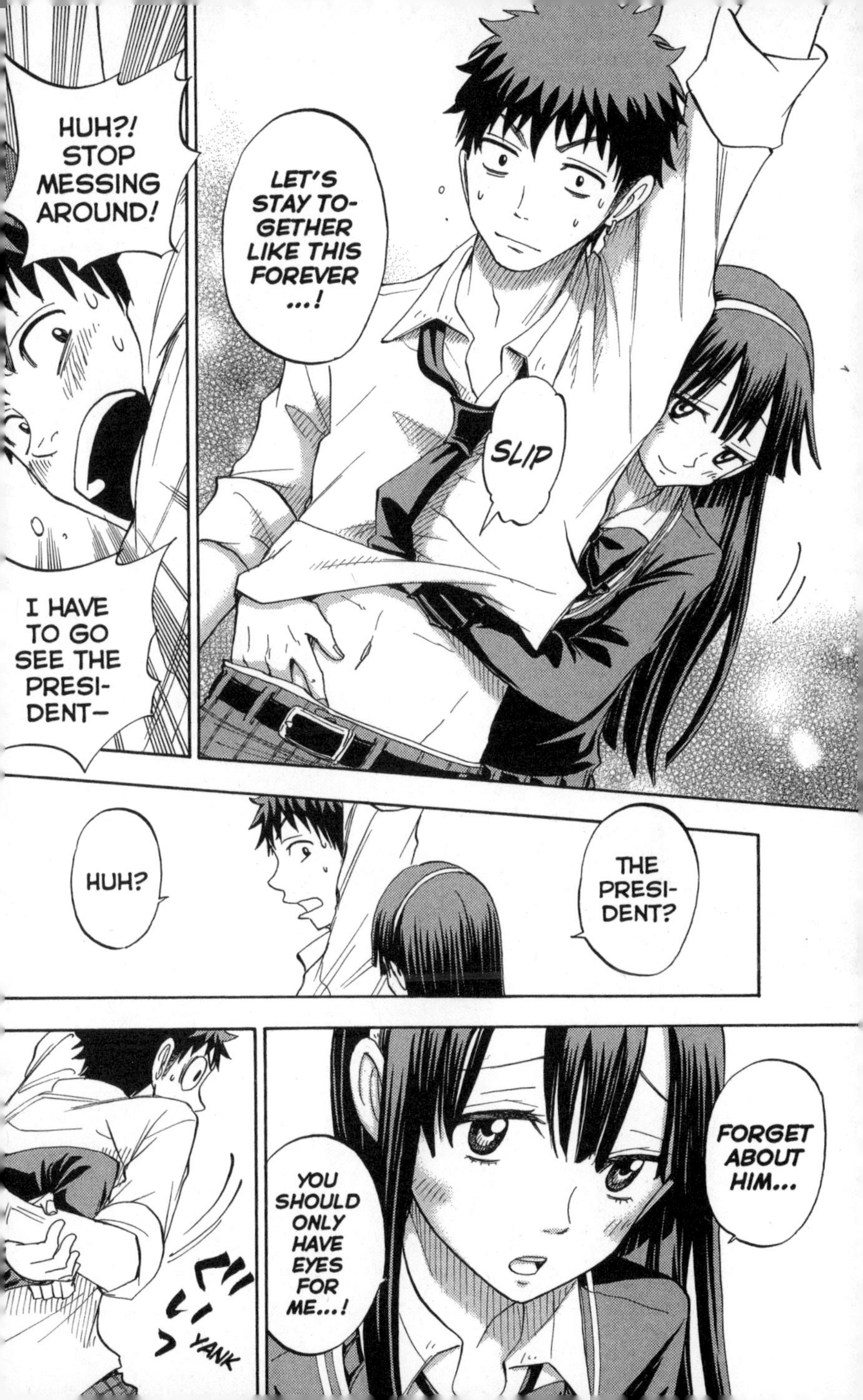
LET'S STAY TOGETHER LIKE THIS FOREVER ...!
SLIP
HUH?! STOP MESSING AROUND!
I HAVE TO GO SEE THE PRESIDENT—
THE PRESIDENT?
HUH?
FORGET ABOUT HIM...
YOU SHOULD ONLY HAVE EYES FOR ME...!
YANK

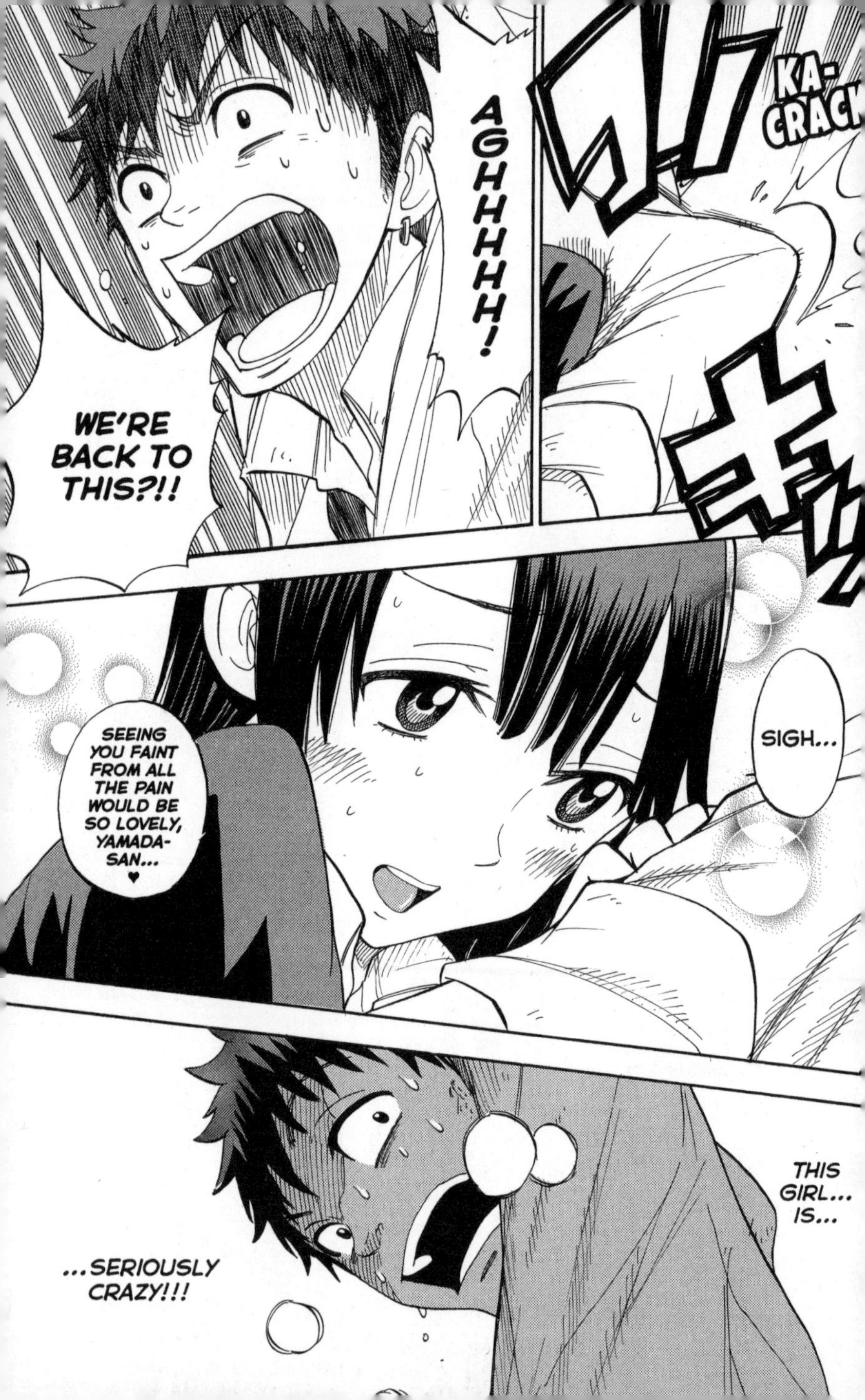
KA-CRACK
AGHHHHHH!
WE'RE BACK TO THIS?!!
SIGH...
SEEING YOU FAINT FROM ALL THE PAIN WOULD BE SO LOVELY, YAMADA-SAN... ♥
THIS GIRL... IS...
...SERIOUSLY CRAZY!!!

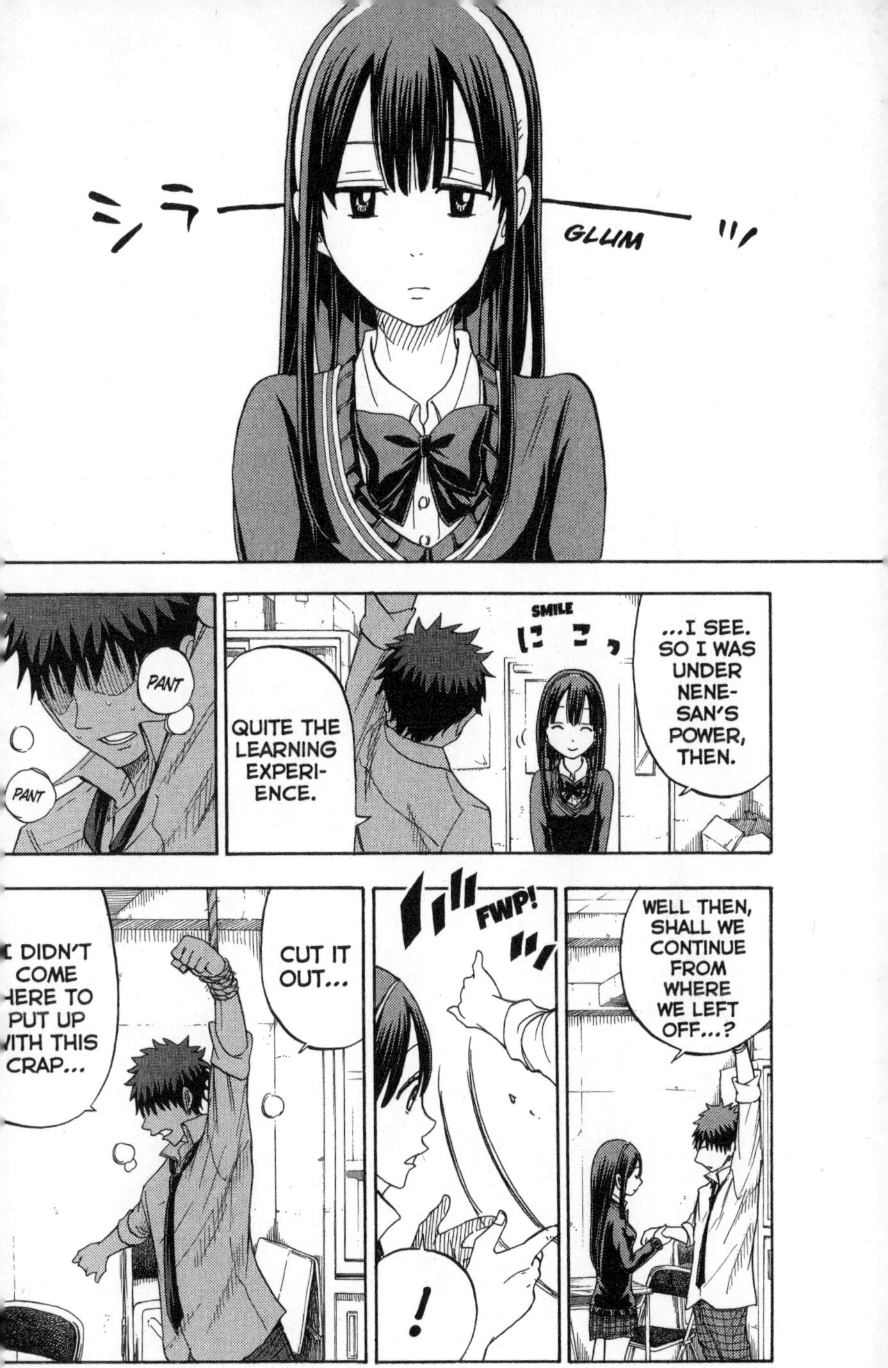
シラー
GLUM
SMILE
にこっ
...I SEE. SO I WAS UNDER NENE-SAN'S POWER, THEN.
QUITE THE LEARNING EXPERIENCE.
PANT
PANT
WELL THEN, SHALL WE CONTINUE FROM WHERE WE LEFT OFF...?
FWP!
!
CUT IT OUT...
I DIDN'T COME HERE TO PUT UP WITH THIS CRAP...

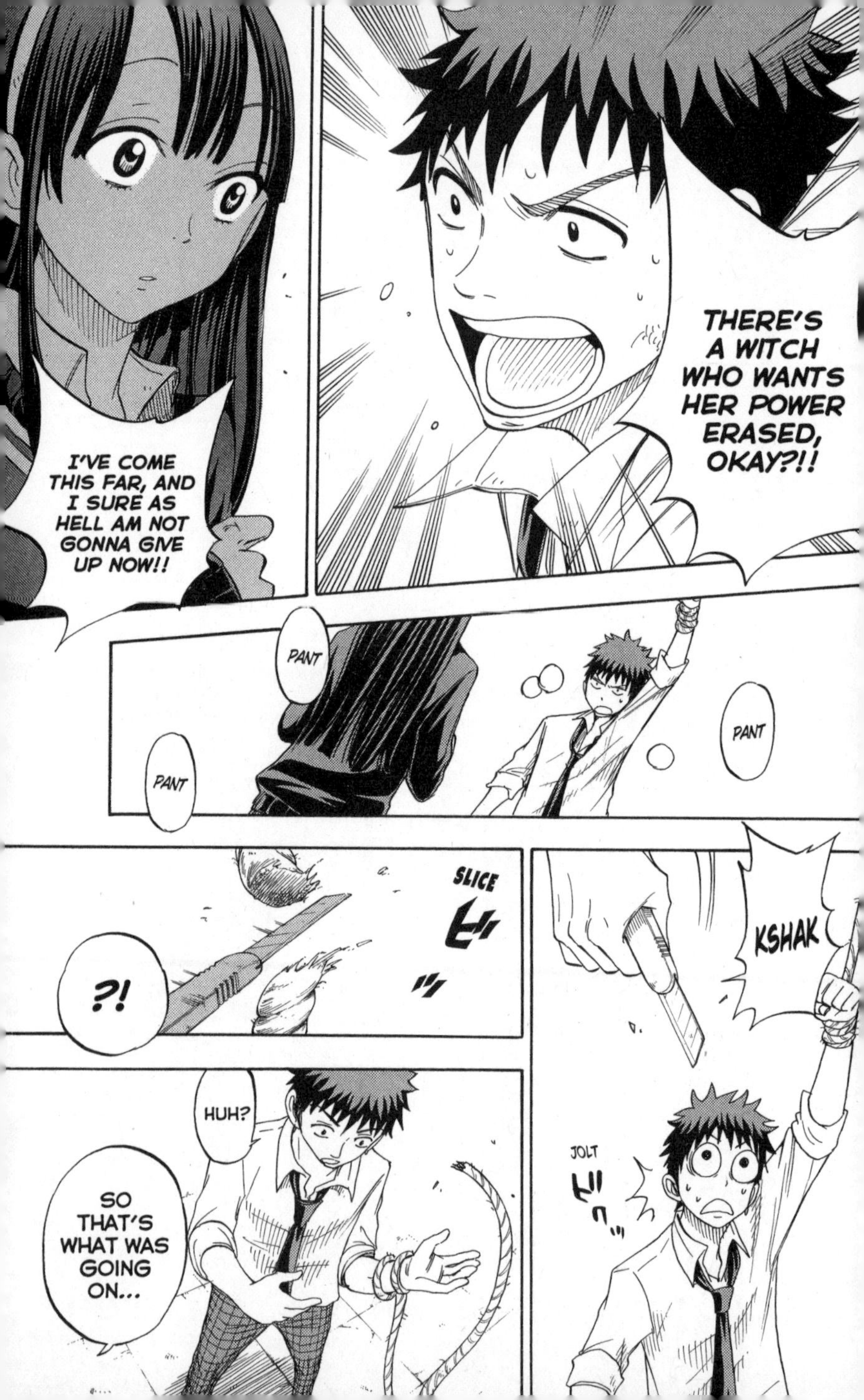
THERE'S A WITCH WHO WANTS HER POWER ERASED, OKAY?!!
I'VE COME THIS FAR, AND I SURE AS HELL AM NOT GONNA GIVE UP NOW!!
PANT
PANT
PANT
KSHAK
JOLT
SLICE
?!
HUH?
SO THAT'S WHAT WAS GOING ON...

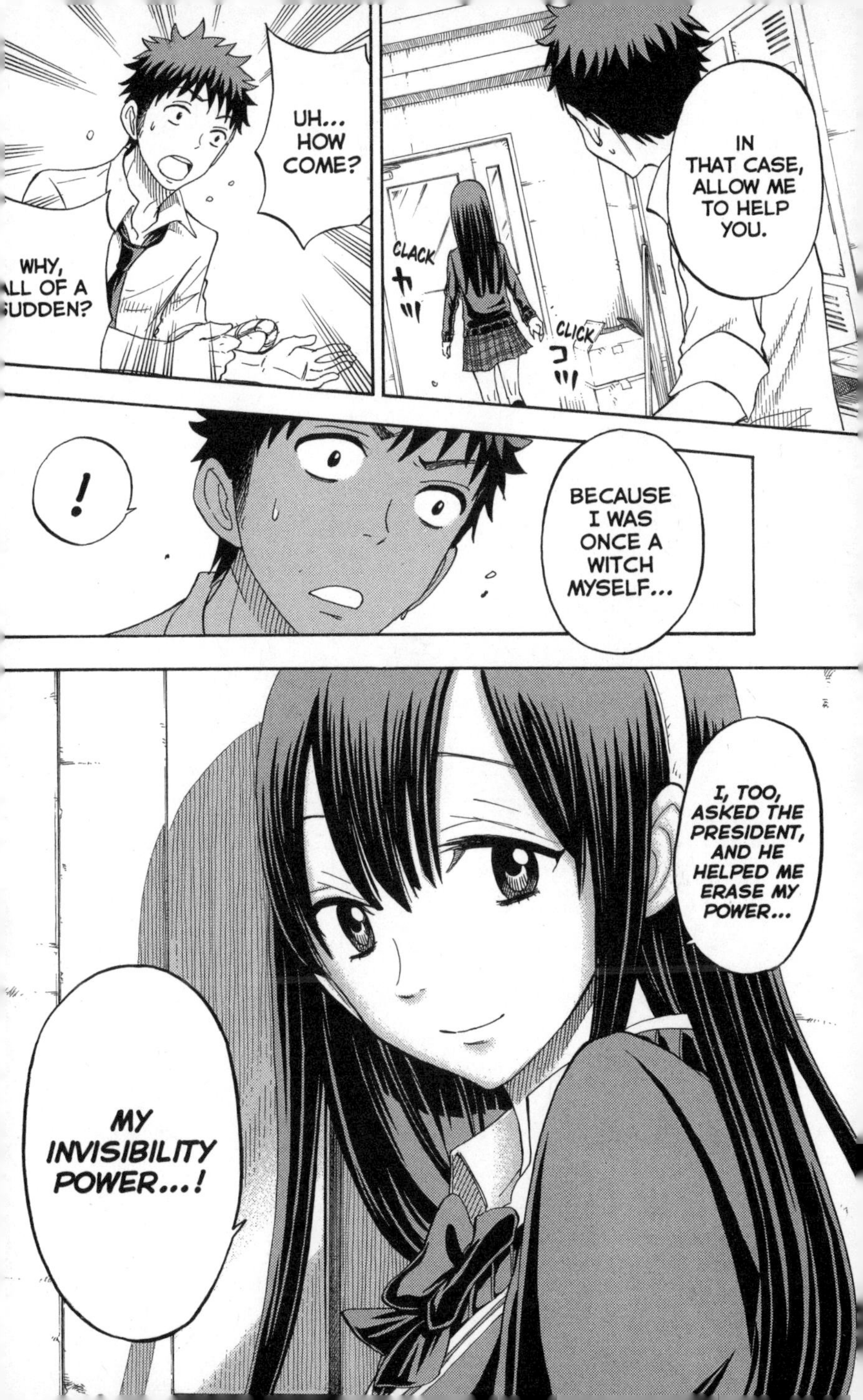

IN THAT CASE, ALLOW ME TO HELP YOU.
CLACK
CLICK
UH... HOW COME?
WHY, ALL OF A SUDDEN?
BECAUSE I WAS ONCE A WITCH MYSELF...
!
I, TOO, ASKED THE PRESIDENT, AND HE HELPED ME ERASE MY POWER...
MY INVISIBILITY POWER...!

CHAPTER 56: Is that how you see them, Yamada-san...?

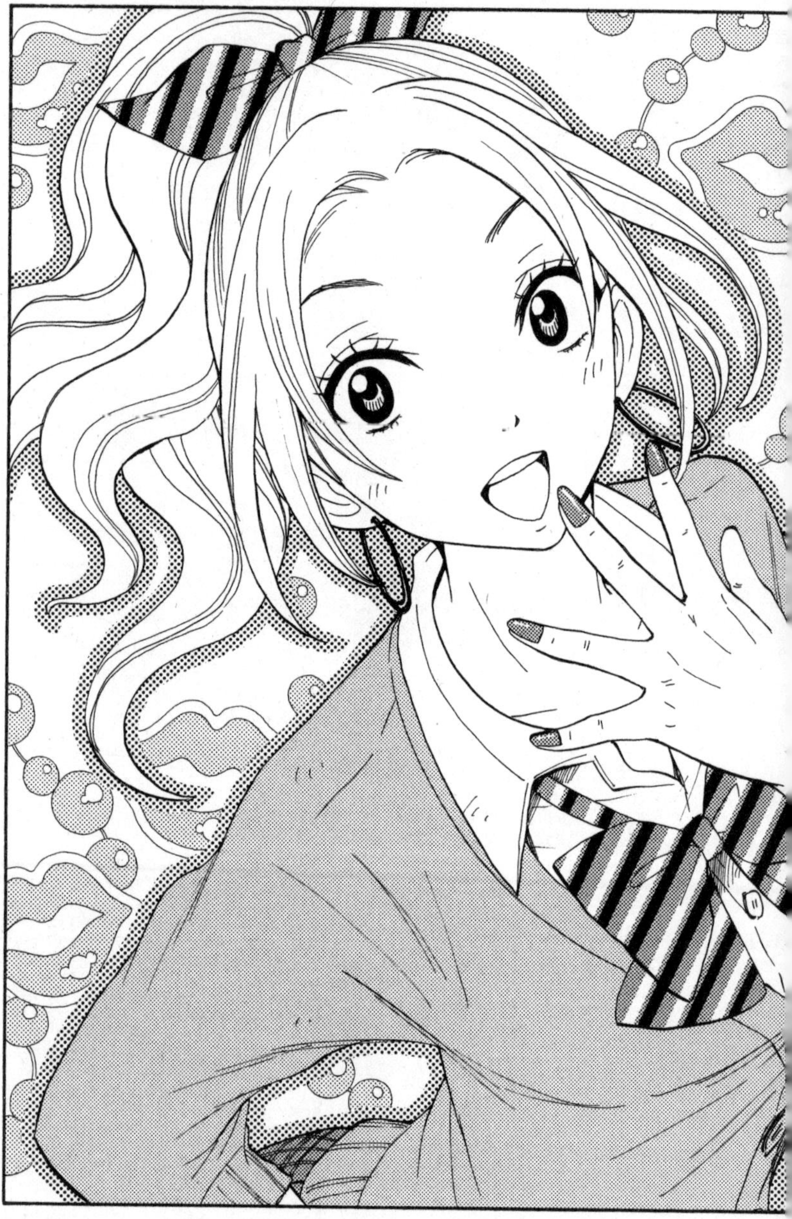

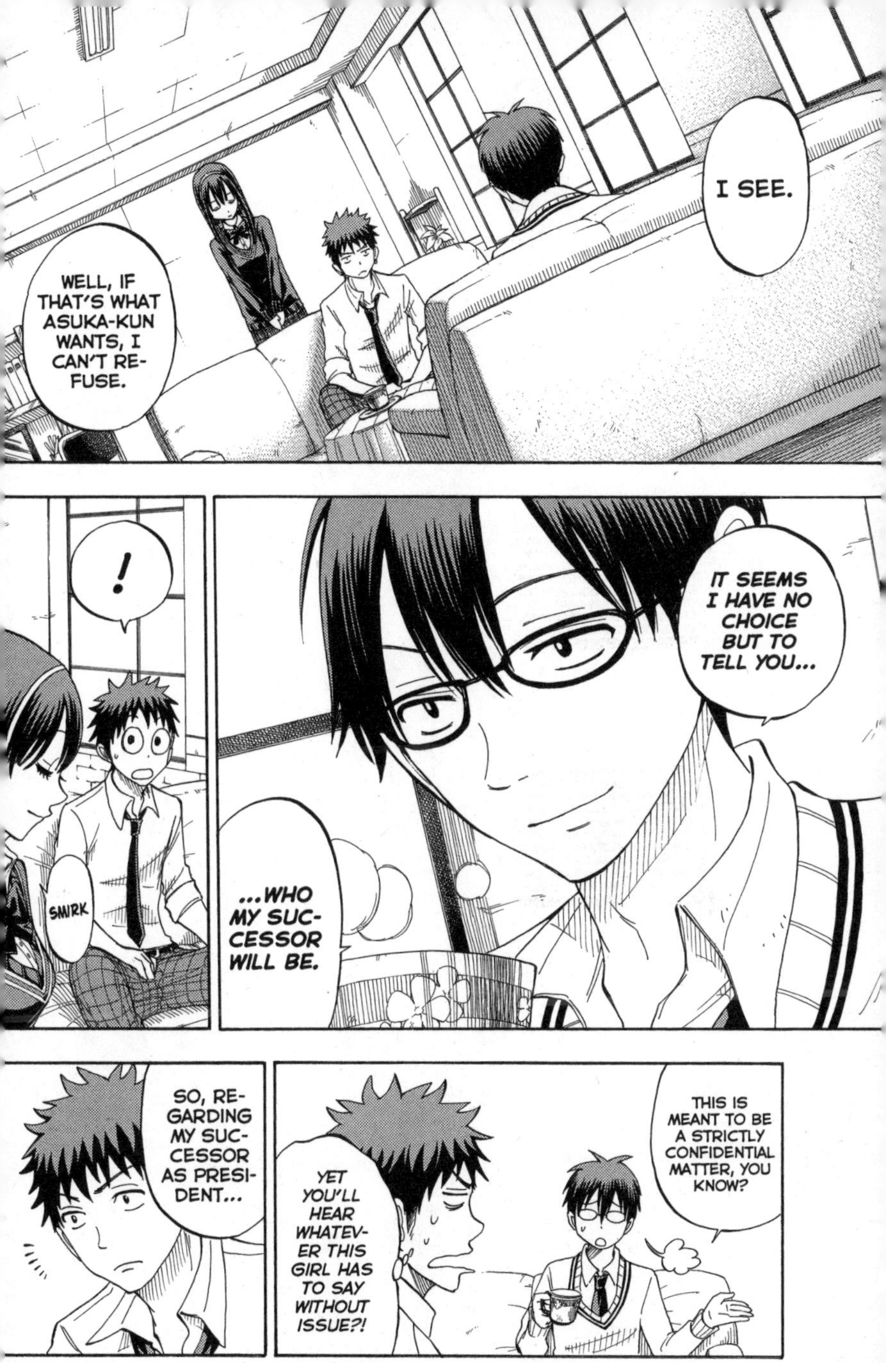
I SEE.
WELL, IF THAT'S WHAT ASUKA-KUN WANTS, I CAN'T REFUSE.
IT SEEMS I HAVE NO CHOICE BUT TO TELL YOU...
...WHO MY SUCCESSOR WILL BE.
!
SMIRK
THIS IS MEANT TO BE A STRICTLY CONFIDENTIAL MATTER, YOU KNOW?
YET YOU'LL HEAR WHATEVER THIS GIRL HAS TO SAY WITHOUT ISSUE?!
SO, REGARDING MY SUCCESSOR AS PRESIDENT...

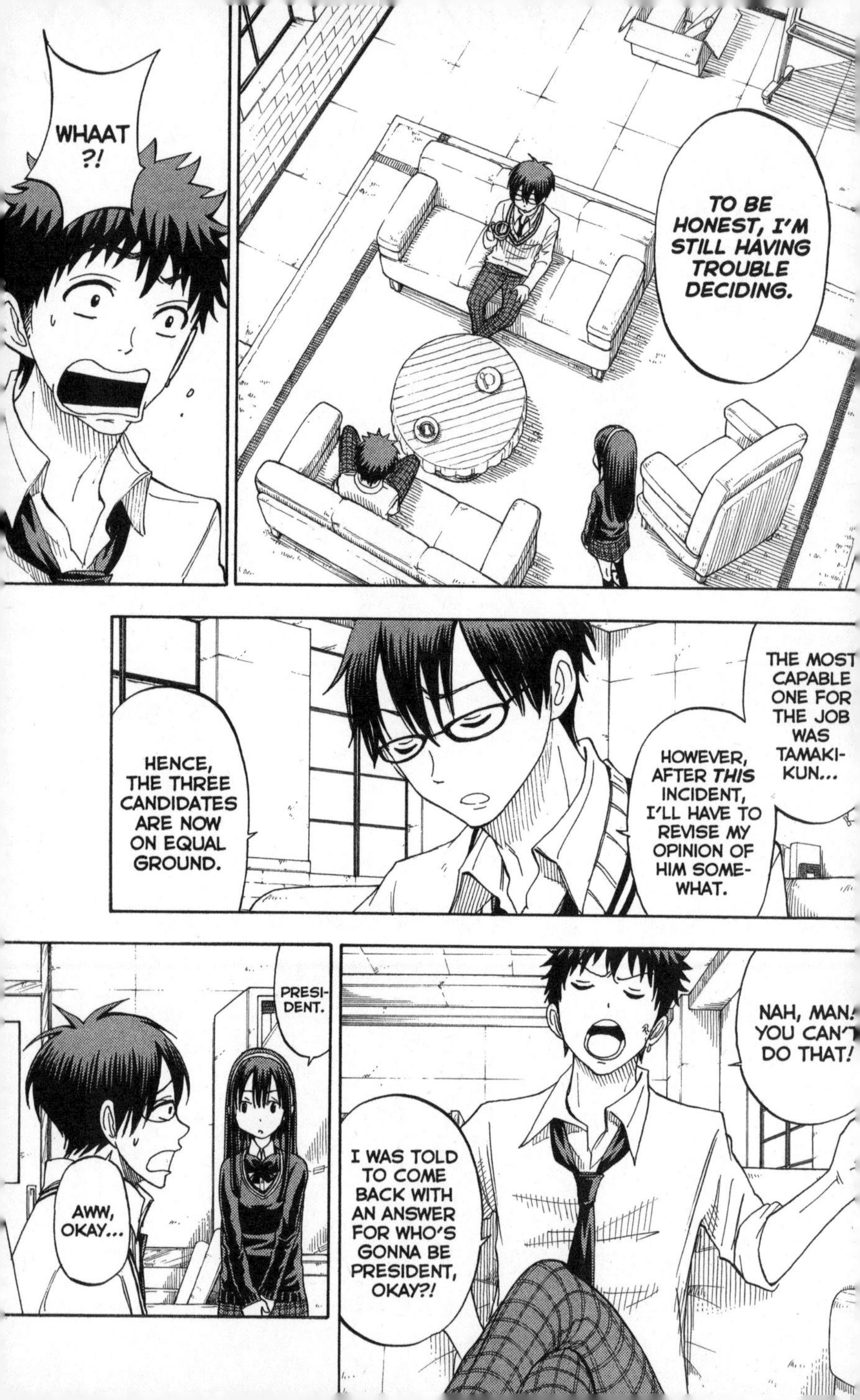
TO BE HONEST, I'M STILL HAVING TROUBLE DECIDING.
WHAAT ?!
THE MOST CAPABLE ONE FOR THE JOB WAS TAMAKI-KUN...
HOWEVER, AFTER *THIS* INCIDENT, I'LL HAVE TO REVISE MY OPINION OF HIM SOME-WHAT.
HENCE, THE THREE CANDIDATES ARE NOW ON EQUAL GROUND.
NAH, MAN! YOU CAN'T DO THAT!
I WAS TOLD TO COME BACK WITH AN ANSWER FOR WHO'S GONNA BE PRESIDENT, OKAY?!
PRESI-DENT.
AWW, OKAY...

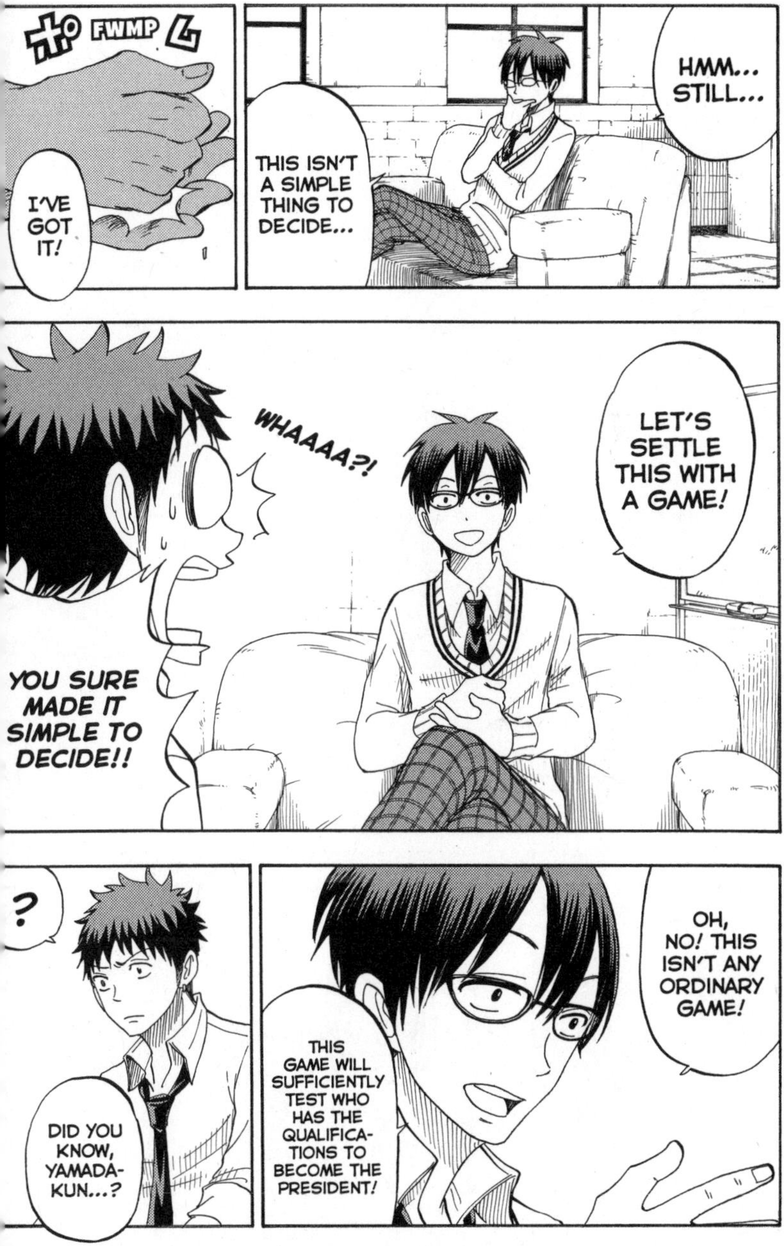
HMM... STILL...
THIS ISN'T A SIMPLE THING TO DECIDE...
FWMP
I'VE GOT IT!
LET'S SETTLE THIS WITH A GAME!
WHAAAA?!
YOU SURE MADE IT SIMPLE TO DECIDE!!
OH, NO! THIS ISN'T ANY ORDINARY GAME!
THIS GAME WILL SUFFICIENTLY TEST WHO HAS THE QUALIFICA-TIONS TO BECOME THE PRESIDENT!
?
DID YOU KNOW, YAMADA-KUN...?

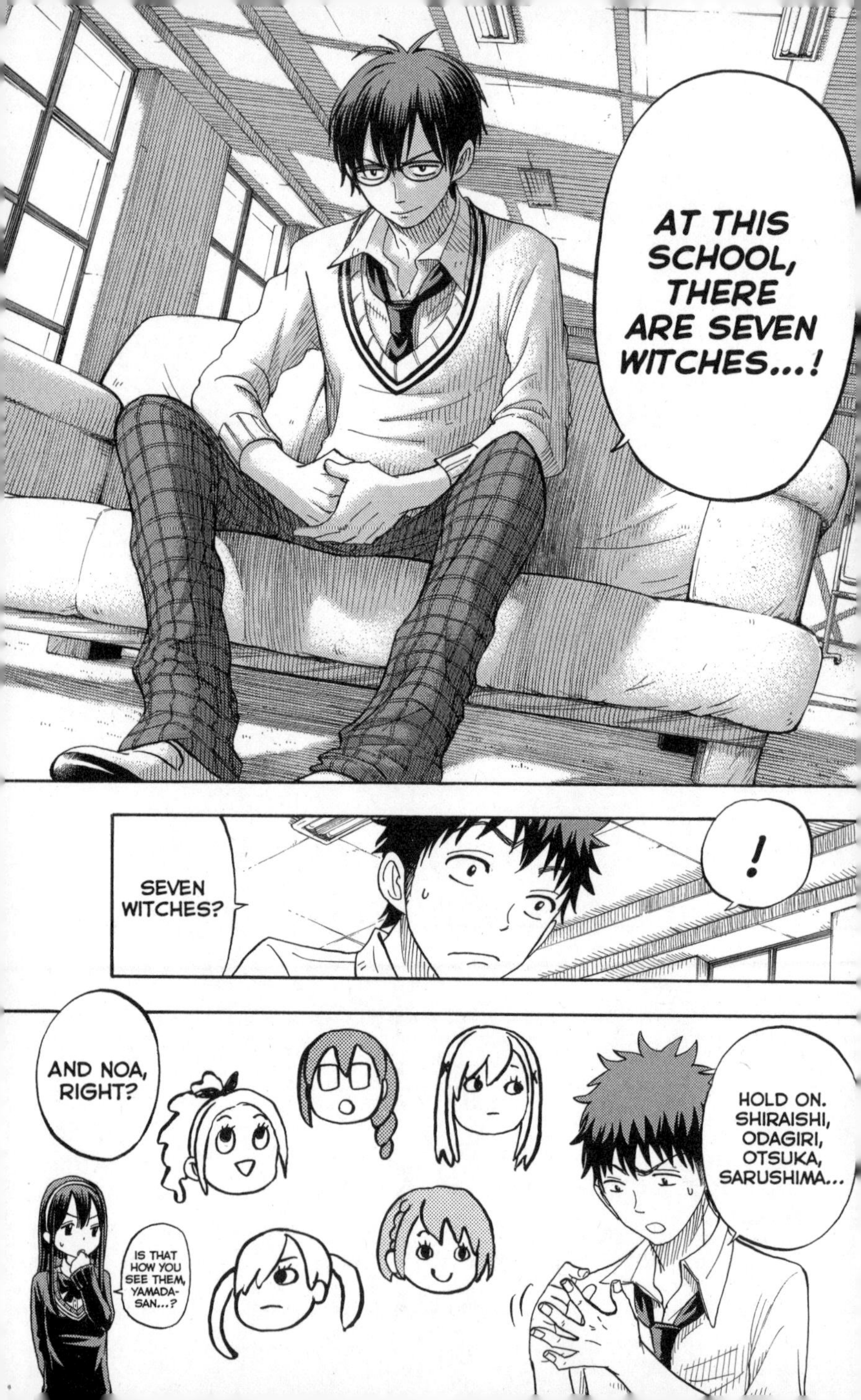
AT THIS SCHOOL, THERE ARE SEVEN WITCHES...!
!
SEVEN WITCHES?
HOLD ON. SHIRAISHI, ODAGIRI, OTSUKA, SARUSHIMA...
AND NOA, RIGHT?
IS THAT HOW YOU SEE THEM, YAMADA-SAN...?

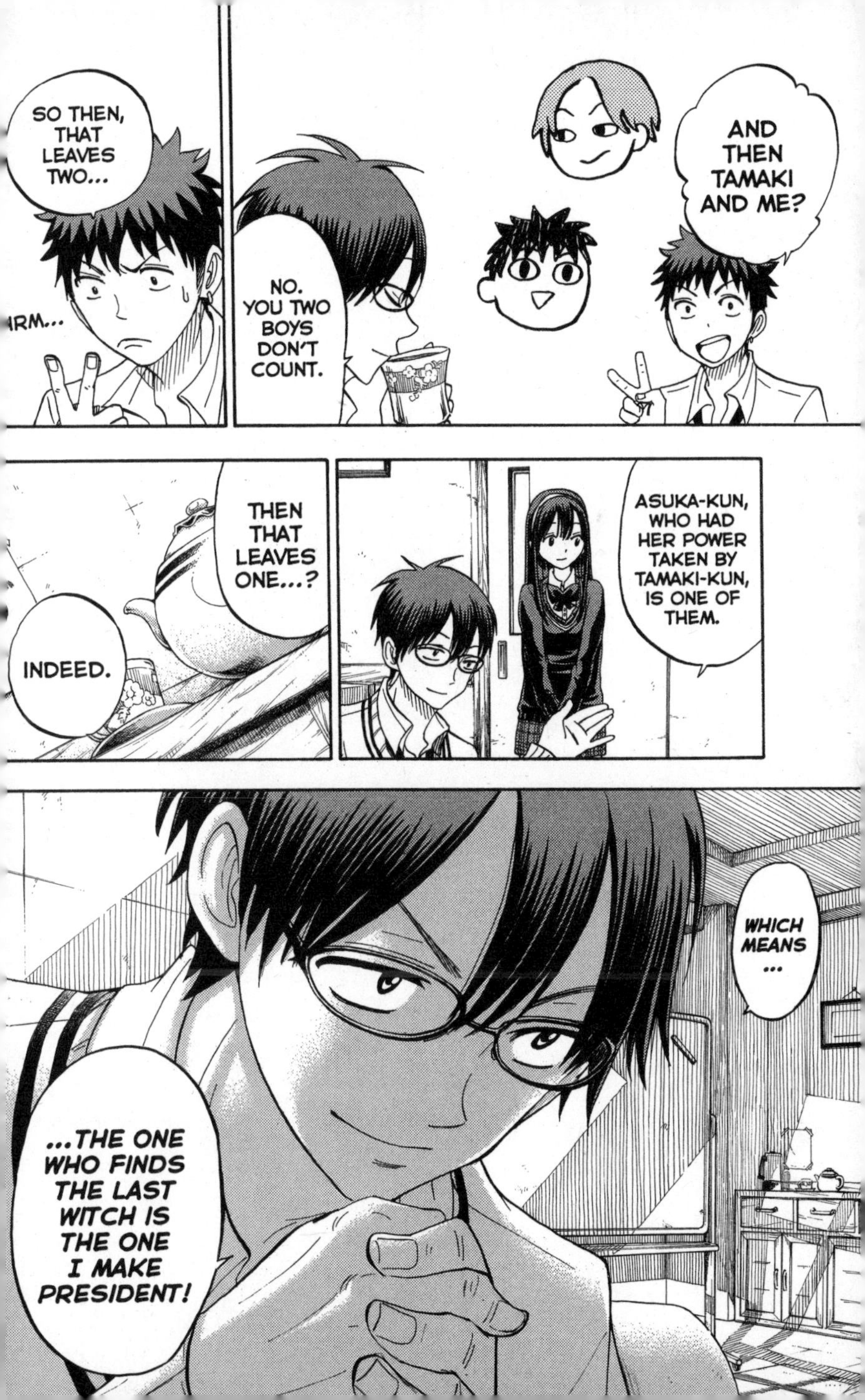
AND THEN TAMAKI AND ME?
NO. YOU TWO BOYS DON'T COUNT.
SO THEN, THAT LEAVES TWO...
HRM...
ASUKA-KUN, WHO HAD HER POWER TAKEN BY TAMAKI-KUN, IS ONE OF THEM.
THEN THAT LEAVES ONE...?
INDEED.
WHICH MEANS...
...THE ONE WHO FINDS THE LAST WITCH IS THE ONE I MAKE PRESIDENT!

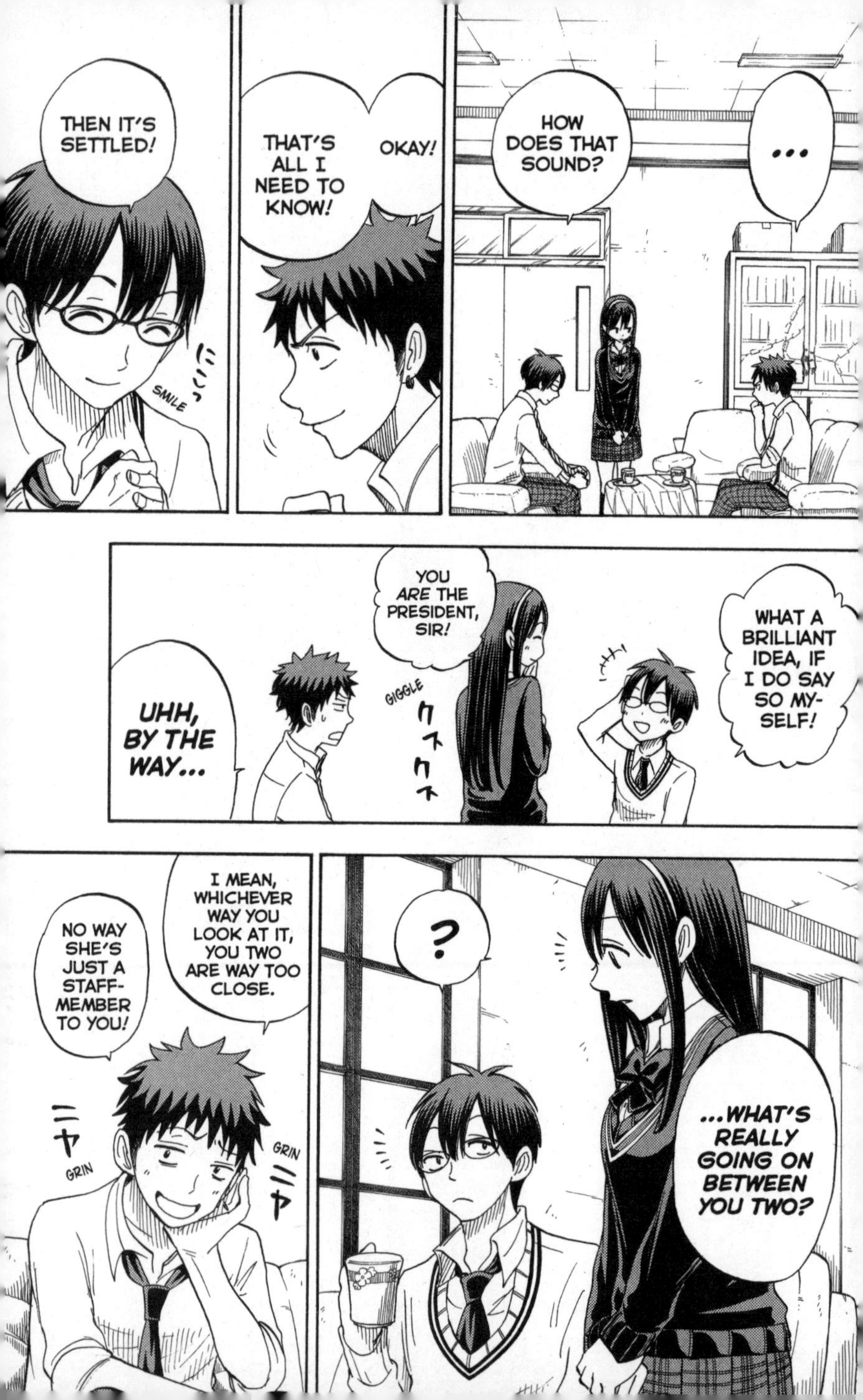
...
HOW DOES THAT SOUND?
OKAY!
THAT'S ALL I NEED TO KNOW!
THEN IT'S SETTLED!
にこっ
SMILE
WHAT A BRILLIANT IDEA, IF I DO SAY SO MY-SELF!
YOU ARE THE PRESIDENT, SIR!
クスクス
GIGGLE
UHH, BY THE WAY...
...WHAT'S REALLY GOING ON BETWEEN YOU TWO?
?
I MEAN, WHICHEVER WAY YOU LOOK AT IT, YOU TWO ARE WAY TOO CLOSE.
NO WAY SHE'S JUST A STAFF-MEMBER TO YOU!
ニヤ
GRIN
ニヤ
GRIN

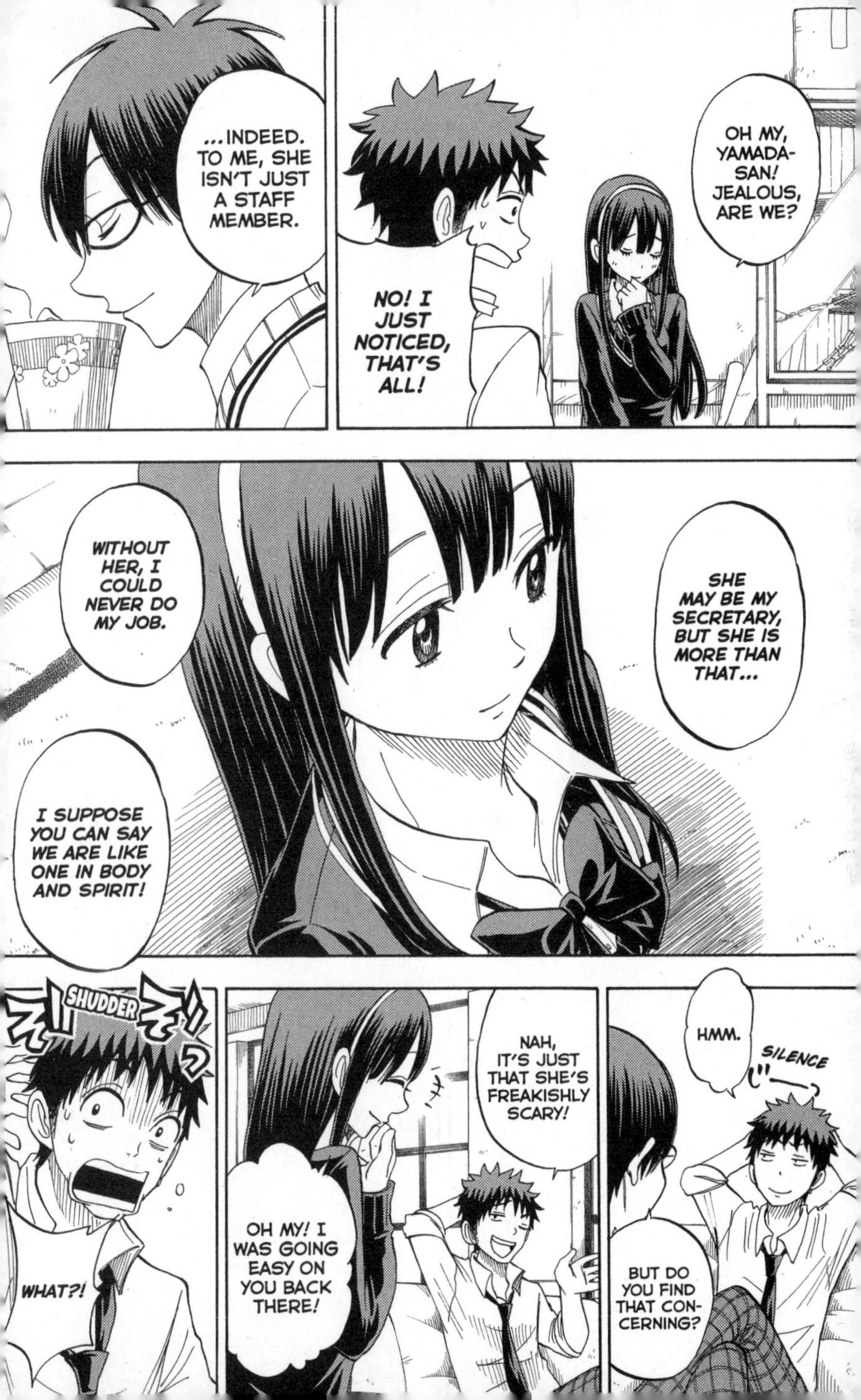
OH MY, YAMADA-SAN! JEALOUS, ARE WE?
NO! I JUST NOTICED, THAT'S ALL!
...INDEED. TO ME, SHE ISN'T JUST A STAFF MEMBER.
SHE MAY BE MY SECRETARY, BUT SHE IS MORE THAN THAT...
WITHOUT HER, I COULD NEVER DO MY JOB.
I SUPPOSE YOU CAN SAY WE ARE LIKE ONE IN BODY AND SPIRIT!
HMM.
SILENCE
BUT DO YOU FIND THAT CONCERNING?
NAH, IT'S JUST THAT SHE'S FREAKISHLY SCARY!
OH MY! I WAS GOING EASY ON YOU BACK THERE!
SHUDDER
WHAT?!

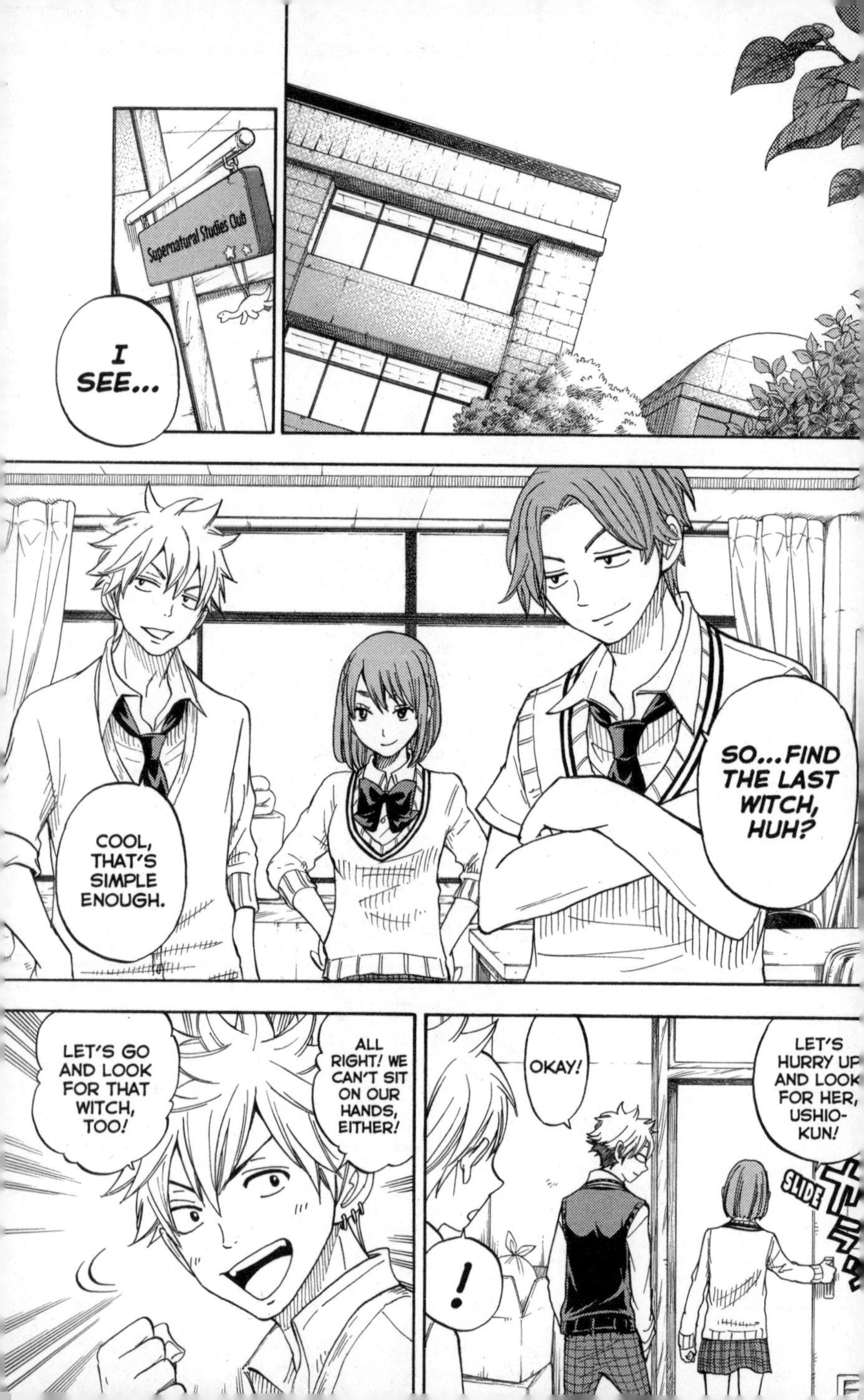
Supernatural Studies Club
I SEE...
SO...FIND THE LAST WITCH, HUH?
COOL, THAT'S SIMPLE ENOUGH.
LET'S HURRY UP AND LOOK FOR HER, USHIO-KUN!
SLIDE
OKAY!
!
ALL RIGHT! WE CAN'T SIT ON OUR HANDS, EITHER!
LET'S GO AND LOOK FOR THAT WITCH, TOO!

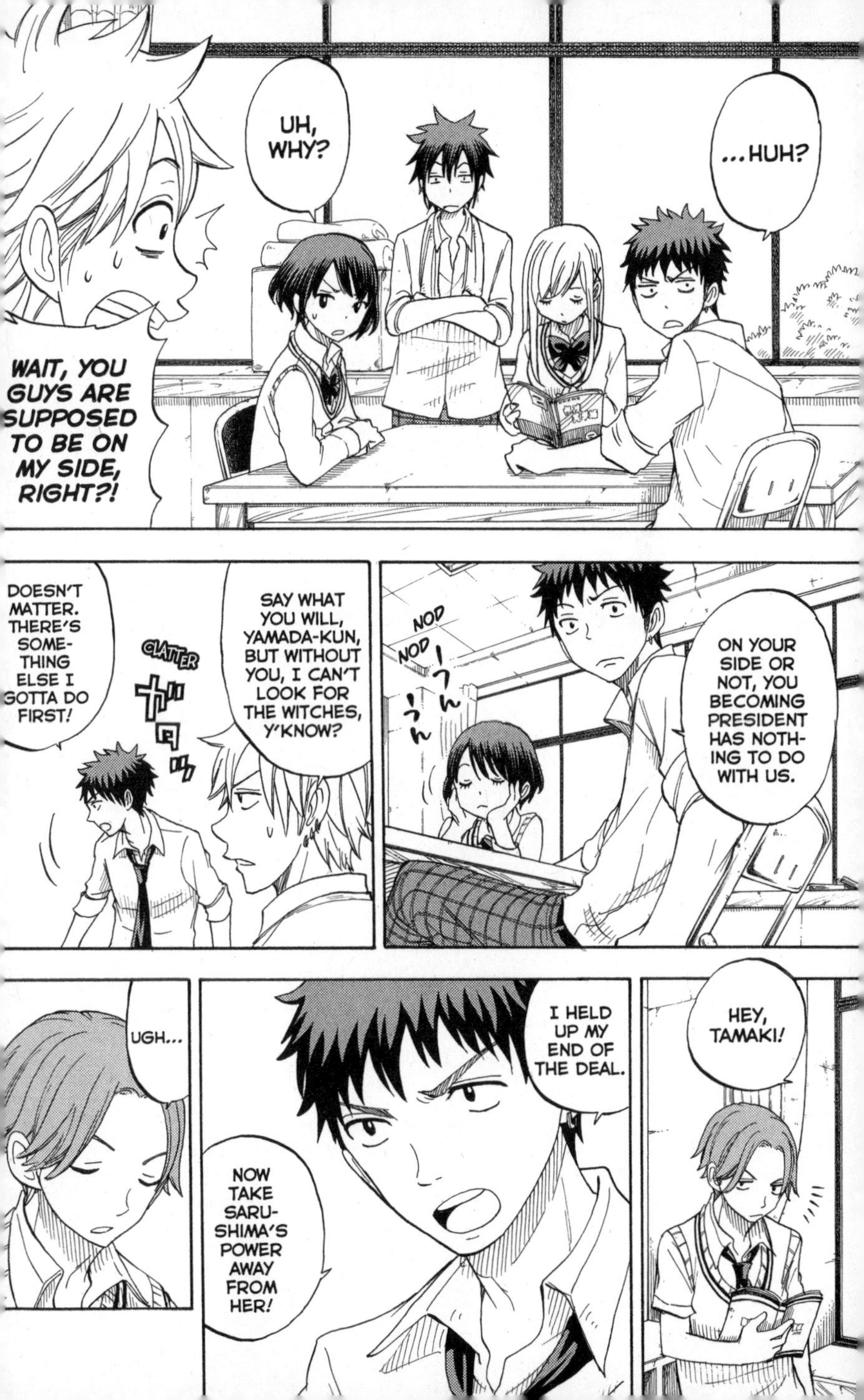
...HUH?
UH, WHY?
WAIT, YOU GUYS ARE SUPPOSED TO BE ON MY SIDE, RIGHT?!
ON YOUR SIDE OR NOT, YOU BECOMING PRESIDENT HAS NOTHING TO DO WITH US.
NOD NOD
SAY WHAT YOU WILL, YAMADA-KUN, BUT WITHOUT YOU, I CAN'T LOOK FOR THE WITCHES, Y'KNOW?
CLATTER
DOESN'T MATTER. THERE'S SOMETHING ELSE I GOTTA DO FIRST!
HEY, TAMAKI!
I HELD UP MY END OF THE DEAL.
NOW TAKE SARUSHIMA'S POWER AWAY FROM HER!
UGH...

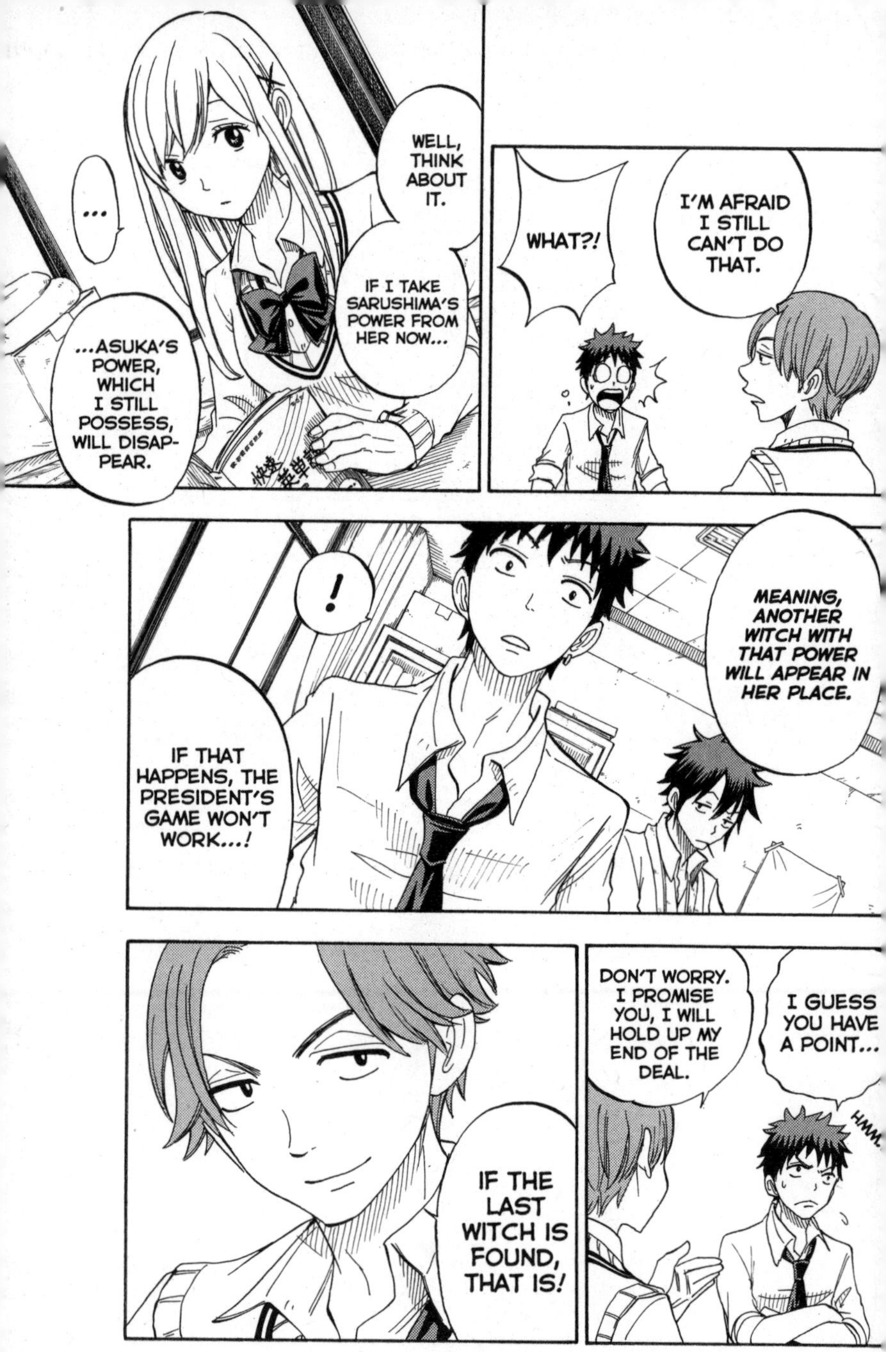
I'M AFRAID I STILL CAN'T DO THAT.
WHAT?!
WELL, THINK ABOUT IT.
IF I TAKE SARUSHIMA'S POWER FROM HER NOW...
...ASUKA'S POWER, WHICH I STILL POSSESS, WILL DISAPPEAR.
...
MEANING, ANOTHER WITCH WITH THAT POWER WILL APPEAR IN HER PLACE.
!
IF THAT HAPPENS, THE PRESIDENT'S GAME WON'T WORK...!
I GUESS YOU HAVE A POINT...
HMM.
DON'T WORRY. I PROMISE YOU, I WILL HOLD UP MY END OF THE DEAL.
IF THE LAST WITCH IS FOUND, THAT IS!

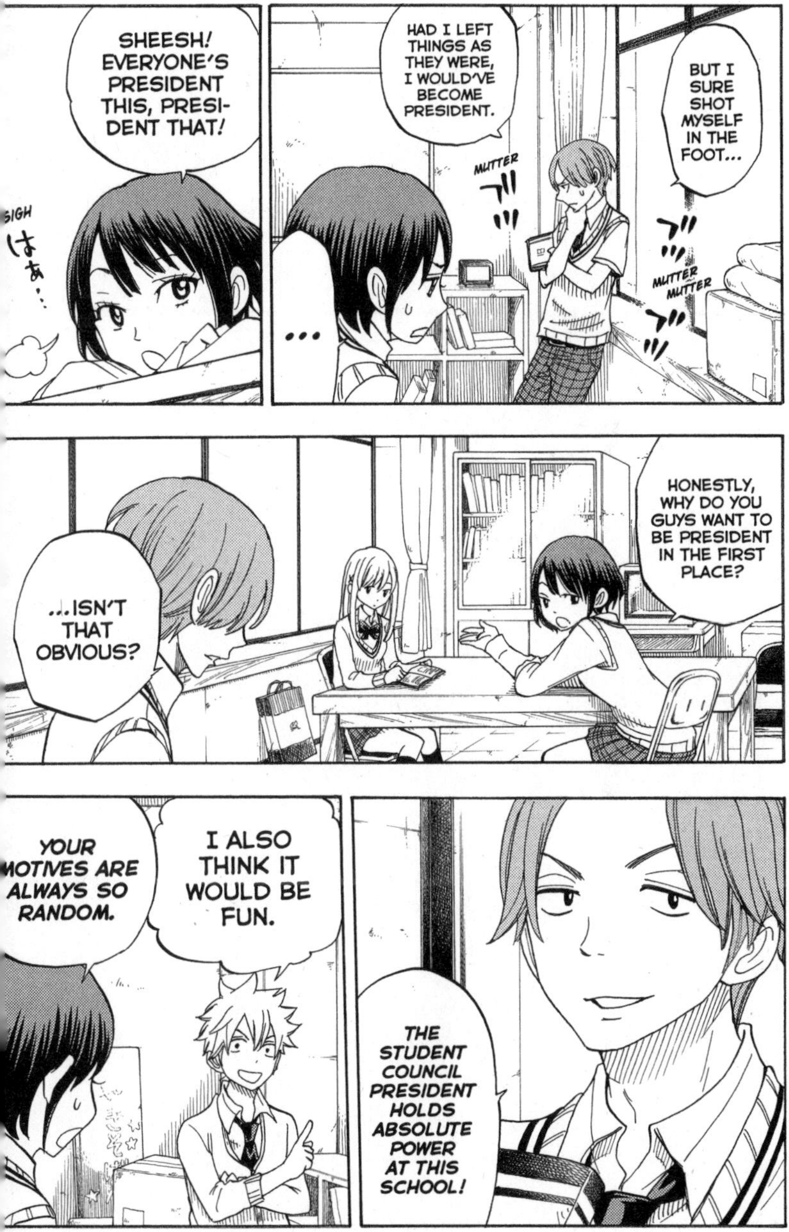

BUT I SURE SHOT MYSELF IN THE FOOT...
MUTTER MUTTER
ブツ ブツ
HAD I LEFT THINGS AS THEY WERE, I WOULD'VE BECOME PRESIDENT.
MUTTER
ブツ
...
SHEESH! EVERYONE'S PRESIDENT THIS, PRESI- DENT THAT!
SIGH
はぁ…
HONESTLY, WHY DO YOU GUYS WANT TO BE PRESIDENT IN THE FIRST PLACE?
...ISN'T THAT OBVIOUS?
THE STUDENT COUNCIL PRESIDENT HOLDS ABSOLUTE POWER AT THIS SCHOOL!
I ALSO THINK IT WOULD BE FUN.
YOUR MOTIVES ARE ALWAYS SO RANDOM.

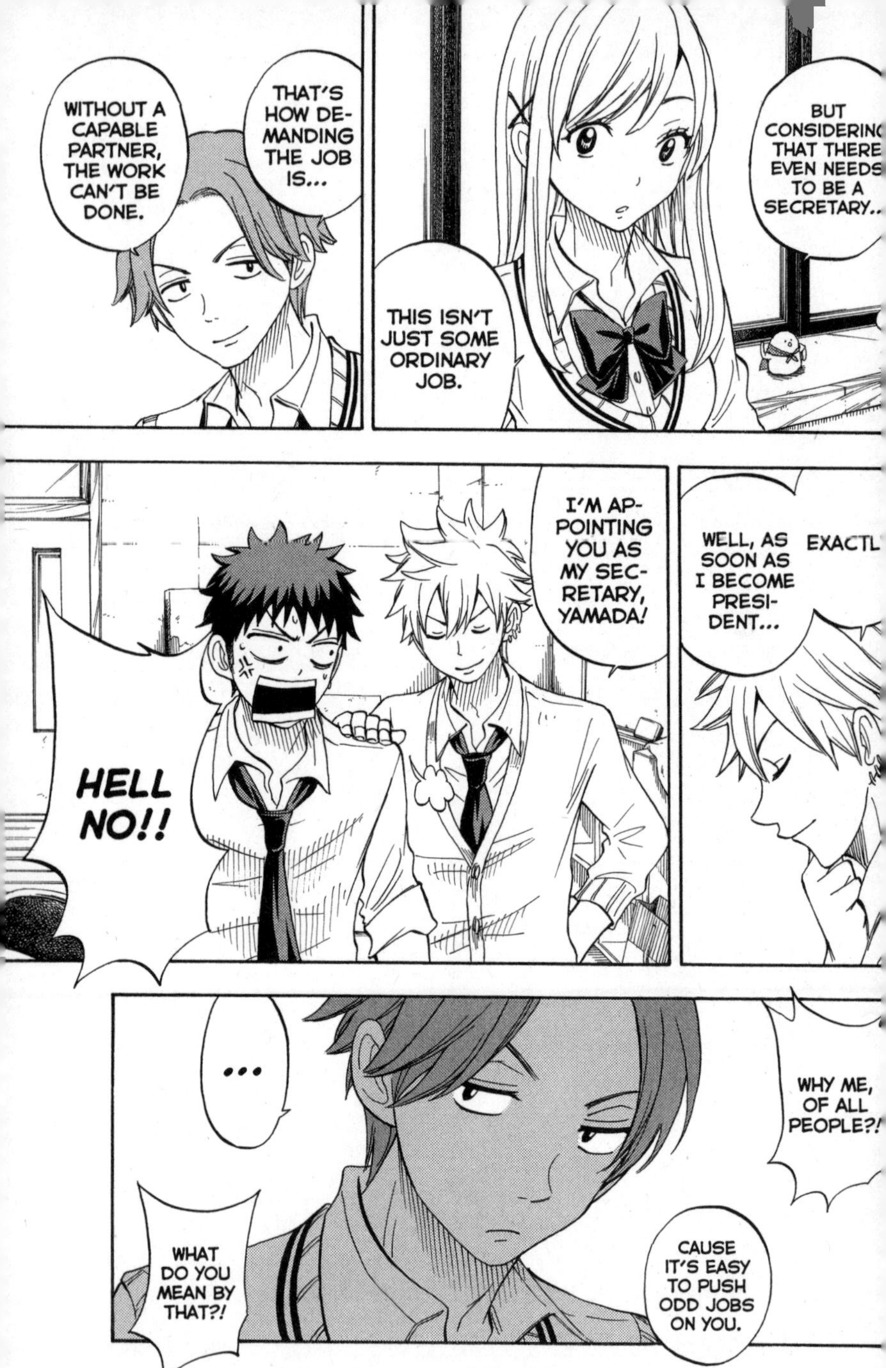
BUT CONSIDERIN THAT THERE EVEN NEEDS TO BE A SECRETARY..
THIS ISN'T JUST SOME ORDINARY JOB.
THAT'S HOW DE-MANDING THE JOB IS...
WITHOUT A CAPABLE PARTNER, THE WORK CAN'T BE DONE.
EXACTL
WELL, AS SOON AS I BECOME PRESI-DENT...
I'M AP-POINTING YOU AS MY SEC-RETARY, YAMADA!
HELL NO!!
WHY ME, OF ALL PEOPLE?!
...
CAUSE IT'S EASY TO PUSH ODD JOBS ON YOU.
WHAT DO YOU MEAN BY THAT?!

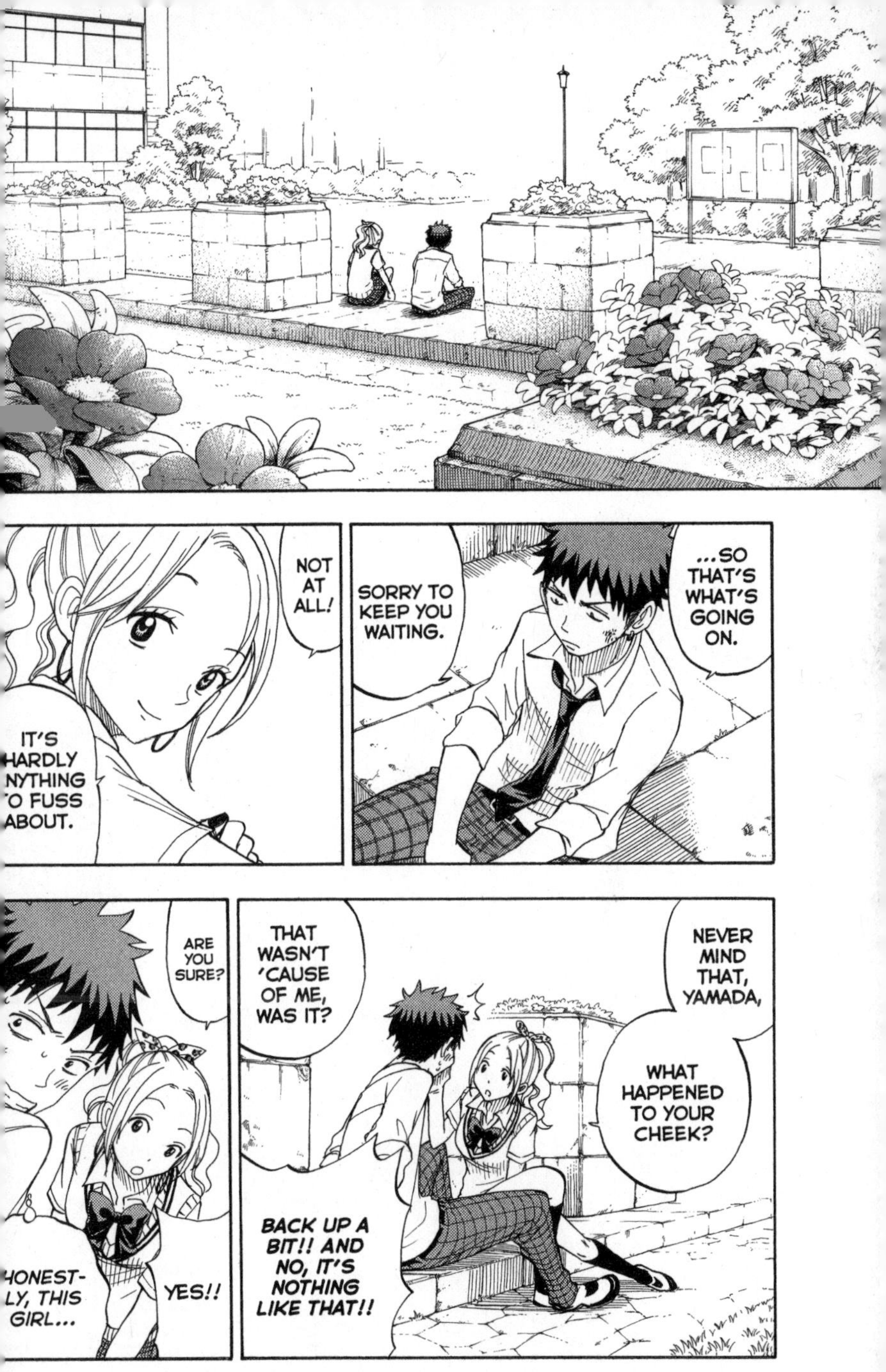

...SO THAT'S WHAT'S GOING ON.
SORRY TO KEEP YOU WAITING.
NOT AT ALL!
IT'S HARDLY NYTHING 'O FUSS ABOUT.
NEVER MIND THAT, YAMADA,
WHAT HAPPENED TO YOUR CHEEK?
THAT WASN'T 'CAUSE OF ME, WAS IT?
BACK UP A BIT!! AND NO, IT'S NOTHING LIKE THAT!!
ARE YOU SURE?
YES!!
HONEST-LY, THIS GIRL...

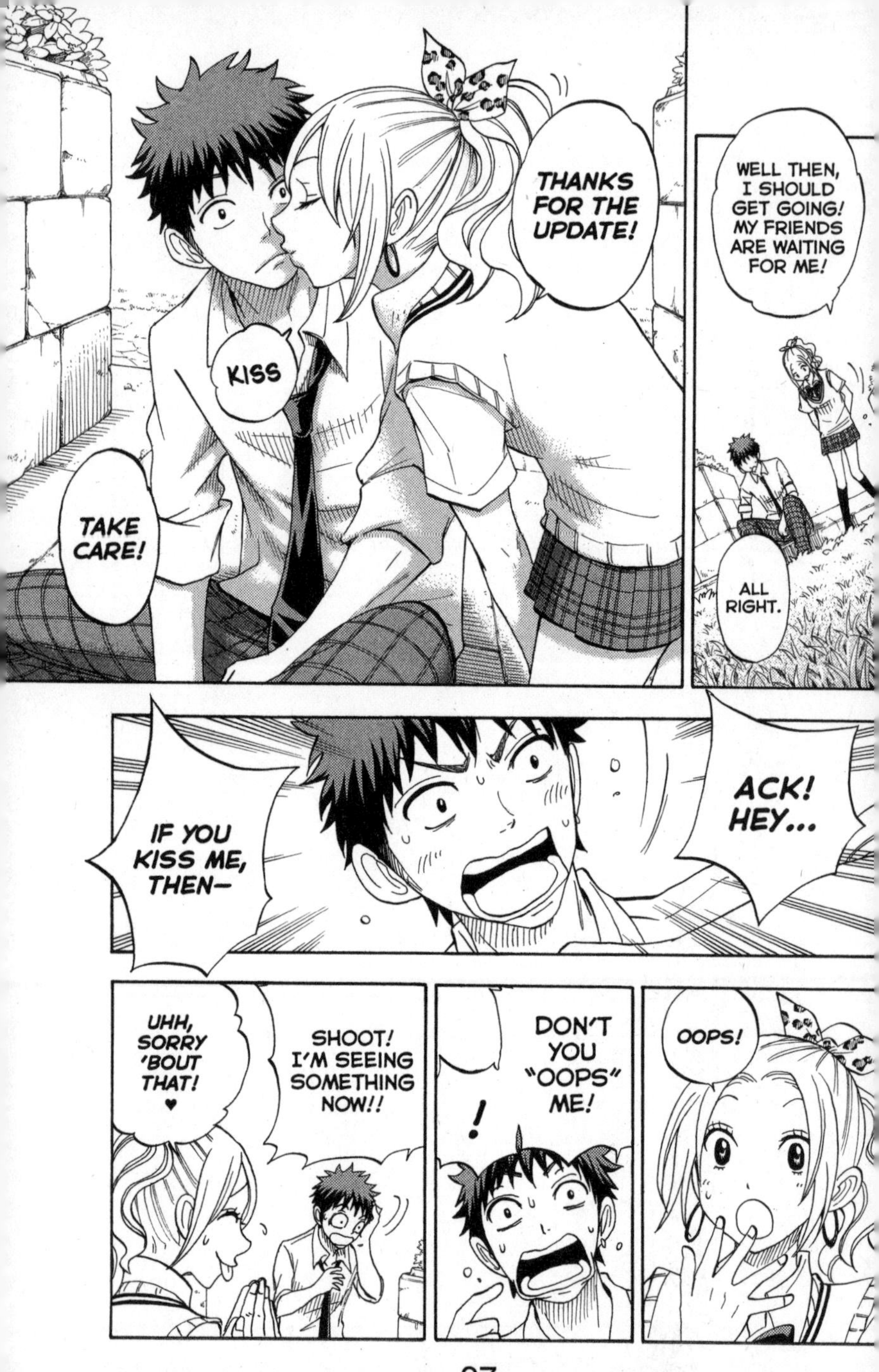
WELL THEN, I SHOULD GET GOING! MY FRIENDS ARE WAITING FOR ME!
ALL RIGHT.
THANKS FOR THE UPDATE!
KISS
TAKE CARE!
ACK! HEY...
IF YOU KISS ME, THEN—
OOPS!
DON'T YOU "OOPS" ME!
!
SHOOT! I'M SEEING SOMETHING NOW!!
UHH, SORRY 'BOUT THAT! ♥

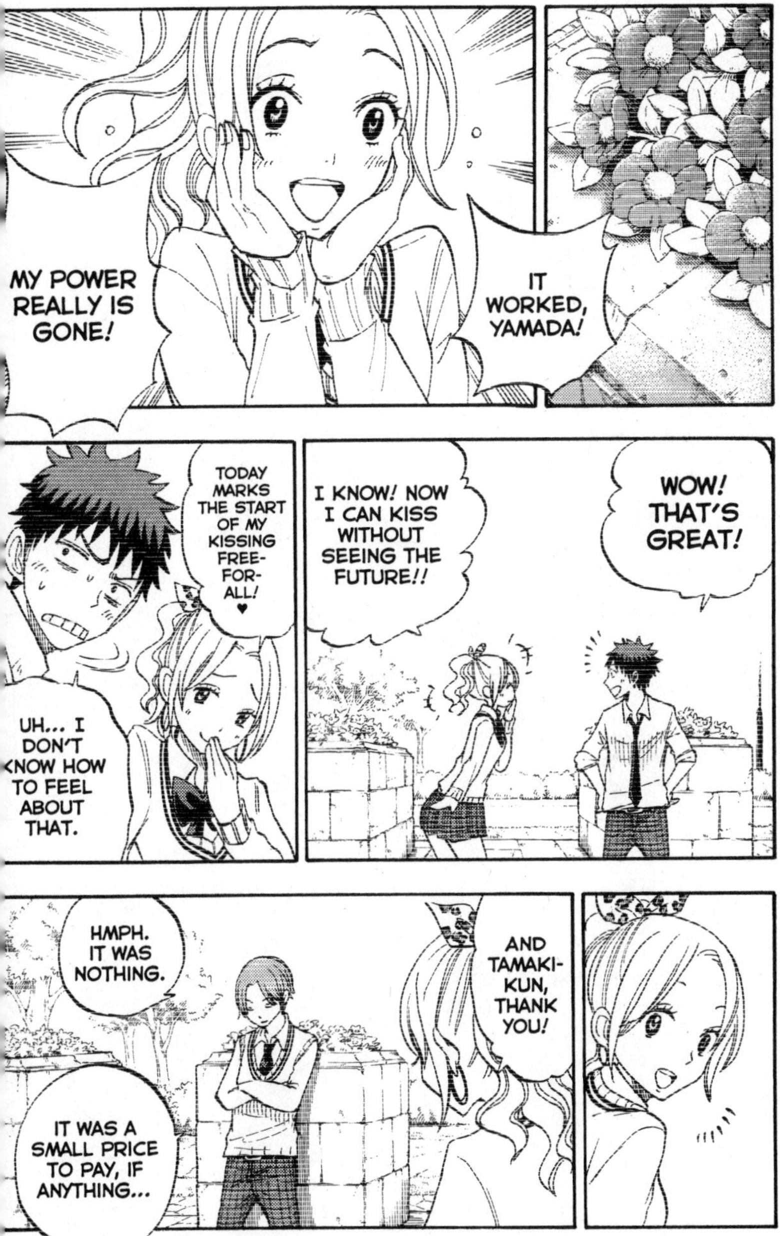
IT WORKED, YAMADA!
MY POWER REALLY IS GONE!
WOW! THAT'S GREAT!
I KNOW! NOW I CAN KISS WITHOUT SEEING THE FUTURE!!
TODAY MARKS THE START OF MY KISSING FREE-FOR-ALL! ♥
UH... I DON'T KNOW HOW TO FEEL ABOUT THAT.
AND TAMAKI-KUN, THANK YOU!
HMPH. IT WAS NOTHING.
IT WAS A SMALL PRICE TO PAY, IF ANYTHING...

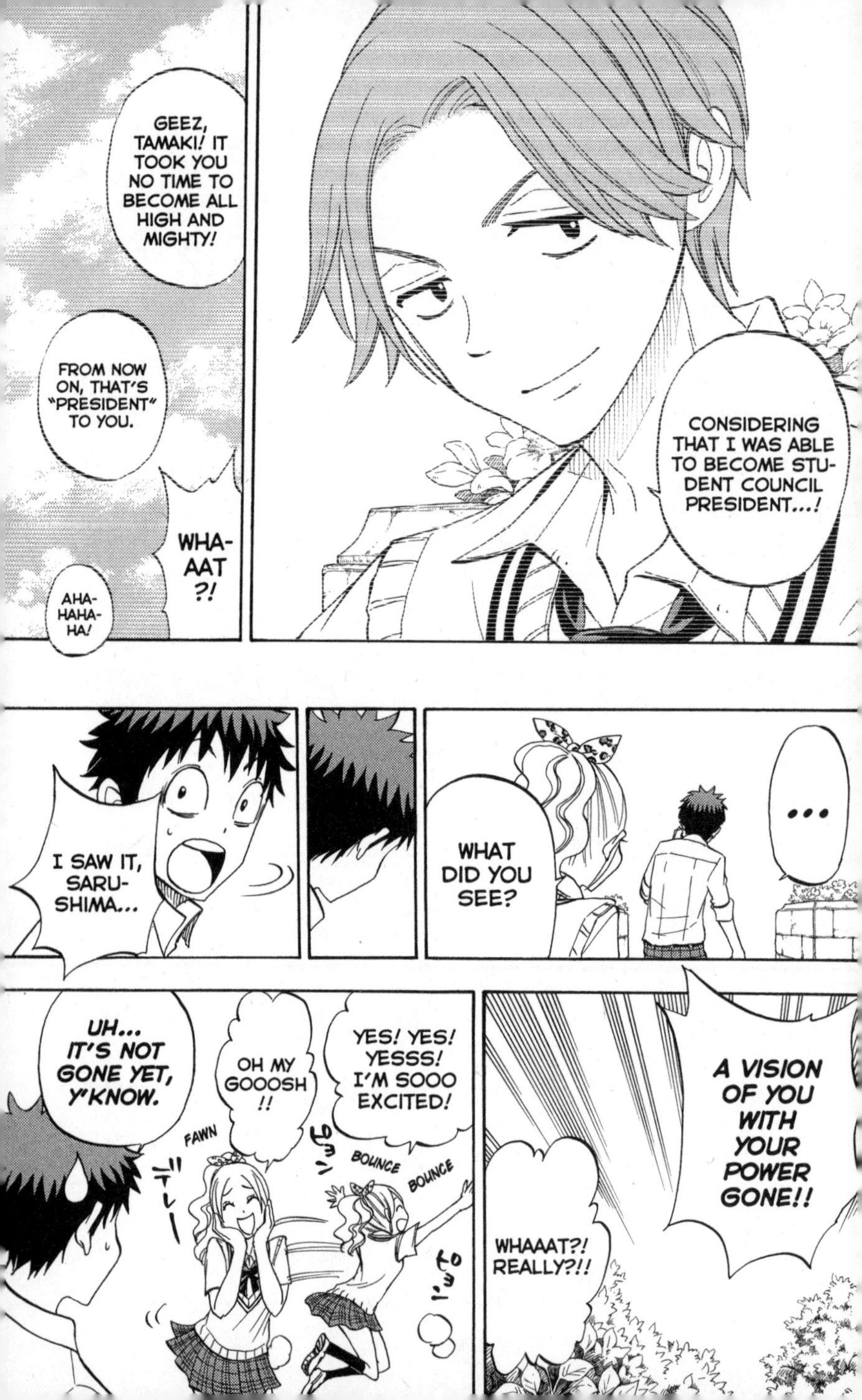
CONSIDERING THAT I WAS ABLE TO BECOME STU-DENT COUNCIL PRESIDENT...!
GEEZ, TAMAKI! IT TOOK YOU NO TIME TO BECOME ALL HIGH AND MIGHTY!
FROM NOW ON, THAT'S "PRESIDENT" TO YOU.
WHA-AAT?!
AHA-HAHA-HA!
...
WHAT DID YOU SEE?
I SAW IT, SARU-SHIMA...
A VISION OF YOU WITH YOUR POWER GONE!!
WHAAAT?! REALLY?!!
YES! YES! YESSS! I'M SOOO EXCITED!
BOUNCE
BOUNCE
OH MY GOOOSH!!
FAWN
UH... IT'S NOT GONE YET, Y'KNOW.

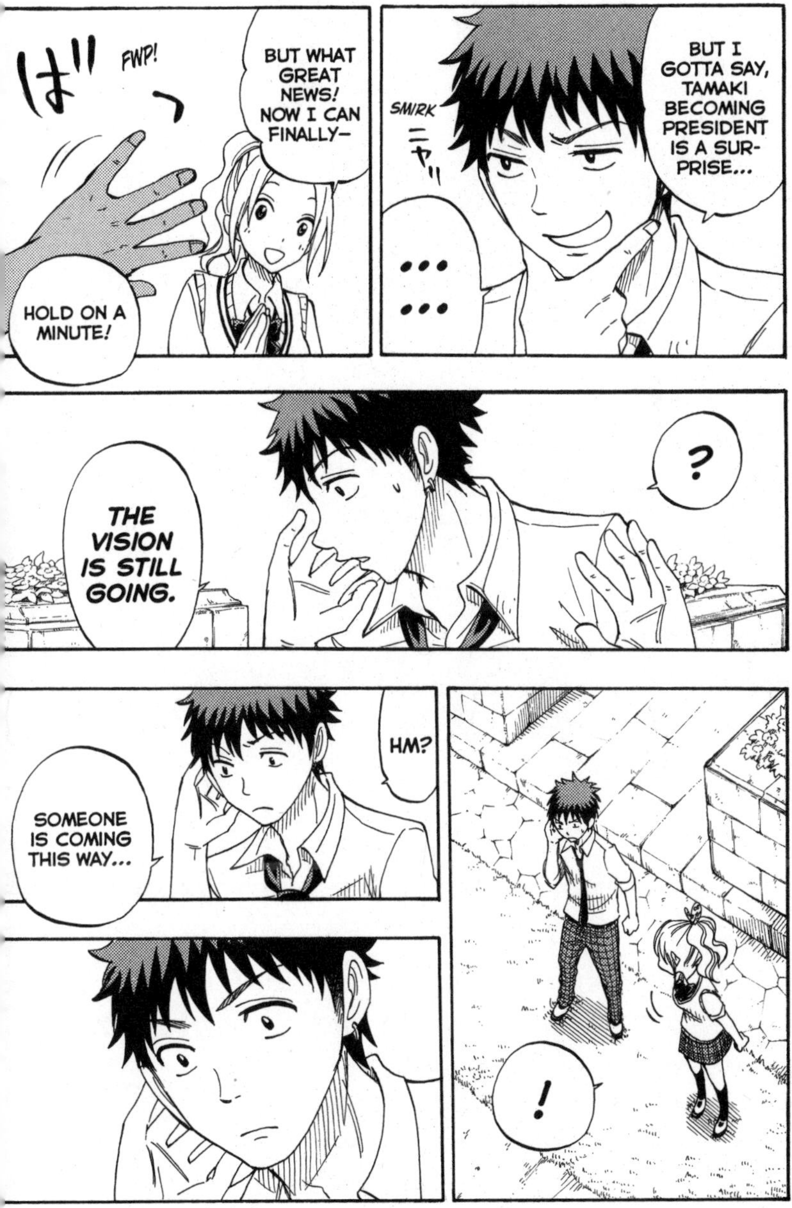
BUT I GOTTA SAY, TAMAKI BECOMING PRESIDENT IS A SURPRISE...
SMIRK
ニヤッ
......
BUT WHAT GREAT NEWS! NOW I CAN FINALLY—
FWP!
ばッ
HOLD ON A MINUTE!
?
THE VISION IS STILL GOING.
!
HM?
SOMEONE IS COMING THIS WAY...

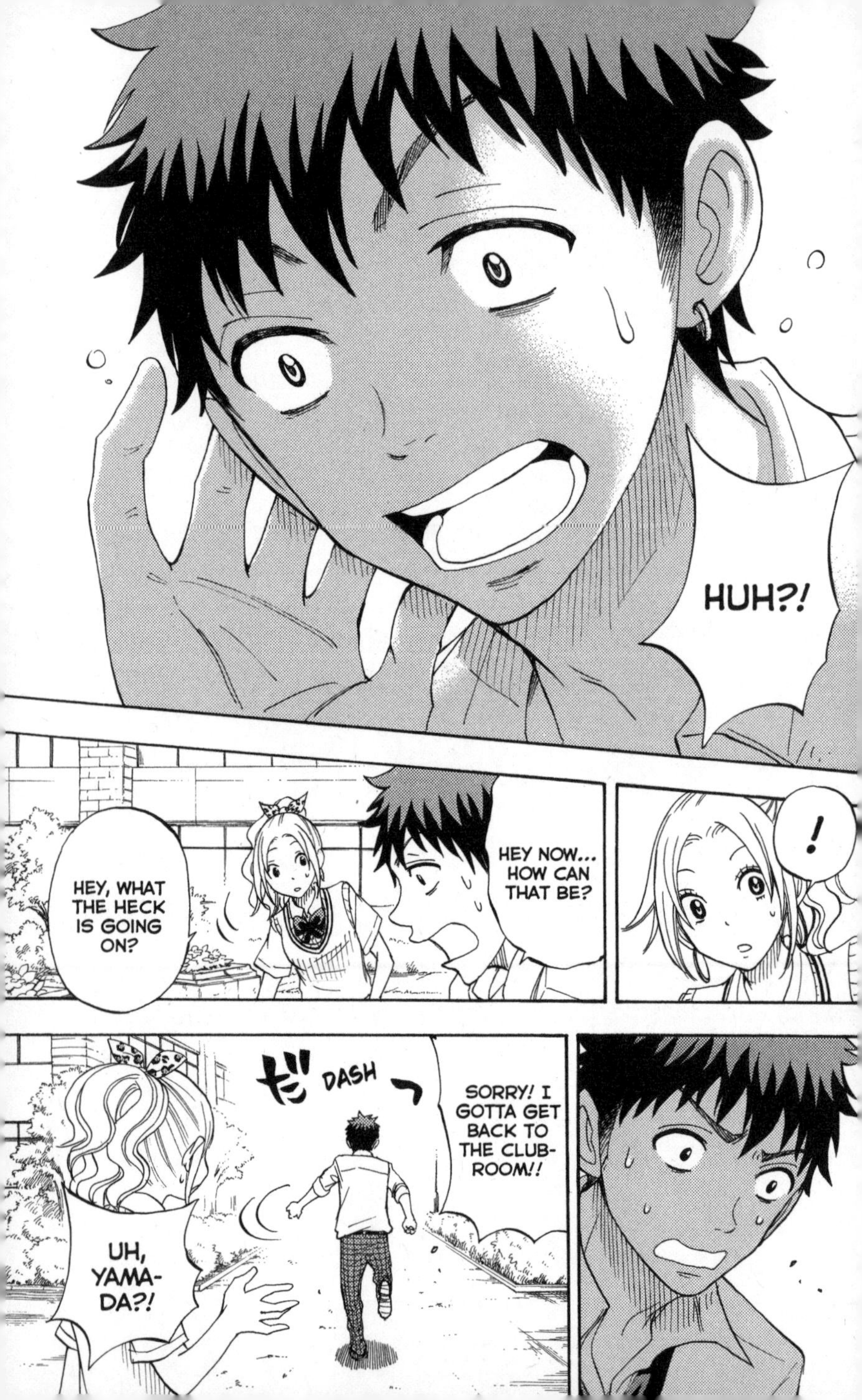
HUH?!
!
HEY NOW... HOW CAN THAT BE?
HEY, WHAT THE HECK IS GOING ON?
SORRY! I GOTTA GET BACK TO THE CLUB-ROOM!!
DASH
UH, YAMA-DA?!

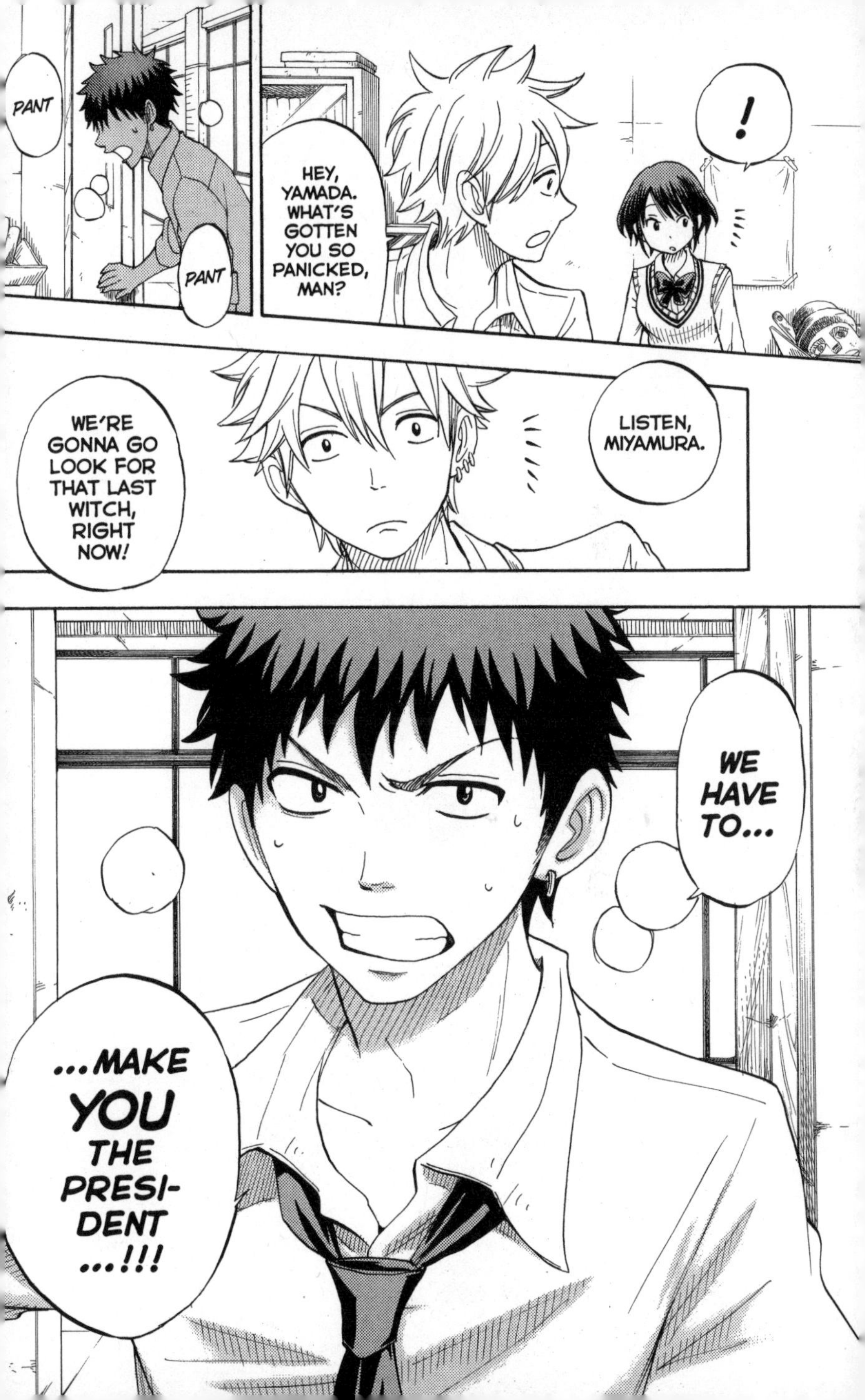
!
HEY, YAMADA. WHAT'S GOTTEN YOU SO PANICKED, MAN?
PANT
PANT
LISTEN, MIYAMURA.
WE'RE GONNA GO LOOK FOR THAT LAST WITCH, RIGHT NOW!
WE HAVE TO...
...MAKE YOU THE PRESIDENT...!!!

CHAPTER 57: Yeah, I do.

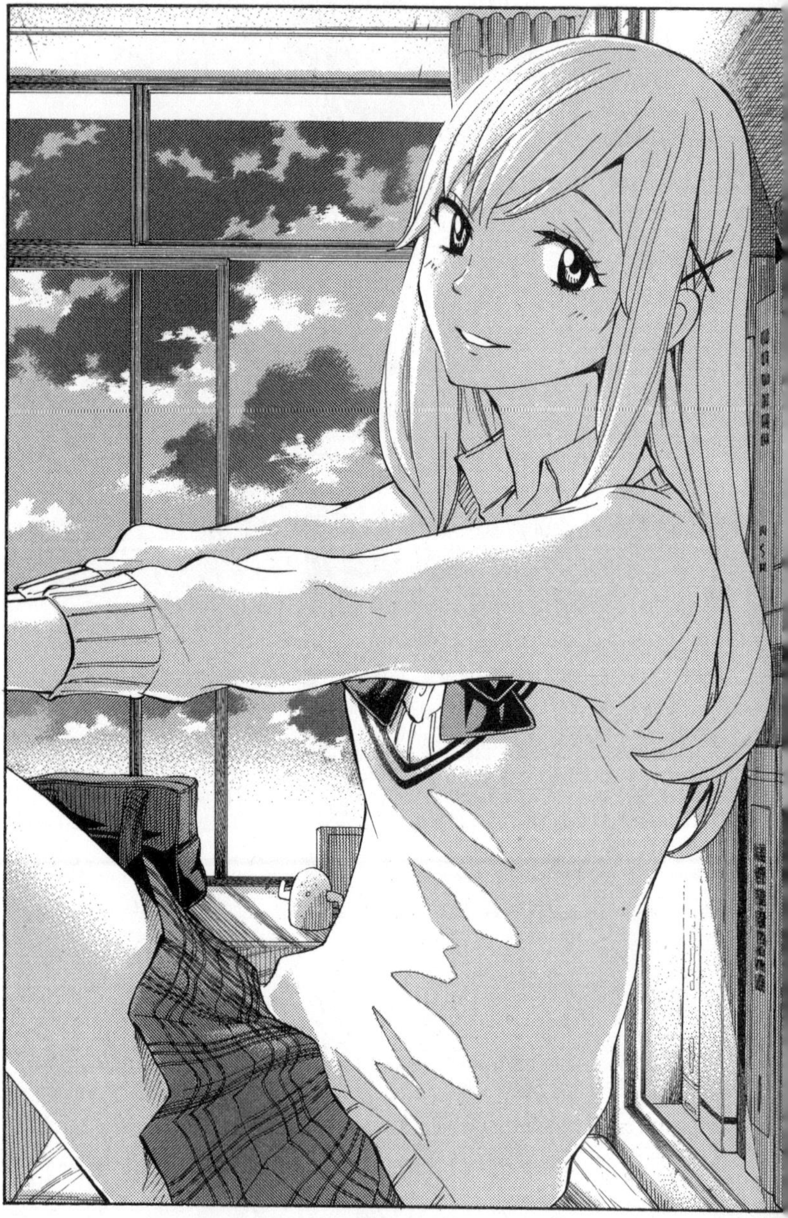

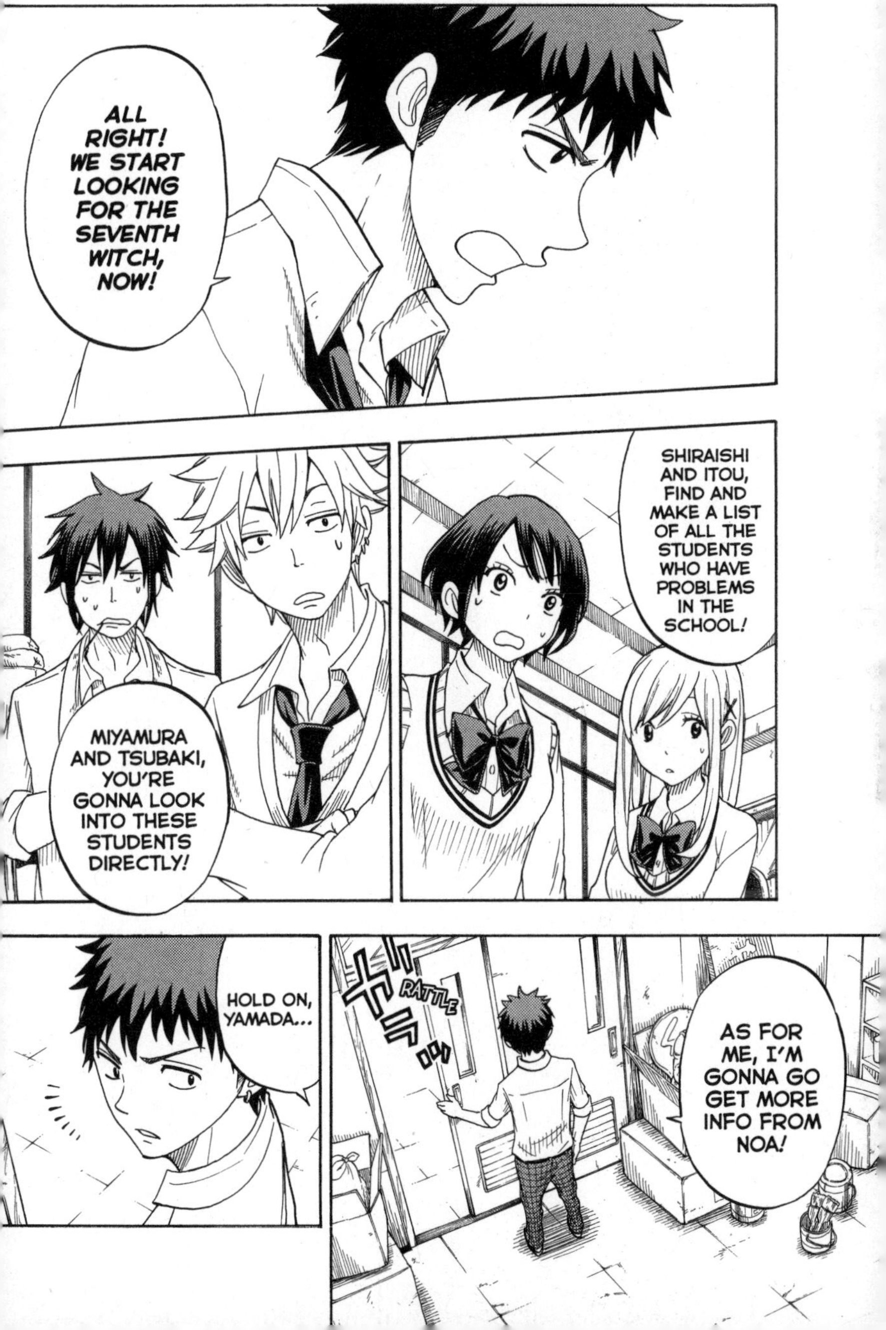
ALL RIGHT! WE START LOOKING FOR THE SEVENTH WITCH, NOW!
SHIRAISHI AND ITOU, FIND AND MAKE A LIST OF ALL THE STUDENTS WHO HAVE PROBLEMS IN THE SCHOOL!
MIYAMURA AND TSUBAKI, YOU'RE GONNA LOOK INTO THESE STUDENTS DIRECTLY!
RATTLE
AS FOR ME, I'M GONNA GO GET MORE INFO FROM NOA!
HOLD ON, YAMADA...

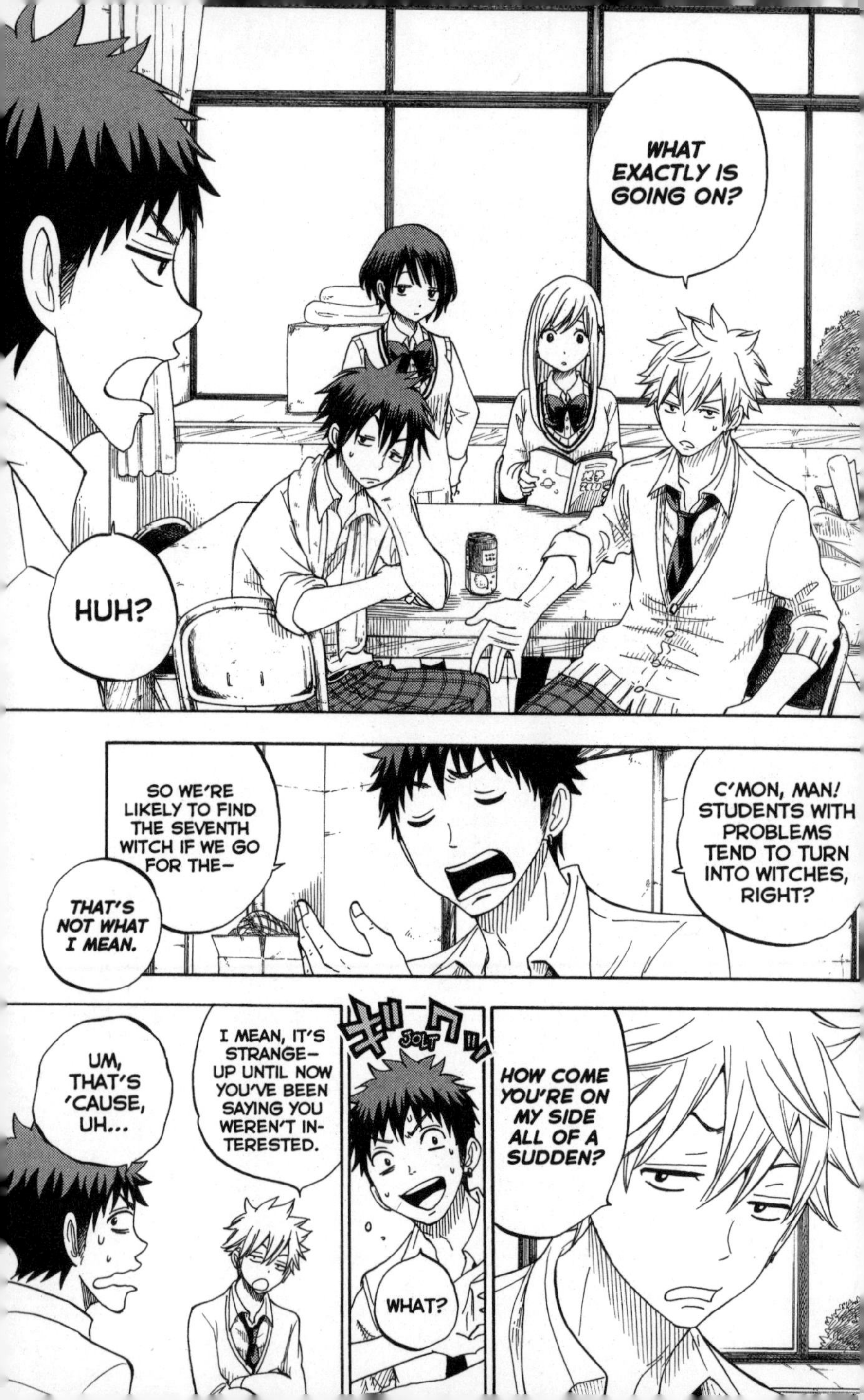
WHAT EXACTLY IS GOING ON?
HUH?
C'MON, MAN! STUDENTS WITH PROBLEMS TEND TO TURN INTO WITCHES, RIGHT?
SO WE'RE LIKELY TO FIND THE SEVENTH WITCH IF WE GO FOR THE–
THAT'S NOT WHAT I MEAN.
HOW COME YOU'RE ON MY SIDE ALL OF A SUDDEN?
JOLT
WHAT?
I MEAN, IT'S STRANGE– UP UNTIL NOW YOU'VE BEEN SAYING YOU WEREN'T IN-TERESTED.
UM, THAT'S 'CAUSE, UH...

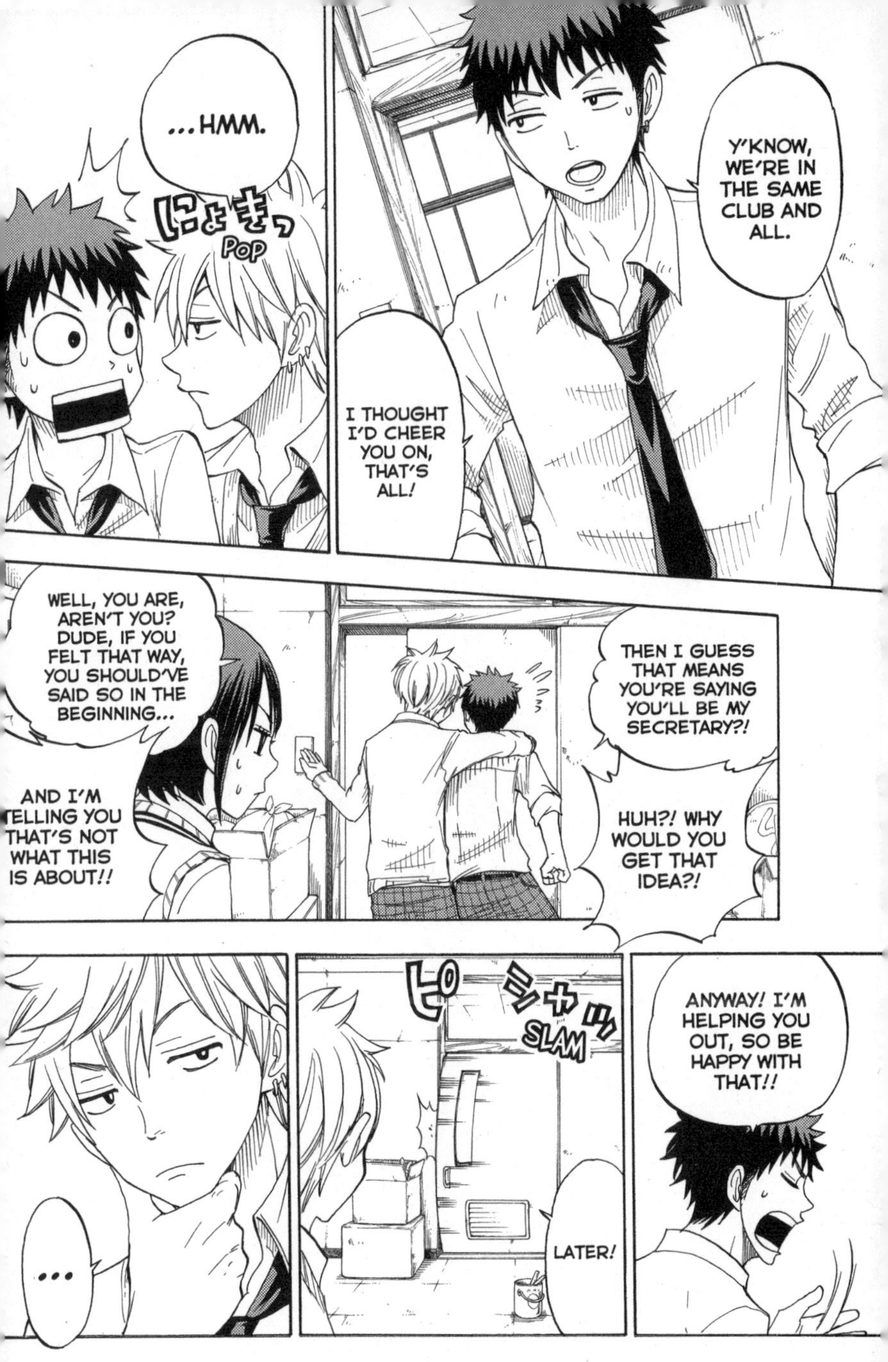
Y'KNOW, WE'RE IN THE SAME CLUB AND ALL.
I THOUGHT I'D CHEER YOU ON, THAT'S ALL!
...HMM.
にょきっ
POP
THEN I GUESS THAT MEANS YOU'RE SAYING YOU'LL BE MY SECRETARY?!
HUH?! WHY WOULD YOU GET THAT IDEA?!
WELL, YOU ARE, AREN'T YOU? DUDE, IF YOU FELT THAT WAY, YOU SHOULD'VE SAID SO IN THE BEGINNING...
AND I'M TELLING YOU THAT'S NOT WHAT THIS IS ABOUT!!
ANYWAY! I'M HELPING YOU OUT, SO BE HAPPY WITH THAT!!
LATER!
ピシャッ
SLAM
...

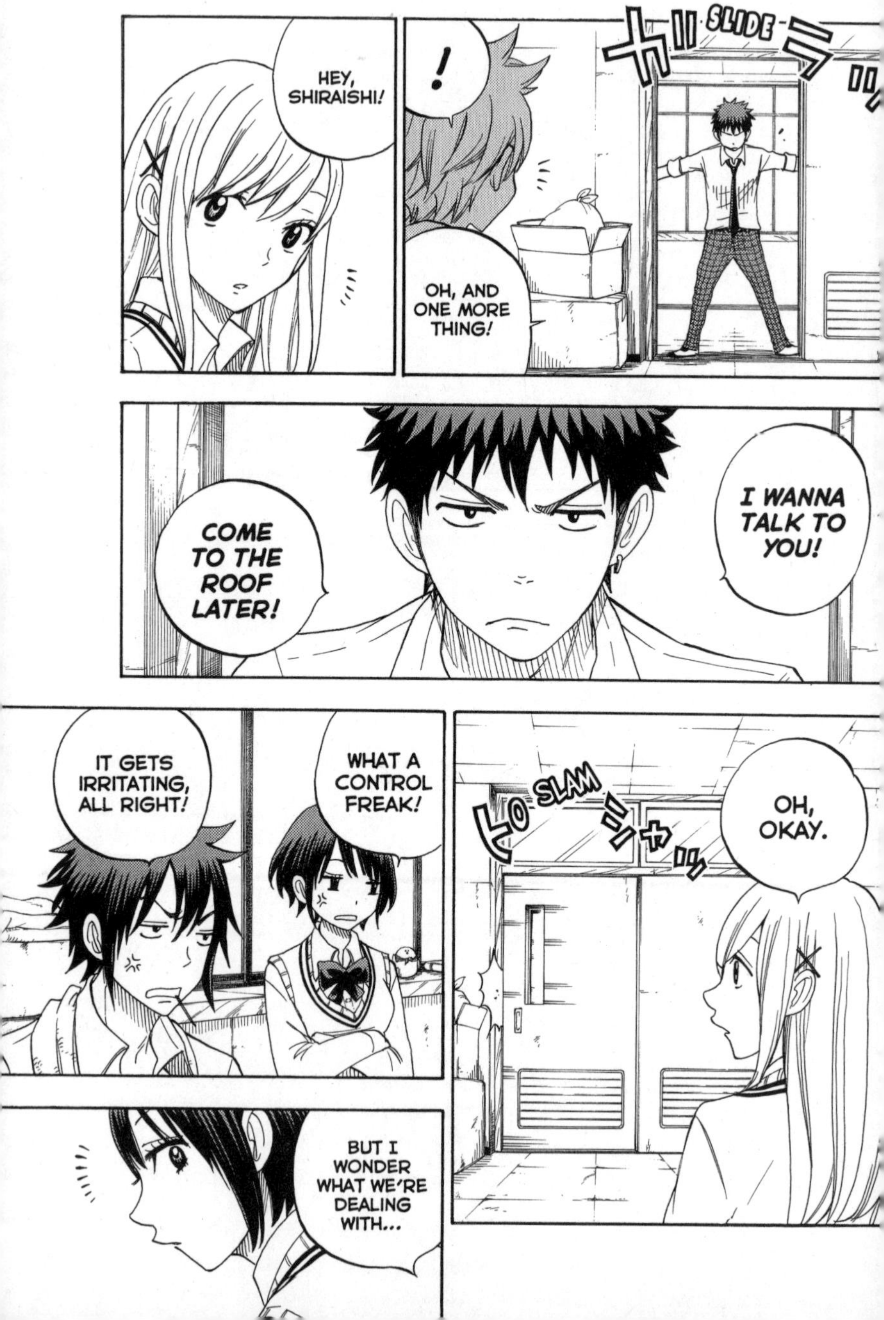
SLIDE
!
OH, AND ONE MORE THING!
HEY, SHIRAISHI!
I WANNA TALK TO YOU!
COME TO THE ROOF LATER!
OH, OKAY.
SLAM
WHAT A CONTROL FREAK!
IT GETS IRRITATING, ALL RIGHT!
BUT I WONDER WHAT WE'RE DEALING WITH...

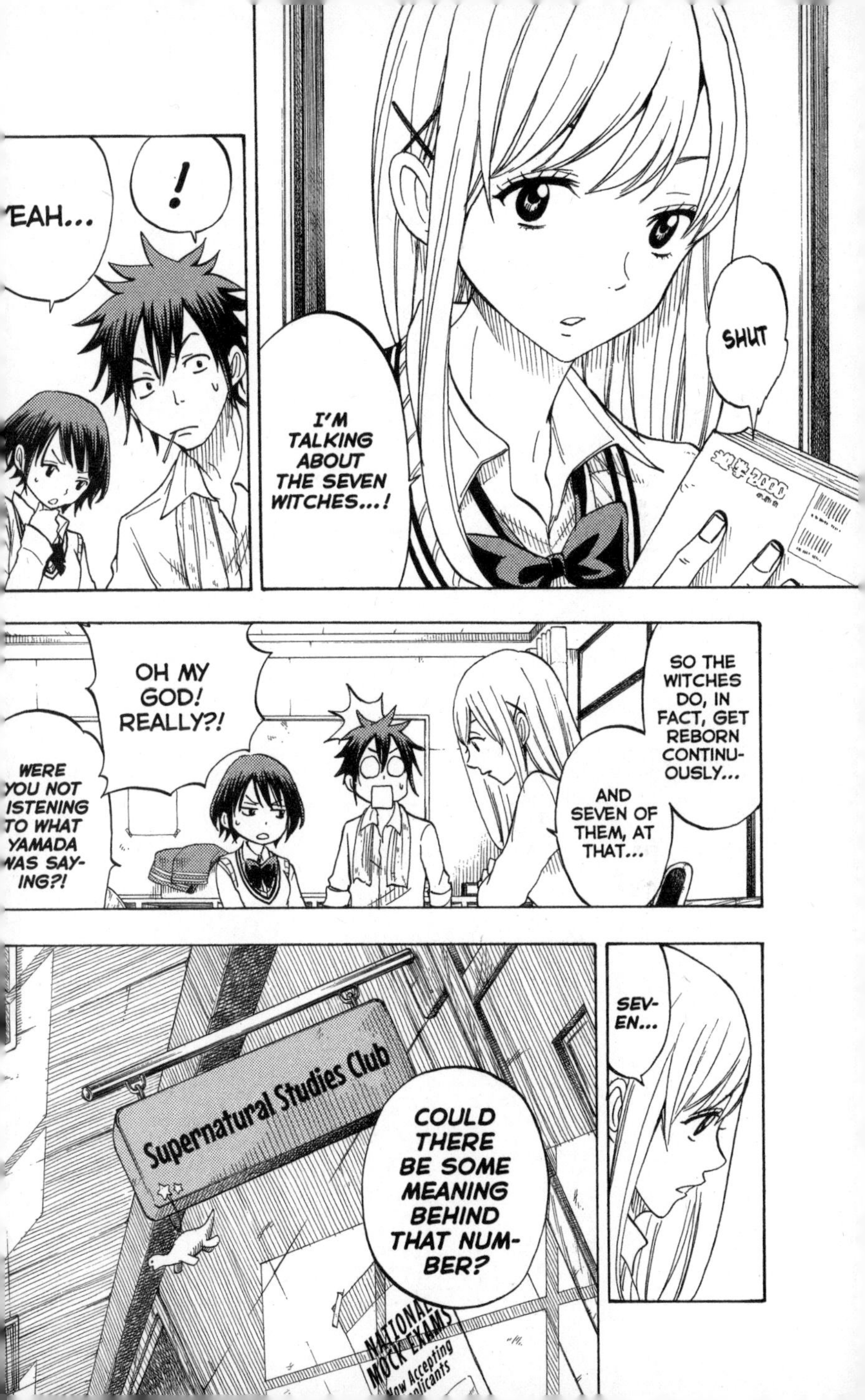
SHUT
I'M TALKING ABOUT THE SEVEN WITCHES...!
!
EAH...
SO THE WITCHES DO, IN FACT, GET REBORN CONTINUOUSLY...
AND SEVEN OF THEM, AT THAT...
OH MY GOD! REALLY?!
WERE YOU NOT ISTENING TO WHAT YAMADA WAS SAYING?!
SEVEN...
COULD THERE BE SOME MEANING BEHIND THAT NUMBER?
Supernatural Studies Club
NATIONAL MOCK EXAMS
Now Accepting
plicants

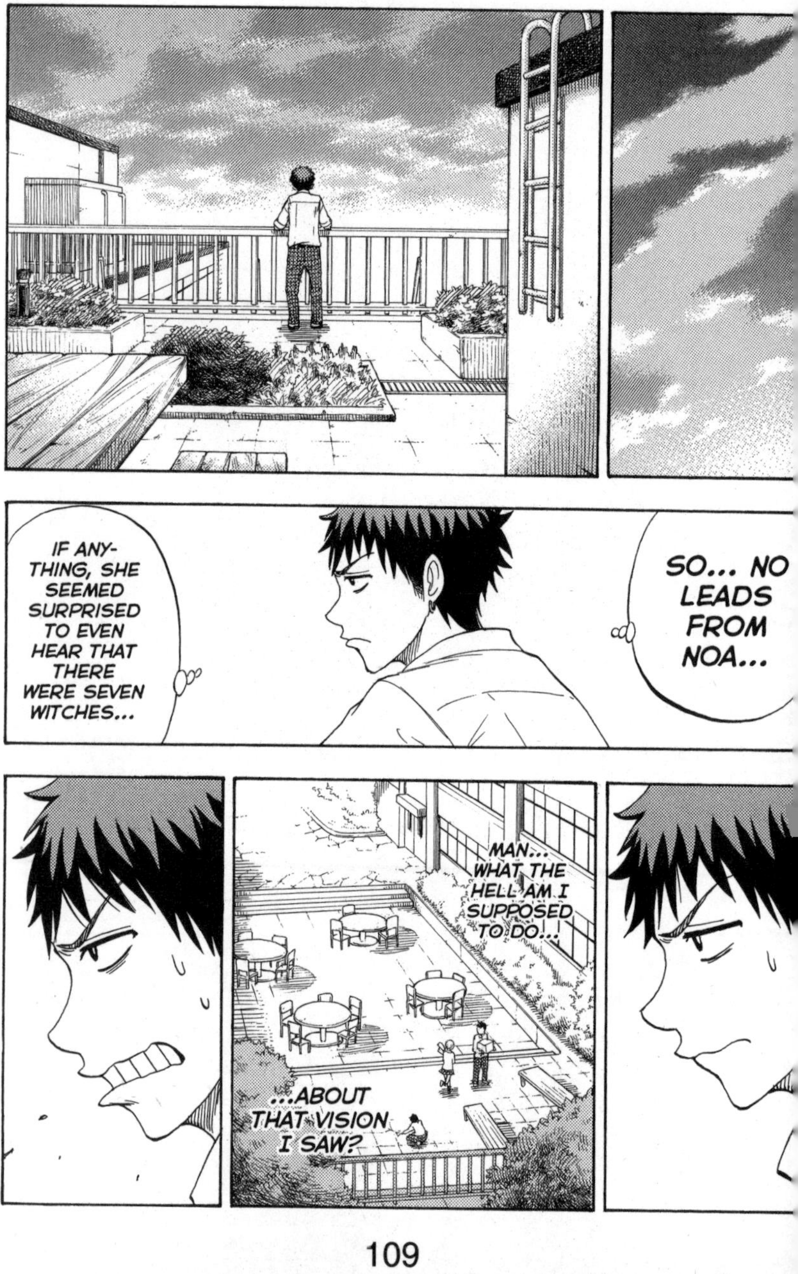
SO... NO LEADS FROM NOA...
IF ANY-THING, SHE SEEMED SURPRISED TO EVEN HEAR THAT THERE WERE SEVEN WITCHES...
MAN... WHAT THE HELL AM I SUPPOSED TO DO...
...ABOUT THAT VISION I SAW?

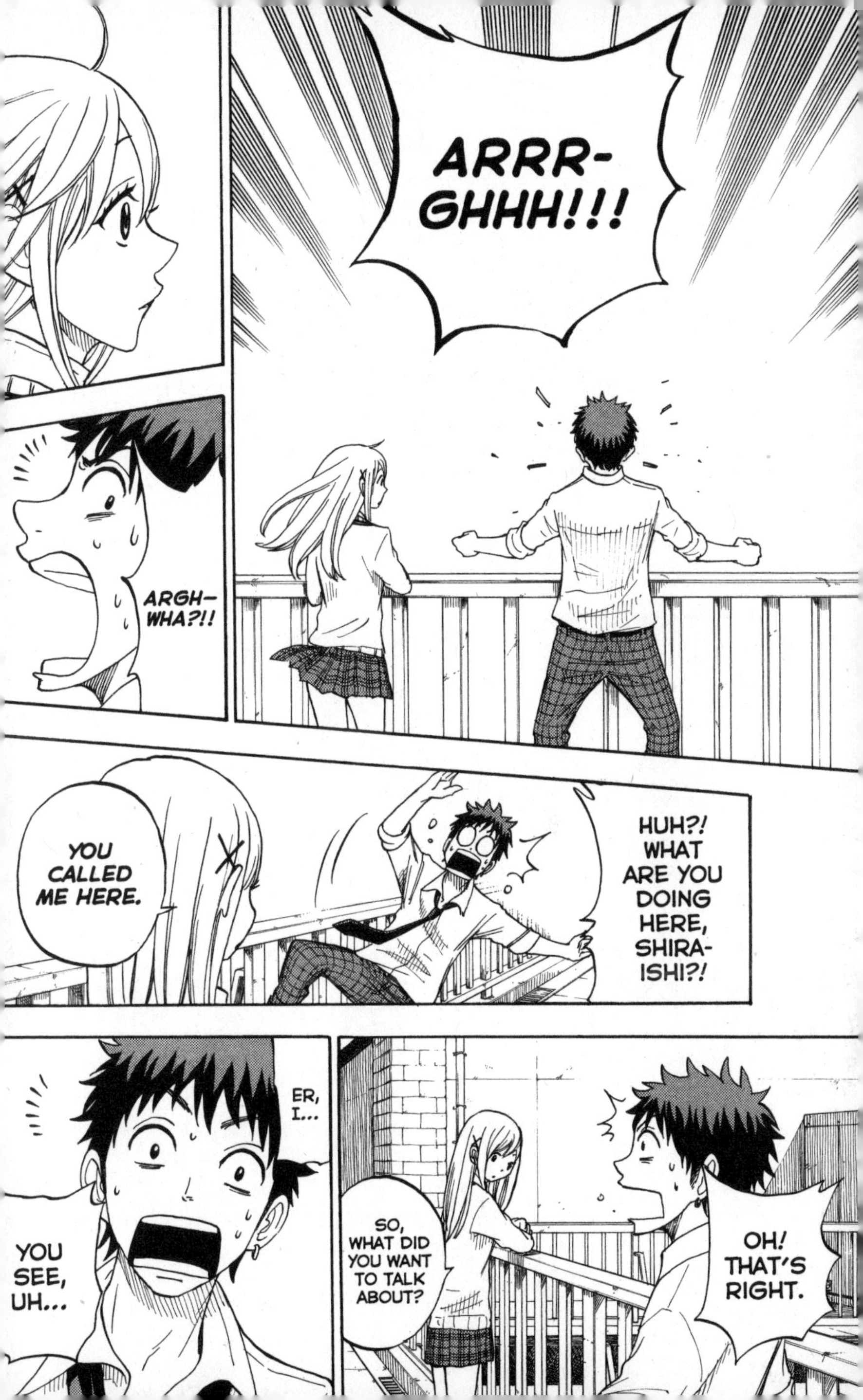
ARRR-
GHHH!!!
ARGH—
WHA?!!
HUH?! WHAT ARE YOU DOING HERE, SHIRAISHI?!
YOU CALLED ME HERE.
OH! THAT'S RIGHT.
SO, WHAT DID YOU WANT TO TALK ABOUT?
ER, I...
YOU SEE, UH...

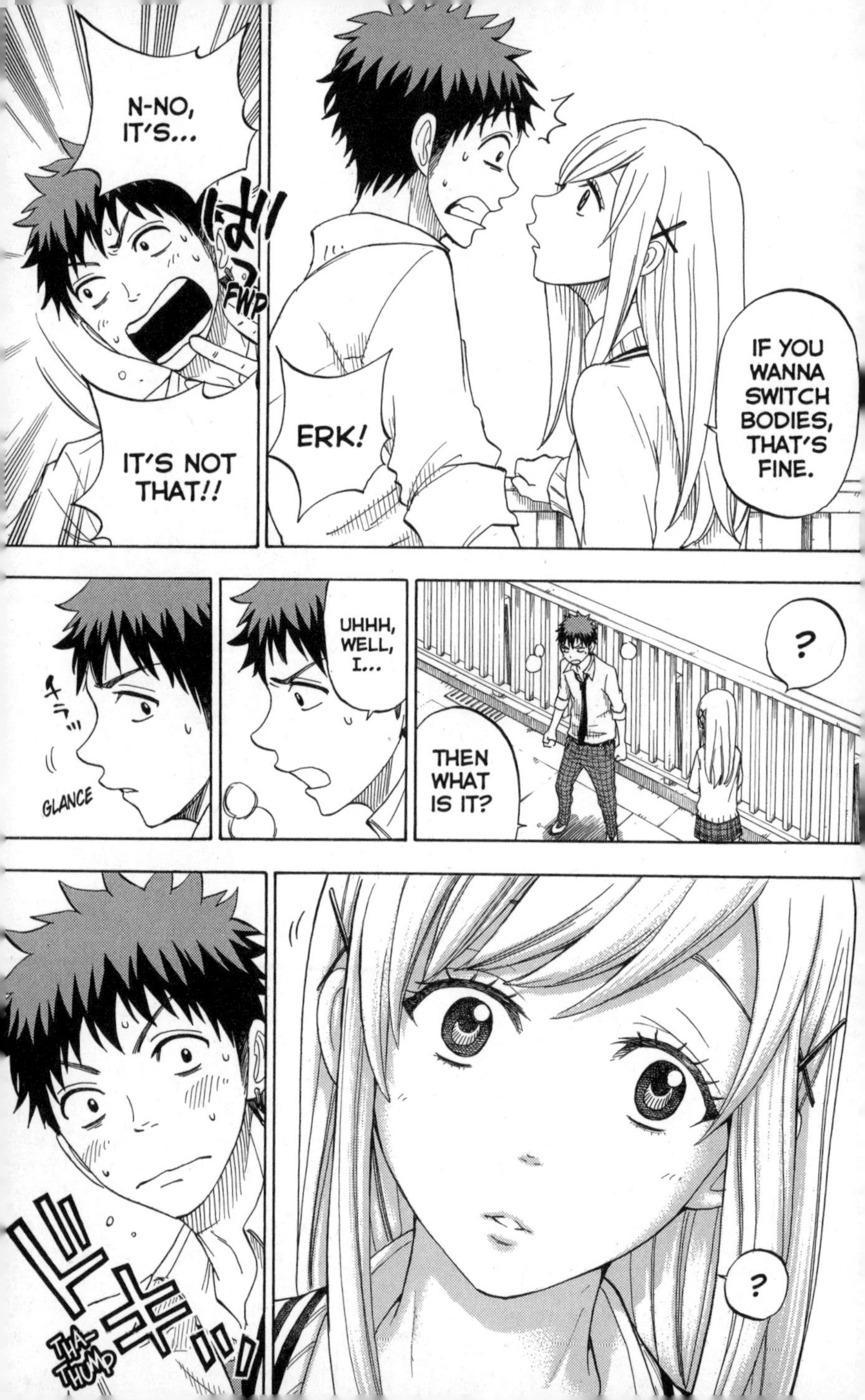
IF YOU WANNA SWITCH BODIES, THAT'S FINE.
ERK!
N-NO, IT'S...
FWP
IT'S NOT THAT!!
?
THEN WHAT IS IT?
UHHH, WELL, I...
GLANCE
?
THA-THUMP

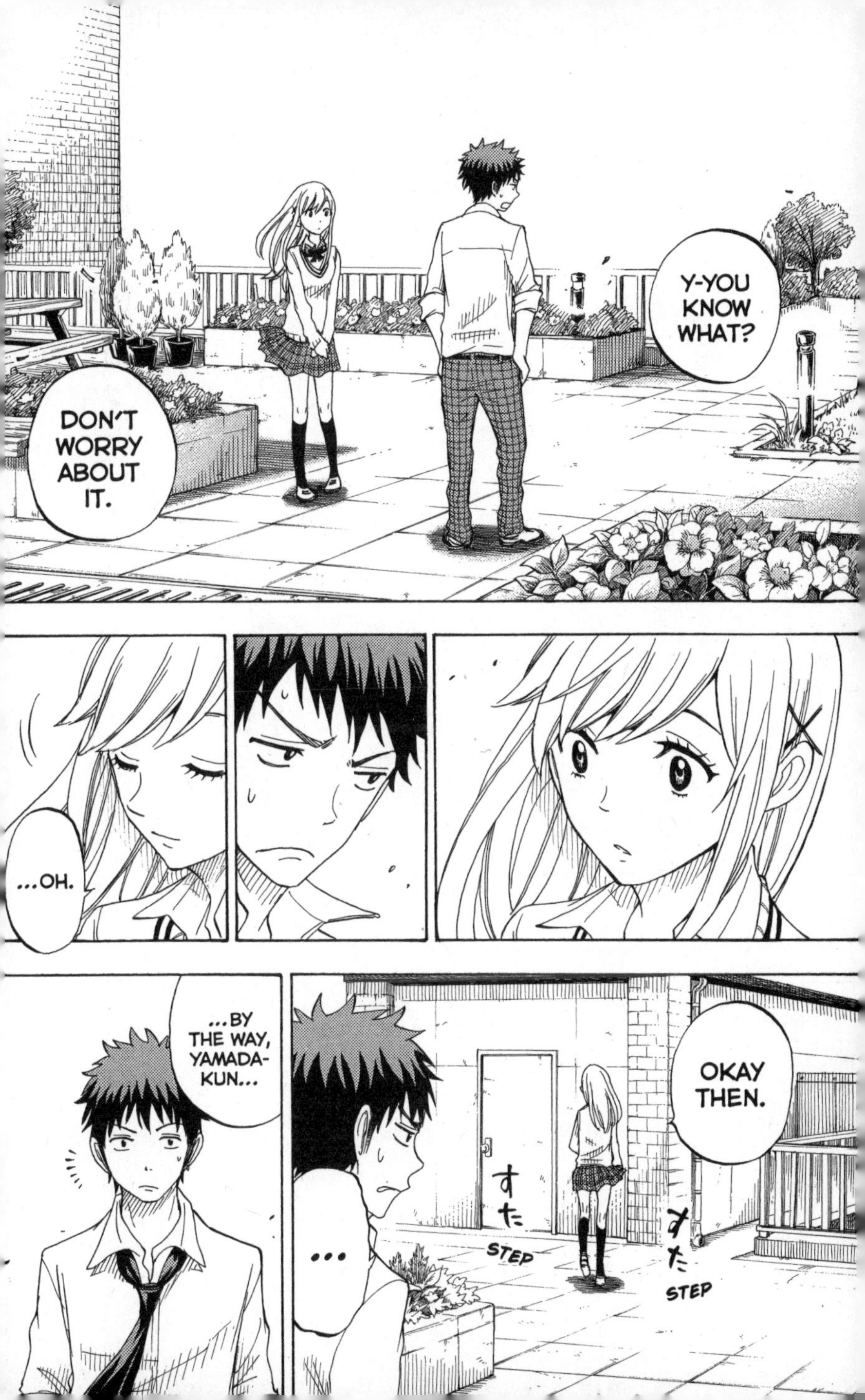
Y-YOU KNOW WHAT?
DON'T WORRY ABOUT IT.
...OH.
OKAY THEN.
すた
STEP
すた
STEP
...
...BY THE WAY, YAMADA-KUN...

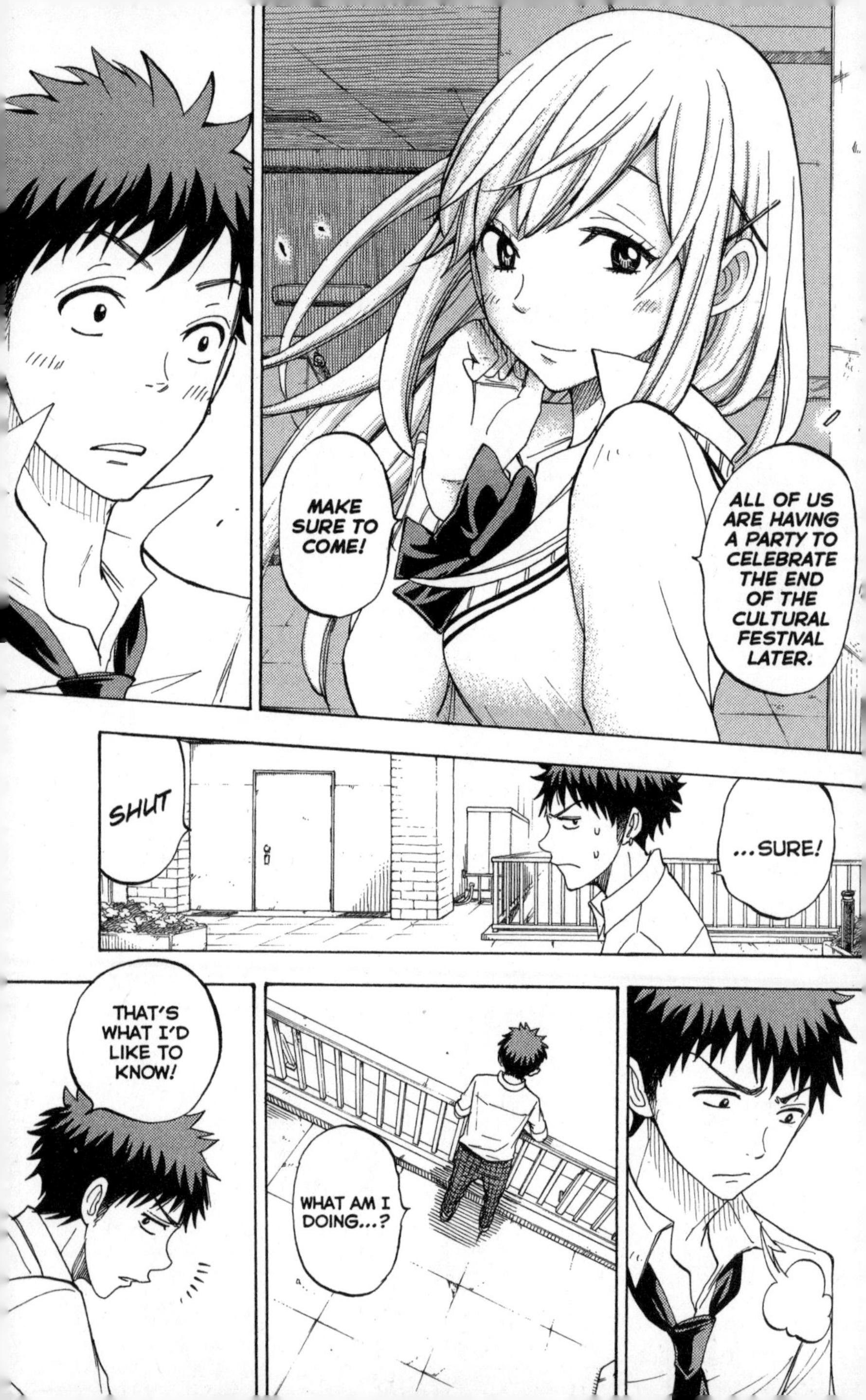
ALL OF US ARE HAVING A PARTY TO CELEBRATE THE END OF THE CULTURAL FESTIVAL LATER.
MAKE SURE TO COME!
...SURE!
SHUT
WHAT AM I DOING...?
THAT'S WHAT I'D LIKE TO KNOW!

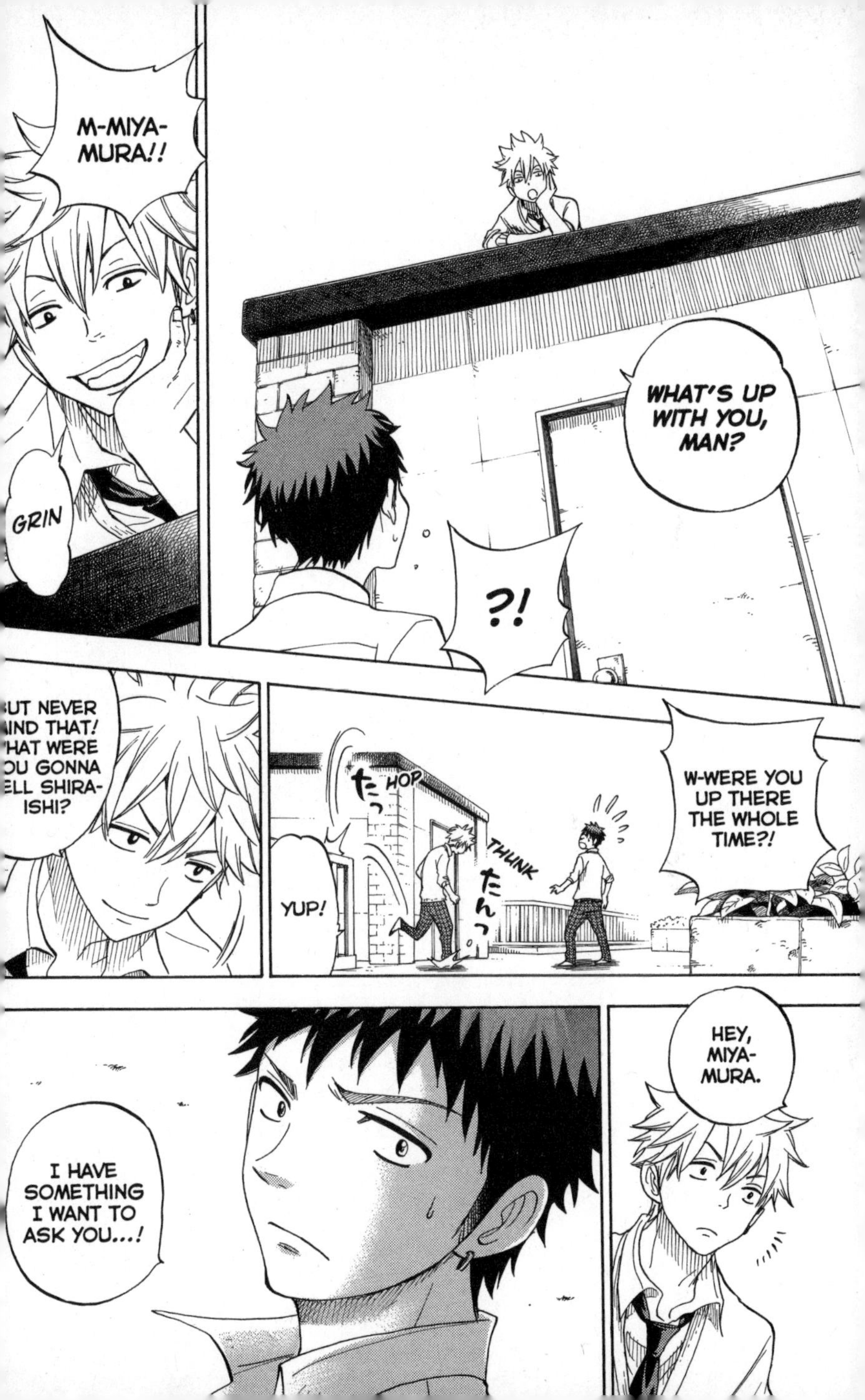
WHAT'S UP WITH YOU, MAN?
?!
M-MIYA-MURA!!
GRIN
W-WERE YOU UP THERE THE WHOLE TIME?!
たっ HOP
THUNK たんっ
YUP!
UT NEVER IND THAT! HAT WERE OU GONNA ELL SHIRA-ISHI?
HEY, MIYA-MURA.
I HAVE SOMETHING I WANT TO ASK YOU...!

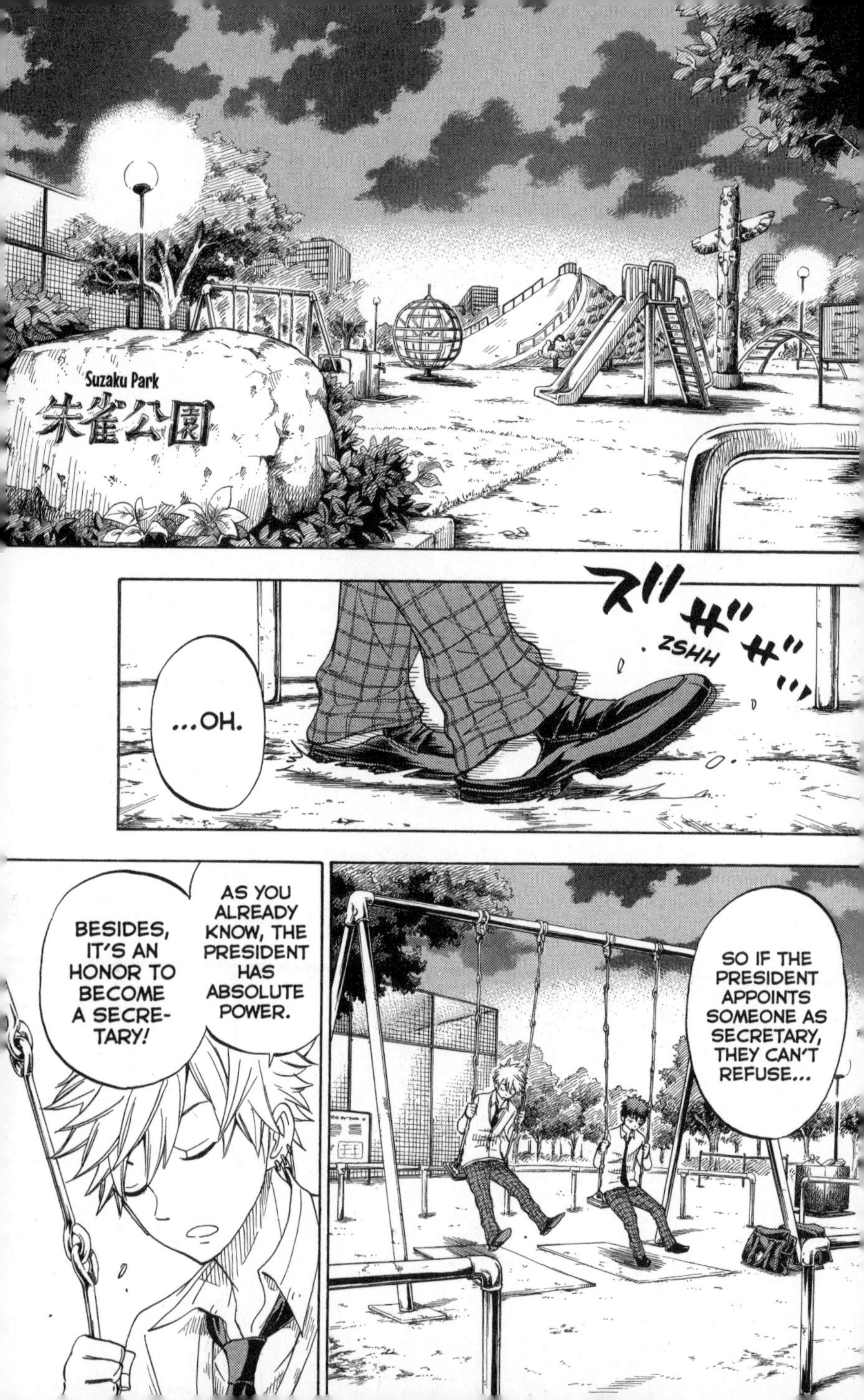
Suzaku Park
朱雀公園
ZSHH
...OH.
SO IF THE PRESIDENT APPOINTS SOMEONE AS SECRETARY, THEY CAN'T REFUSE...
AS YOU ALREADY KNOW, THE PRESIDENT HAS ABSOLUTE POWER.
BESIDES, IT'S AN HONOR TO BECOME A SECRE-TARY!

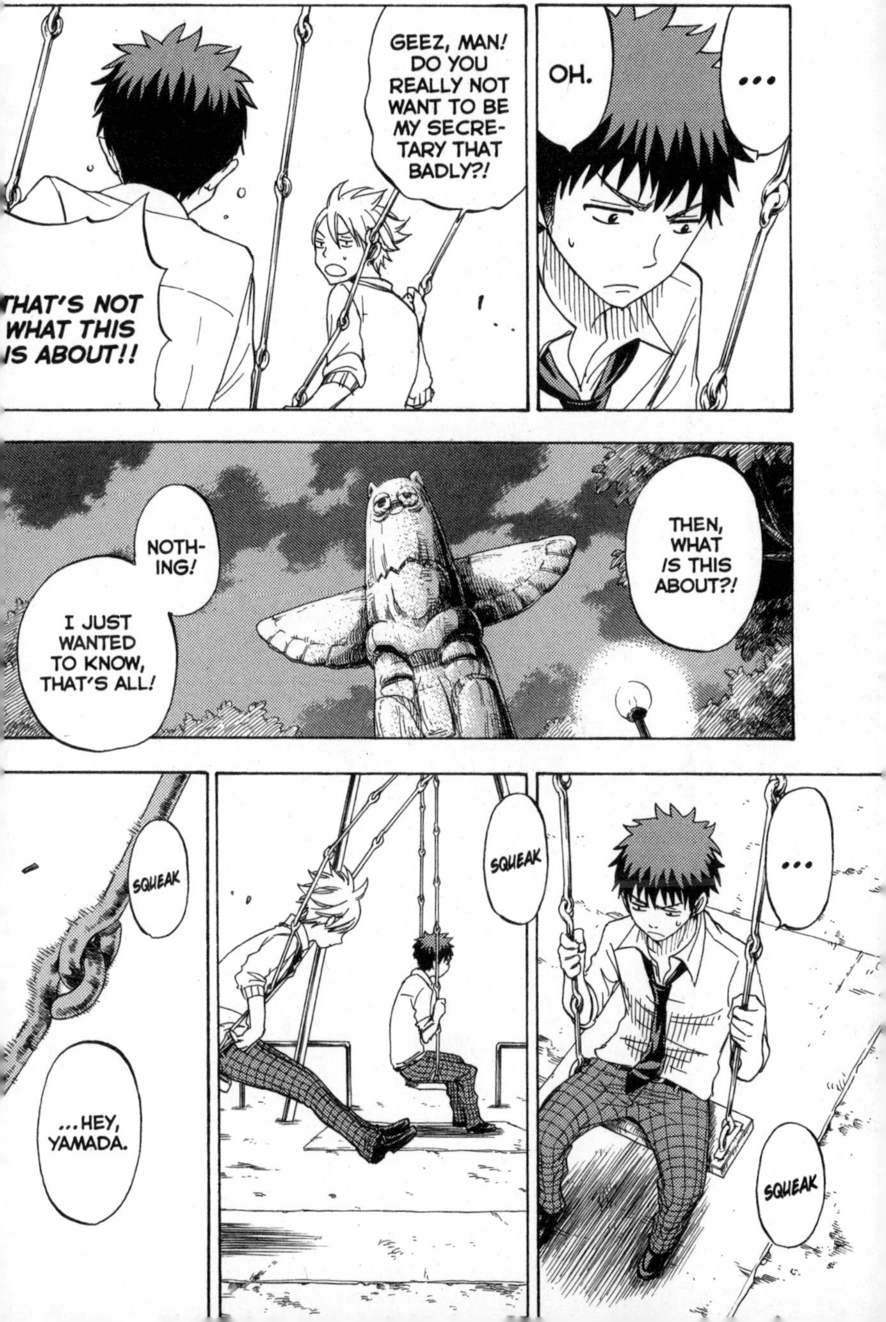
...
OH.
GEEZ, MAN! DO YOU REALLY NOT WANT TO BE MY SECRETARY THAT BADLY?!
THAT'S NOT WHAT THIS IS ABOUT!!
THEN, WHAT IS THIS ABOUT?!
NOTH-ING!
I JUST WANTED TO KNOW, THAT'S ALL!
...
SQUEAK
SQUEAK
SQUEAK
...HEY, YAMADA.

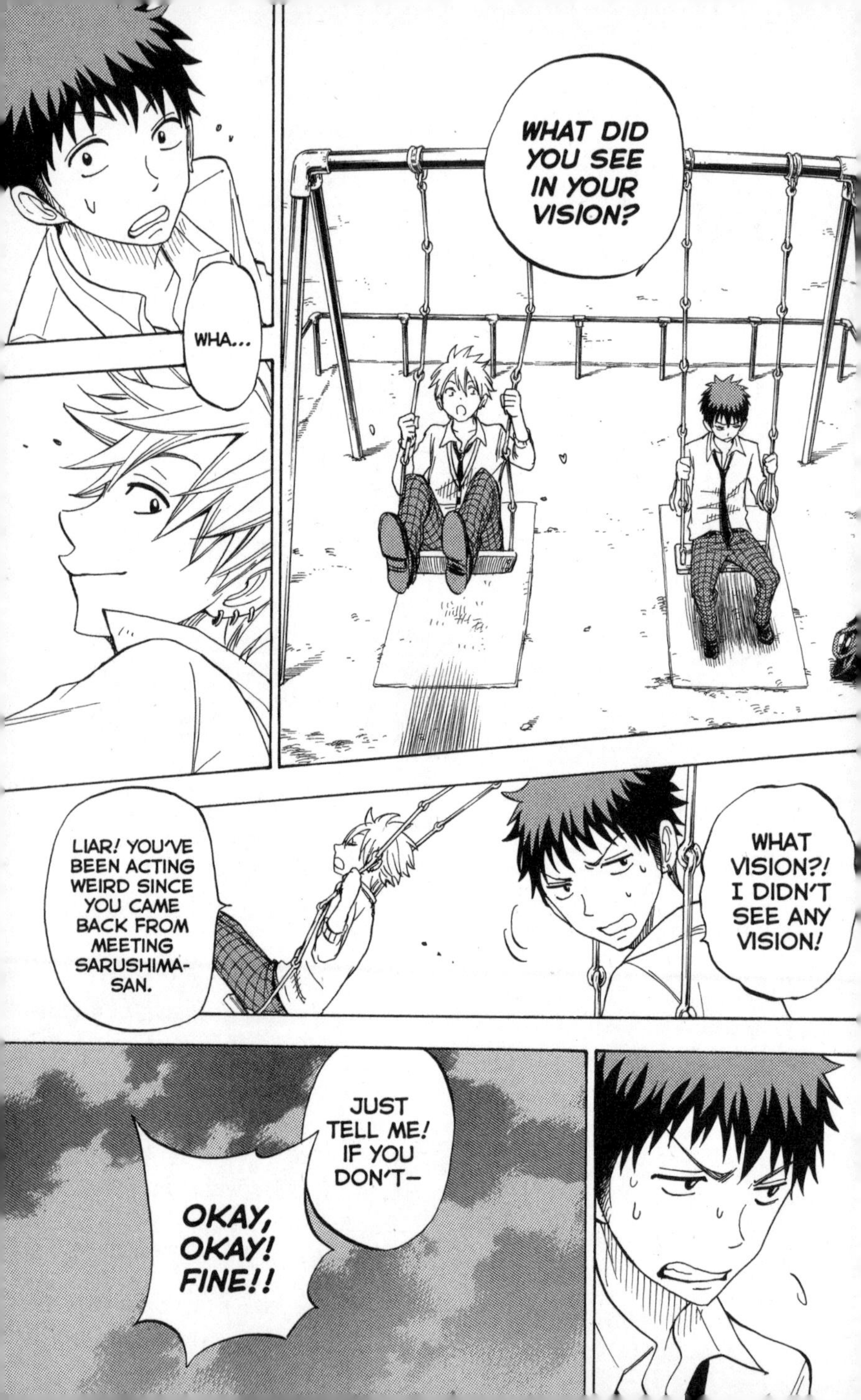
WHAT DID YOU SEE IN YOUR VISION?
WHA...
WHAT VISION?! I DIDN'T SEE ANY VISION!
LIAR! YOU'VE BEEN ACTING WEIRD SINCE YOU CAME BACK FROM MEETING SARUSHIMA-SAN.
JUST TELL ME! IF YOU DON'T—
OKAY, OKAY! FINE!!

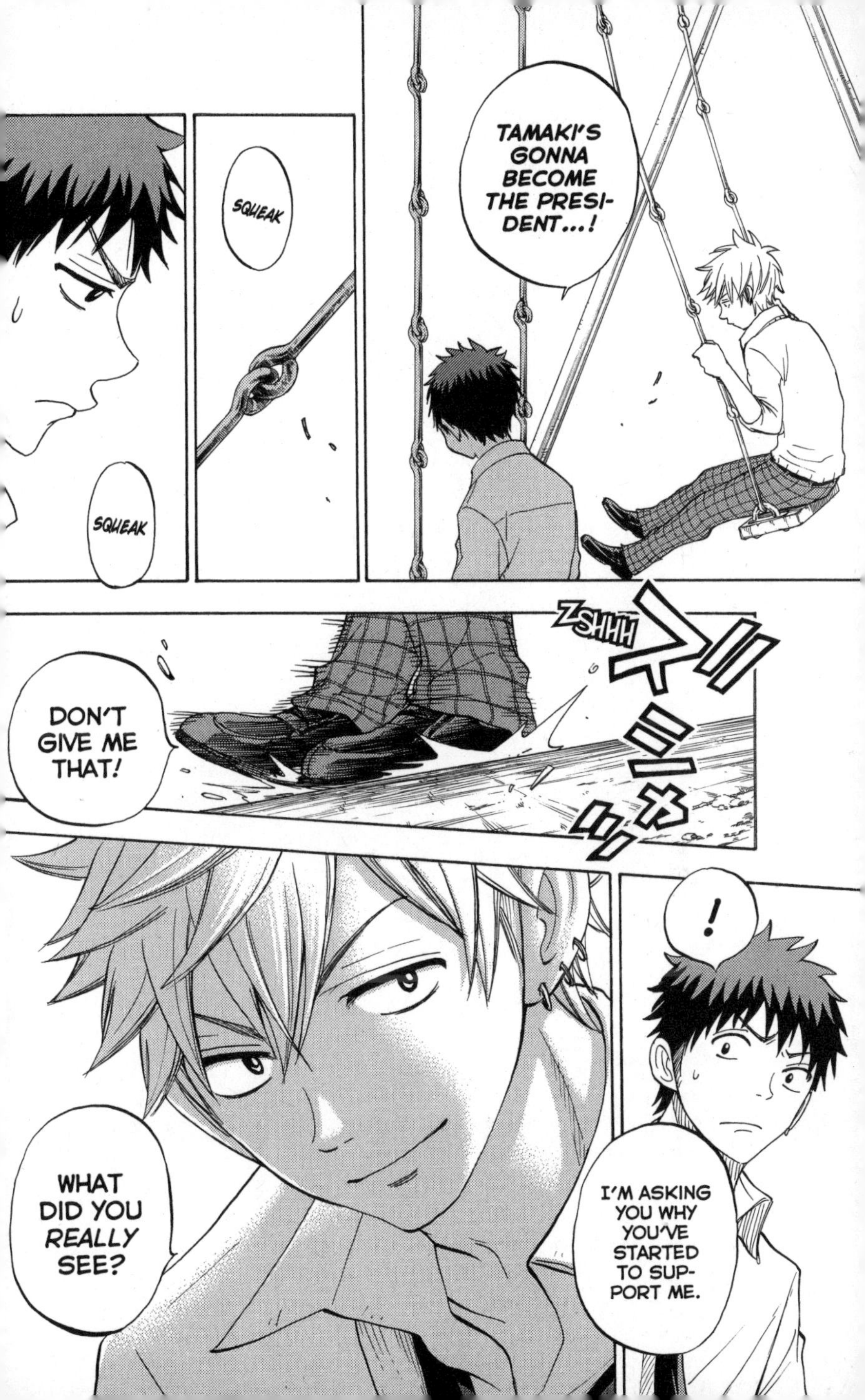
TAMAKI'S GONNA BECOME THE PRESI- DENT...!
SQUEAK
SQUEAK
ZSHHH
DON'T GIVE ME THAT!
!
I'M ASKING YOU WHY YOU'VE STARTED TO SUP- PORT ME.
WHAT DID YOU REALLY SEE?

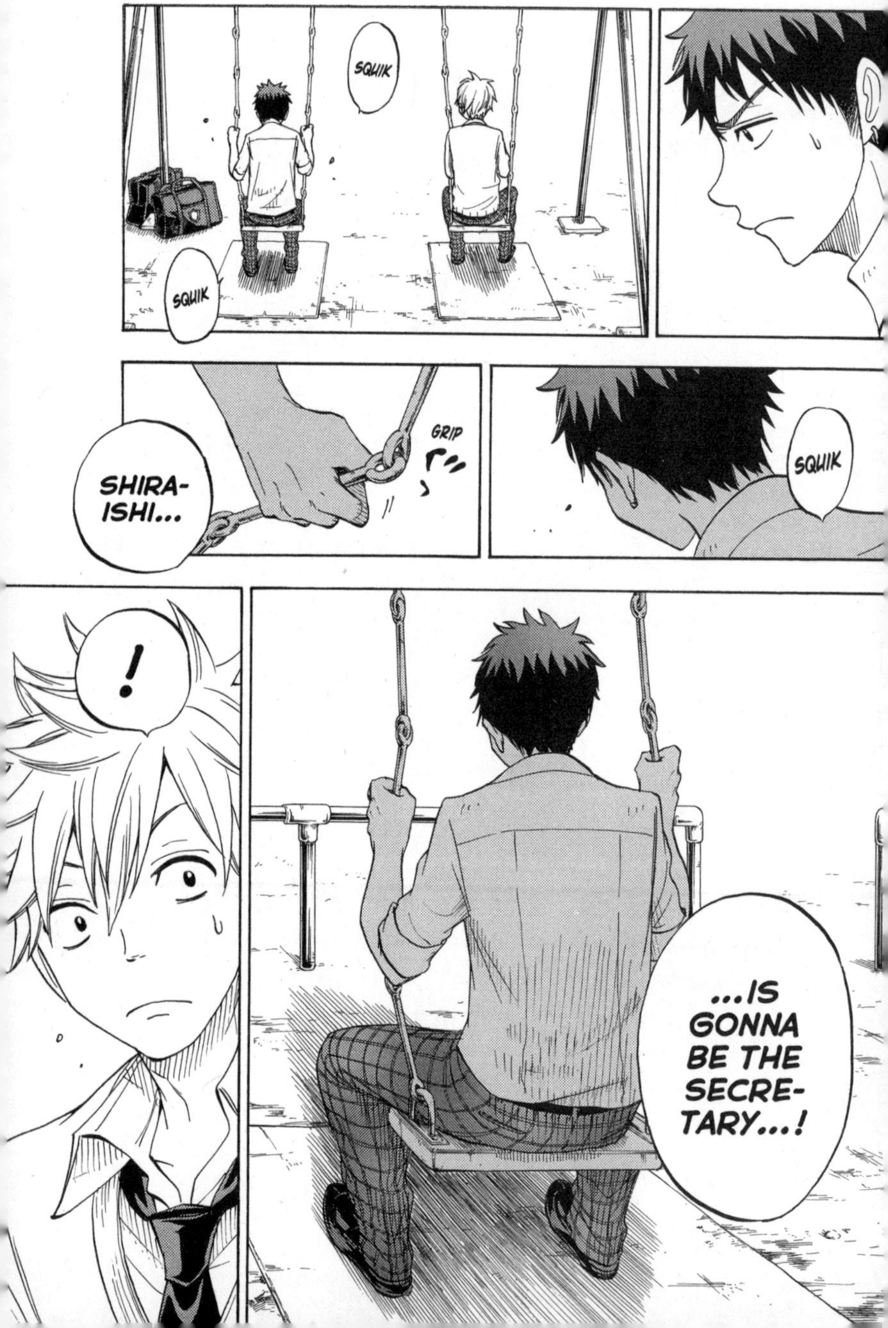
SQUIK
SQUIK
SQUIK
GRIP
SHIRA-ISHI...
...IS GONNA BE THE SECRETARY...!
!

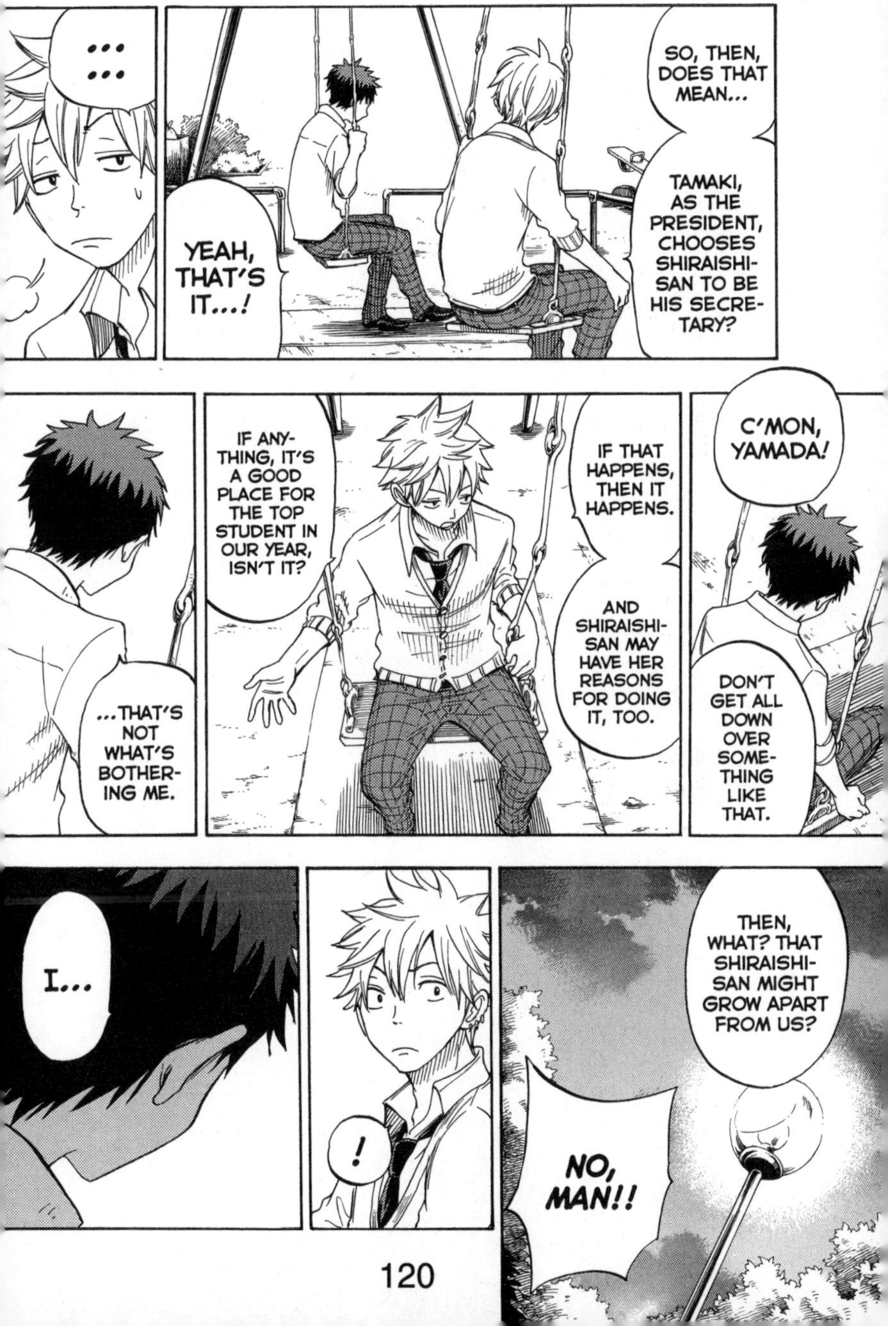
SO, THEN, DOES THAT MEAN...
TAMAKI, AS THE PRESIDENT, CHOOSES SHIRAISHI-SAN TO BE HIS SECRETARY?
YEAH, THAT'S IT...!
...
...
C'MON, YAMADA!
DON'T GET ALL DOWN OVER SOMETHING LIKE THAT.
IF THAT HAPPENS, THEN IT HAPPENS.
IF ANYTHING, IT'S A GOOD PLACE FOR THE TOP STUDENT IN OUR YEAR, ISN'T IT?
AND SHIRAISHI-SAN MAY HAVE HER REASONS FOR DOING IT, TOO.
...THAT'S NOT WHAT'S BOTHERING ME.
THEN, WHAT? THAT SHIRAISHI-SAN MIGHT GROW APART FROM US?
NO, MAN!!
!
I...

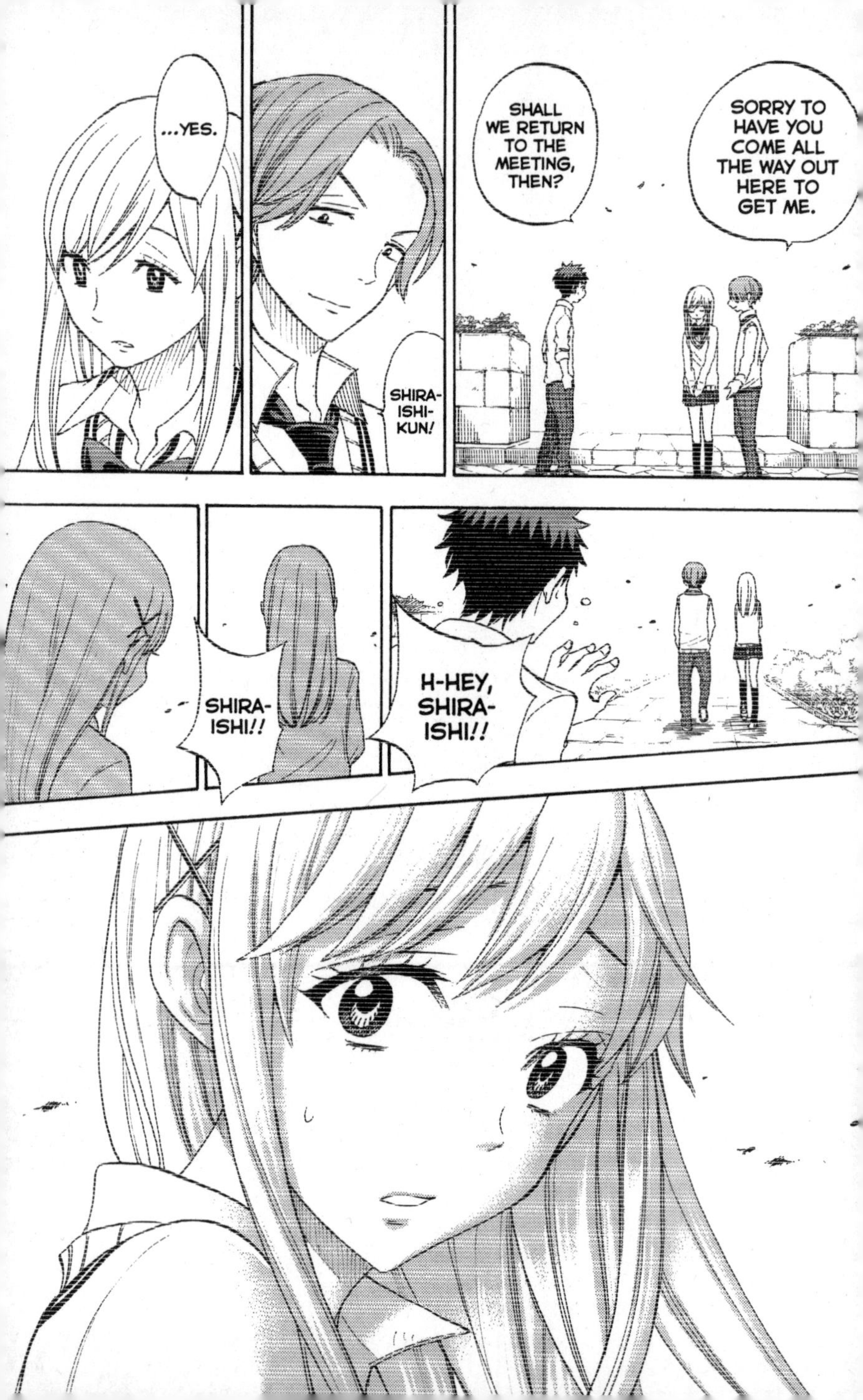
SORRY TO HAVE YOU COME ALL THE WAY OUT HERE TO GET ME.
SHALL WE RETURN TO THE MEETING, THEN?
SHIRA-ISHI-KUN!
...YES.
H-HEY, SHIRA-ISHI!!
SHIRA-ISHI!!

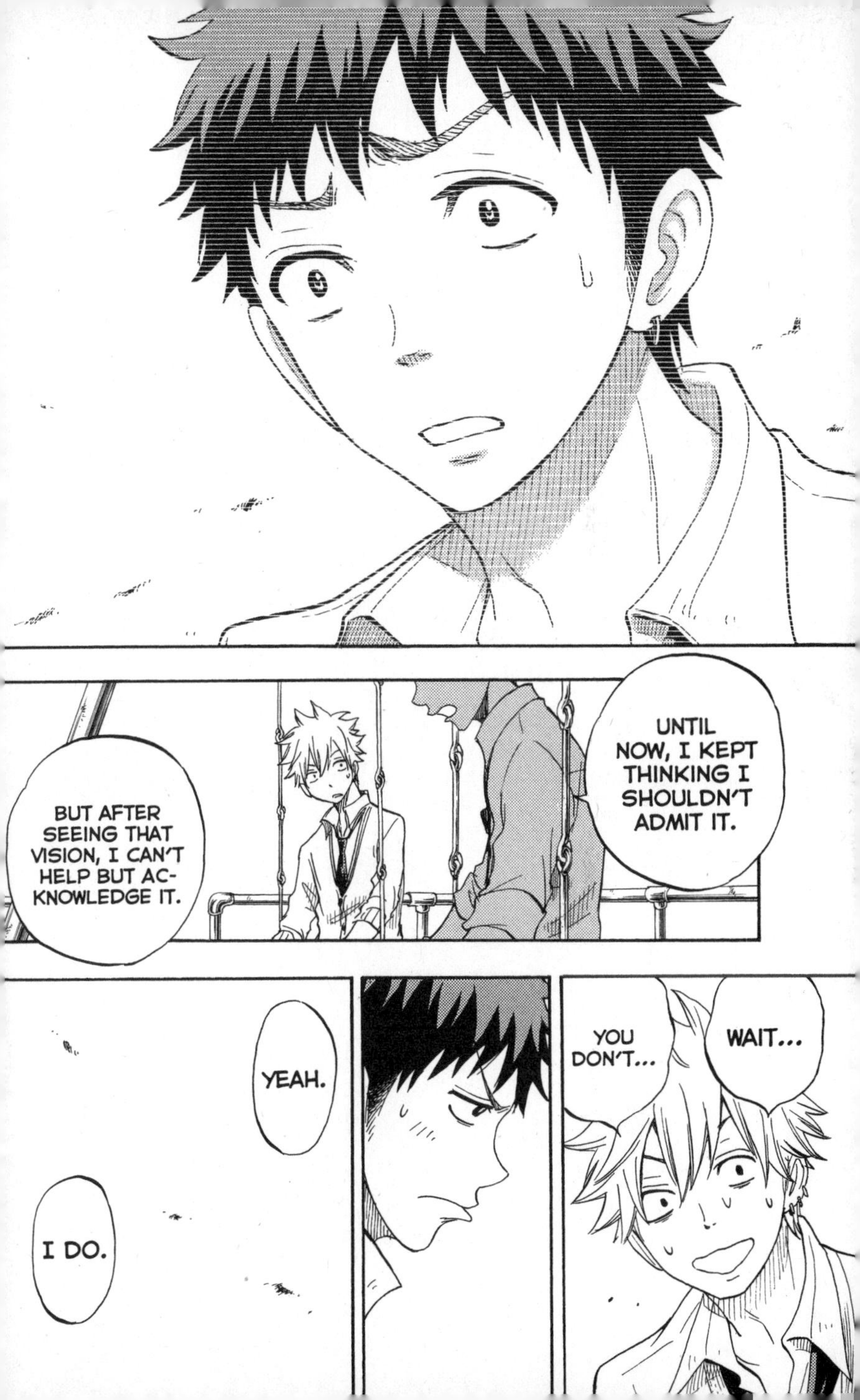
UNTIL NOW, I KEPT THINKING I SHOULDN'T ADMIT IT.
BUT AFTER SEEING THAT VISION, I CAN'T HELP BUT AC-KNOWLEDGE IT.
WAIT...
YOU DON'T...
YEAH.
I DO.

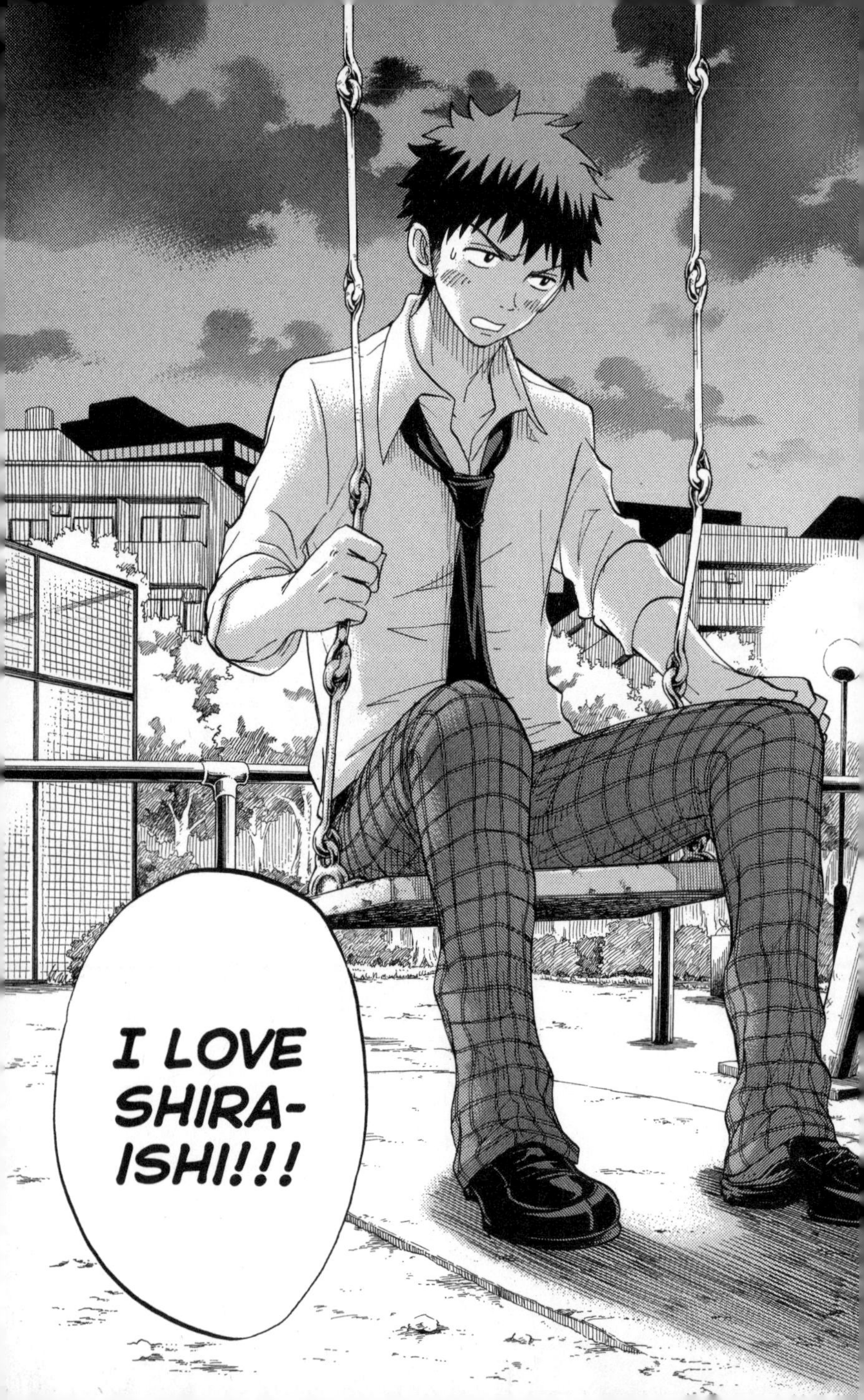
I LOVE SHIRA-ISHI!!!

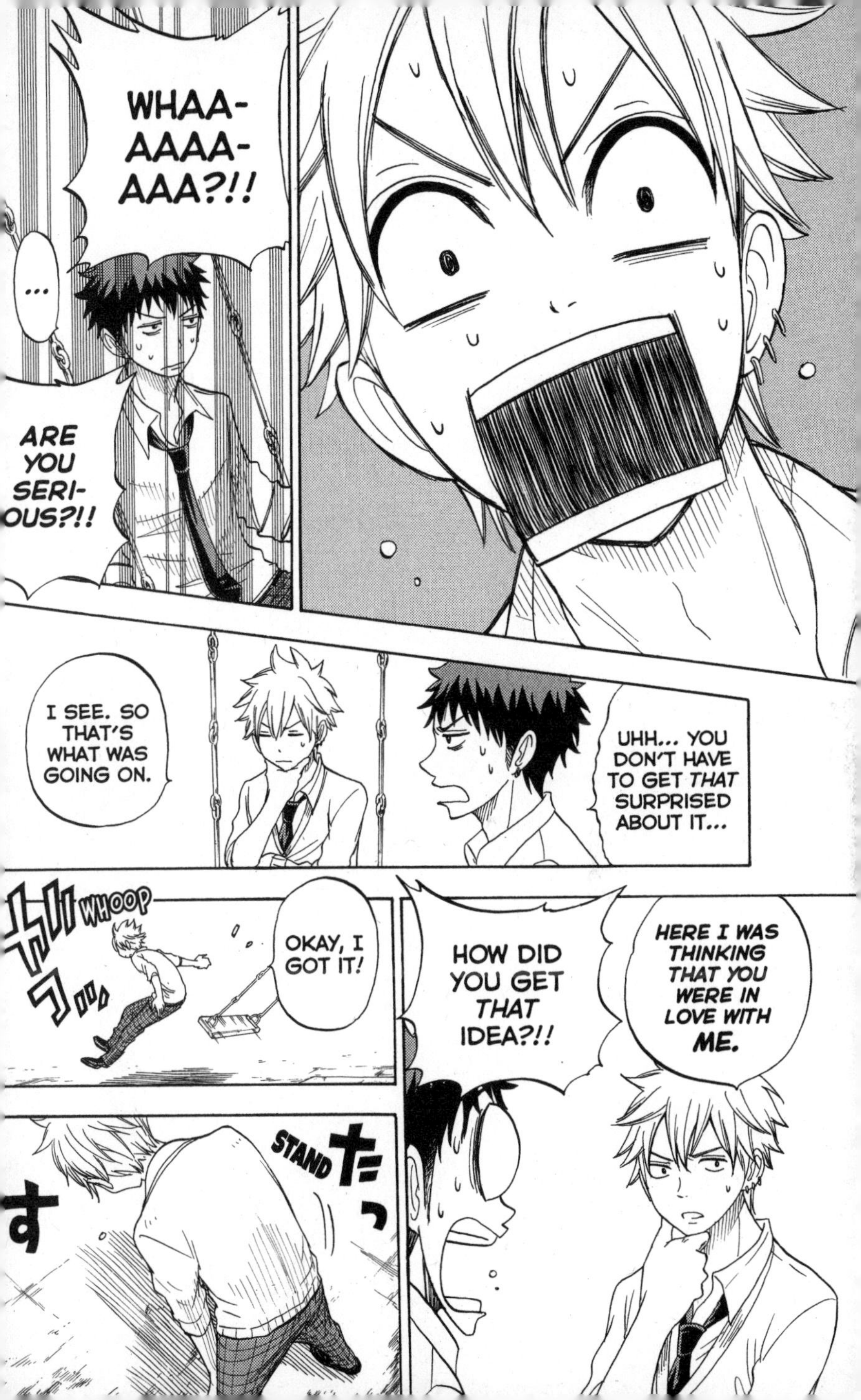
WHAA-AAAA-AAA?!!
...
ARE YOU SERI-OUS?!!
UHH... YOU DON'T HAVE TO GET THAT SURPRISED ABOUT IT...
I SEE. SO THAT'S WHAT WAS GOING ON.
WHOOP
OKAY, I GOT IT!
STAND
HERE I WAS THINKING THAT YOU WERE IN LOVE WITH ME.
HOW DID YOU GET THAT IDEA?!!

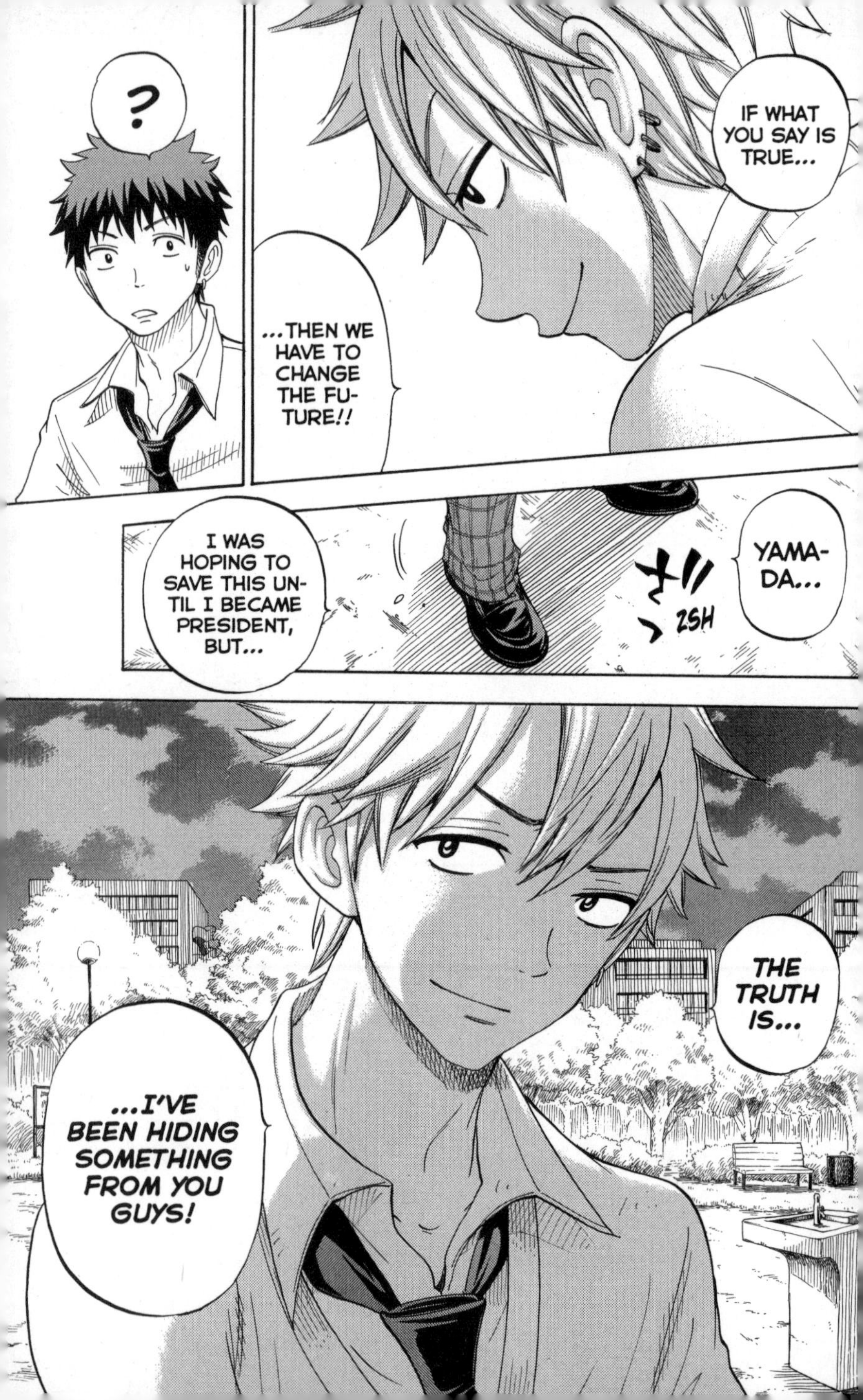
IF WHAT YOU SAY IS TRUE...
...THEN WE HAVE TO CHANGE THE FUTURE!!
?
YAMADA...
ZSH
I WAS HOPING TO SAVE THIS UNTIL I BECAME PRESIDENT, BUT...
THE TRUTH IS...
...I'VE BEEN HIDING SOMETHING FROM YOU GUYS!

Yamada-kun
AND THE
Seven Witches

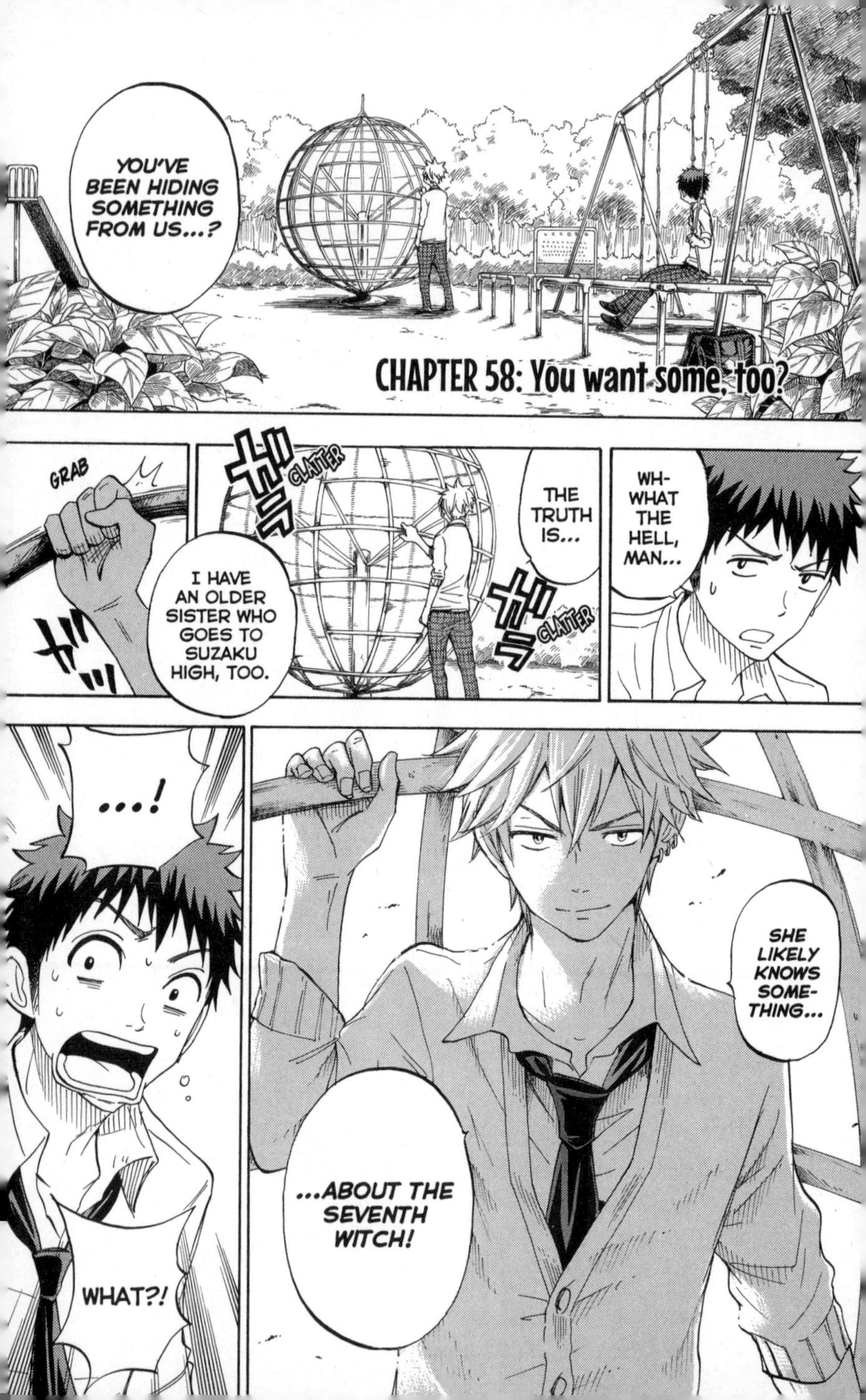
YOU'VE BEEN HIDING SOMETHING FROM US...?
CHAPTER 58: You want some, too?
WH-WHAT THE HELL, MAN...
THE TRUTH IS...
CLATTER
CLATTER
I HAVE AN OLDER SISTER WHO GOES TO SUZAKU HIGH, TOO.
GRAB
SHE LIKELY KNOWS SOMETHING...
...ABOUT THE SEVENTH WITCH!
...!
WHAT?!

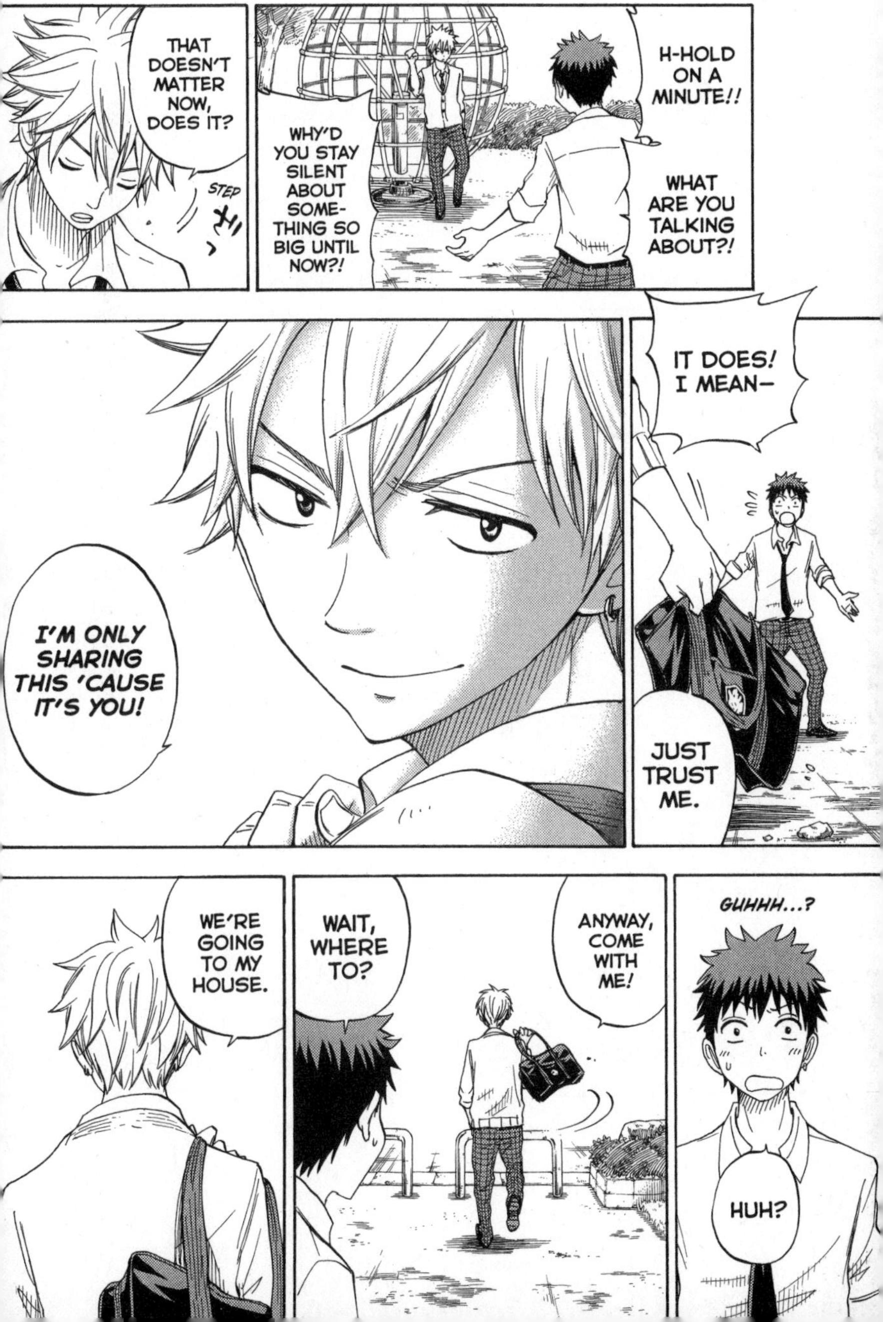
H-HOLD ON A MINUTE!!
WHAT ARE YOU TALKING ABOUT?!
WHY'D YOU STAY SILENT ABOUT SOME-THING SO BIG UNTIL NOW?!
THAT DOESN'T MATTER NOW, DOES IT?
STEP
IT DOES! I MEAN—
JUST TRUST ME.
I'M ONLY SHARING THIS 'CAUSE IT'S YOU!
GUHHH...?
HUH?
ANYWAY, COME WITH ME!
WAIT, WHERE TO?
WE'RE GOING TO MY HOUSE.

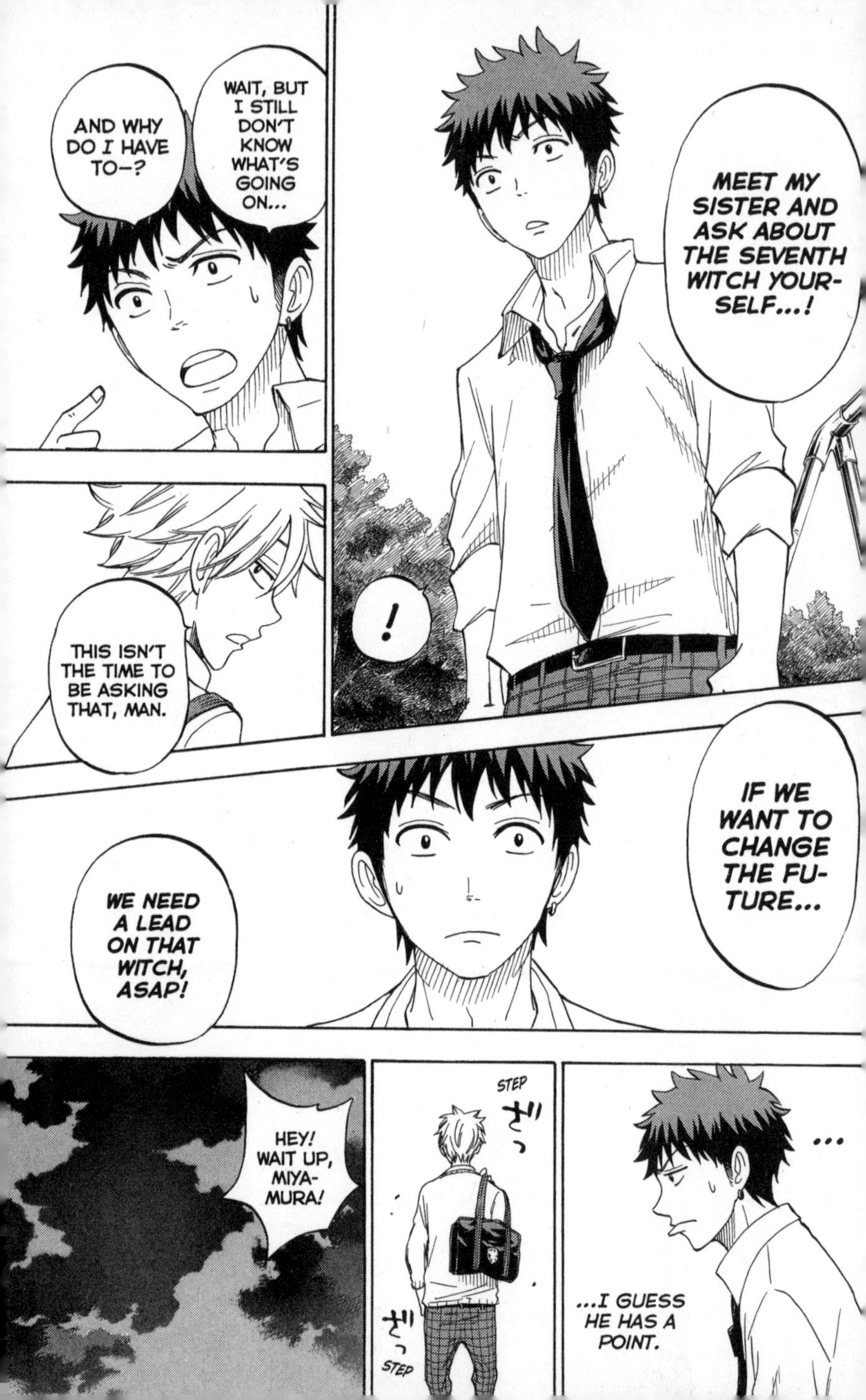
MEET MY SISTER AND ASK ABOUT THE SEVENTH WITCH YOURSELF...!
!
WAIT, BUT I STILL DON'T KNOW WHAT'S GOING ON...
AND WHY DO I HAVE TO-?
THIS ISN'T THE TIME TO BE ASKING THAT, MAN.
IF WE WANT TO CHANGE THE FUTURE...
WE NEED A LEAD ON THAT WITCH, ASAP!
...
...I GUESS HE HAS A POINT.
STEP ざっ
ざっ STEP
HEY! WAIT UP, MIYAMURA!

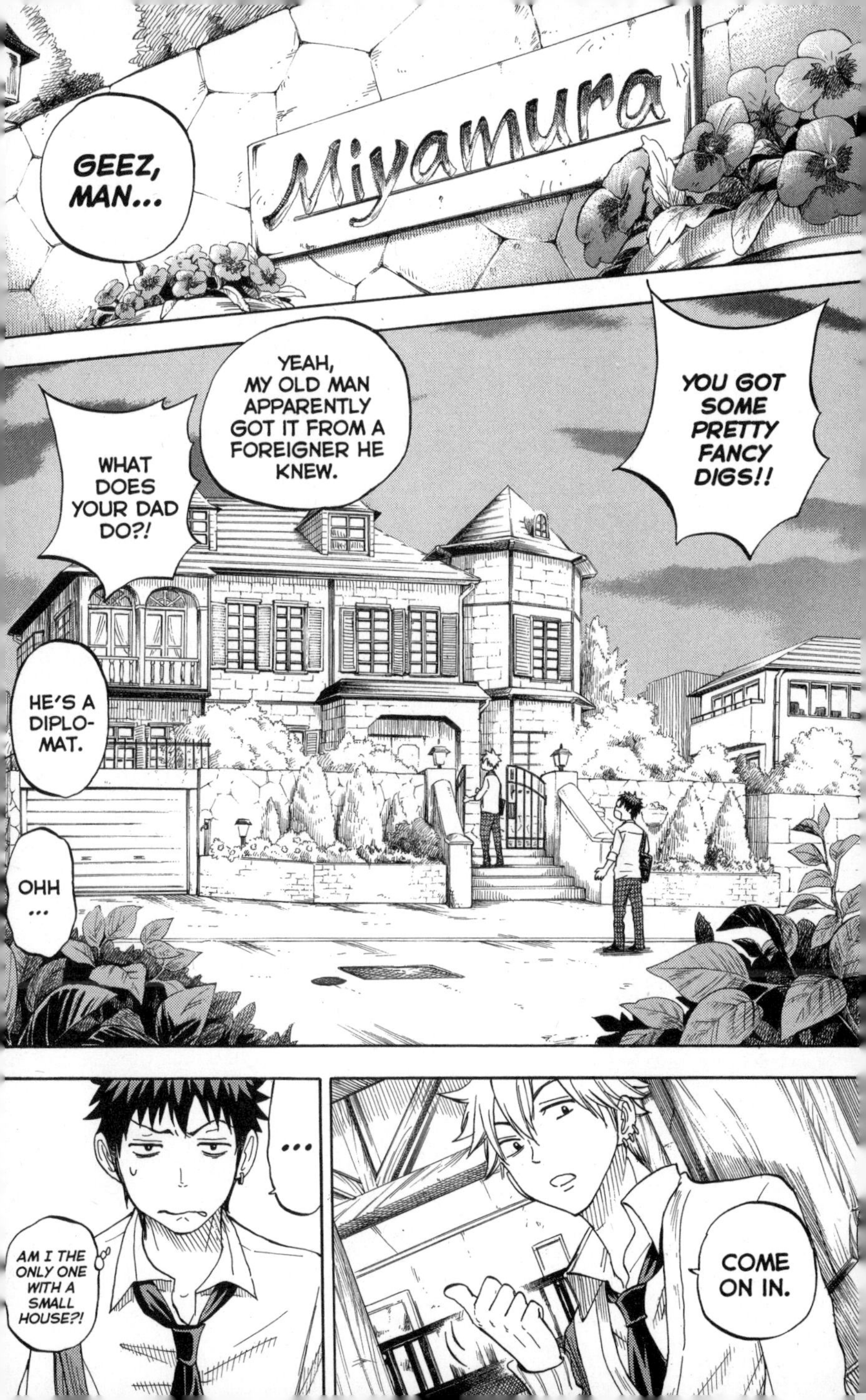

Miyamura
GEEZ, MAN...
YOU GOT SOME PRETTY FANCY DIGS!!
YEAH, MY OLD MAN APPARENTLY GOT IT FROM A FOREIGNER HE KNEW.
WHAT DOES YOUR DAD DO?!
HE'S A DIPLO-MAT.
OHH...
COME ON IN.
...
AM I THE ONLY ONE WITH A SMALL HOUSE?!

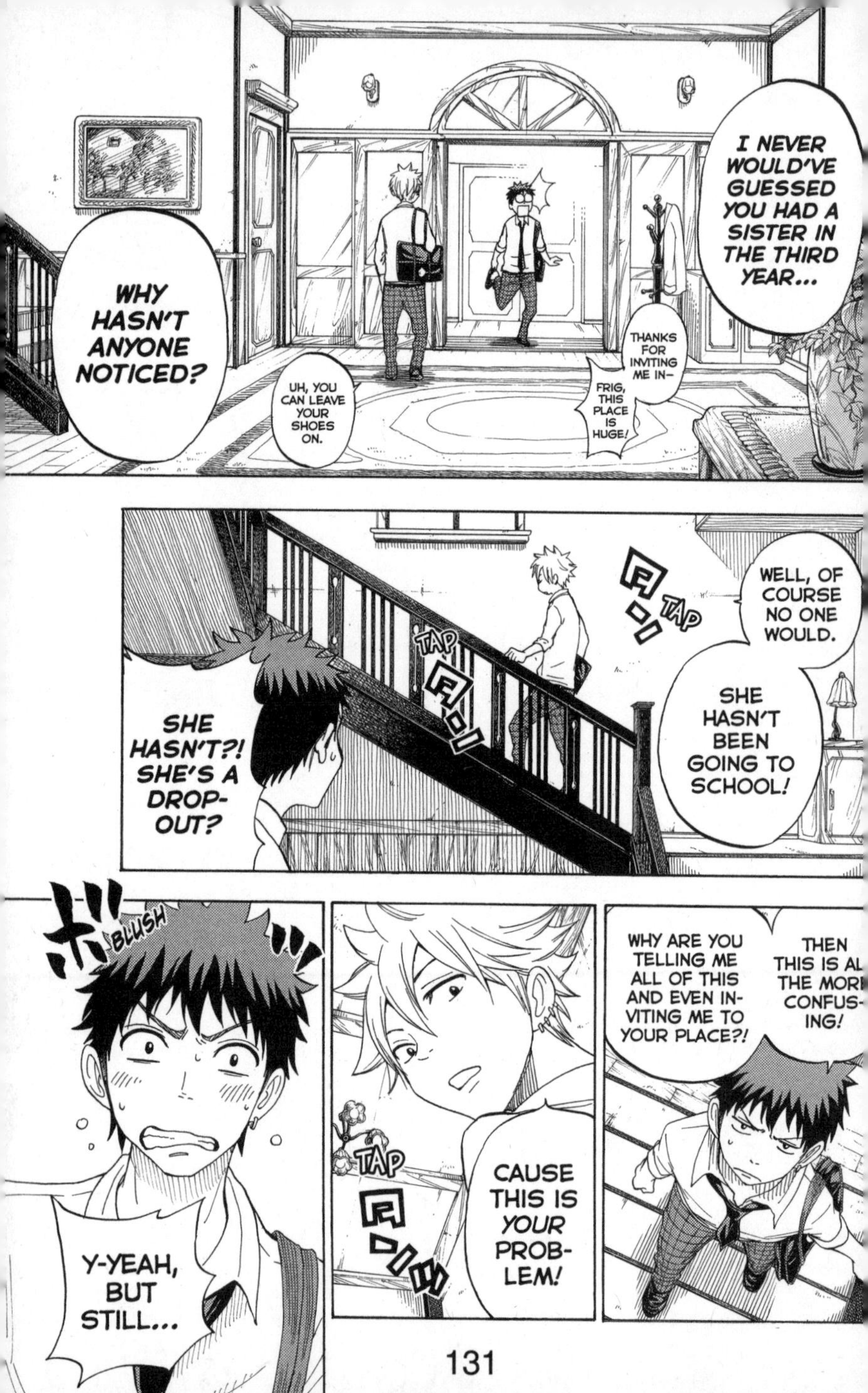
I NEVER WOULD'VE GUESSED YOU HAD A SISTER IN THE THIRD YEAR...
THANKS FOR INVITING ME IN—
FRIG, THIS PLACE IS HUGE!
UH, YOU CAN LEAVE YOUR SHOES ON.
WHY HASN'T ANYONE NOTICED?
WELL, OF COURSE NO ONE WOULD.
TAP
TAP
SHE HASN'T BEEN GOING TO SCHOOL!
SHE HASN'T?! SHE'S A DROP-OUT?
THEN THIS IS AL THE MORI CONFUS-ING!
WHY ARE YOU TELLING ME ALL OF THIS AND EVEN IN-VITING ME TO YOUR PLACE?!
TAP
CAUSE THIS IS *YOUR* PROB-LEM!
BLUSH
Y-YEAH, BUT STILL...

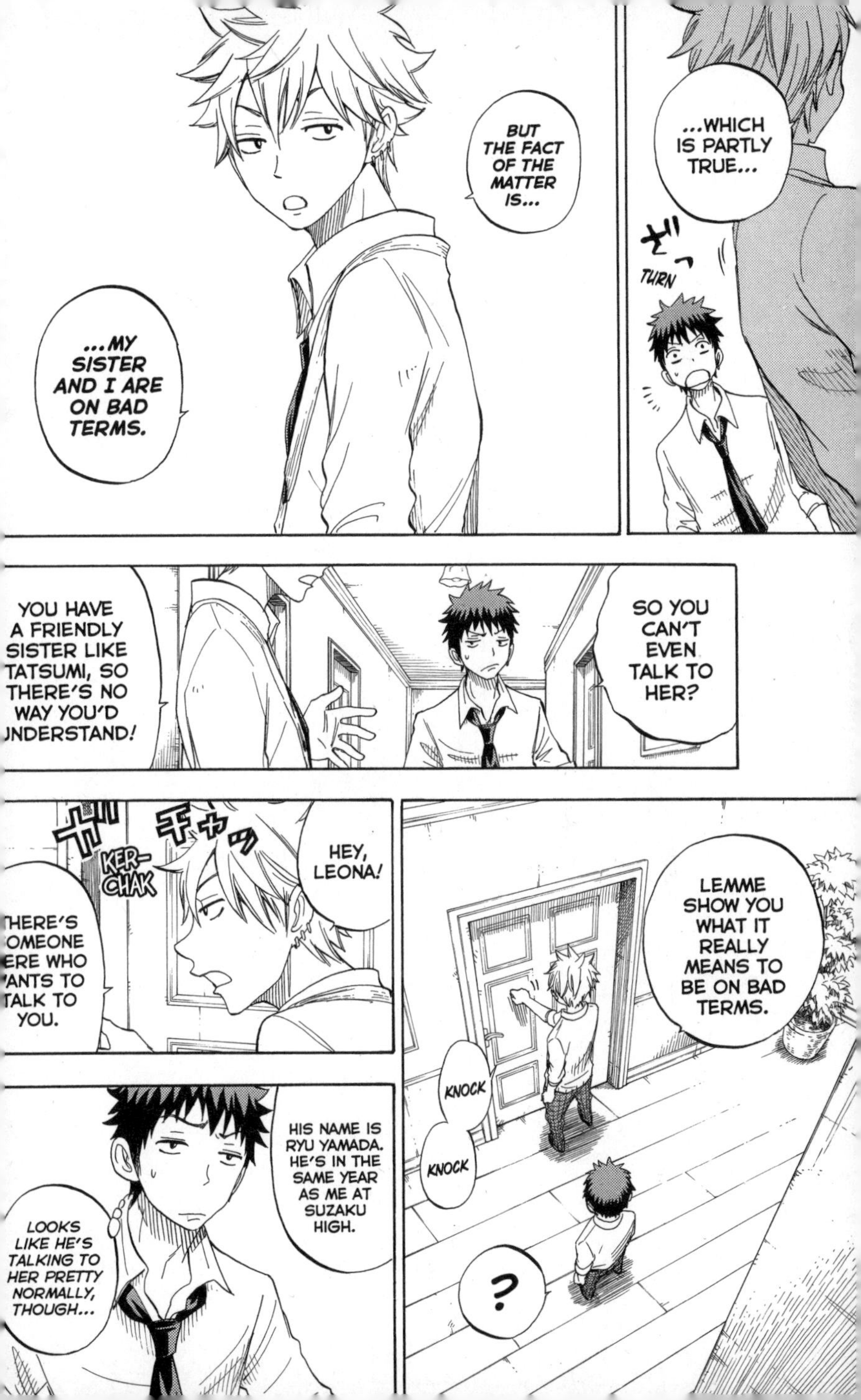
...WHICH IS PARTLY TRUE...
ぞっ
TURN
BUT THE FACT OF THE MATTER IS...
...MY SISTER AND I ARE ON BAD TERMS.
SO YOU CAN'T EVEN TALK TO HER?
YOU HAVE A FRIENDLY SISTER LIKE TATSUMI, SO THERE'S NO WAY YOU'D NDERSTAND!
LEMME SHOW YOU WHAT IT REALLY MEANS TO BE ON BAD TERMS.
KNOCK
KNOCK
?
HEY, LEONA!
ガチャ
KER-CHAK
THERE'S OMEONE ERE WHO ANTS TO TALK TO YOU.
HIS NAME IS RYU YAMADA. HE'S IN THE SAME YEAR AS ME AT SUZAKU HIGH.
LOOKS LIKE HE'S TALKING TO HER PRETTY NORMALLY, THOUGH...

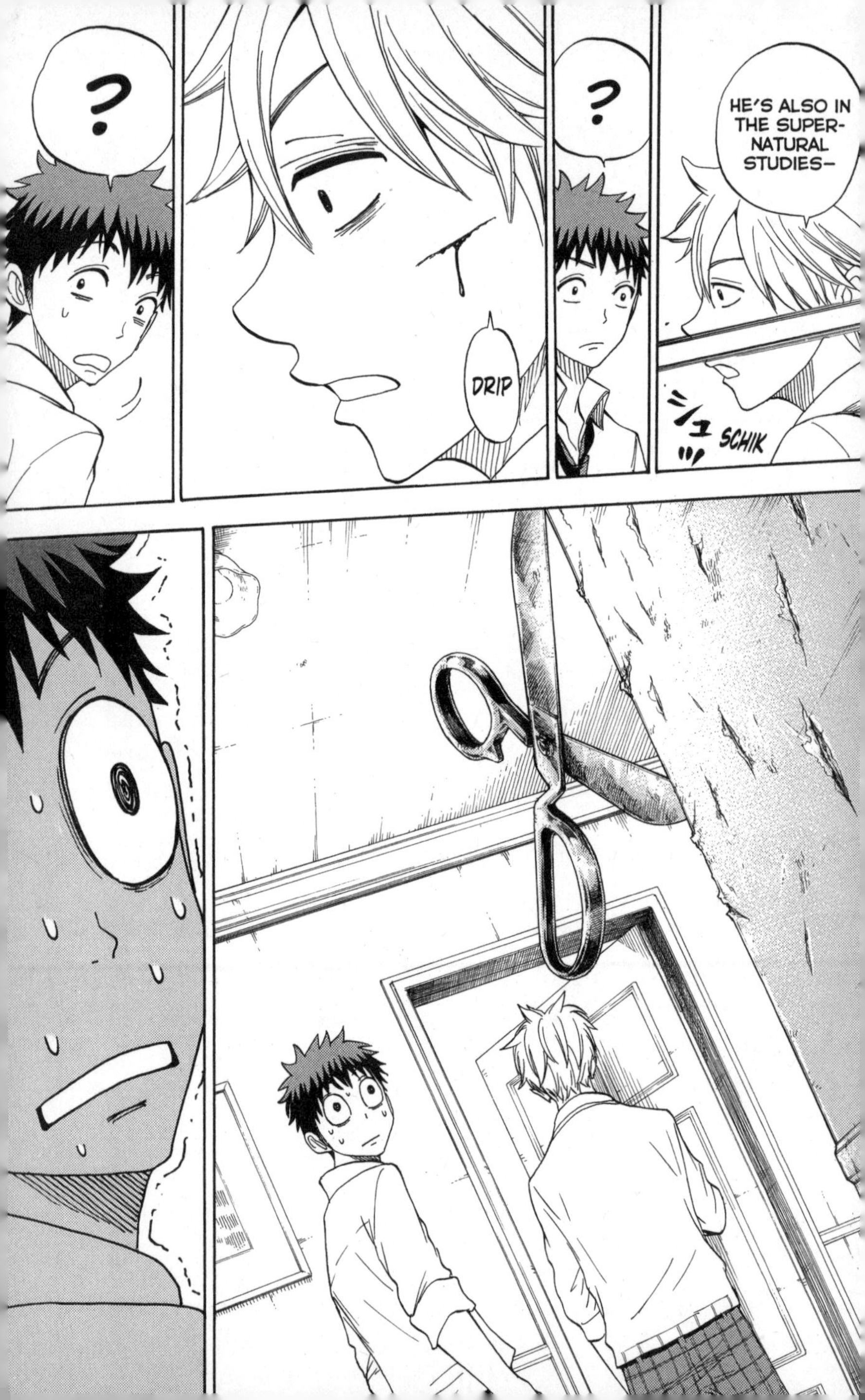
HE'S ALSO IN THE SUPER-NATURAL STUDIES—
シュッ
SCHIK
?
DRIP
?

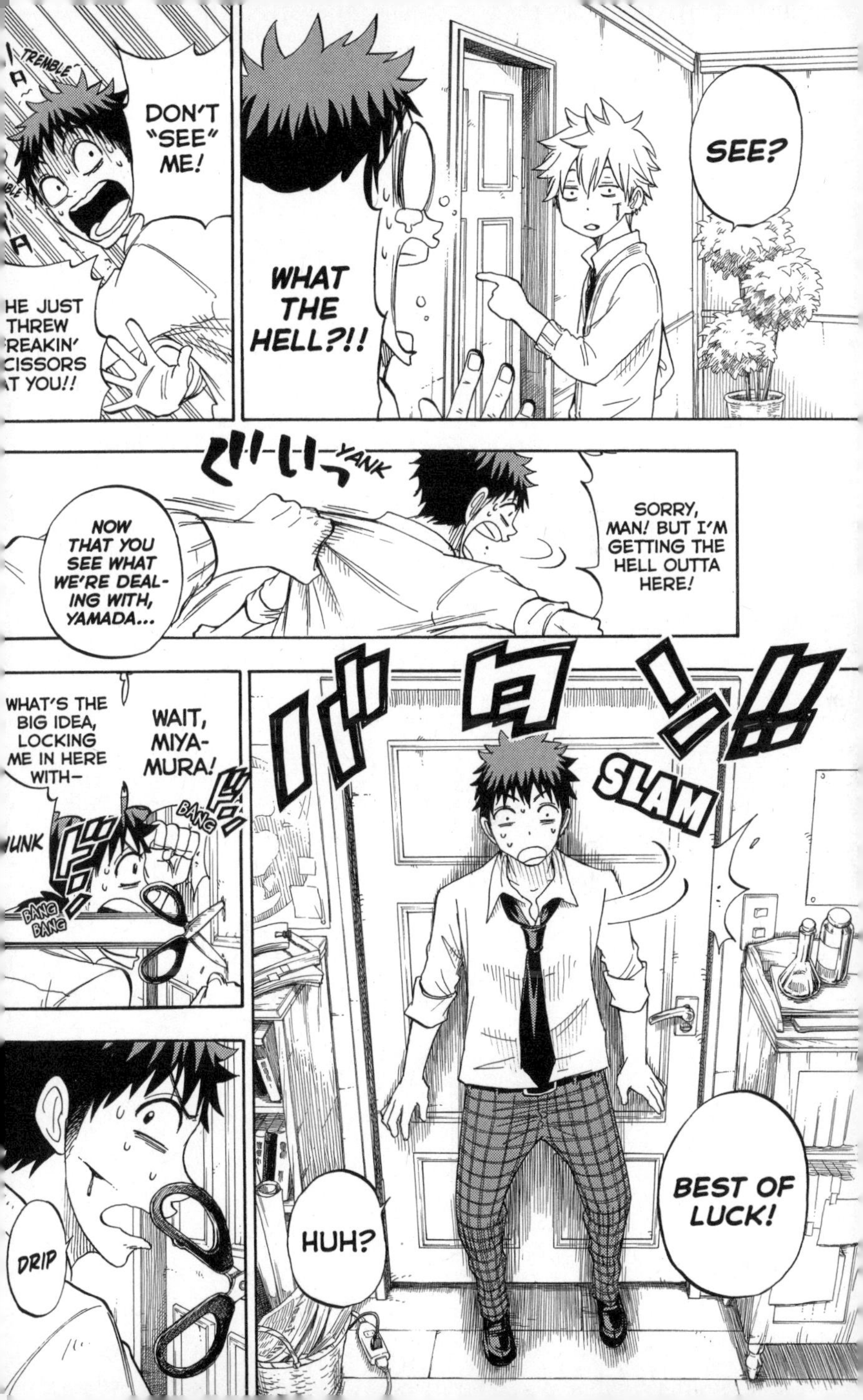

SEE?
WHAT THE HELL?!!
TREMBLE
DON'T "SEE" ME!
HE JUST THREW REAKIN' CISSORS T YOU!!
YANK
SORRY, MAN! BUT I'M GETTING THE HELL OUTTA HERE!
NOW THAT YOU SEE WHAT WE'RE DEAL-ING WITH, YAMADA...
SLAM
BEST OF LUCK!
HUH?
WAIT, MIYA-MURA!
WHAT'S THE BIG IDEA, LOCKING ME IN HERE WITH—
BANG
UNK
BANG BANG
DRIP

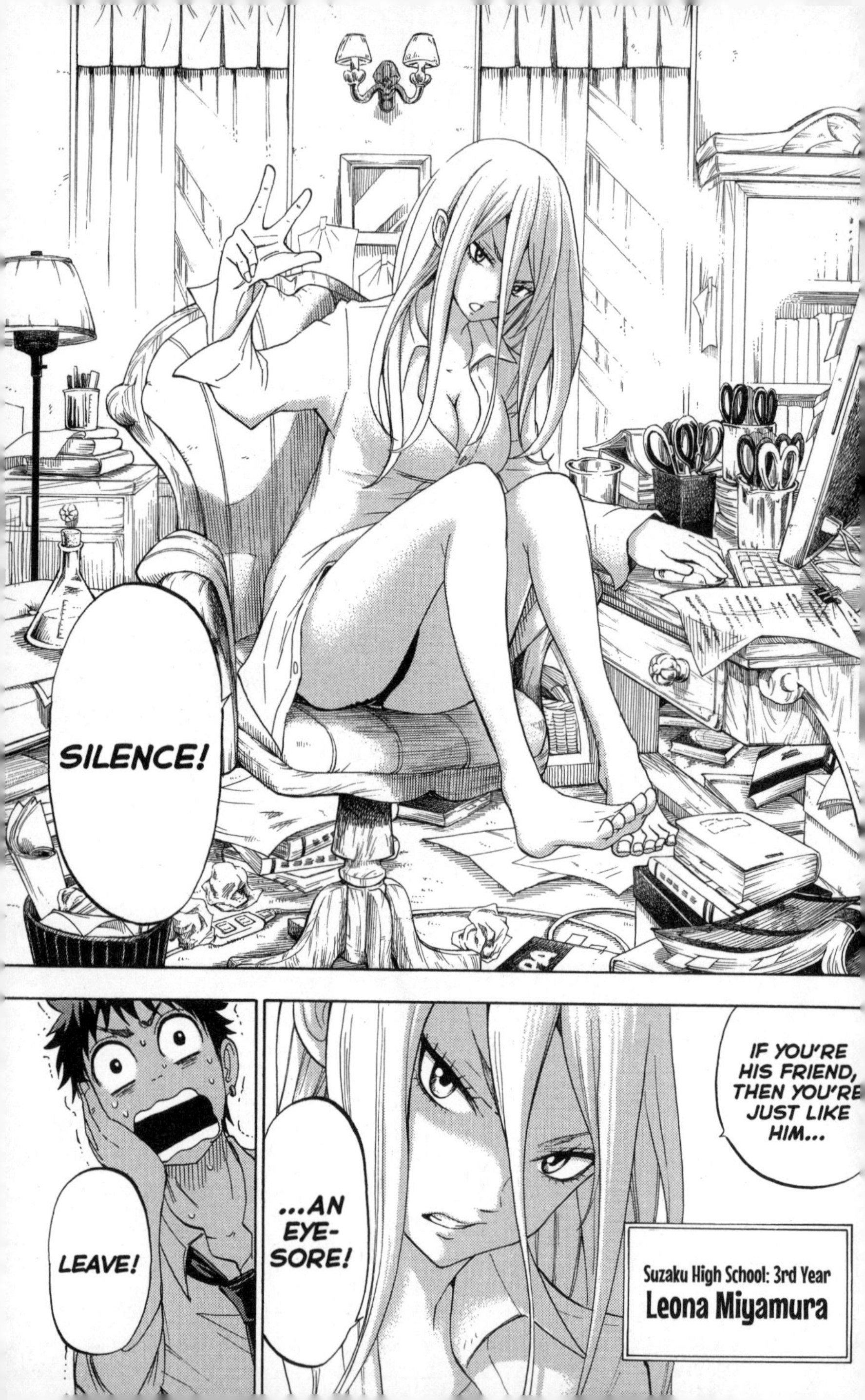

SILENCE!
IF YOU'RE HIS FRIEND, THEN YOU'RE JUST LIKE HIM...
...AN EYE-SORE!
Suzaku High School: 3rd Year
Leona Miyamura
LEAVE!

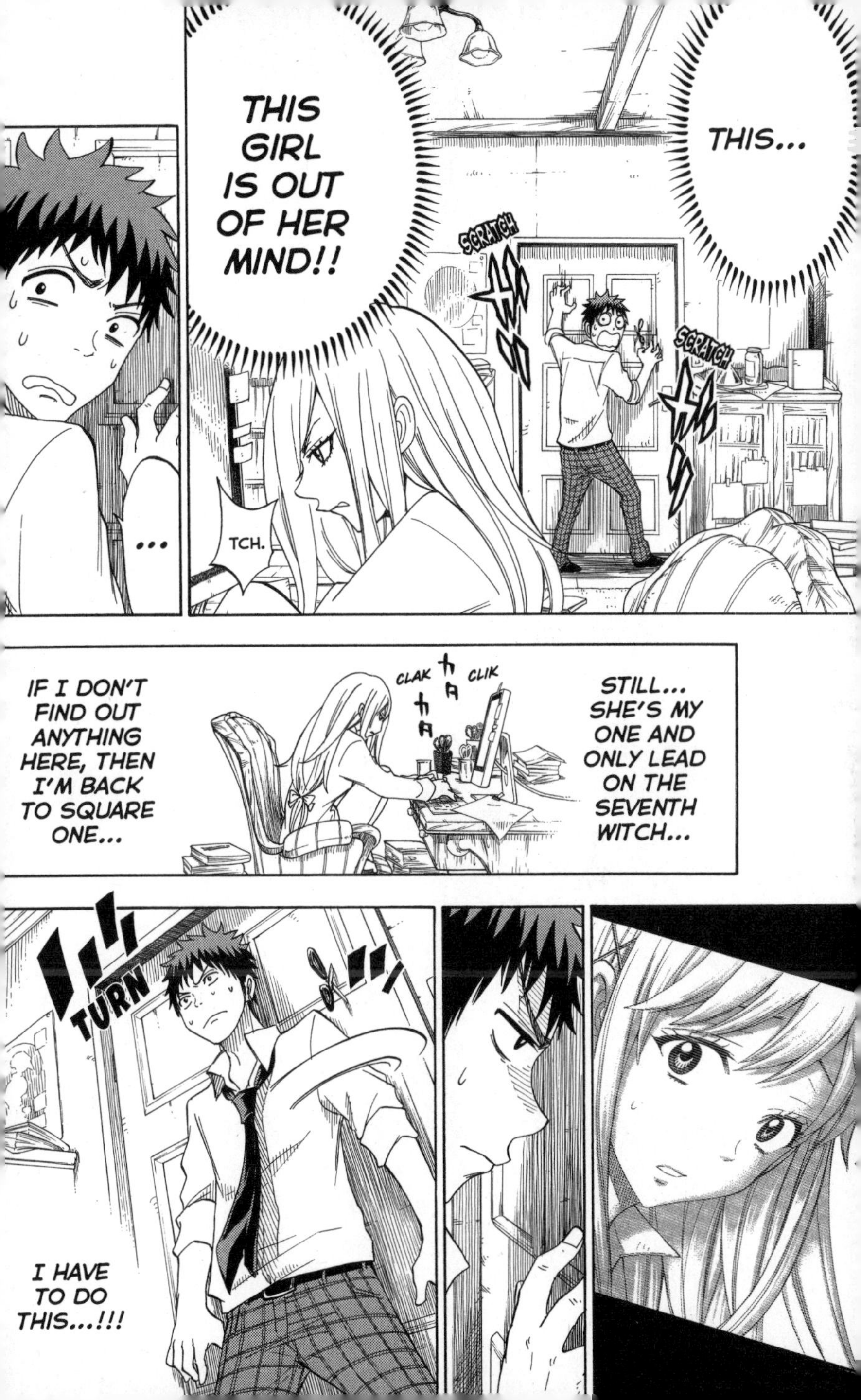
THIS...
THIS GIRL IS OUT OF HER MIND!!
SCRATCH
SCRATCH
TCH.
...
STILL... SHE'S MY ONE AND ONLY LEAD ON THE SEVENTH WITCH...
CLIK
CLAK
IF I DON'T FIND OUT ANYTHING HERE, THEN I'M BACK TO SQUARE ONE...
TURN
I HAVE TO DO THIS...!!!

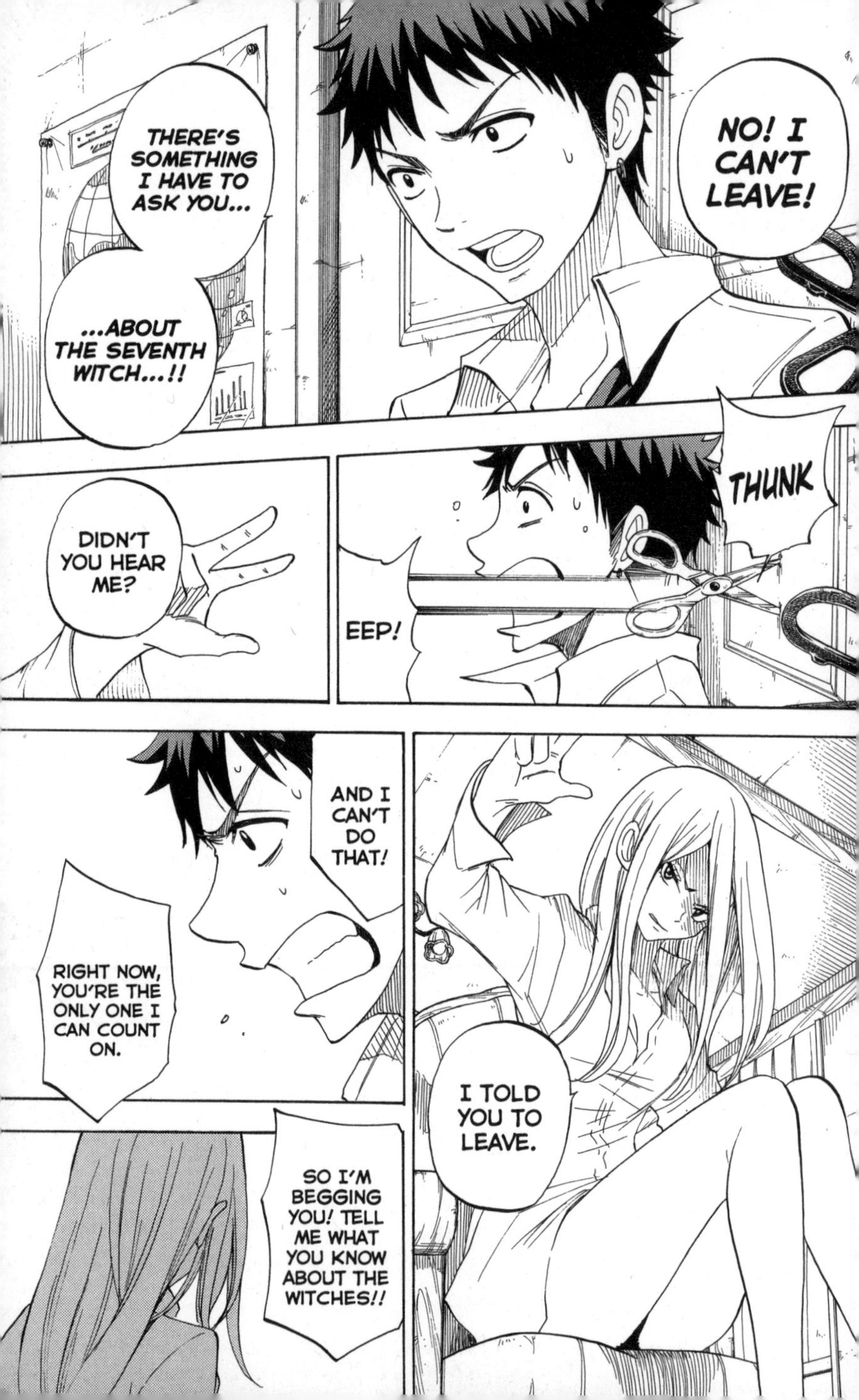
NO! I CAN'T LEAVE!
THERE'S SOMETHING I HAVE TO ASK YOU...
...ABOUT THE SEVENTH WITCH...!!
THUNK
EEP!
DIDN'T YOU HEAR ME?
I TOLD YOU TO LEAVE.
AND I CAN'T DO THAT!
RIGHT NOW, YOU'RE THE ONLY ONE I CAN COUNT ON.
SO I'M BEGGING YOU! TELL ME WHAT YOU KNOW ABOUT THE WITCHES!!

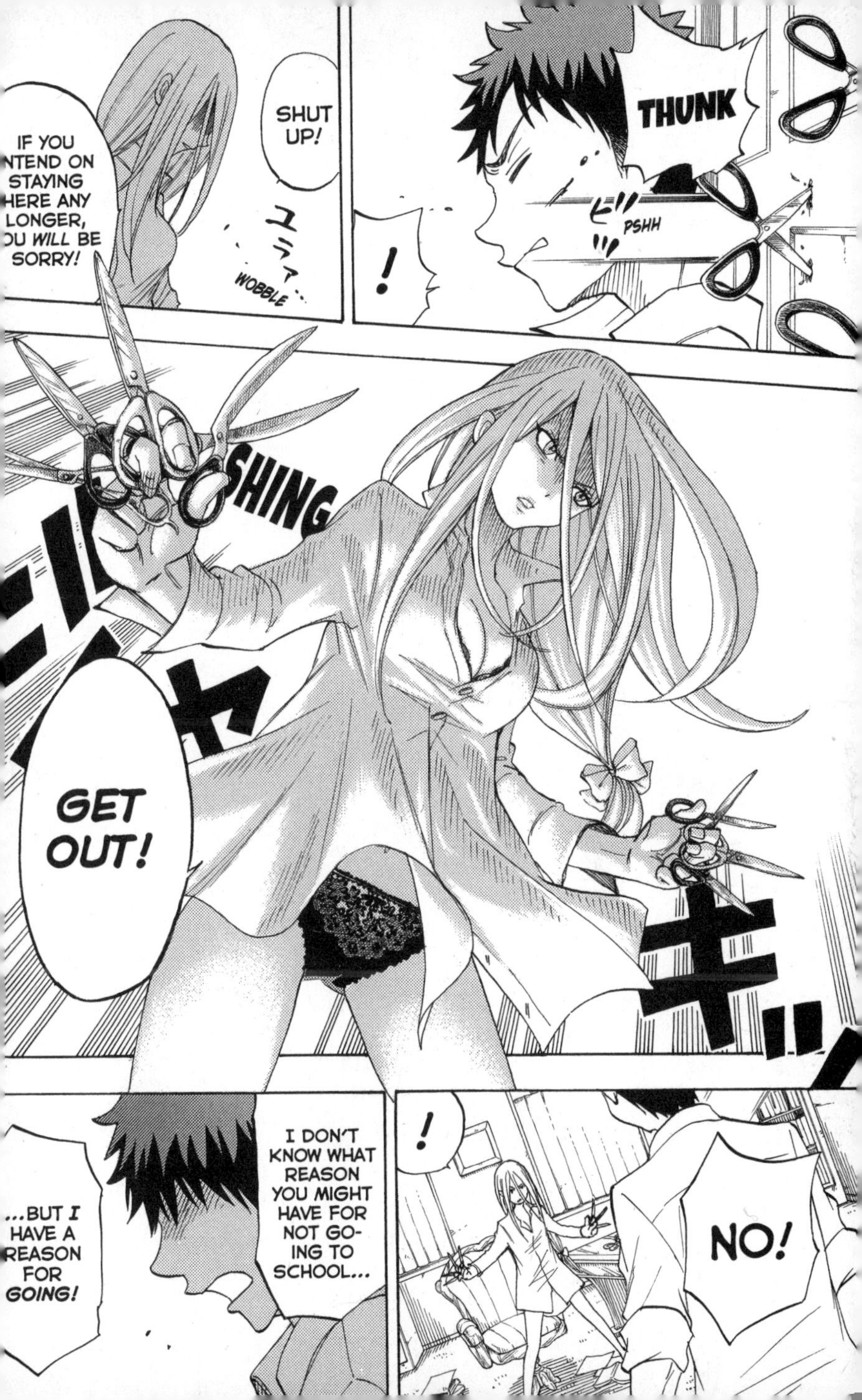
THUNK
ビッ
PSHH
!
SHUT UP!
ユラァ
WOBBLE
IF YOU NTEND ON STAYING HERE ANY LONGER, OU WILL BE SORRY!
SHING
GET OUT!
!
NO!
I DON'T KNOW WHAT REASON YOU MIGHT HAVE FOR NOT GO-ING TO SCHOOL...
...BUT I HAVE A REASON FOR GOING!

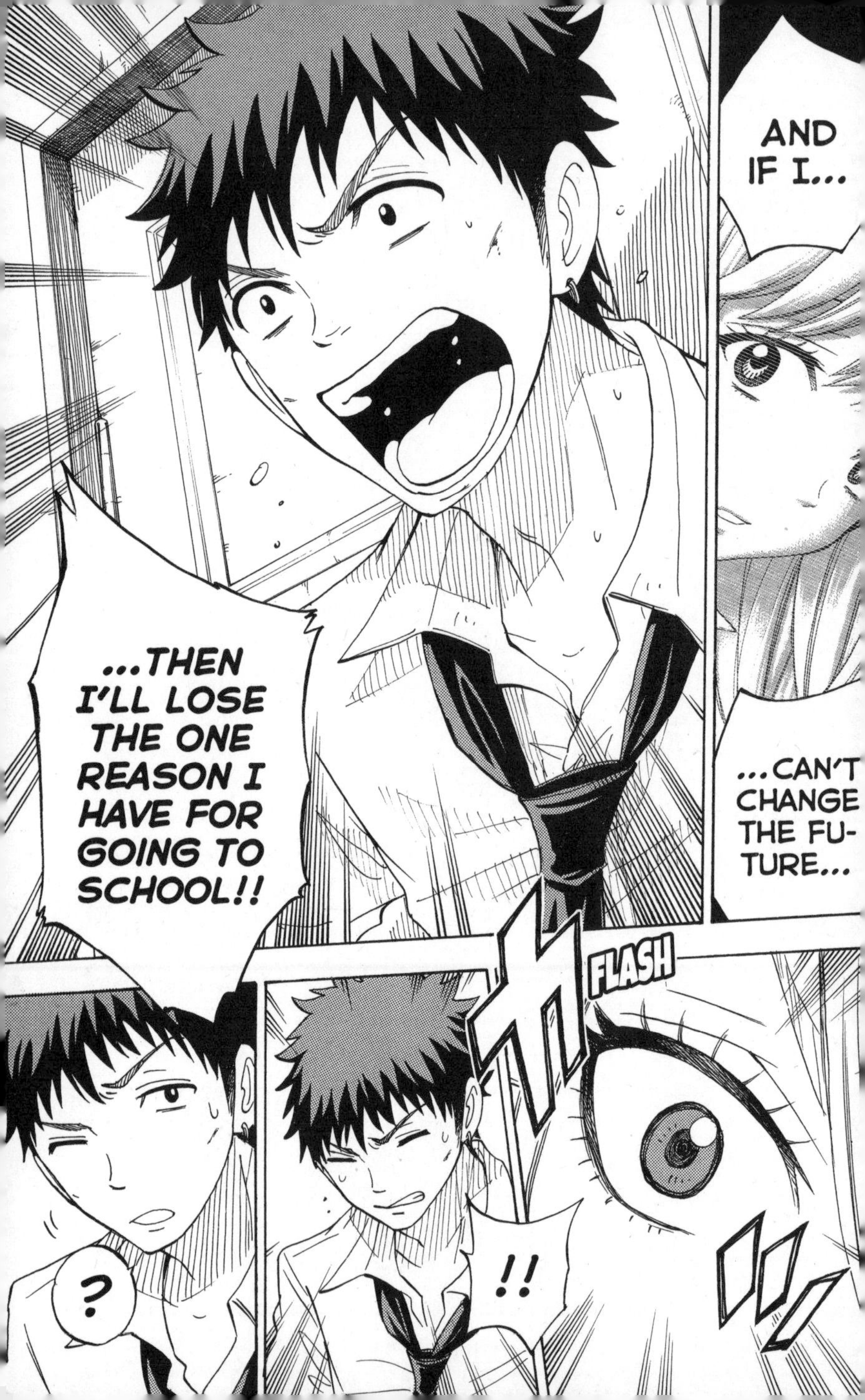
AND IF I...
...CAN'T CHANGE THE FU-TURE...
...THEN I'LL LOSE THE ONE REASON I HAVE FOR GOING TO SCHOOL!!
FLASH
!!
?

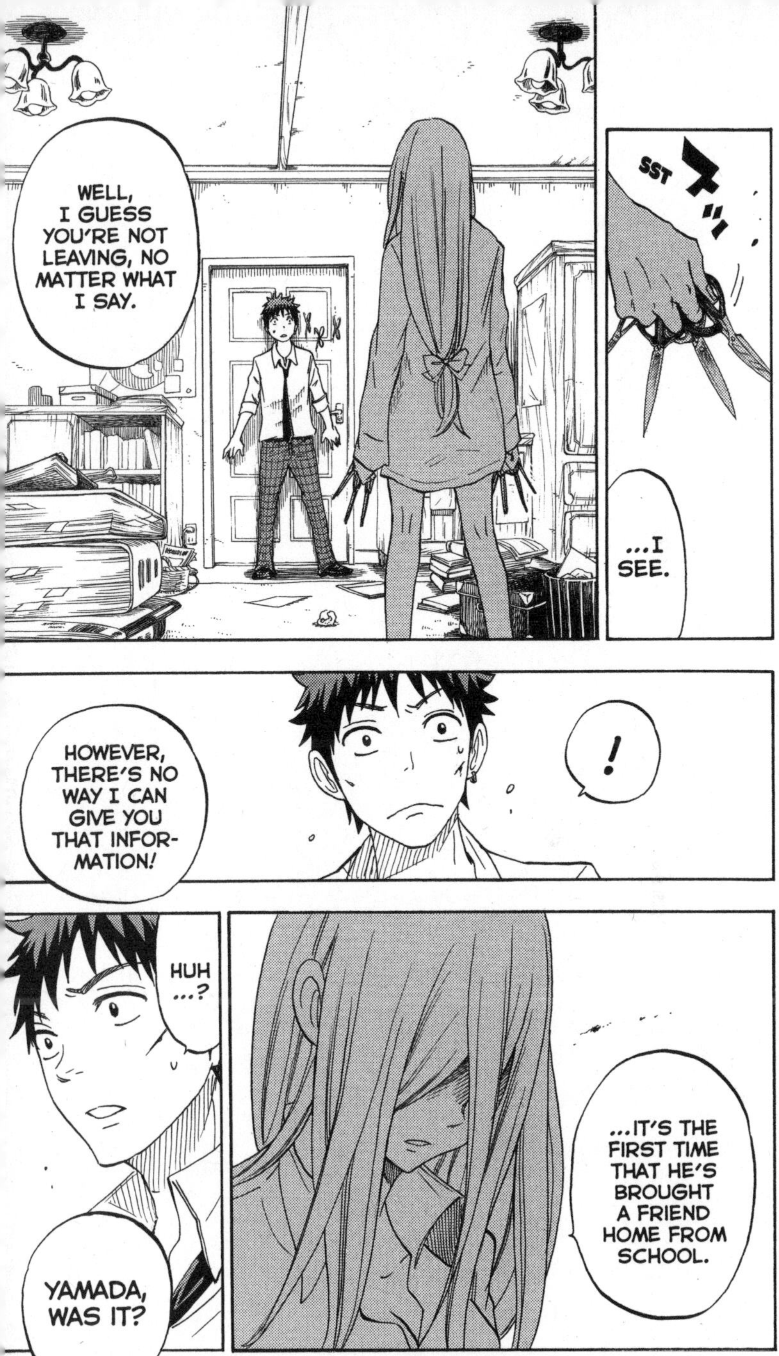
SST
...I SEE.
WELL, I GUESS YOU'RE NOT LEAVING, NO MATTER WHAT I SAY.
!
HOWEVER, THERE'S NO WAY I CAN GIVE YOU THAT INFOR-MATION!
...IT'S THE FIRST TIME THAT HE'S BROUGHT A FRIEND HOME FROM SCHOOL.
HUH ...?
YAMADA, WAS IT?

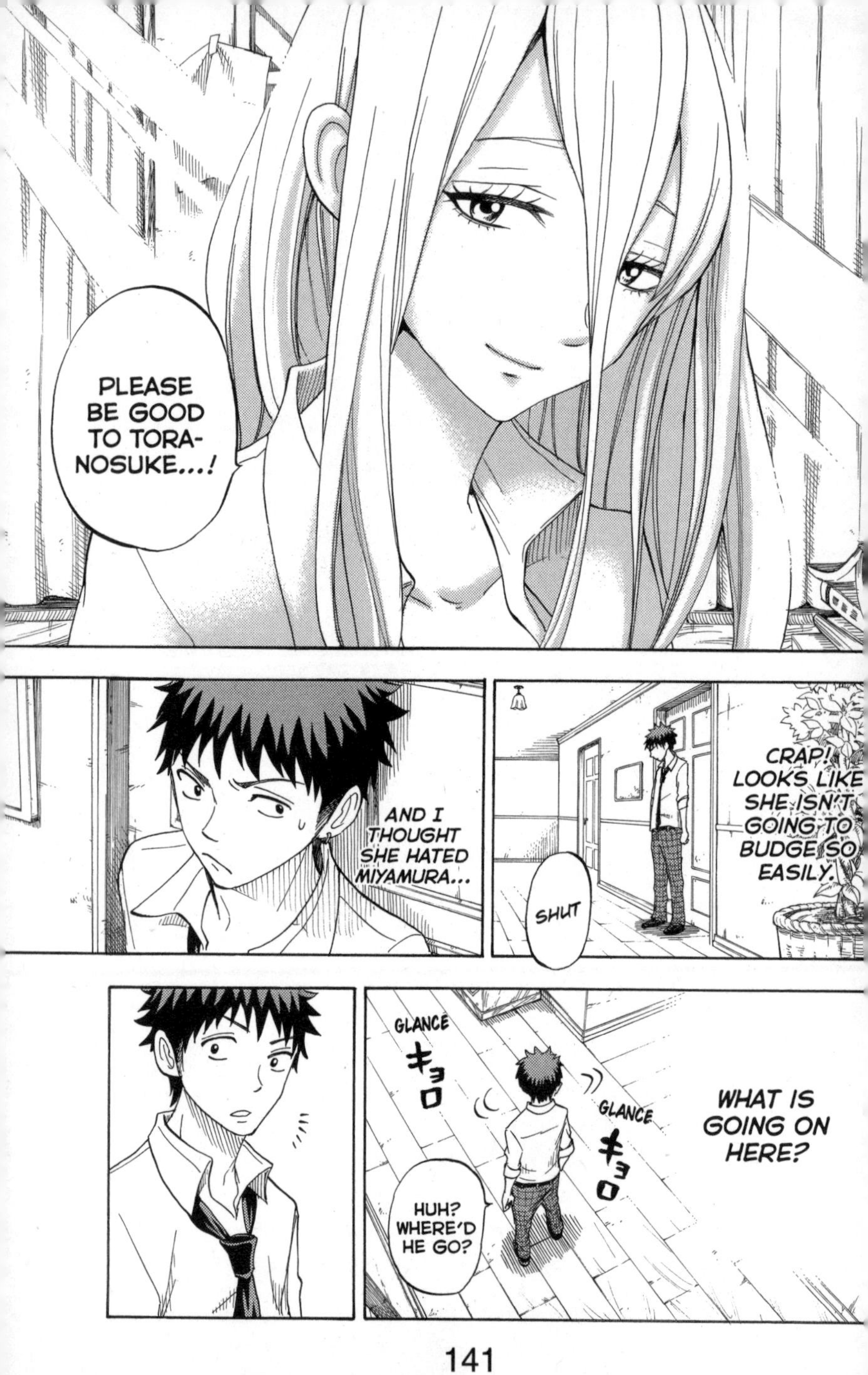
PLEASE BE GOOD TO TORA-NOSUKE...!
CRAP! LOOKS LIKE SHE ISN'T GOING TO BUDGE SO EASILY.
SHUT
AND I THOUGHT SHE HATED MIYAMURA...
WHAT IS GOING ON HERE?
GLANCE キョロ
GLANCE キョロ
HUH? WHERE'D HE GO?

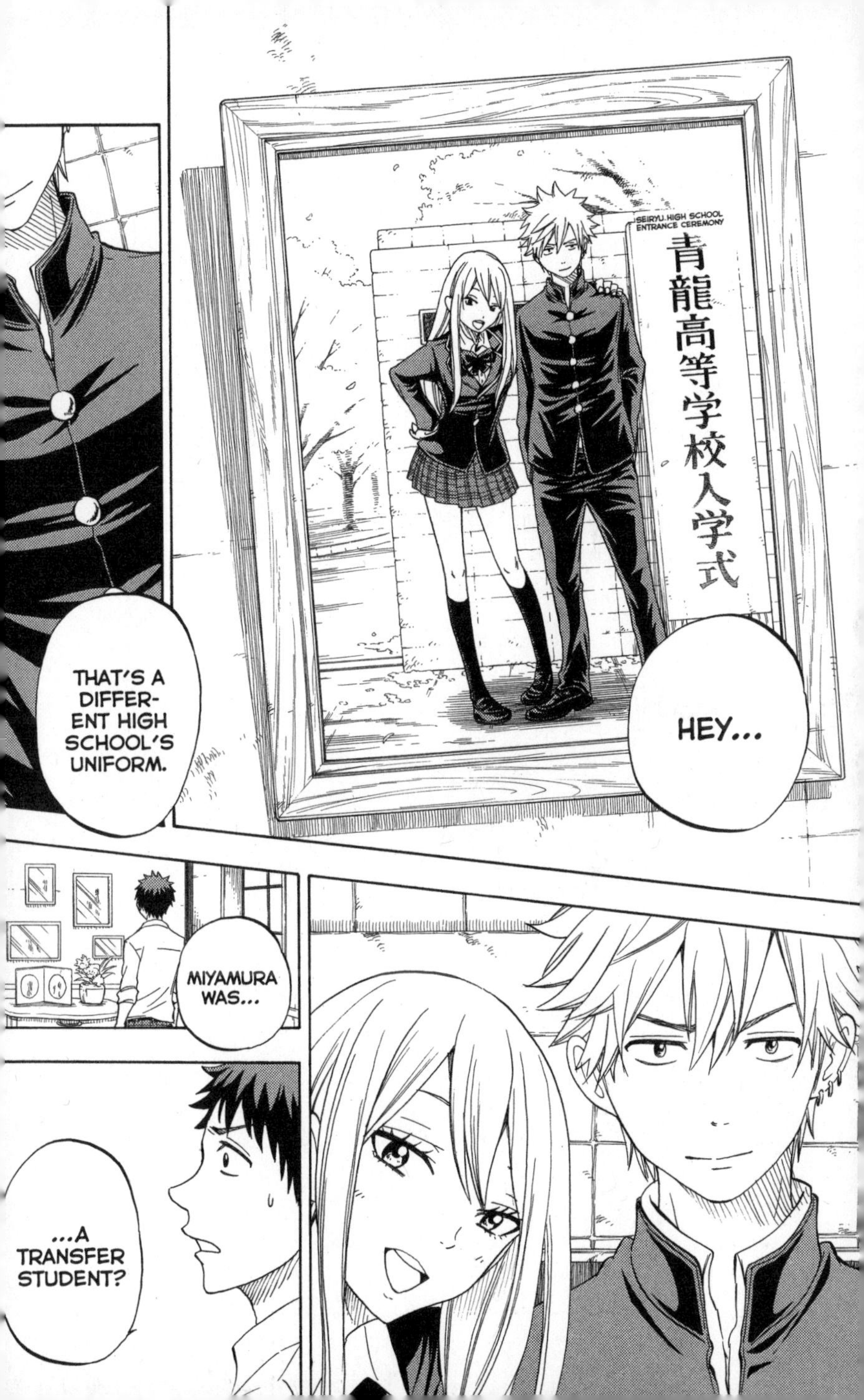
SEIRYU HIGH SCHOOL ENTRANCE CEREMONY
青龍高等学校入学式
HEY...
THAT'S A DIFFERENT HIGH SCHOOL'S UNIFORM.
MIYAMURA WAS...
...A TRANSFER STUDENT?

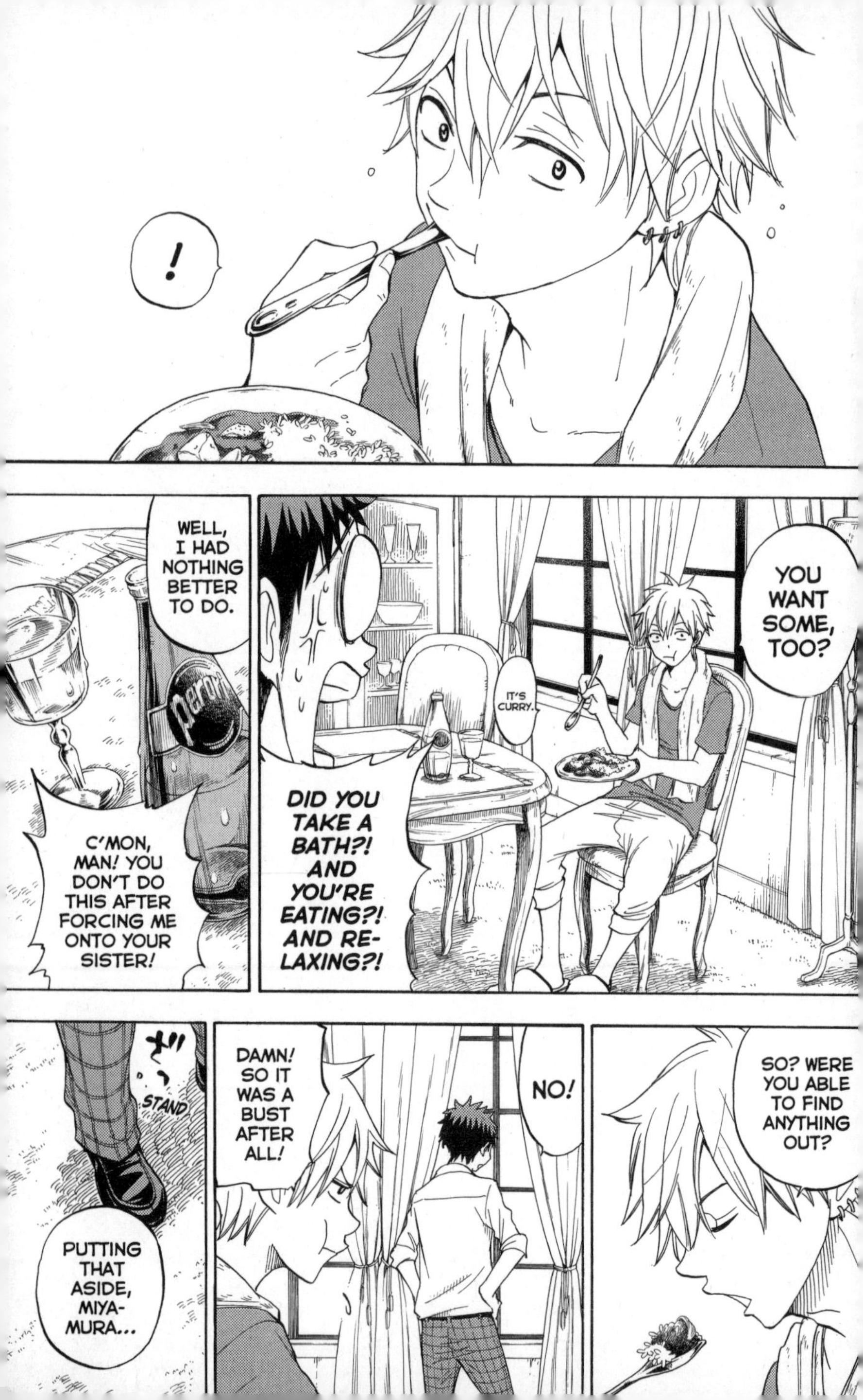
!
YOU WANT SOME, TOO?
IT'S CURRY.
DID YOU TAKE A BATH?! AND YOU'RE EATING?! AND RE-LAXING?!
WELL, I HAD NOTHING BETTER TO DO.
C'MON, MAN! YOU DON'T DO THIS AFTER FORCING ME ONTO YOUR SISTER!
SO? WERE YOU ABLE TO FIND ANYTHING OUT?
NO!
DAMN! SO IT WAS A BUST AFTER ALL!
STAND
PUTTING THAT ASIDE, MIYA-MURA...

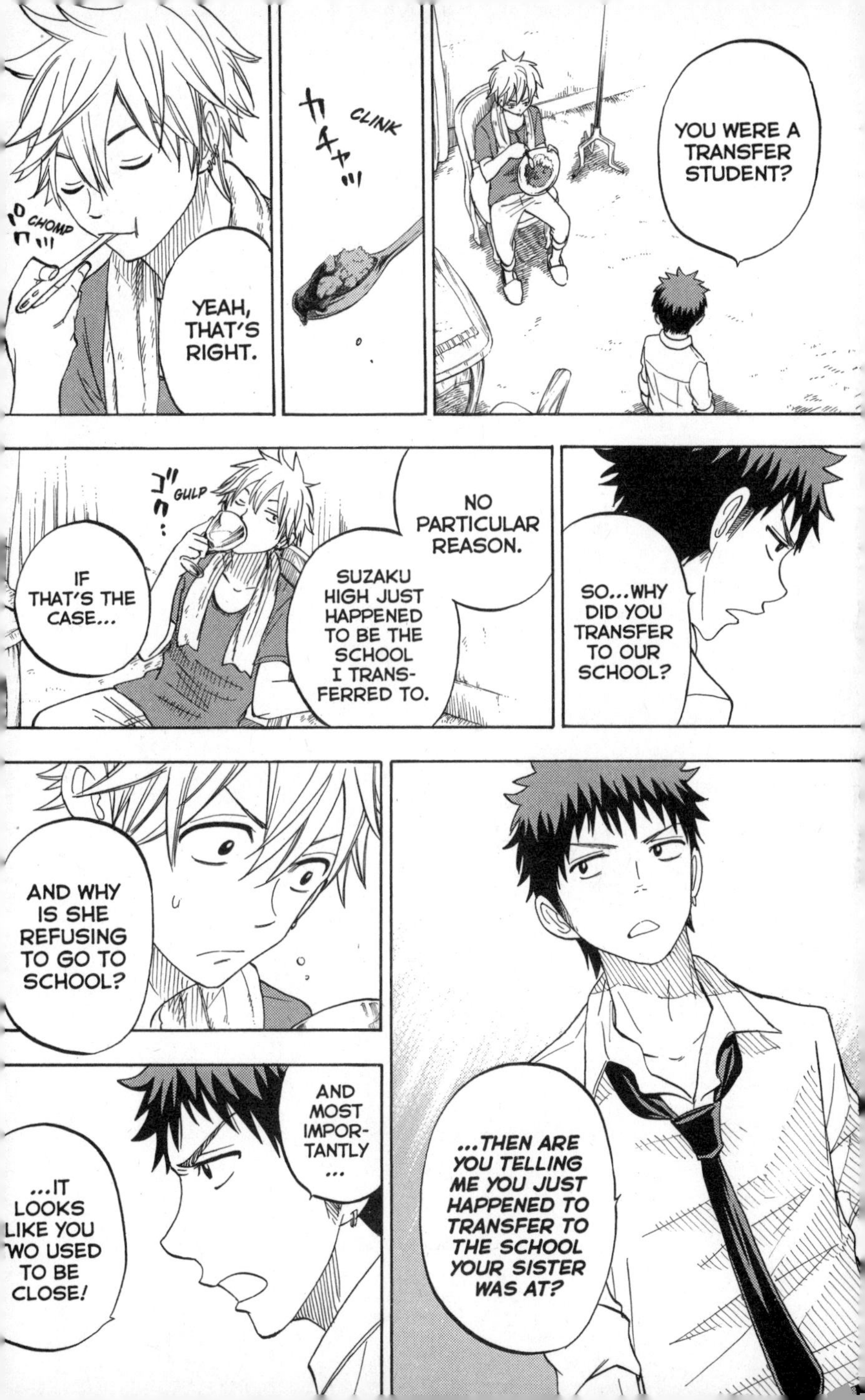
YOU WERE A TRANSFER STUDENT?
CLINK
CHOMP
YEAH, THAT'S RIGHT.
SO...WHY DID YOU TRANSFER TO OUR SCHOOL?
NO PARTICULAR REASON.
SUZAKU HIGH JUST HAPPENED TO BE THE SCHOOL I TRANS-FERRED TO.
GULP
IF THAT'S THE CASE...
...THEN ARE YOU TELLING ME YOU JUST HAPPENED TO TRANSFER TO THE SCHOOL YOUR SISTER WAS AT?
AND WHY IS SHE REFUSING TO GO TO SCHOOL?
AND MOST IMPOR-TANTLY...
...IT LOOKS LIKE YOU WO USED TO BE CLOSE!

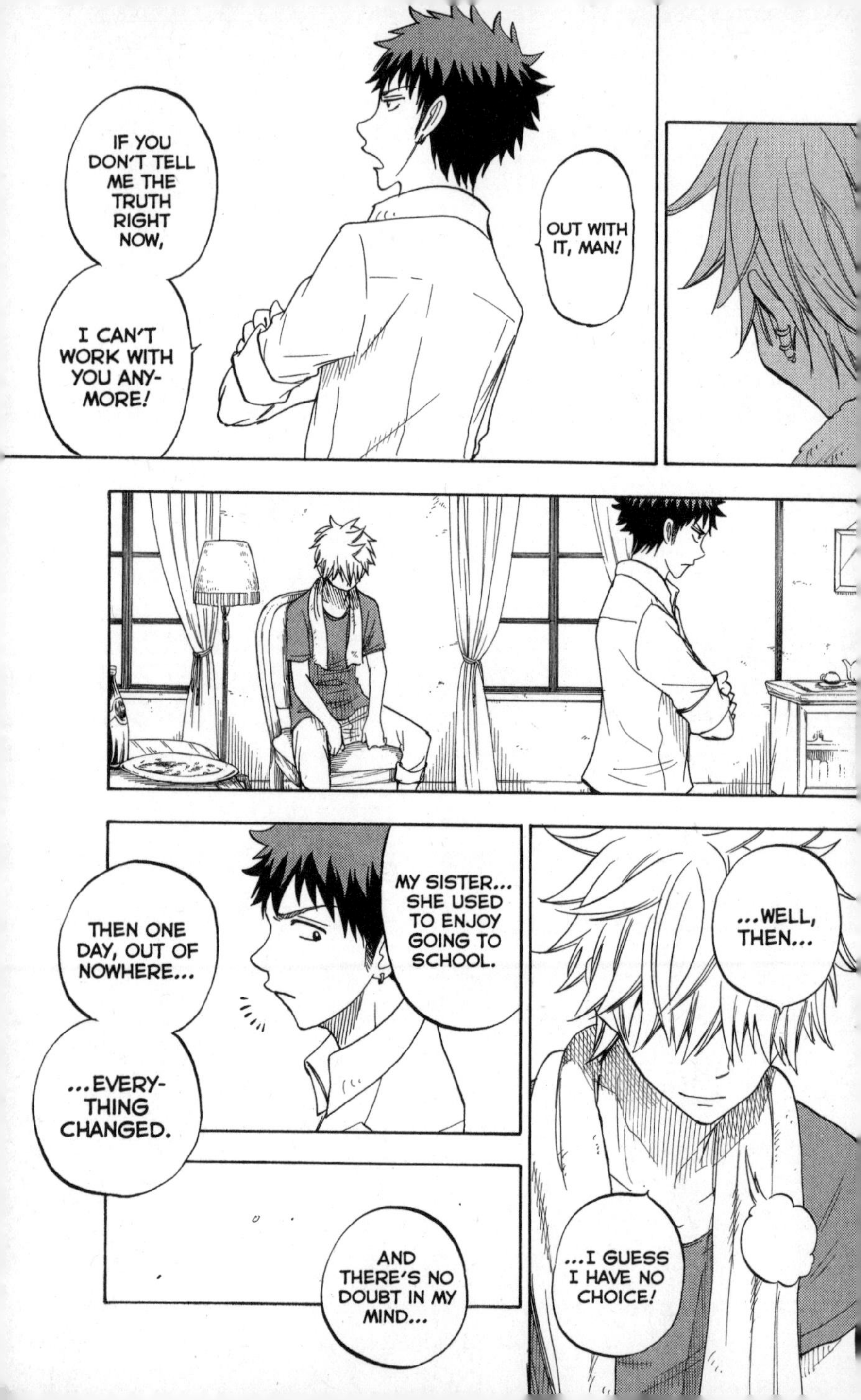
OUT WITH IT, MAN!
IF YOU DON'T TELL ME THE TRUTH RIGHT NOW,
I CAN'T WORK WITH YOU ANYMORE!
...WELL, THEN...
...I GUESS I HAVE NO CHOICE!
MY SISTER... SHE USED TO ENJOY GOING TO SCHOOL.
THEN ONE DAY, OUT OF NOWHERE...
...EVERYTHING CHANGED.
AND THERE'S NO DOUBT IN MY MIND...

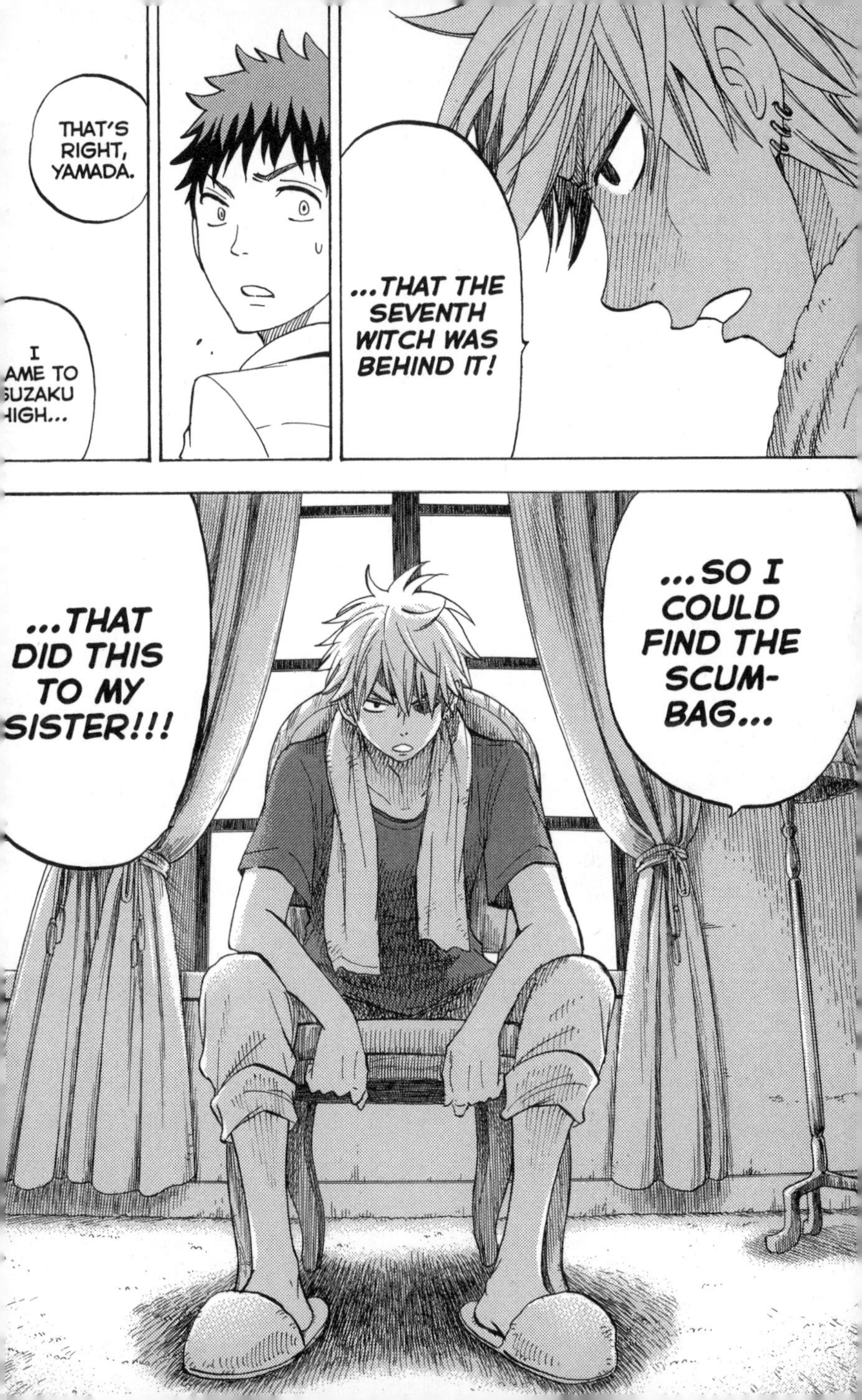
...THAT THE SEVENTH WITCH WAS BEHIND IT!
THAT'S RIGHT, YAMADA.
I AME TO UZAKU IGH...
...SO I COULD FIND THE SCUM-BAG...
...THAT DID THIS TO MY SISTER!!!

CHAPTER 59: Smooth talker, that one...!!

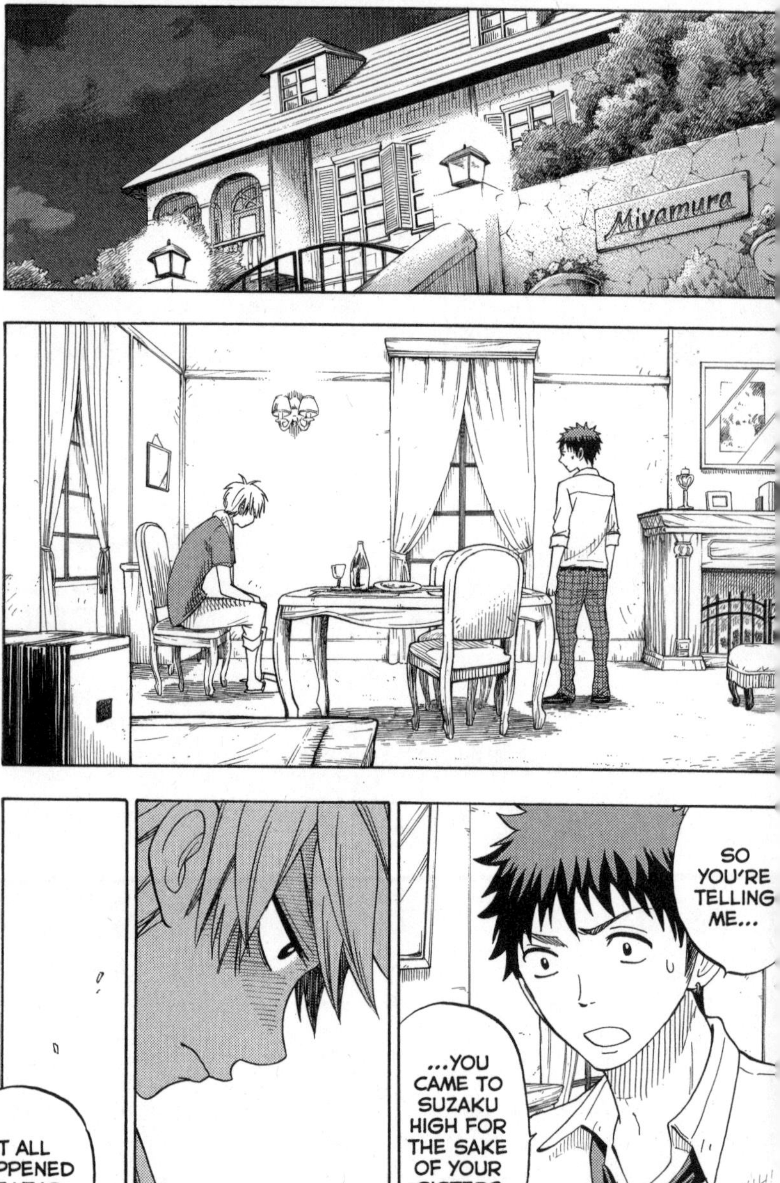
Miyamura
SO YOU'RE TELLING ME...
...YOU CAME TO SUZAKU HIGH FOR THE SAKE OF YOUR SISTER?
IT ALL HAPPENED LAST YEAR...

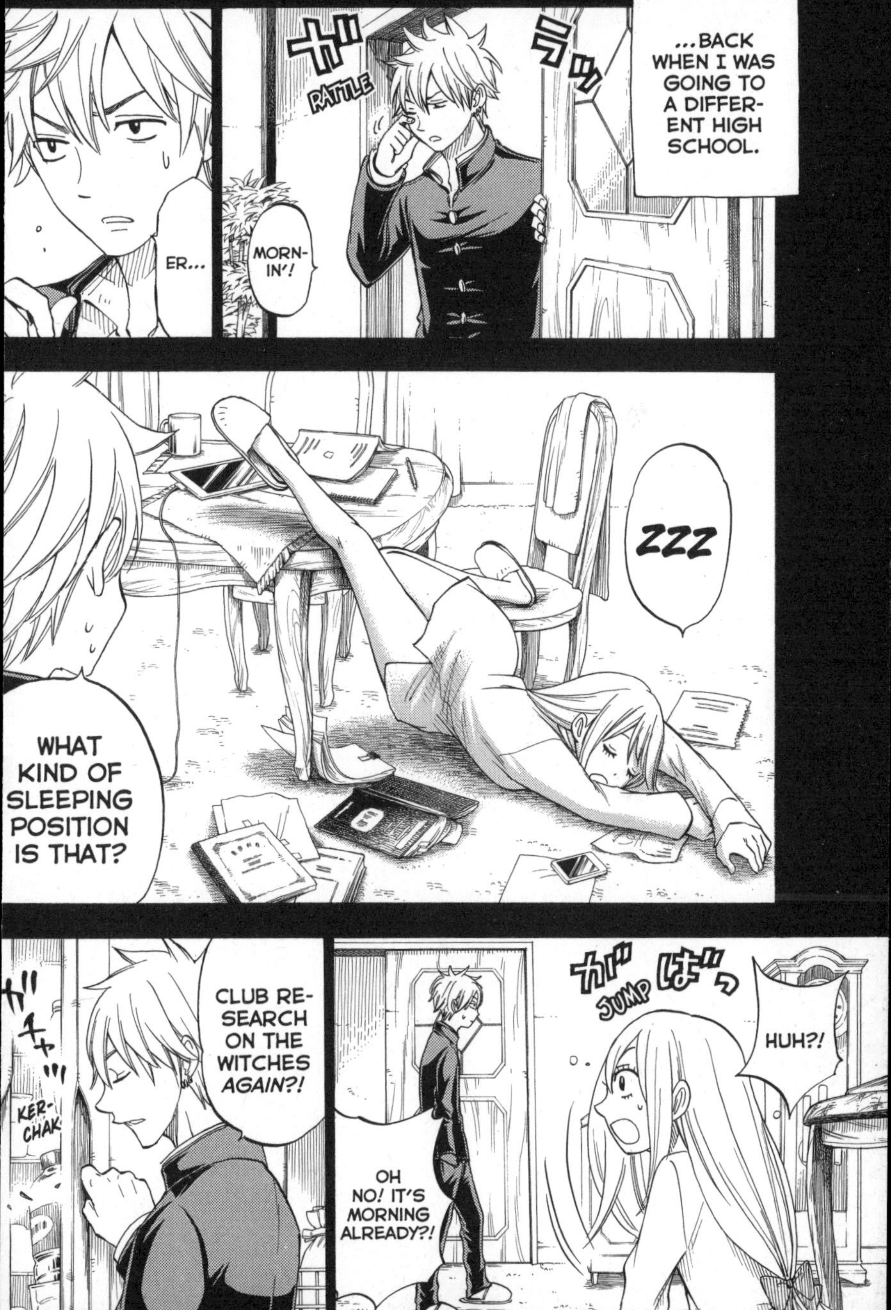
...BACK WHEN I WAS GOING TO A DIFFERENT HIGH SCHOOL.
ガラッ
RATTLE
MORNIN'!
ER...
ZZZ
WHAT KIND OF SLEEPING POSITION IS THAT?
がばっ
JUMP
HUH?!
OH NO! IT'S MORNING ALREADY?!
CLUB RESEARCH ON THE WITCHES *AGAIN*?!
ガチャ
KER-CHAK

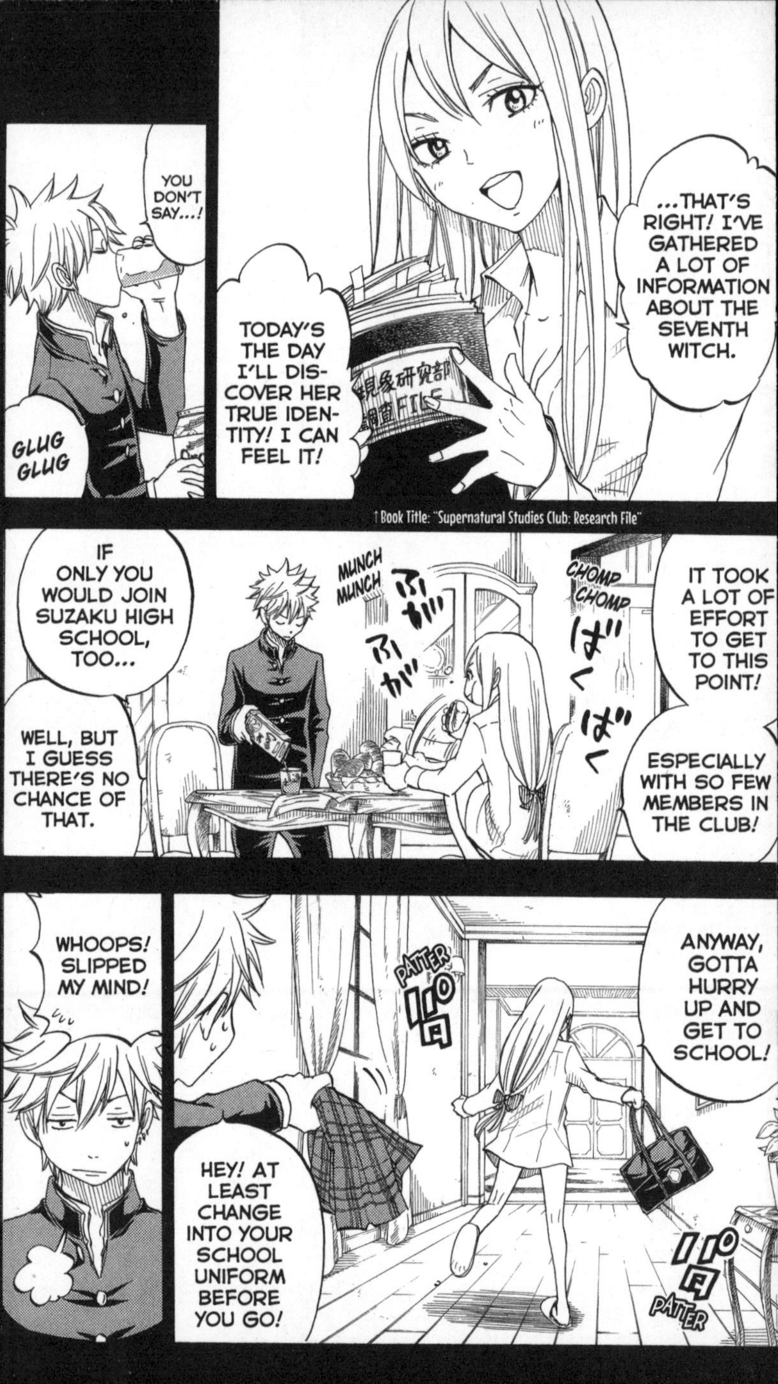
...THAT'S RIGHT! I'VE GATHERED A LOT OF INFORMATION ABOUT THE SEVENTH WITCH.
TODAY'S THE DAY I'LL DISCOVER HER TRUE IDENTITY! I CAN FEEL IT!
YOU DON'T SAY...!
GLUG GLUG
↑Book Title: "Supernatural Studies Club: Research File"
IT TOOK A LOT OF EFFORT TO GET TO THIS POINT!
CHOMP CHOMP
ばくばく
ESPECIALLY WITH SO FEW MEMBERS IN THE CLUB!
MUNCH MUNCH
ふがふが
IF ONLY YOU WOULD JOIN SUZAKU HIGH SCHOOL, TOO...
WELL, BUT I GUESS THERE'S NO CHANCE OF THAT.
ANYWAY, GOTTA HURRY UP AND GET TO SCHOOL!
PATTER
PATTER
HEY! AT LEAST CHANGE INTO YOUR SCHOOL UNIFORM BEFORE YOU GO!
WHOOPS! SLIPPED MY MIND!

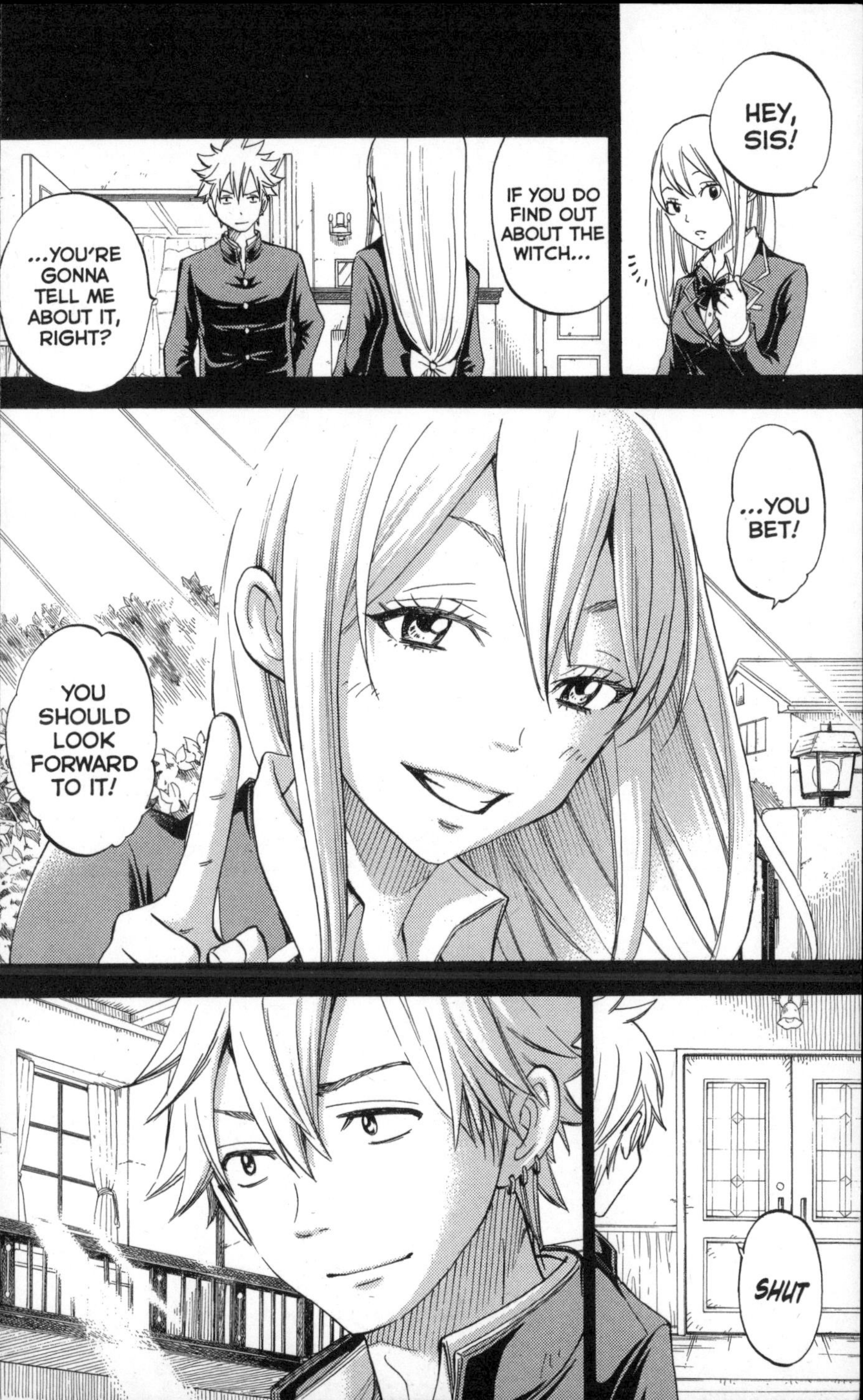
HEY, SIS!
IF YOU DO FIND OUT ABOUT THE WITCH...
...YOU'RE GONNA TELL ME ABOUT IT, RIGHT?
...YOU BET!
YOU SHOULD LOOK FORWARD TO IT!
SHUT

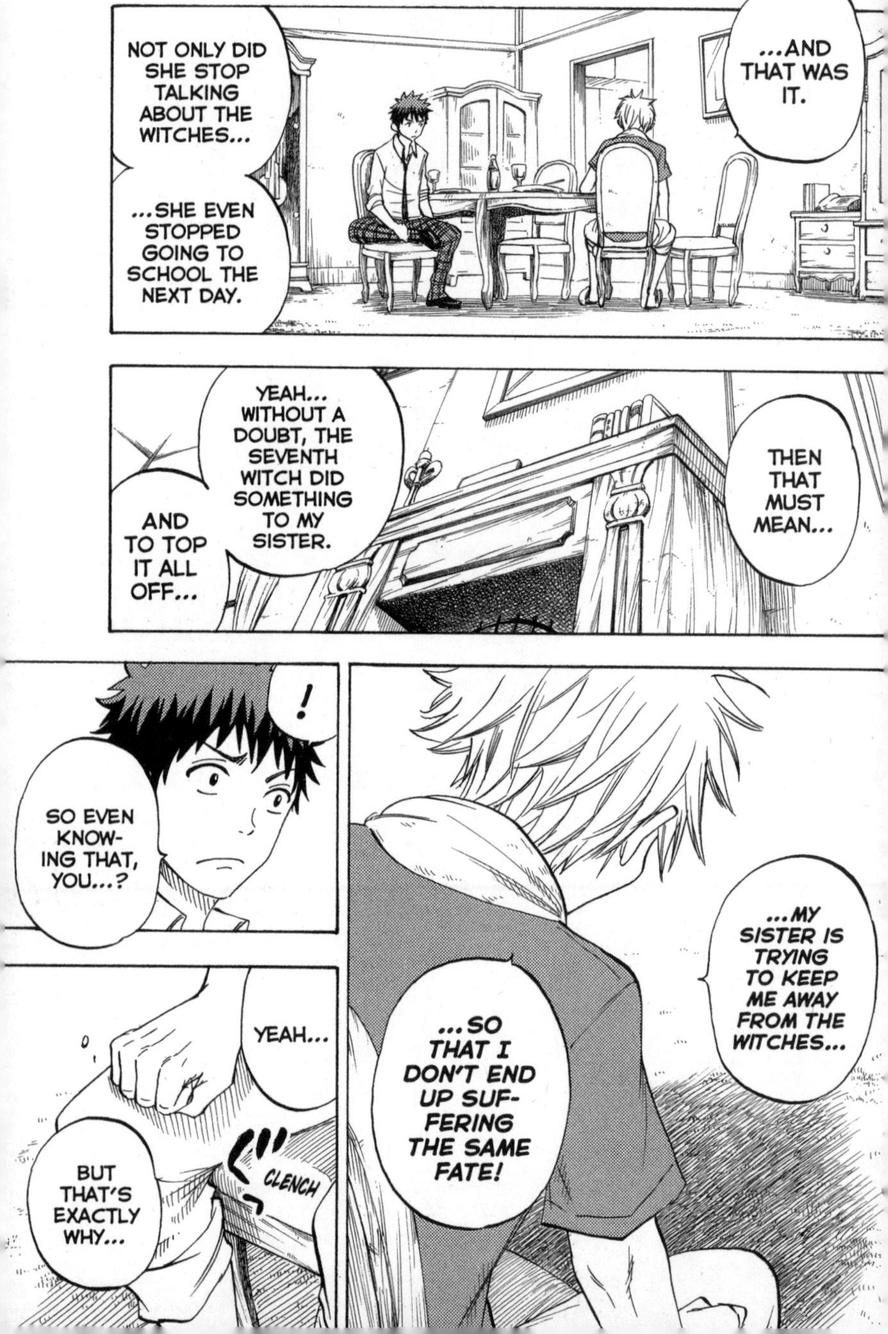
...AND THAT WAS IT.
NOT ONLY DID SHE STOP TALKING ABOUT THE WITCHES...
...SHE EVEN STOPPED GOING TO SCHOOL THE NEXT DAY.
THEN THAT MUST MEAN...
YEAH... WITHOUT A DOUBT, THE SEVENTH WITCH DID SOMETHING TO MY SISTER.
AND TO TOP IT ALL OFF...
...MY SISTER IS TRYING TO KEEP ME AWAY FROM THE WITCHES...
...SO THAT I DON'T END UP SUF-FERING THE SAME FATE!
!
SO EVEN KNOW-ING THAT, YOU...?
YEAH...
CLENCH
BUT THAT'S EXACTLY WHY...

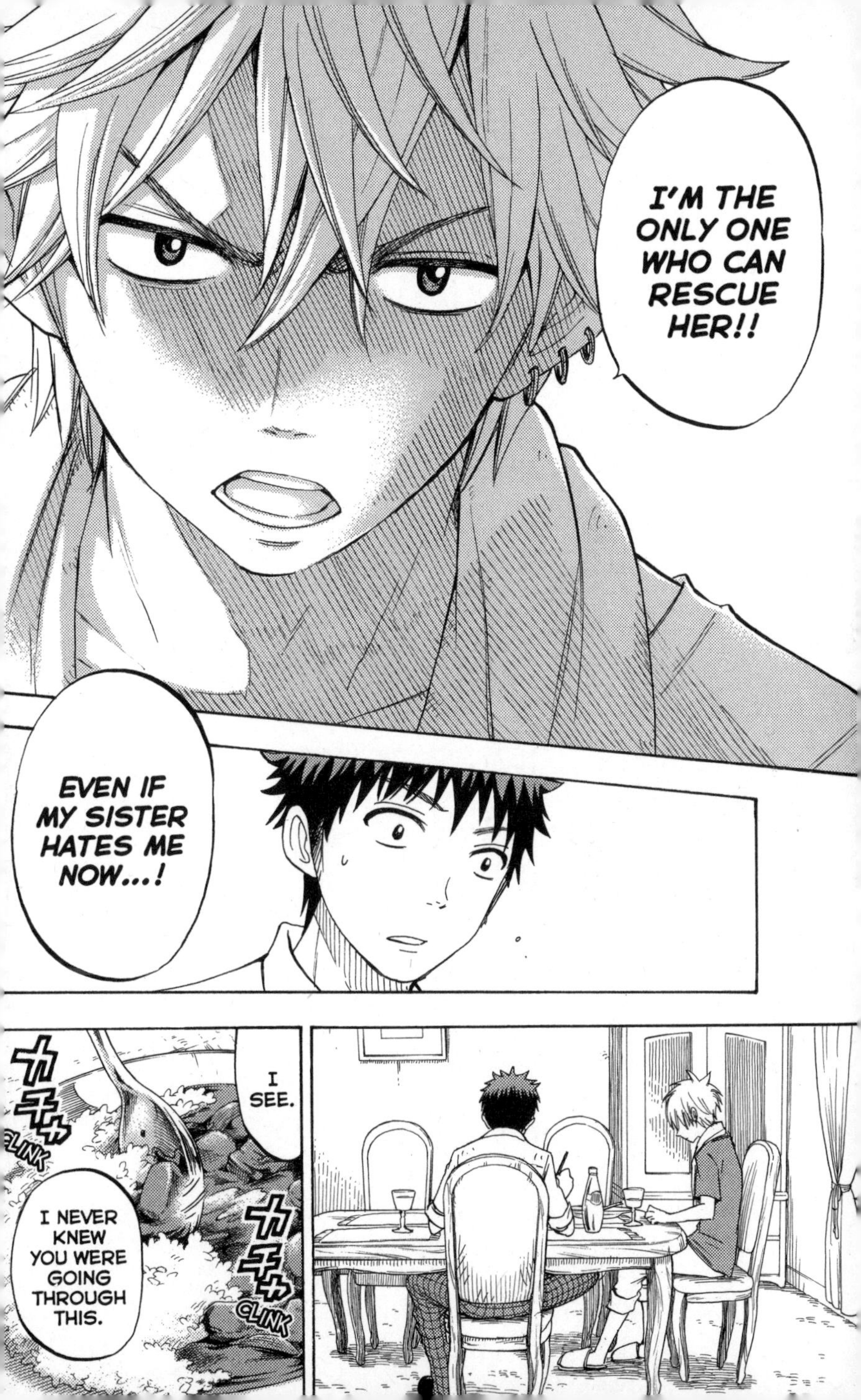
I'M THE ONLY ONE WHO CAN RESCUE HER!!
EVEN IF MY SISTER HATES ME NOW...!
I SEE.
カチャ
CLINK
I NEVER KNEW YOU WERE GOING THROUGH THIS.
カチャ
CLINK

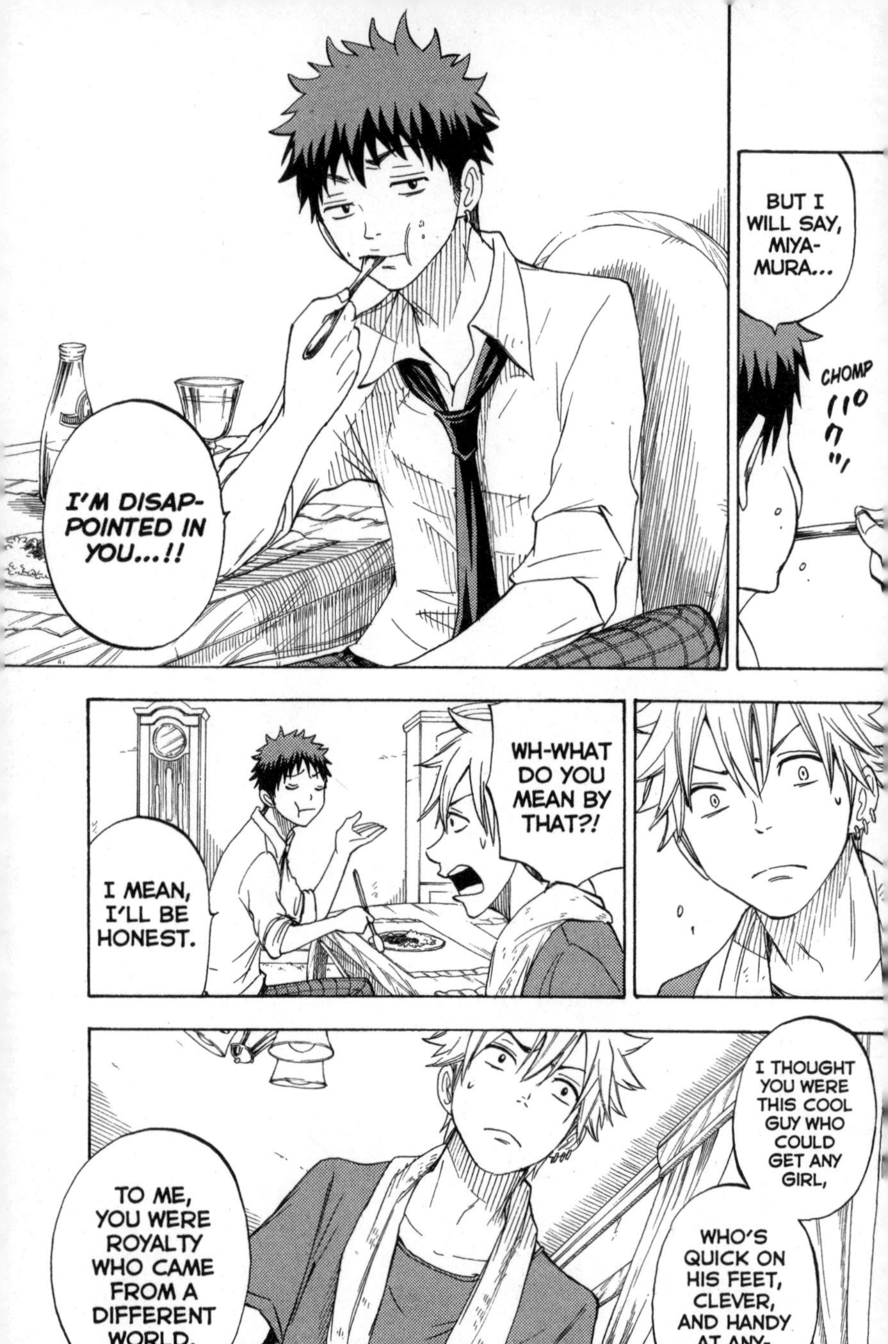
BUT I WILL SAY, MIYA-MURA...
CHOMP
I'M DISAP-POINTED IN YOU...!!
WH-WHAT DO YOU MEAN BY THAT?!
I MEAN, I'LL BE HONEST.
I THOUGHT YOU WERE THIS COOL GUY WHO COULD GET ANY GIRL,
WHO'S QUICK ON HIS FEET, CLEVER, AND HANDY AT ANY-THING.
TO ME, YOU WERE ROYALTY WHO CAME FROM A DIFFERENT WORLD.

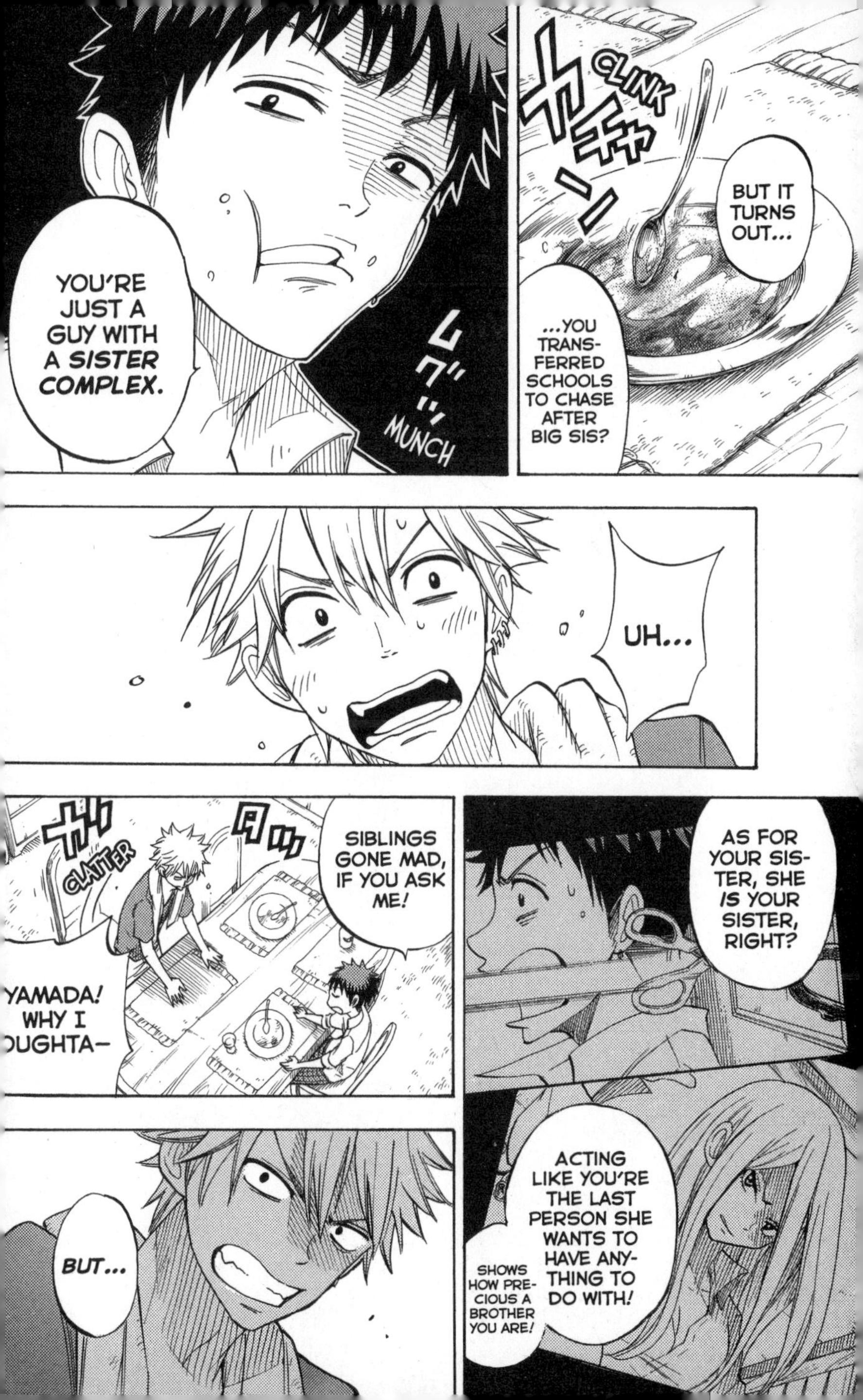
CLINK
BUT IT TURNS OUT...
...YOU TRANSFERRED SCHOOLS TO CHASE AFTER BIG SIS?
YOU'RE JUST A GUY WITH A *SISTER COMPLEX.*
MUNCH
UH...
AS FOR YOUR SISTER, SHE *IS* YOUR SISTER, RIGHT?
CLATTER
SIBLINGS GONE MAD, IF YOU ASK ME!
YAMADA! WHY I OUGHTA—
ACTING LIKE YOU'RE THE LAST PERSON SHE WANTS TO HAVE ANYTHING TO DO WITH!
SHOWS HOW PRECIOUS A BROTHER YOU ARE!
BUT...

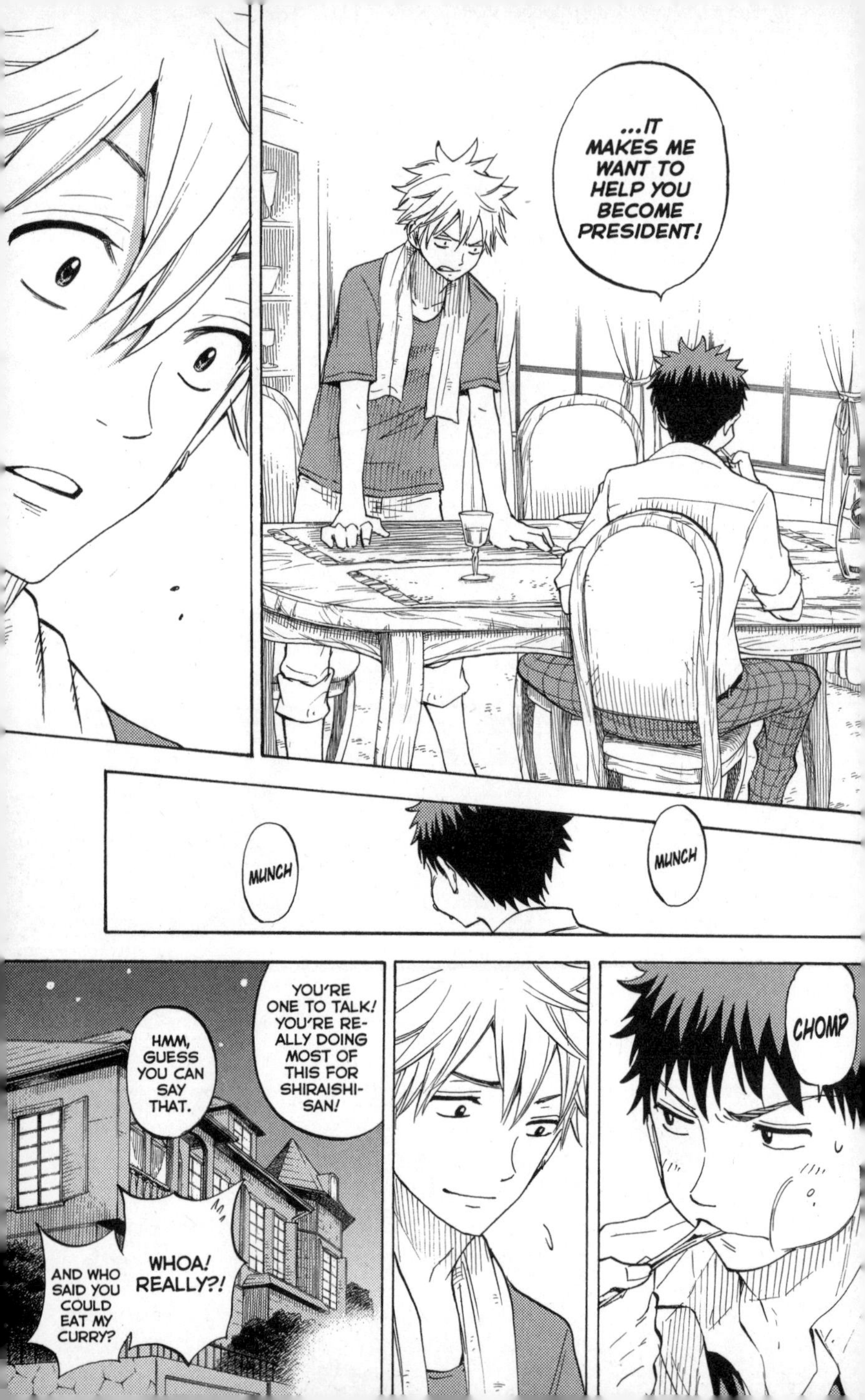
...IT MAKES ME WANT TO HELP YOU BECOME PRESIDENT!
MUNCH
MUNCH
CHOMP
YOU'RE ONE TO TALK! YOU'RE REALLY DOING MOST OF THIS FOR SHIRAISHI-SAN!
HMM, GUESS YOU CAN SAY THAT.
WHOA! REALLY?!
AND WHO SAID YOU COULD EAT MY CURRY?

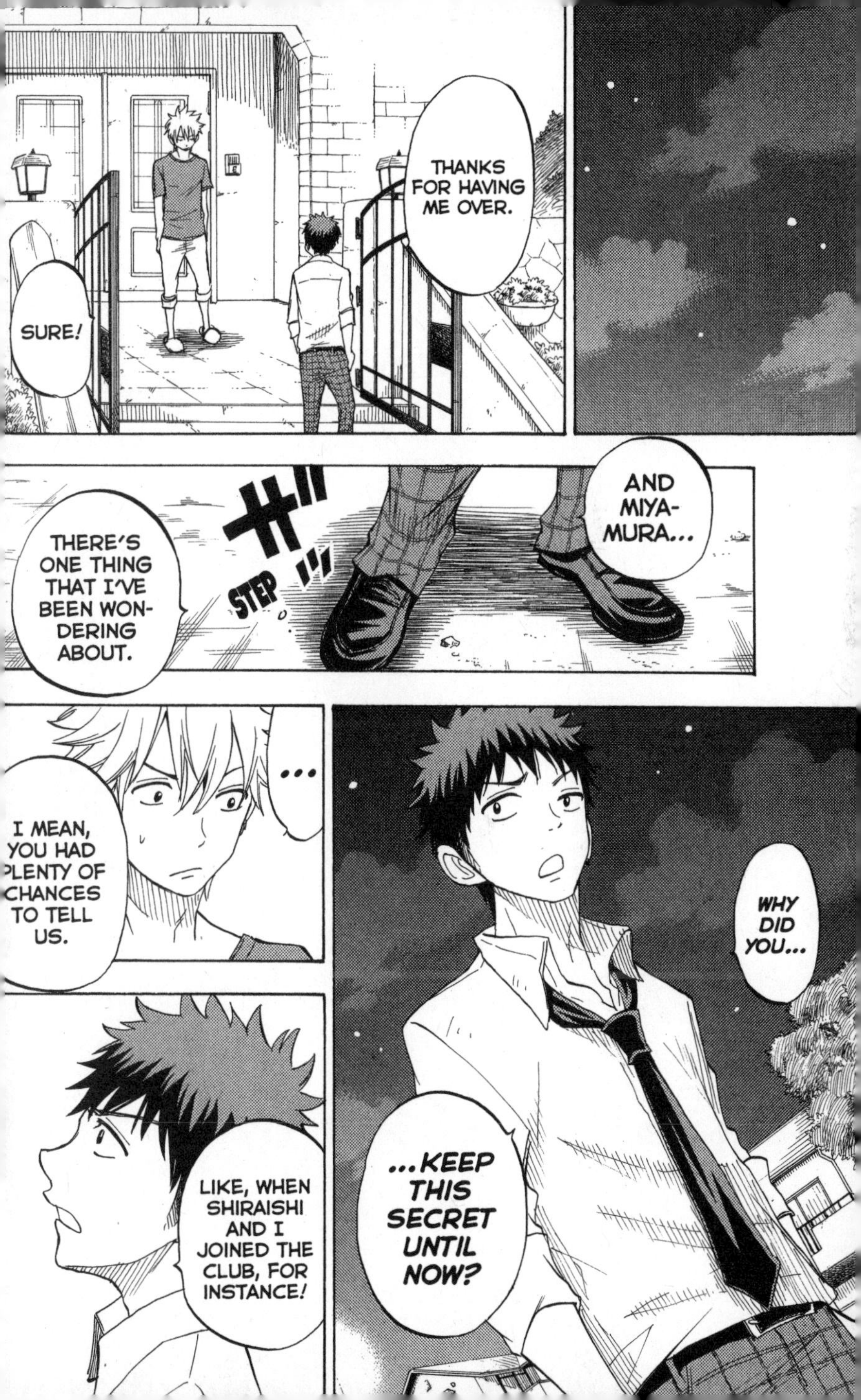
THANKS FOR HAVING ME OVER.
SURE!
AND MIYA-MURA...
STEP
THERE'S ONE THING THAT I'VE BEEN WON-DERING ABOUT.
WHY DID YOU...
...KEEP THIS SECRET UNTIL NOW?
...
I MEAN, YOU HAD PLENTY OF CHANCES TO TELL US.
LIKE, WHEN SHIRAISHI AND I JOINED THE CLUB, FOR INSTANCE!

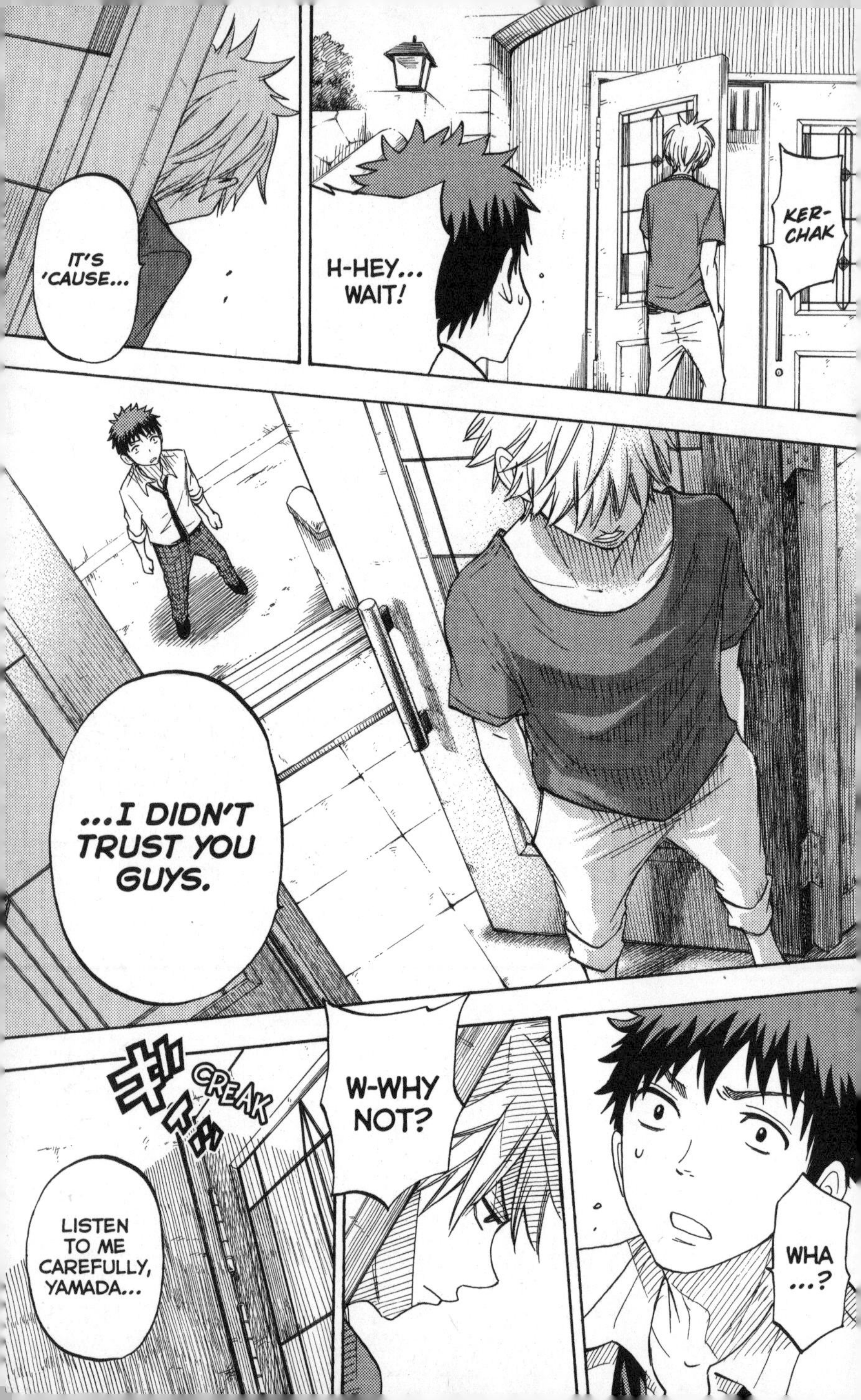
KER-
CHAK
H-HEY... WAIT!
IT'S 'CAUSE...
...I DIDN'T TRUST YOU GUYS.
WHA...?
W-WHY NOT?
CREAK
LISTEN TO ME CAREFULLY, YAMADA...

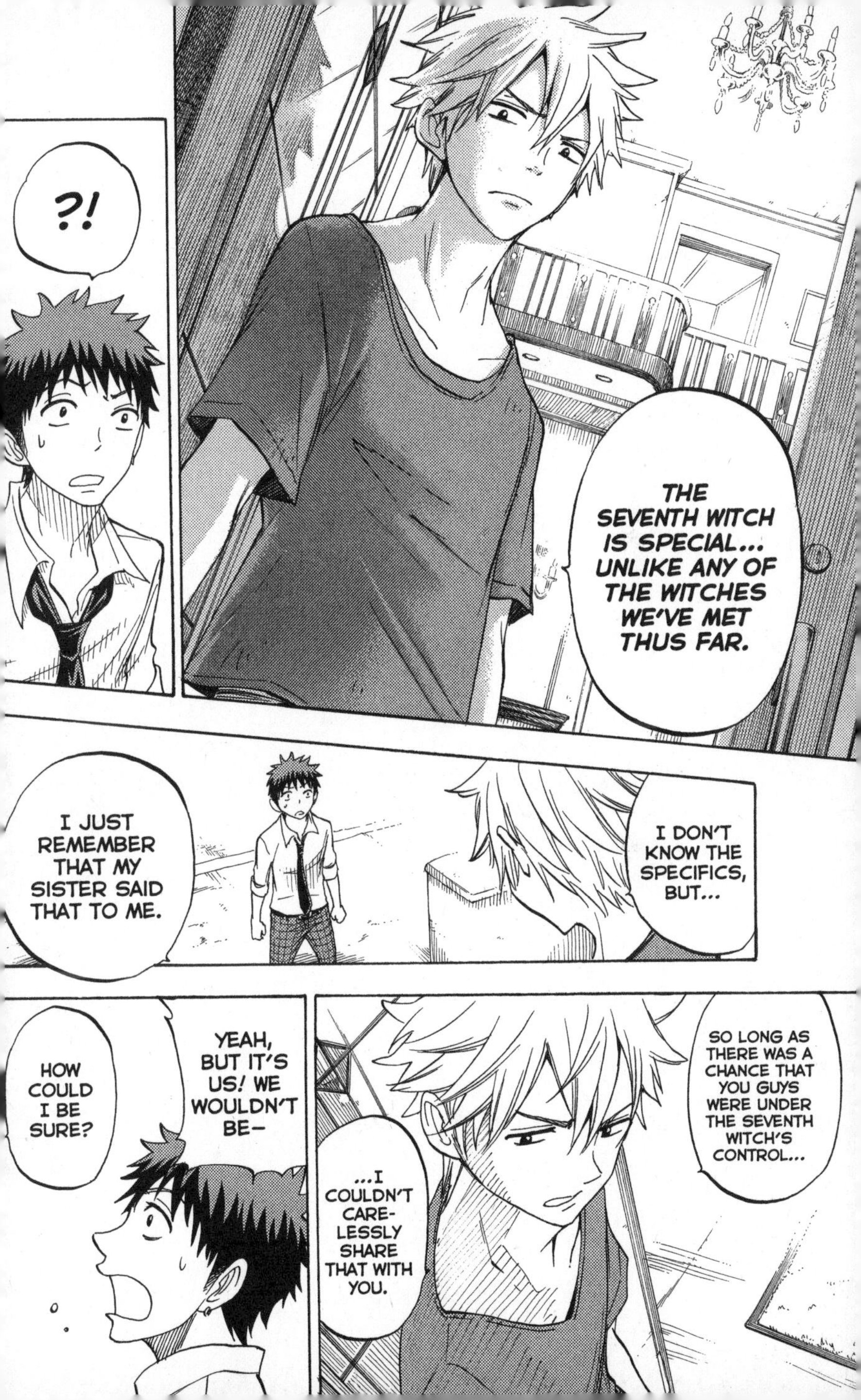
THE SEVENTH WITCH IS SPECIAL... UNLIKE ANY OF THE WITCHES WE'VE MET THUS FAR.
?!
I DON'T KNOW THE SPECIFICS, BUT...
I JUST REMEMBER THAT MY SISTER SAID THAT TO ME.
SO LONG AS THERE WAS A CHANCE THAT YOU GUYS WERE UNDER THE SEVENTH WITCH'S CONTROL...
...I COULDN'T CARELESSLY SHARE THAT WITH YOU.
YEAH, BUT IT'S US! WE WOULDN'T BE–
HOW COULD I BE SURE?

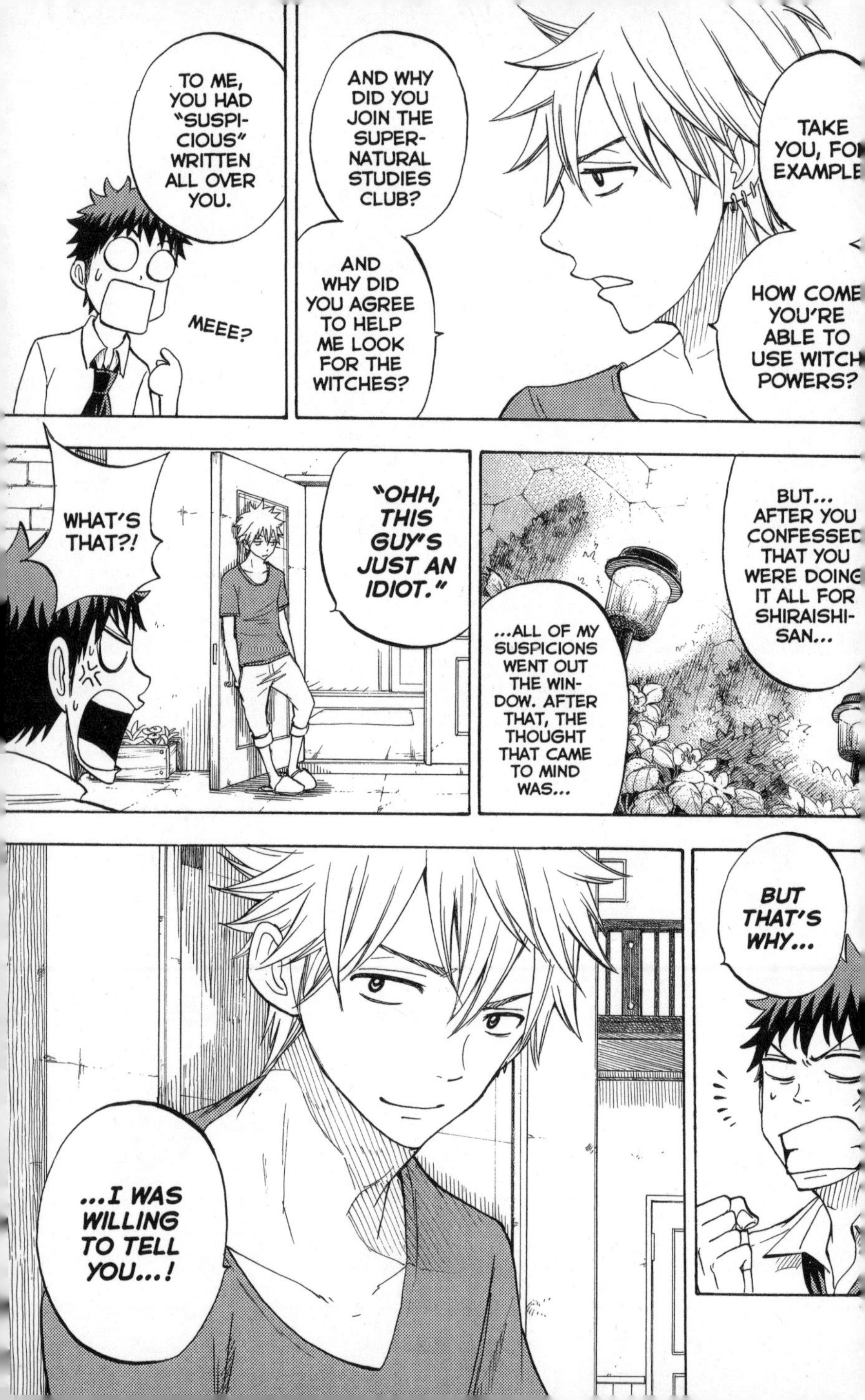
TAKE YOU, FOR EXAMPLE
HOW COME YOU'RE ABLE TO USE WITCH POWERS?
AND WHY DID YOU JOIN THE SUPERNATURAL STUDIES CLUB?
AND WHY DID YOU AGREE TO HELP ME LOOK FOR THE WITCHES?
TO ME, YOU HAD "SUSPICIOUS" WRITTEN ALL OVER YOU.
MEEE?
BUT... AFTER YOU CONFESSED THAT YOU WERE DOING IT ALL FOR SHIRAISHI-SAN...
...ALL OF MY SUSPICIONS WENT OUT THE WINDOW. AFTER THAT, THE THOUGHT THAT CAME TO MIND WAS...
"OHH, THIS GUY'S JUST AN IDIOT."
WHAT'S THAT?!
BUT THAT'S WHY...
...I WAS WILLING TO TELL YOU...!

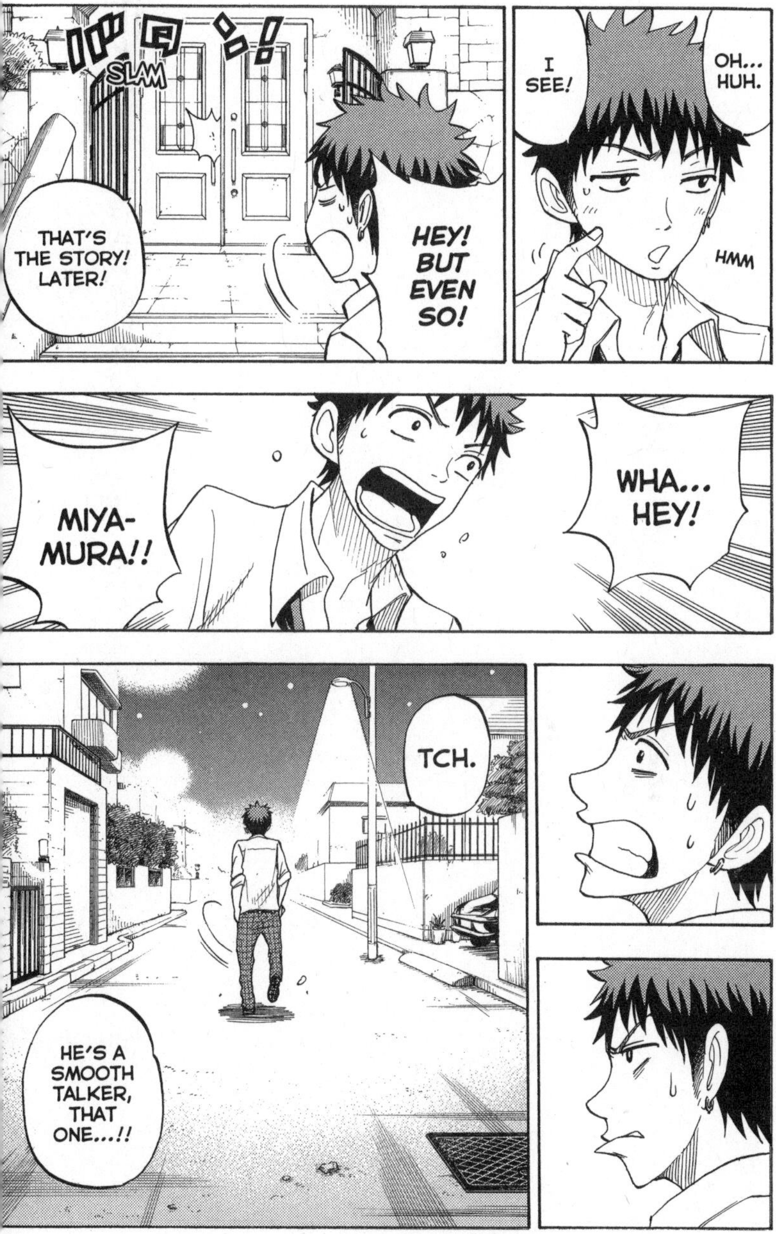
OH... HUH.
I SEE!
HMM
SLAM
HEY! BUT EVEN SO!
THAT'S THE STORY! LATER!
WHA... HEY!
MIYA-MURA!!
TCH.
HE'S A SMOOTH TALKER, THAT ONE...!!

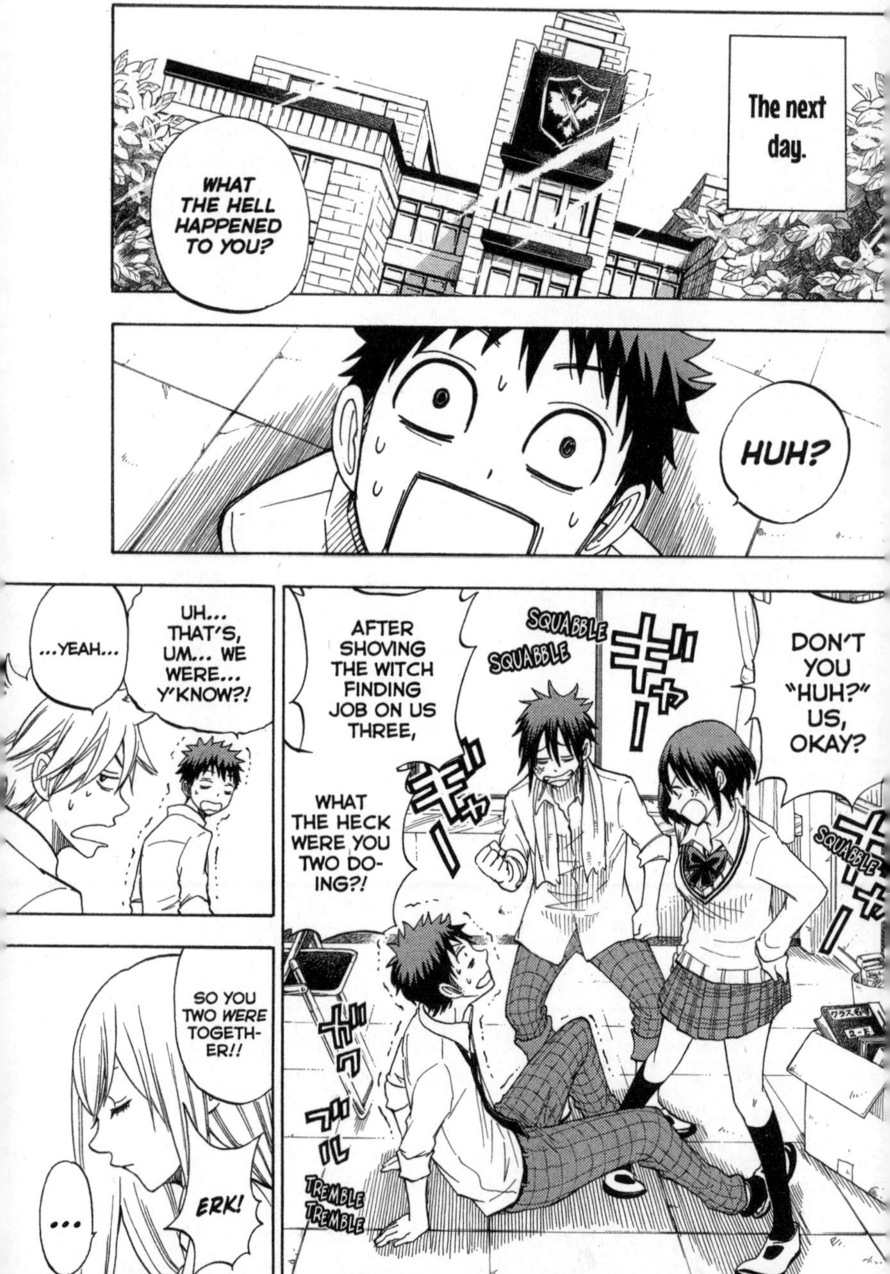
The next day.
WHAT THE HELL HAPPENED TO YOU?
HUH?
DON'T YOU "HUH?" US, OKAY?
SQUABBLE
SQUABBLE
SQUABBLE
AFTER SHOVING THE WITCH FINDING JOB ON US THREE,
WHAT THE HECK WERE YOU TWO DO-ING?!
TREMBLE TREMBLE
UH... THAT'S, UM... WE WERE... Y'KNOW?!
...YEAH...
SO YOU TWO WERE TOGETH-ER!!
ERK!
...

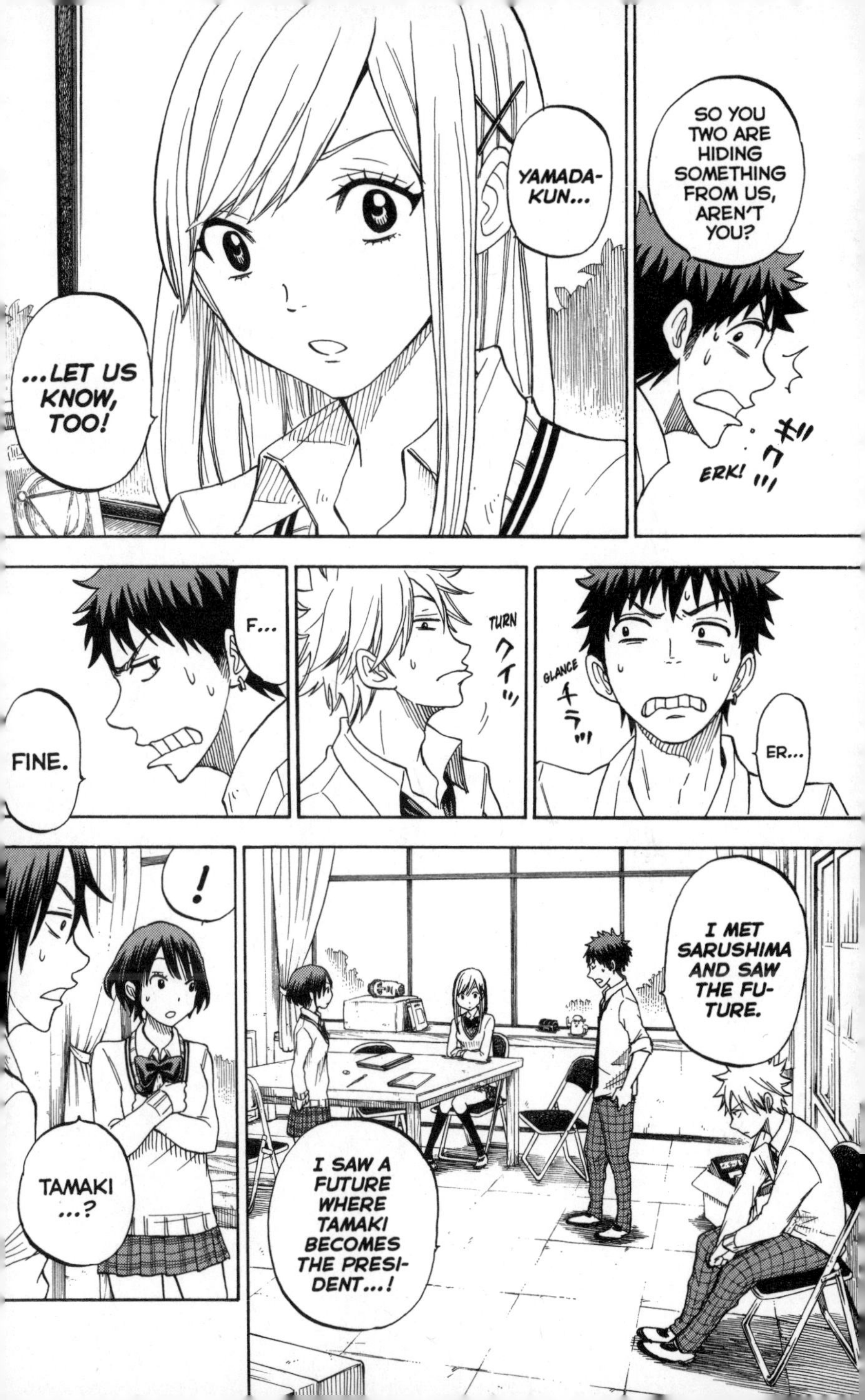
SO YOU TWO ARE HIDING SOMETHING FROM US, AREN'T YOU?
ギクッ
ERK!
YAMADA-KUN...
...LET US KNOW, TOO!
チラッ
GLANCE
ER...
クイッ
TURN
F...
FINE.
I MET SARUSHIMA AND SAW THE FUTURE.
I SAW A FUTURE WHERE TAMAKI BECOMES THE PRESIDENT...!
!
TAMAKI ...?

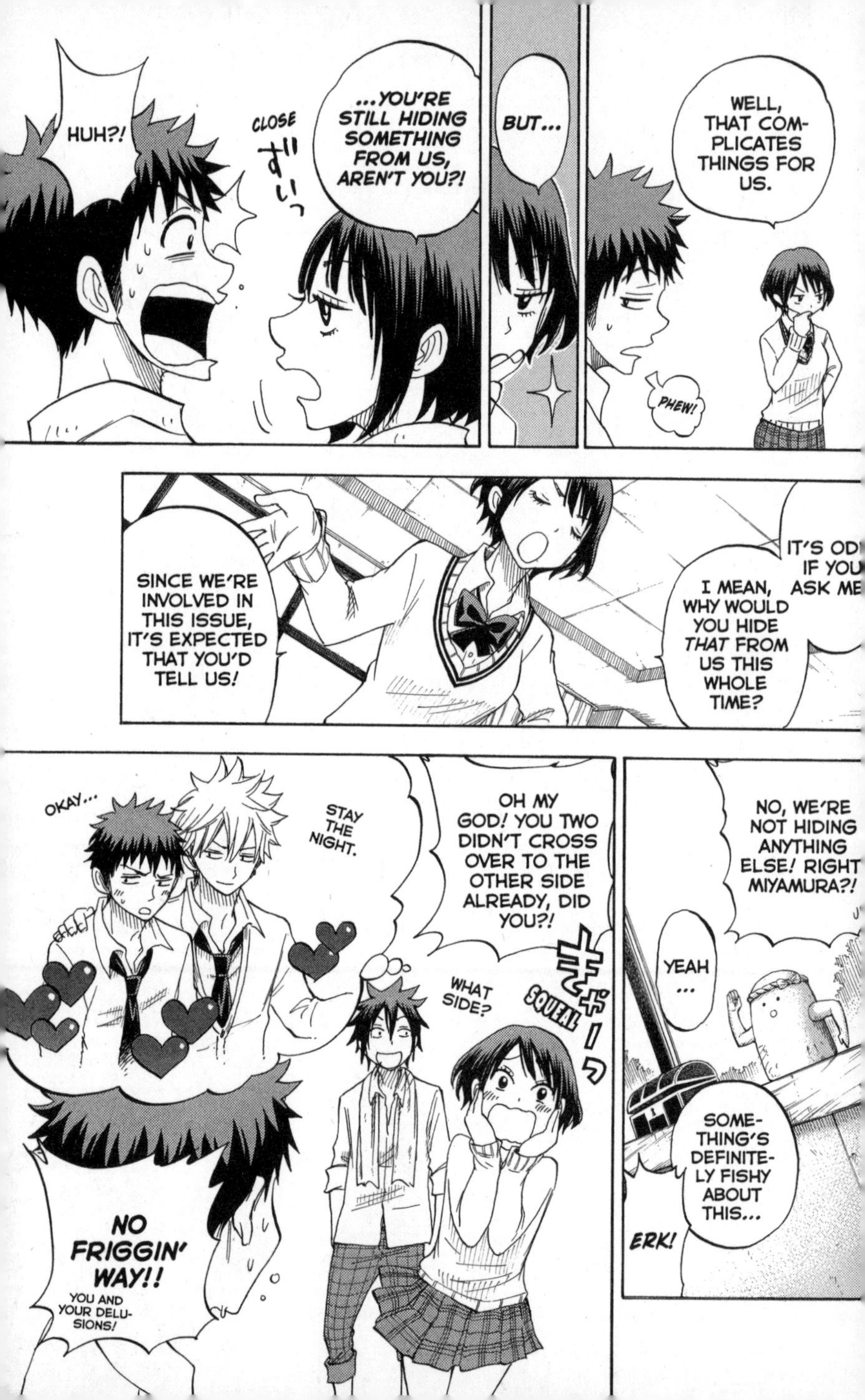
WELL, THAT COMPLICATES THINGS FOR US.
PHEW!
BUT...
...YOU'RE STILL HIDING SOMETHING FROM US, AREN'T YOU?!
CLOSE
ずいっ
HUH?!
IT'S OD IF YOU ASK ME
I MEAN, WHY WOULD YOU HIDE *THAT* FROM US THIS WHOLE TIME?
SINCE WE'RE INVOLVED IN THIS ISSUE, IT'S EXPECTED THAT YOU'D TELL US!
NO, WE'RE NOT HIDING ANYTHING ELSE! RIGHT MIYAMURA?!
YEAH...
SOMETHING'S DEFINITELY FISHY ABOUT THIS...
ERK!
OH MY GOD! YOU TWO DIDN'T CROSS OVER TO THE OTHER SIDE ALREADY, DID YOU?!
SQUEAL
WHAT SIDE?
STAY THE NIGHT.
OKAY...
NO FRIGGIN' WAY!!
YOU AND YOUR DELUSIONS!

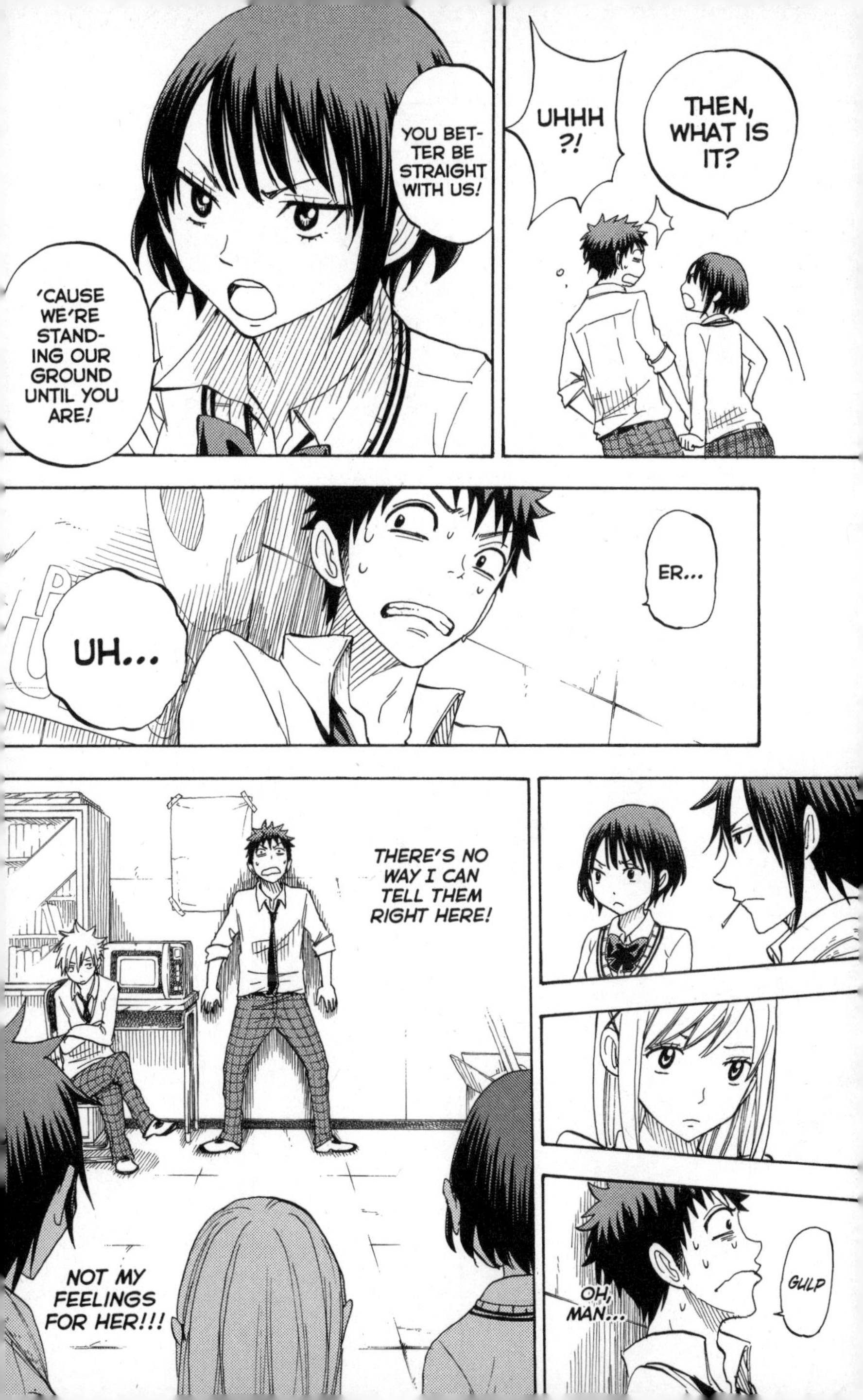
THEN, WHAT IS IT?
UHHH ?!
YOU BETTER BE STRAIGHT WITH US!
'CAUSE WE'RE STANDING OUR GROUND UNTIL YOU ARE!
ER...
UH...
GULP
OH, MAN...
THERE'S NO WAY I CAN TELL THEM RIGHT HERE!
NOT MY FEELINGS FOR HER!!!

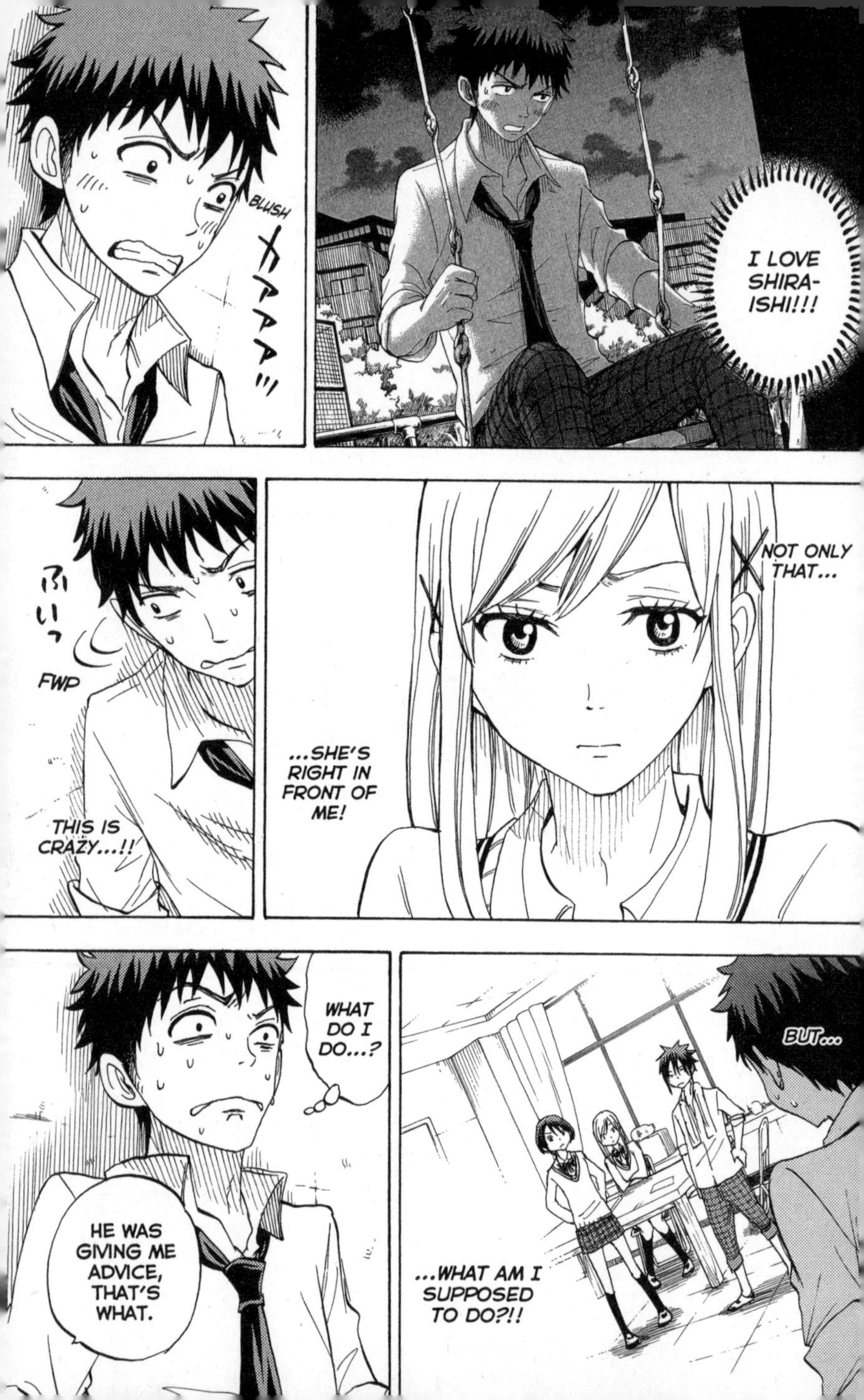

I LOVE SHIRA-ISHI!!!
BLUSH
カァァァッ
NOT ONLY THAT...
...SHE'S RIGHT IN FRONT OF ME!
ふいっ
FWP
THIS IS CRAZY...!!
BUT...
...WHAT AM I SUPPOSED TO DO?!!
WHAT DO I DO...?
HE WAS GIVING ME ADVICE, THAT'S WHAT.

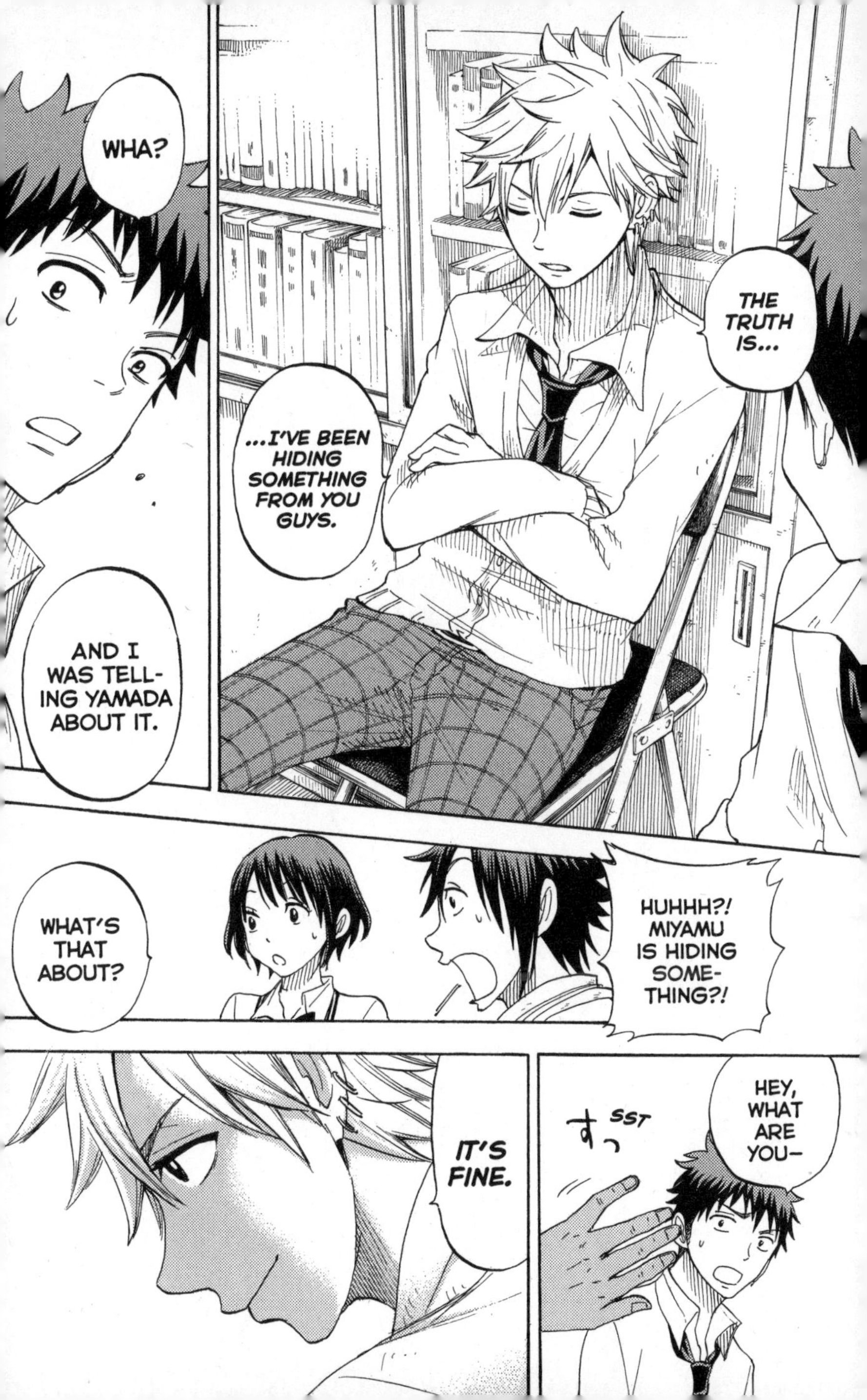

THE TRUTH IS...
...I'VE BEEN HIDING SOMETHING FROM YOU GUYS.
WHA?
AND I WAS TELLING YAMADA ABOUT IT.
HUHHH?! MIYAMU IS HIDING SOMETHING?!
WHAT'S THAT ABOUT?
HEY, WHAT ARE YOU—
すっ SST
IT'S FINE.

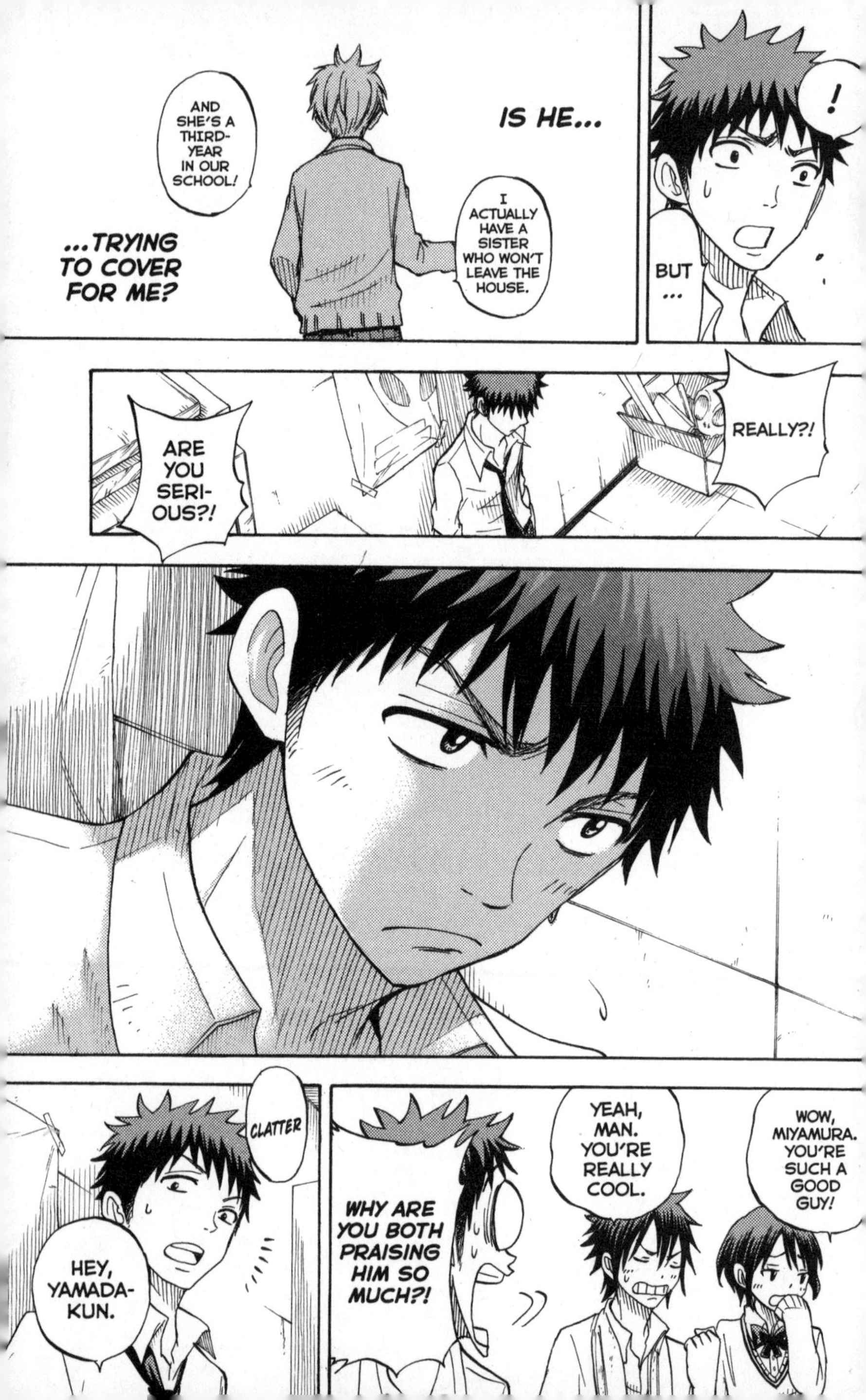
!
BUT ...
IS HE...
I ACTUALLY HAVE A SISTER WHO WON'T LEAVE THE HOUSE.
AND SHE'S A THIRD-YEAR IN OUR SCHOOL!
...TRYING TO COVER FOR ME?
REALLY?!
ARE YOU SERI-OUS?!
WOW, MIYAMURA. YOU'RE SUCH A GOOD GUY!
YEAH, MAN. YOU'RE REALLY COOL.
WHY ARE YOU BOTH PRAISING HIM SO MUCH?!
CLATTER
HEY, YAMADA-KUN.

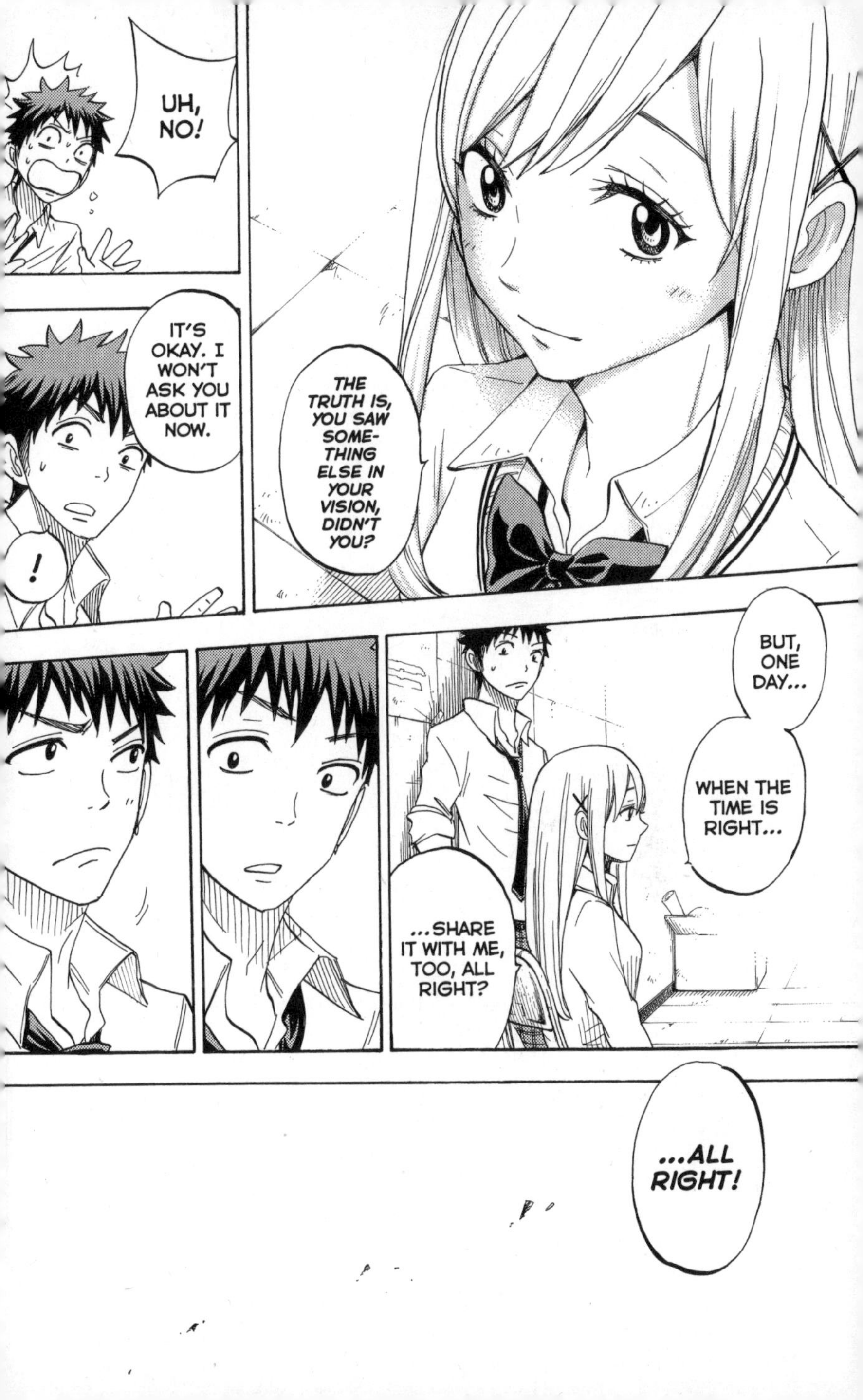
THE TRUTH IS, YOU SAW SOMETHING ELSE IN YOUR VISION, DIDN'T YOU?
UH, NO!
IT'S OKAY. I WON'T ASK YOU ABOUT IT NOW.
!
BUT, ONE DAY...
WHEN THE TIME IS RIGHT...
...SHARE IT WITH ME, TOO, ALL RIGHT?
...ALL RIGHT!

CHAPTER 60: Clang!

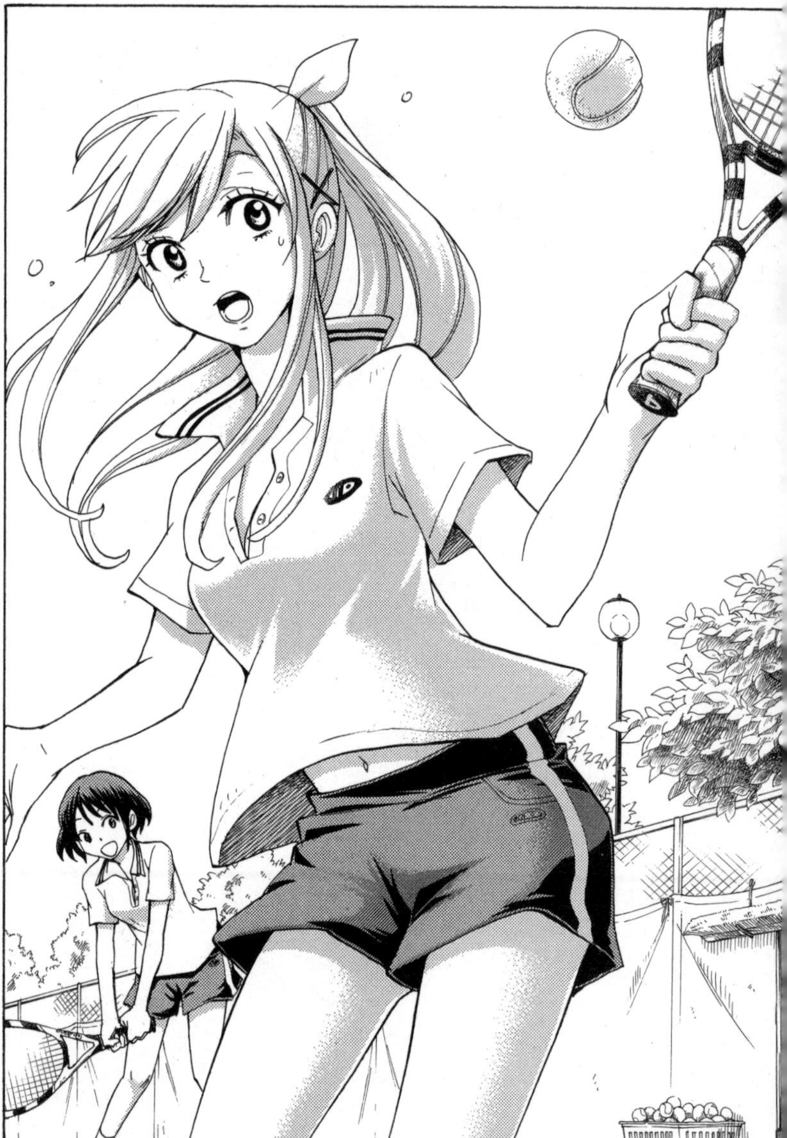

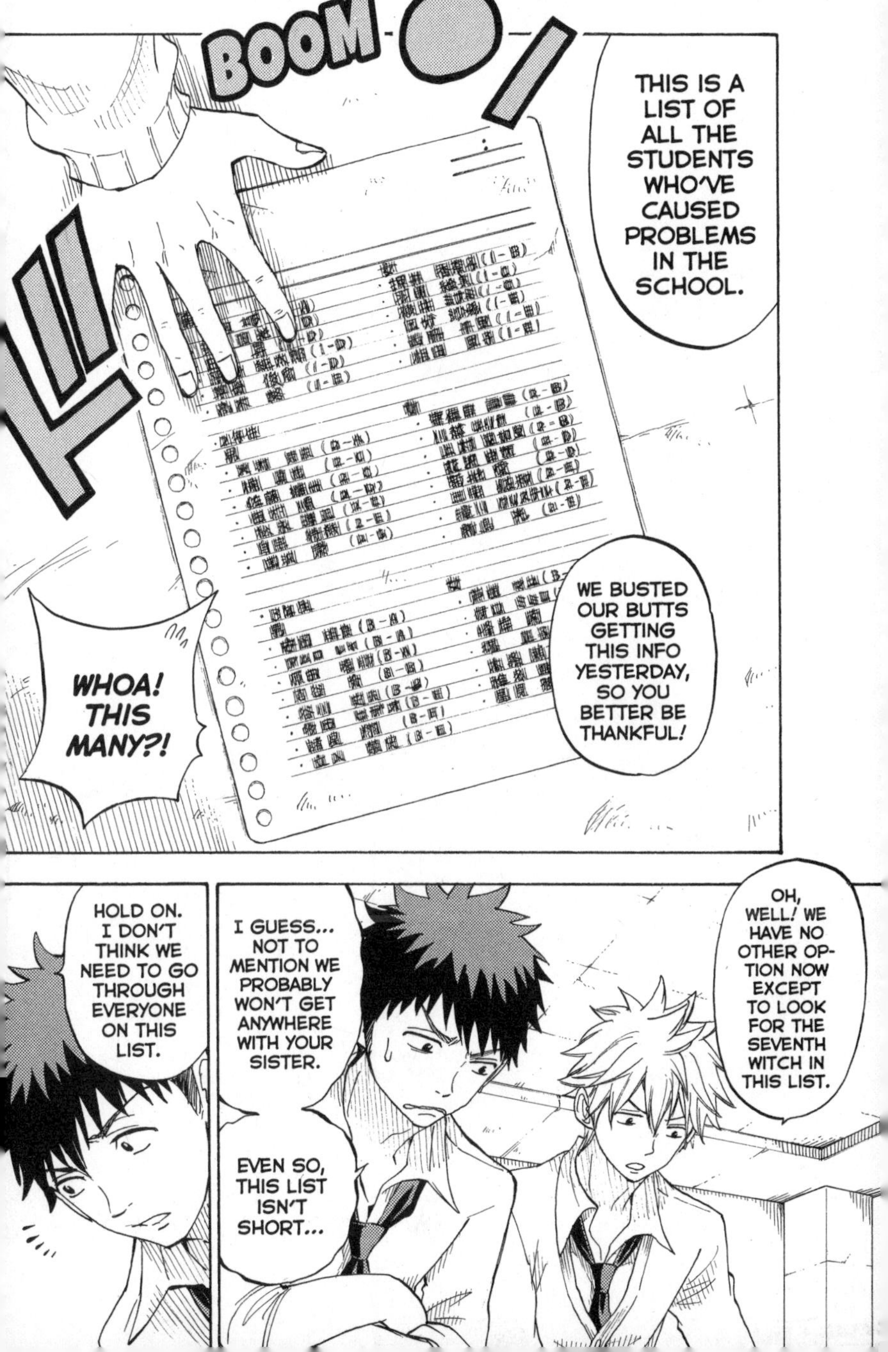
BOOM
THIS IS A LIST OF ALL THE STUDENTS WHO'VE CAUSED PROBLEMS IN THE SCHOOL.
WE BUSTED OUR BUTTS GETTING THIS INFO YESTERDAY, SO YOU BETTER BE THANKFUL!
WHOA! THIS MANY?!
OH, WELL! WE HAVE NO OTHER OPTION NOW EXCEPT TO LOOK FOR THE SEVENTH WITCH IN THIS LIST.
I GUESS... NOT TO MENTION WE PROBABLY WON'T GET ANYWHERE WITH YOUR SISTER.
EVEN SO, THIS LIST ISN'T SHORT...
HOLD ON. I DON'T THINK WE NEED TO GO THROUGH EVERYONE ON THIS LIST.

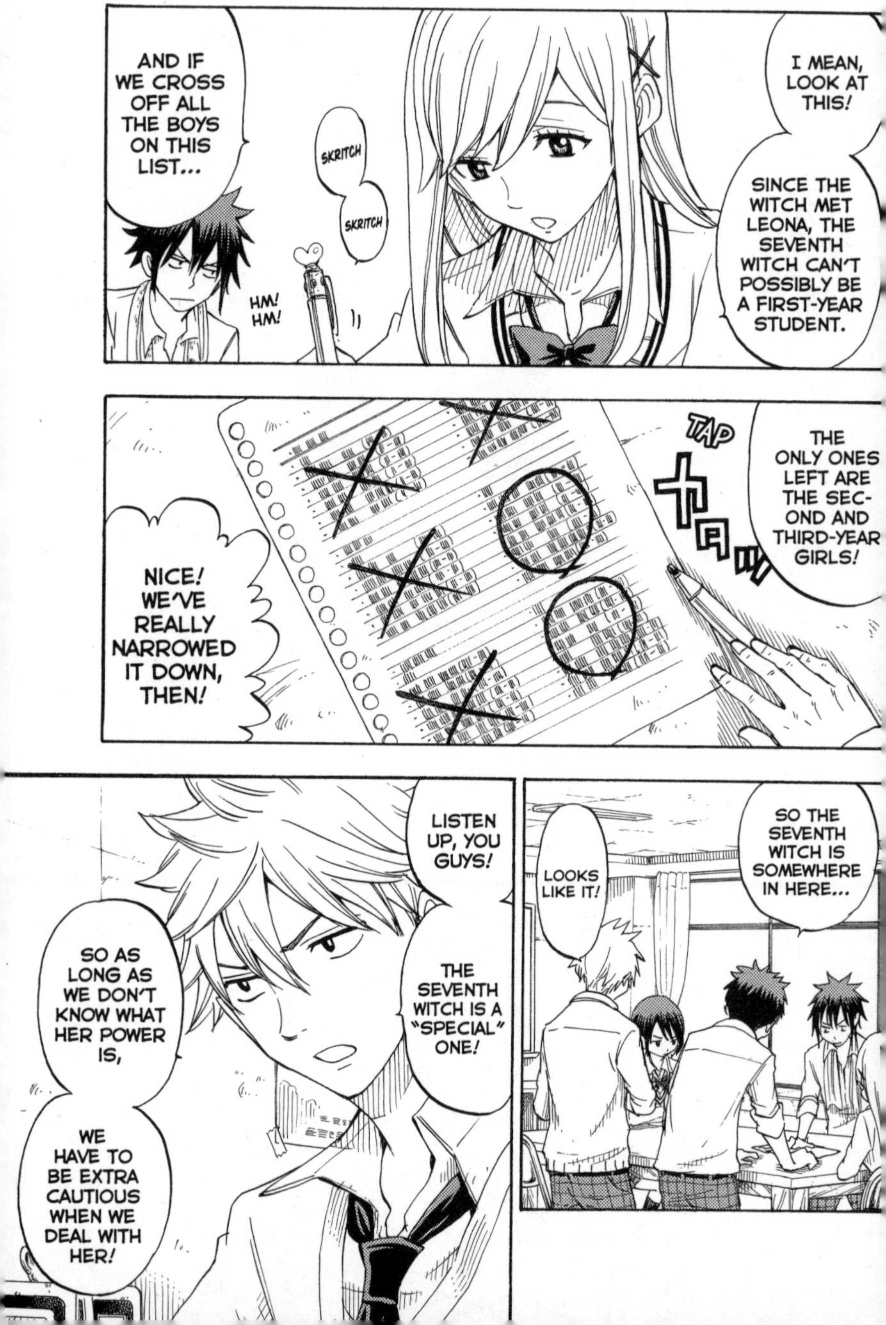
I MEAN, LOOK AT THIS!
SINCE THE WITCH MET LEONA, THE SEVENTH WITCH CAN'T POSSIBLY BE A FIRST-YEAR STUDENT.
AND IF WE CROSS OFF ALL THE BOYS ON THIS LIST...
SKRITCH
SKRITCH
HM! HM!
THE ONLY ONES LEFT ARE THE SEC-OND AND THIRD-YEAR GIRLS!
TAP
NICE! WE'VE REALLY NARROWED IT DOWN, THEN!
SO THE SEVENTH WITCH IS SOMEWHERE IN HERE...
LOOKS LIKE IT!
LISTEN UP, YOU GUYS!
THE SEVENTH WITCH IS A "SPECIAL" ONE!
SO AS LONG AS WE DON'T KNOW WHAT HER POWER IS,
WE HAVE TO BE EXTRA CAUTIOUS WHEN WE DEAL WITH HER!

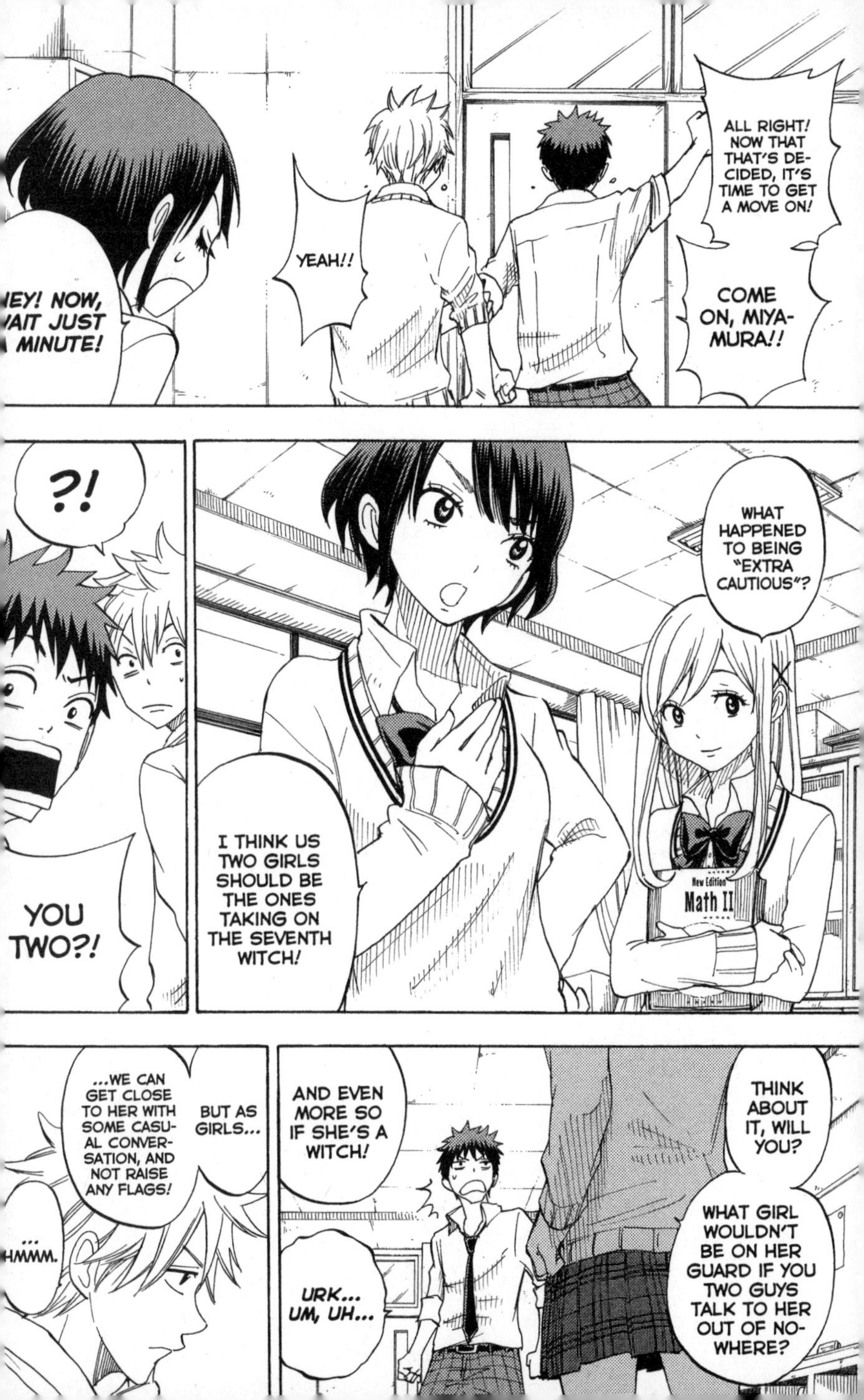
ALL RIGHT! NOW THAT THAT'S DECIDED, IT'S TIME TO GET A MOVE ON!
COME ON, MIYAMURA!!
YEAH!!
EY! NOW, AIT JUST MINUTE!
WHAT HAPPENED TO BEING "EXTRA CAUTIOUS"?
I THINK US TWO GIRLS SHOULD BE THE ONES TAKING ON THE SEVENTH WITCH!
New Edition Math II
?!
YOU TWO?!
THINK ABOUT IT, WILL YOU?
WHAT GIRL WOULDN'T BE ON HER GUARD IF YOU TWO GUYS TALK TO HER OUT OF NOWHERE?
AND EVEN MORE SO IF SHE'S A WITCH!
URK... UM, UH...
BUT AS GIRLS...
...WE CAN GET CLOSE TO HER WITH SOME CASUAL CONVERSATION, AND NOT RAISE ANY FLAGS!
... HMMM.

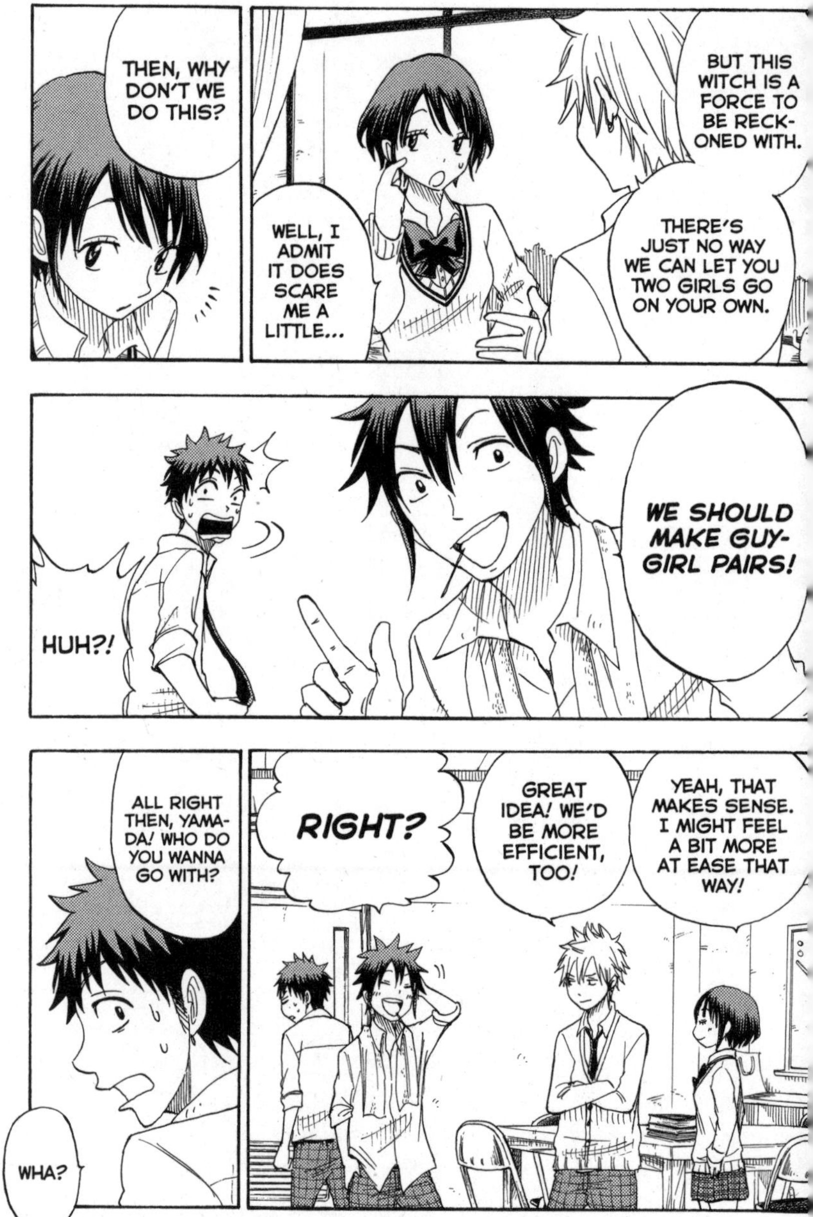
BUT THIS WITCH IS A FORCE TO BE RECKONED WITH.
THERE'S JUST NO WAY WE CAN LET YOU TWO GIRLS GO ON YOUR OWN.
WELL, I ADMIT IT DOES SCARE ME A LITTLE...
THEN, WHY DON'T WE DO THIS?
WE SHOULD MAKE GUY-GIRL PAIRS!
HUH?!
YEAH, THAT MAKES SENSE. I MIGHT FEEL A BIT MORE AT EASE THAT WAY!
GREAT IDEA! WE'D BE MORE EFFICIENT, TOO!
RIGHT?
ALL RIGHT THEN, YAMADA! WHO DO YOU WANNA GO WITH?
WHA?

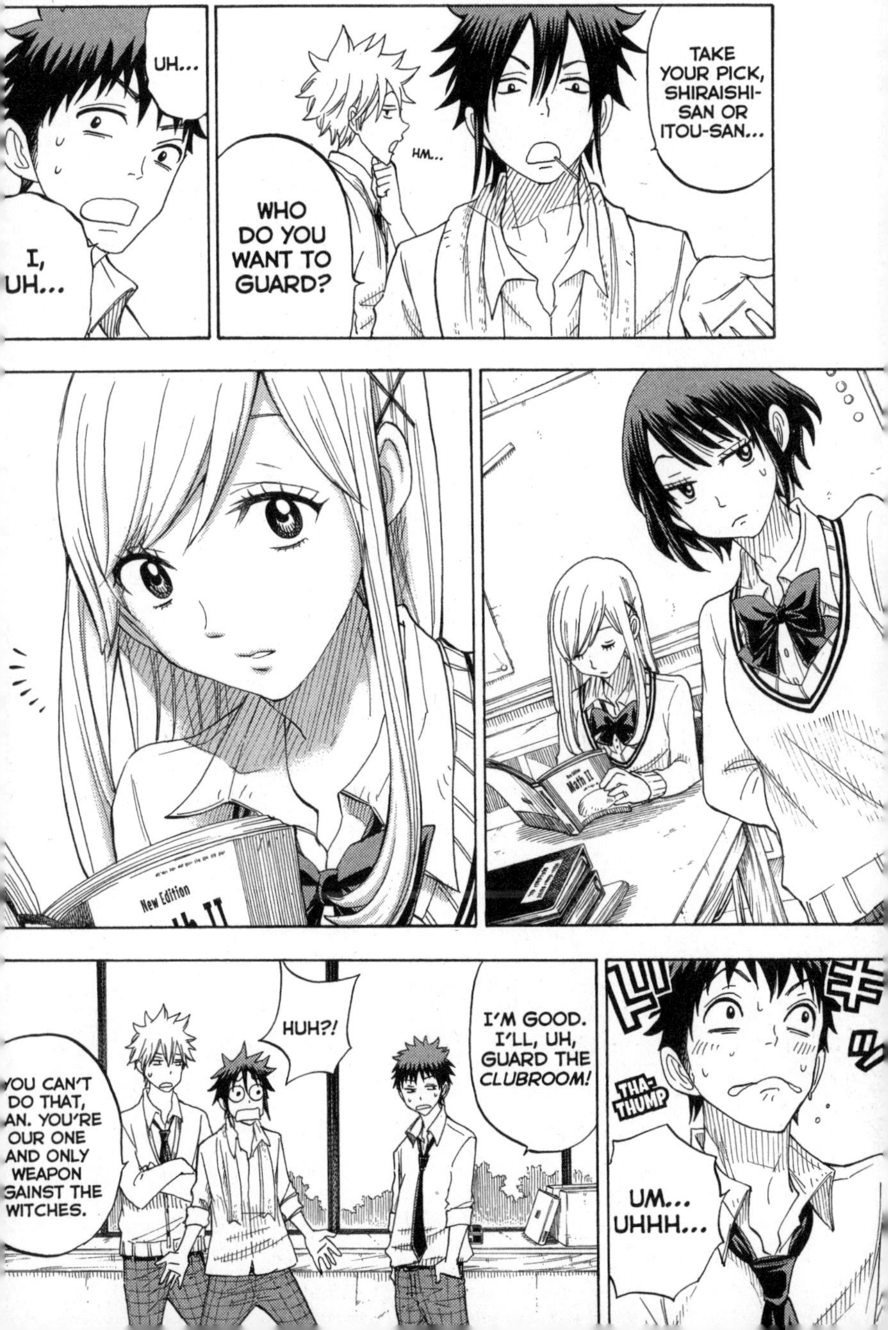
TAKE YOUR PICK, SHIRAISHI-SAN OR ITOU-SAN...
HM...
WHO DO YOU WANT TO GUARD?
UH...
I, UH...
THA-THUMP
UM... UHHH...
I'M GOOD. I'LL, UH, GUARD THE *CLUBROOM!*
HUH?!
YOU CAN'T DO THAT, AN. YOU'RE OUR ONE AND ONLY WEAPON GAINST THE WITCHES.

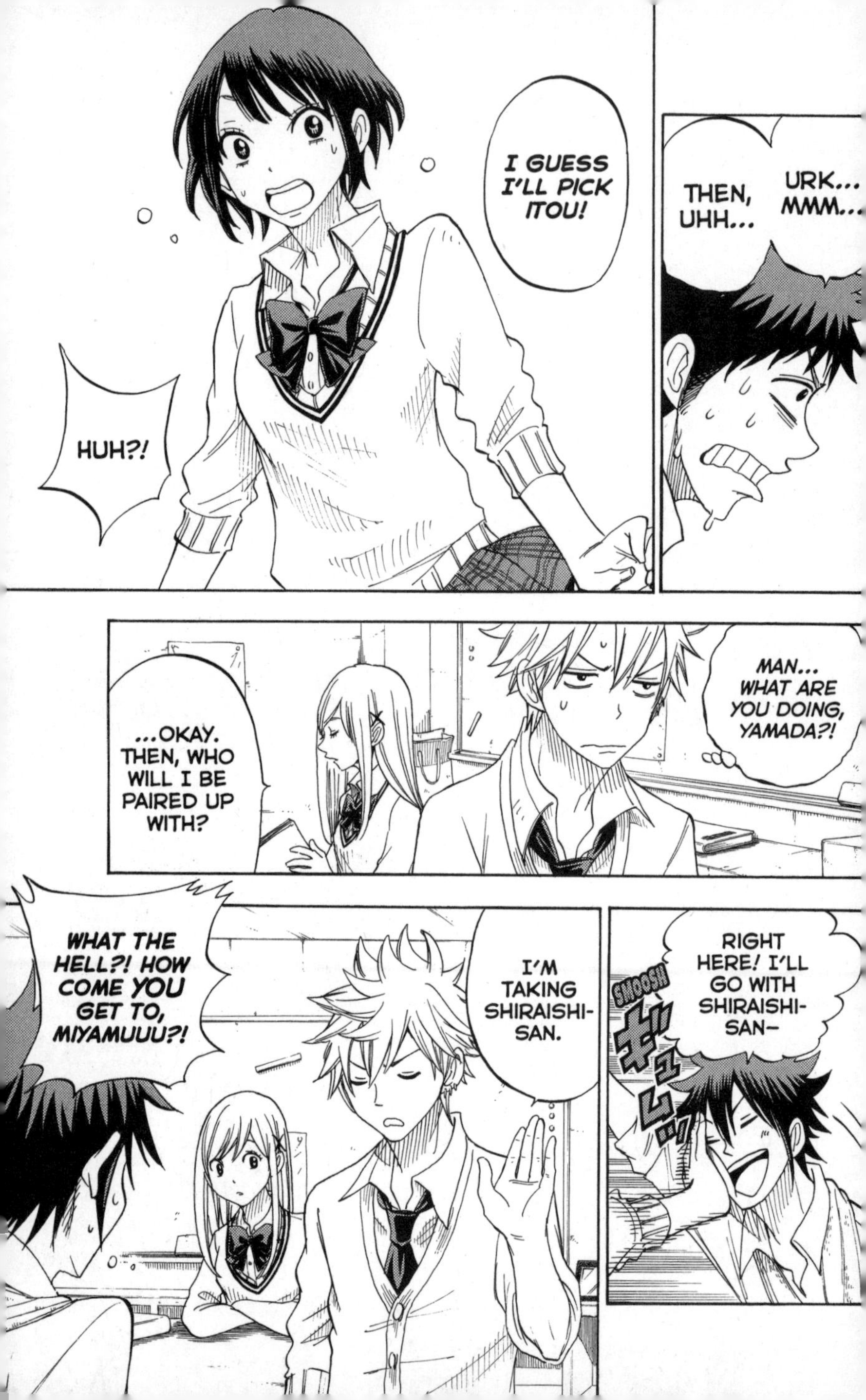
URK... MMM...
THEN, UHH...
I GUESS I'LL PICK ITOU!
HUH?!
MAN... WHAT ARE YOU DOING, YAMADA?!
...OKAY. THEN, WHO WILL I BE PAIRED UP WITH?
RIGHT HERE! I'LL GO WITH SHIRAISHI-SAN–
SMOOSH
I'M TAKING SHIRAISHI-SAN.
WHAT THE HELL?! HOW COME YOU GET TO, MIYAMUUU?!

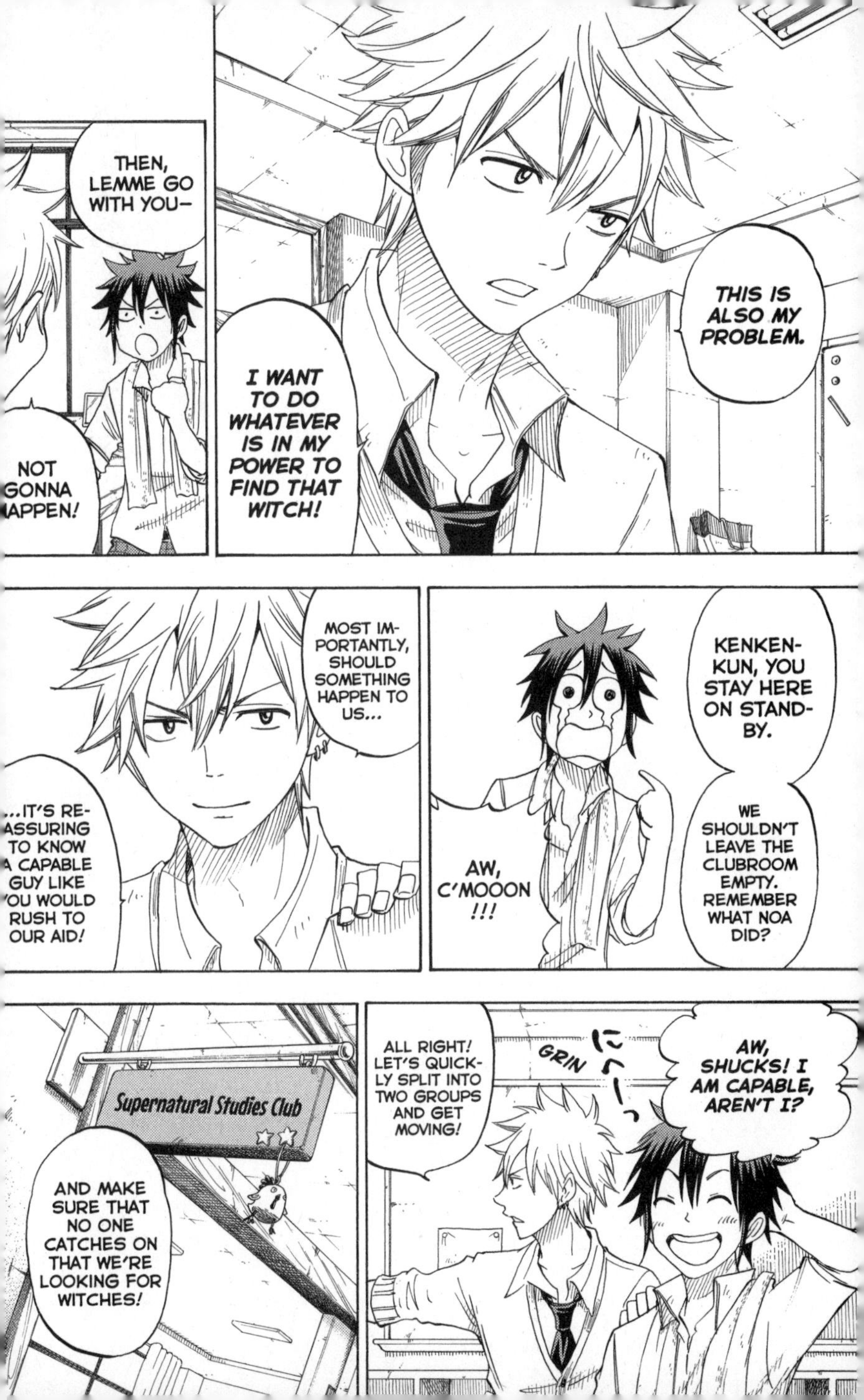
THIS IS ALSO MY PROBLEM.
I WANT TO DO WHATEVER IS IN MY POWER TO FIND THAT WITCH!
THEN, LEMME GO WITH YOU–
NOT GONNA APPEN!
KENKEN-KUN, YOU STAY HERE ON STAND-BY.
WE SHOULDN'T LEAVE THE CLUBROOM EMPTY. REMEMBER WHAT NOA DID?
AW, C'MOOON !!!
MOST IMPORTANTLY, SHOULD SOMETHING HAPPEN TO US...
...IT'S RE-ASSURING TO KNOW A CAPABLE GUY LIKE 'OU WOULD RUSH TO OUR AID!
AW, SHUCKS! I AM CAPABLE, AREN'T I?
GRIN
にへーっ
ALL RIGHT! LET'S QUICKLY SPLIT INTO TWO GROUPS AND GET MOVING!
Supernatural Studies Club
AND MAKE SURE THAT NO ONE CATCHES ON THAT WE'RE LOOKING FOR WITCHES!

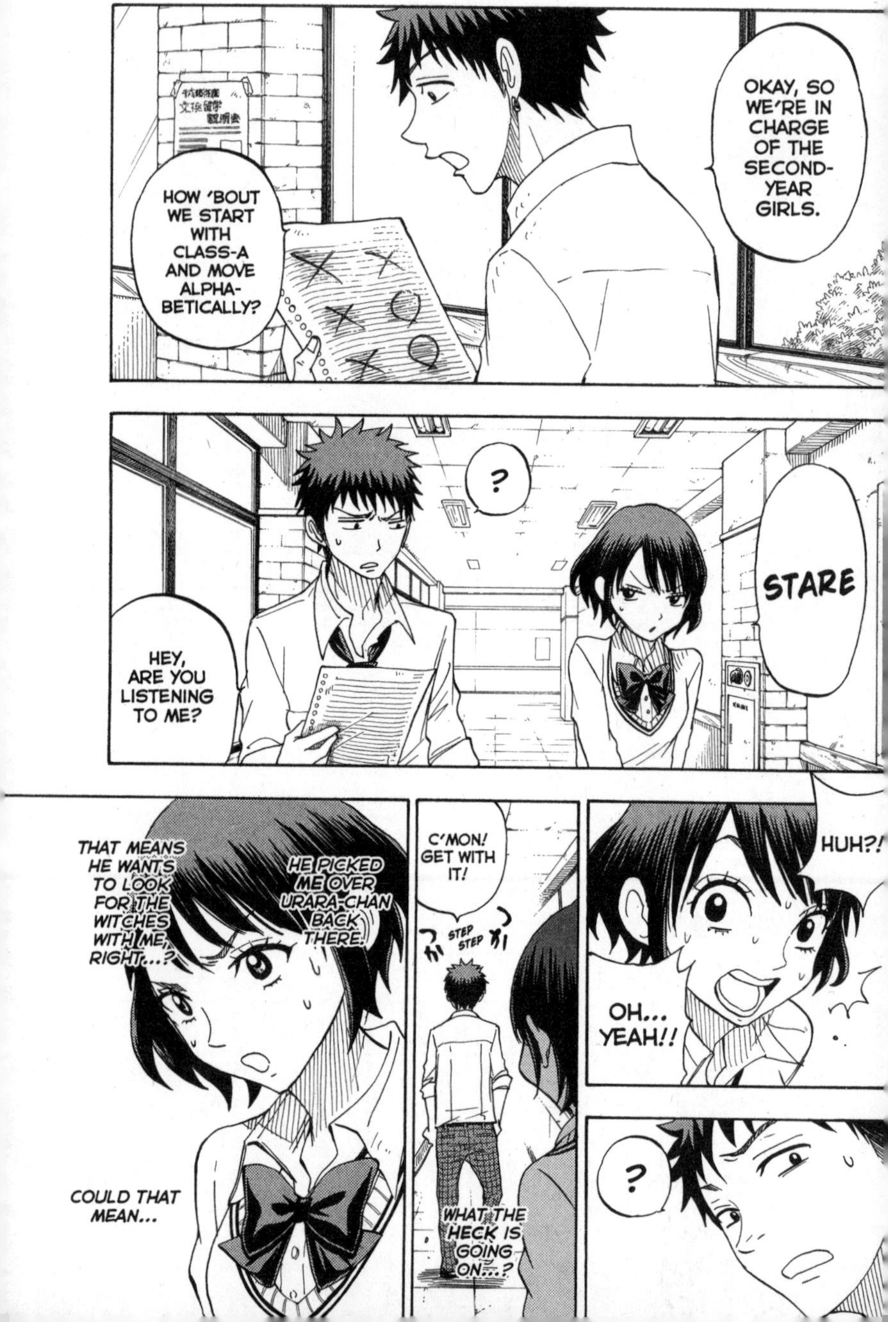
OKAY, SO WE'RE IN CHARGE OF THE SECOND-YEAR GIRLS.
HOW 'BOUT WE START WITH CLASS-A AND MOVE ALPHA-BETICALLY?
STARE
?
HEY, ARE YOU LISTENING TO ME?
HUH?!
OH... YEAH!!
?
C'MON! GET WITH IT!
STEP STEP
WHAT THE HECK IS GOING ON...?
HE PICKED ME OVER URARA-CHAN BACK THERE.
THAT MEANS HE WANTS TO LOOK FOR THE WITCHES WITH ME, RIGHT...?
COULD THAT MEAN...

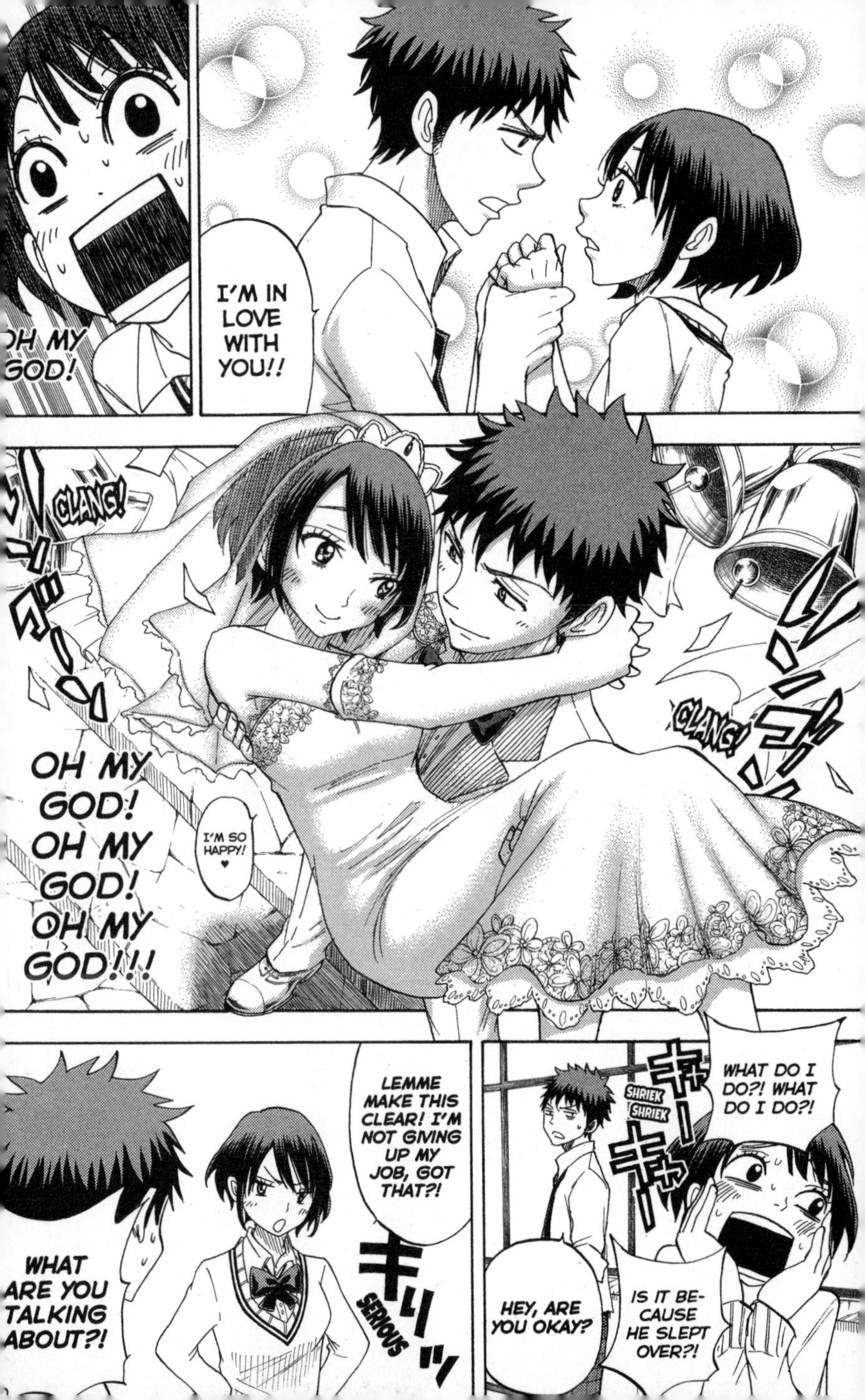

I'M IN LOVE WITH YOU!!
OH MY GOD!
CLANG!
CLANG!
I'M SO HAPPY! ♥
OH MY GOD! OH MY GOD! OH MY GOD!!!
WHAT DO I DO?! WHAT DO I DO?!
SHRIEK SHRIEK
IS IT BE-CAUSE HE SLEPT OVER?!
HEY, ARE YOU OKAY?
LEMME MAKE THIS CLEAR! I'M NOT GIVING UP MY JOB, GOT THAT?!
SERIOUS
WHAT ARE YOU TALKING ABOUT?!

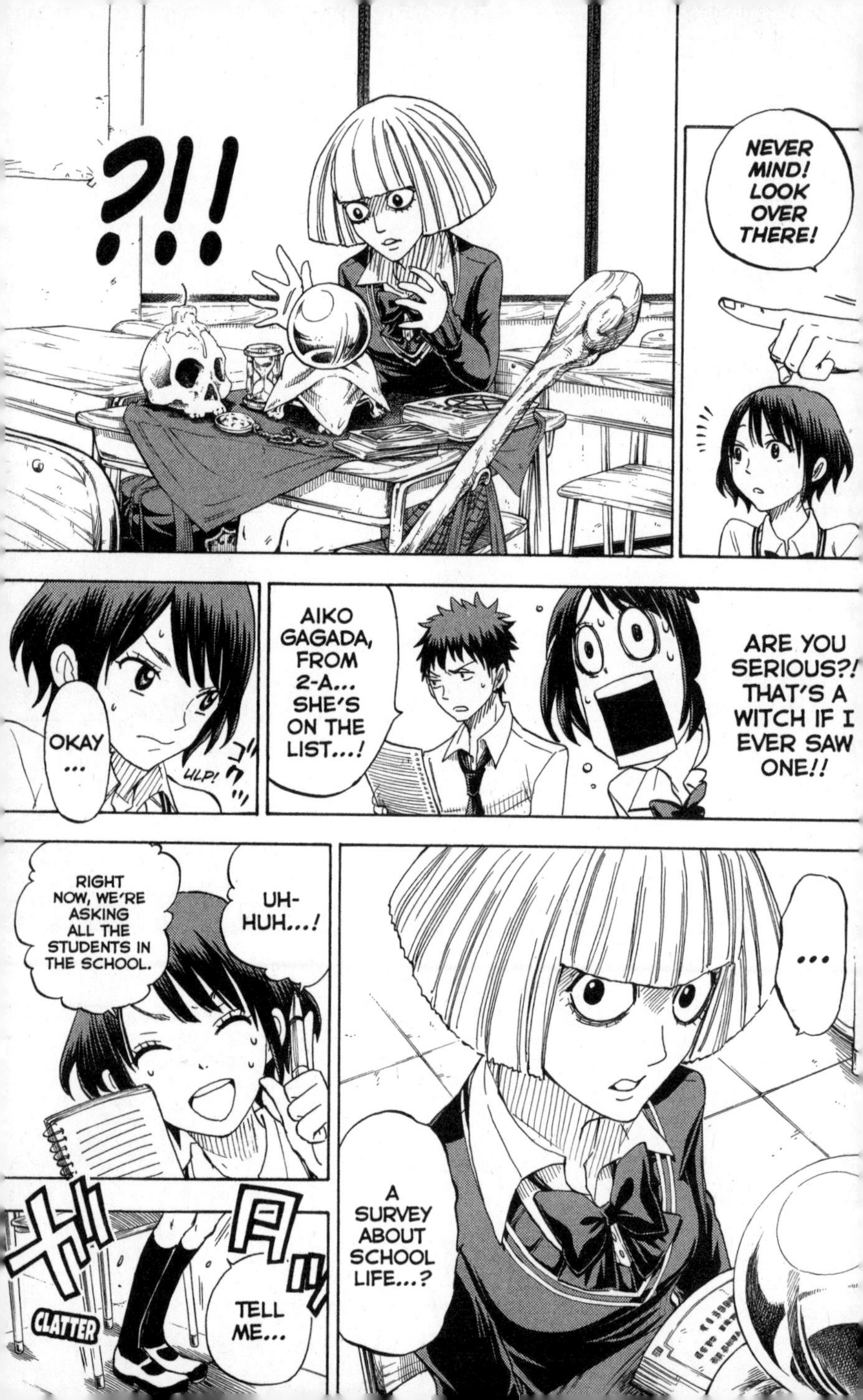
NEVER MIND! LOOK OVER THERE!
?!!
ARE YOU SERIOUS?! THAT'S A WITCH IF I EVER SAW ONE!!
AIKO GAGADA, FROM 2-A... SHE'S ON THE LIST...!
ULP!
OKAY...
...
A SURVEY ABOUT SCHOOL LIFE...?
UH-HUH...!
RIGHT NOW, WE'RE ASKING ALL THE STUDENTS IN THE SCHOOL.
TELL ME...
CLATTER

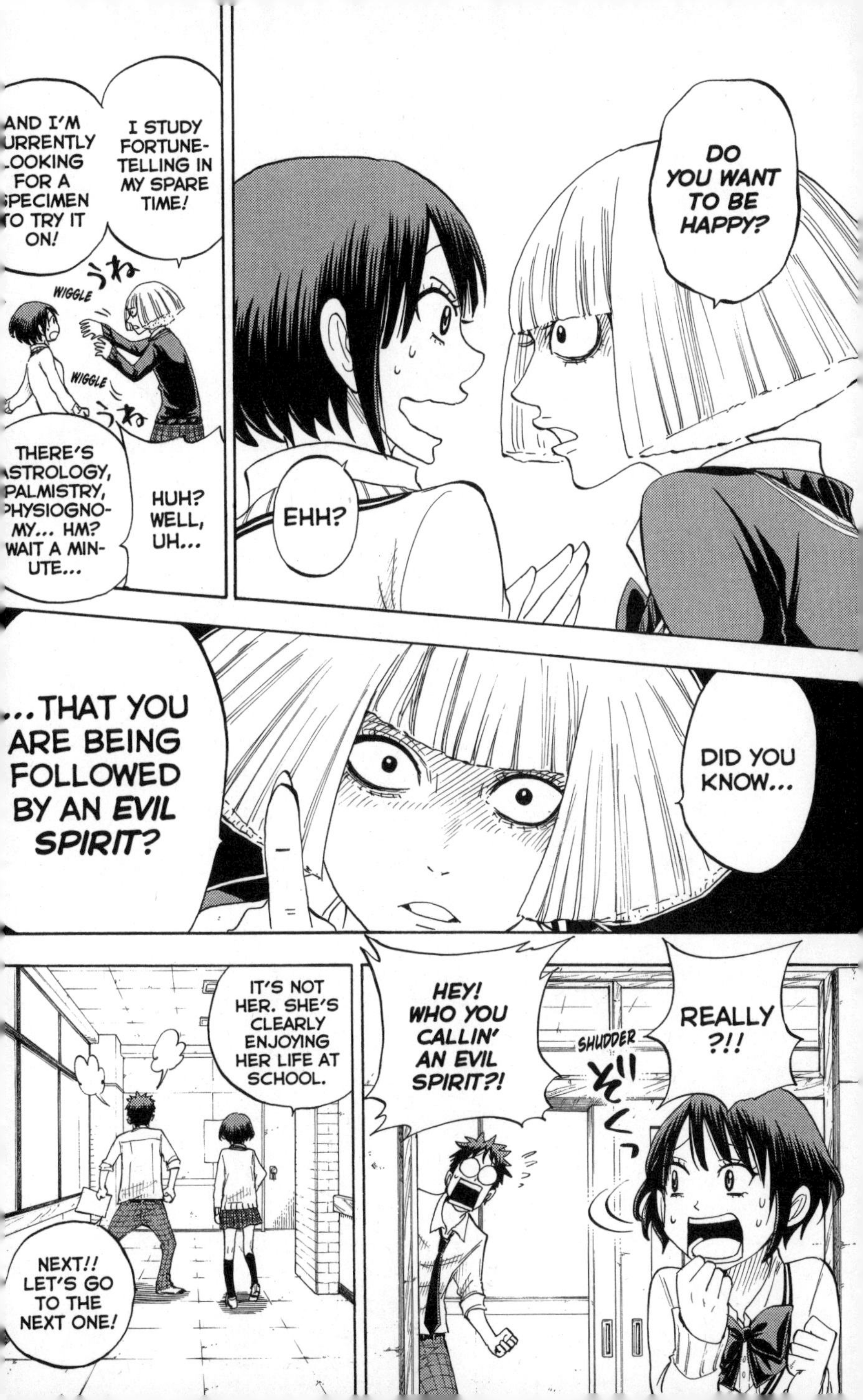
DO YOU WANT TO BE HAPPY?
EHH?
I STUDY FORTUNE-TELLING IN MY SPARE TIME!
AND I'M URRENTLY OOKING FOR A PECIMEN O TRY IT ON!
うね WIGGLE
WIGGLE うね
HUH? WELL, UH...
THERE'S STROLOGY, PALMISTRY, HYSIOGNO-MY... HM? WAIT A MIN-UTE...
DID YOU KNOW...
...THAT YOU ARE BEING FOLLOWED BY AN EVIL SPIRIT?
REALLY ?!!
SHUDDER ぞくっ
HEY! WHO YOU CALLIN' AN EVIL SPIRIT?!
IT'S NOT HER. SHE'S CLEARLY ENJOYING HER LIFE AT SCHOOL.
NEXT!! LET'S GO TO THE NEXT ONE!

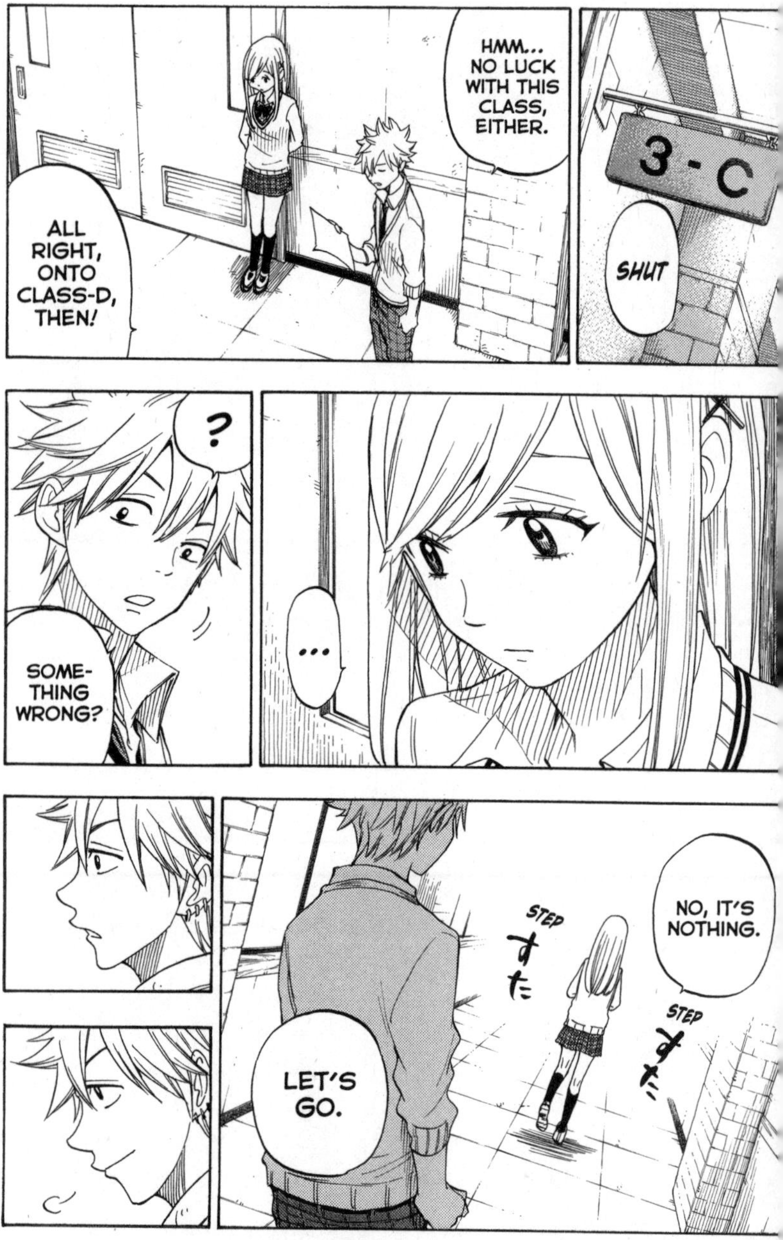
3 - C
SHUT
HMM... NO LUCK WITH THIS CLASS, EITHER.
ALL RIGHT, ONTO CLASS-D, THEN!
...
?
SOME-THING WRONG?
NO, IT'S NOTHING.
STEP すた
STEP すた
LET'S GO.

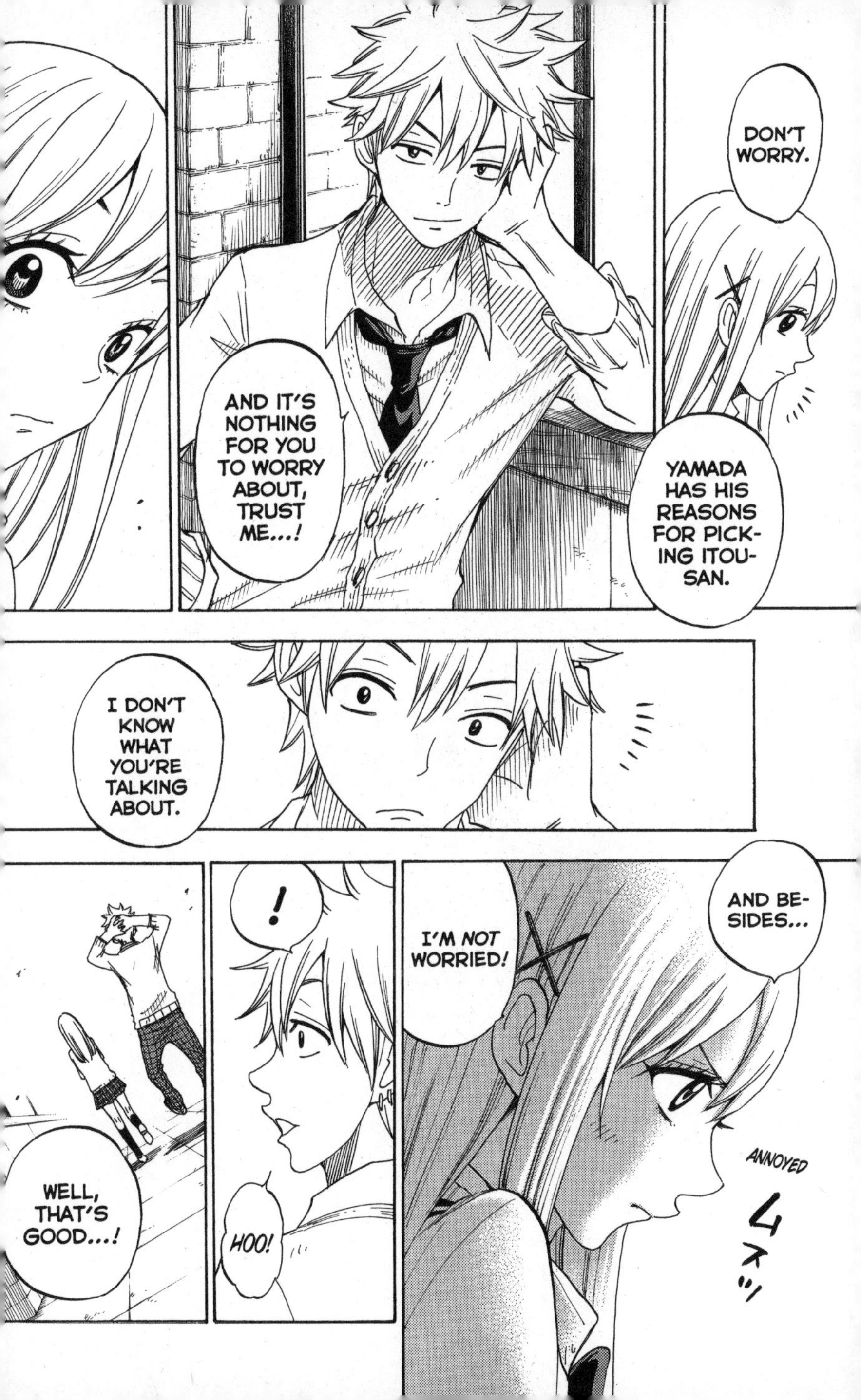
DON'T WORRY.
YAMADA HAS HIS REASONS FOR PICK-ING ITOU-SAN.
AND IT'S NOTHING FOR YOU TO WORRY ABOUT, TRUST ME...!
I DON'T KNOW WHAT YOU'RE TALKING ABOUT.
AND BE-SIDES...
I'M *NOT* WORRIED!
ANNOYED
ムスッ
!
HOO!
WELL, THAT'S GOOD...!

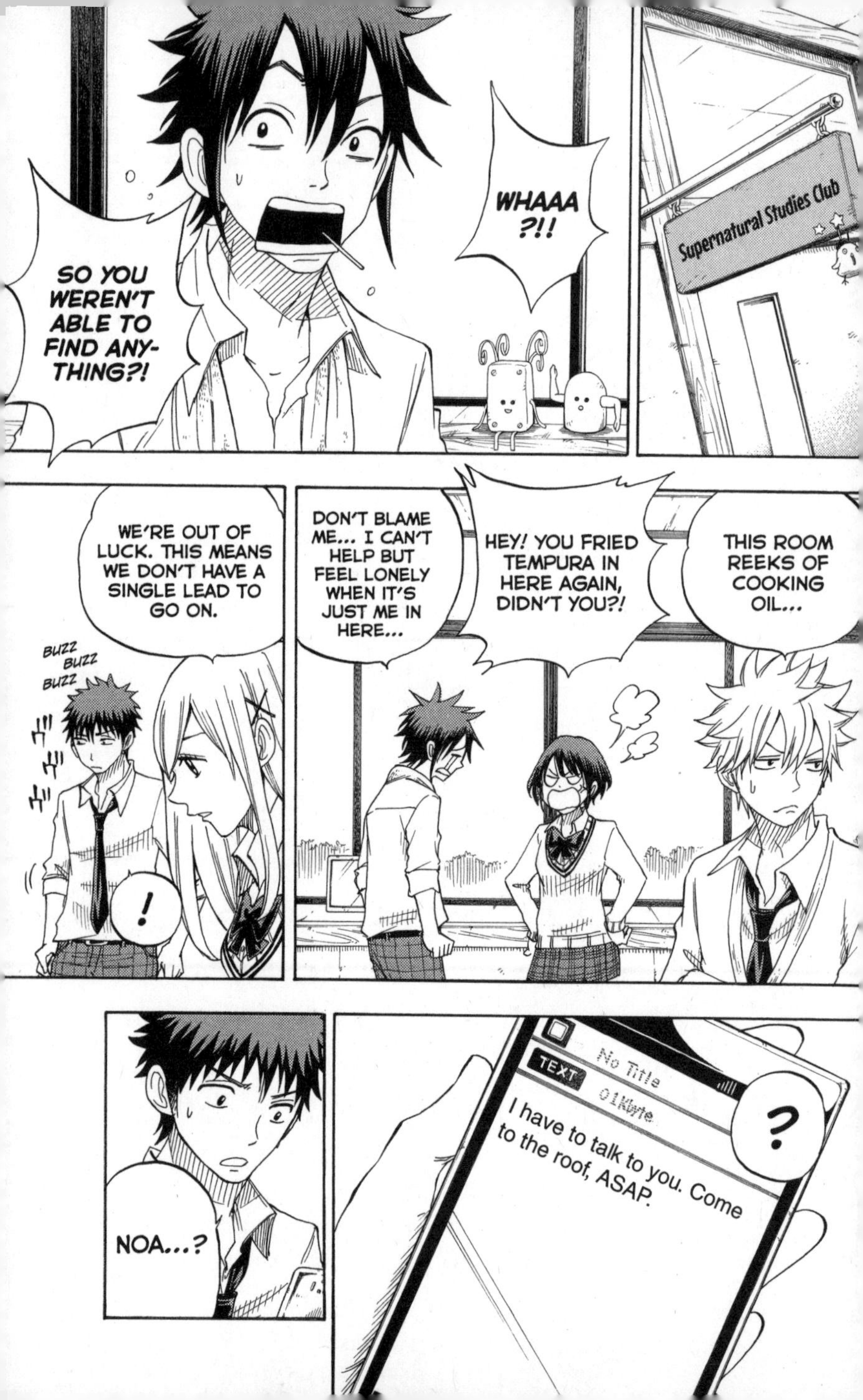
Supernatural Studies Club
WHAAA ?!!
SO YOU WEREN'T ABLE TO FIND ANY-THING?!
THIS ROOM REEKS OF COOKING OIL...
HEY! YOU FRIED TEMPURA IN HERE AGAIN, DIDN'T YOU?!
DON'T BLAME ME... I CAN'T HELP BUT FEEL LONELY WHEN IT'S JUST ME IN HERE...
WE'RE OUT OF LUCK. THIS MEANS WE DON'T HAVE A SINGLE LEAD TO GO ON.
BUZZ BUZZ BUZZ
!
TEXT
No Title
01Kbyte
I have to talk to you. Come to the roof, ASAP.
?
NOA...?

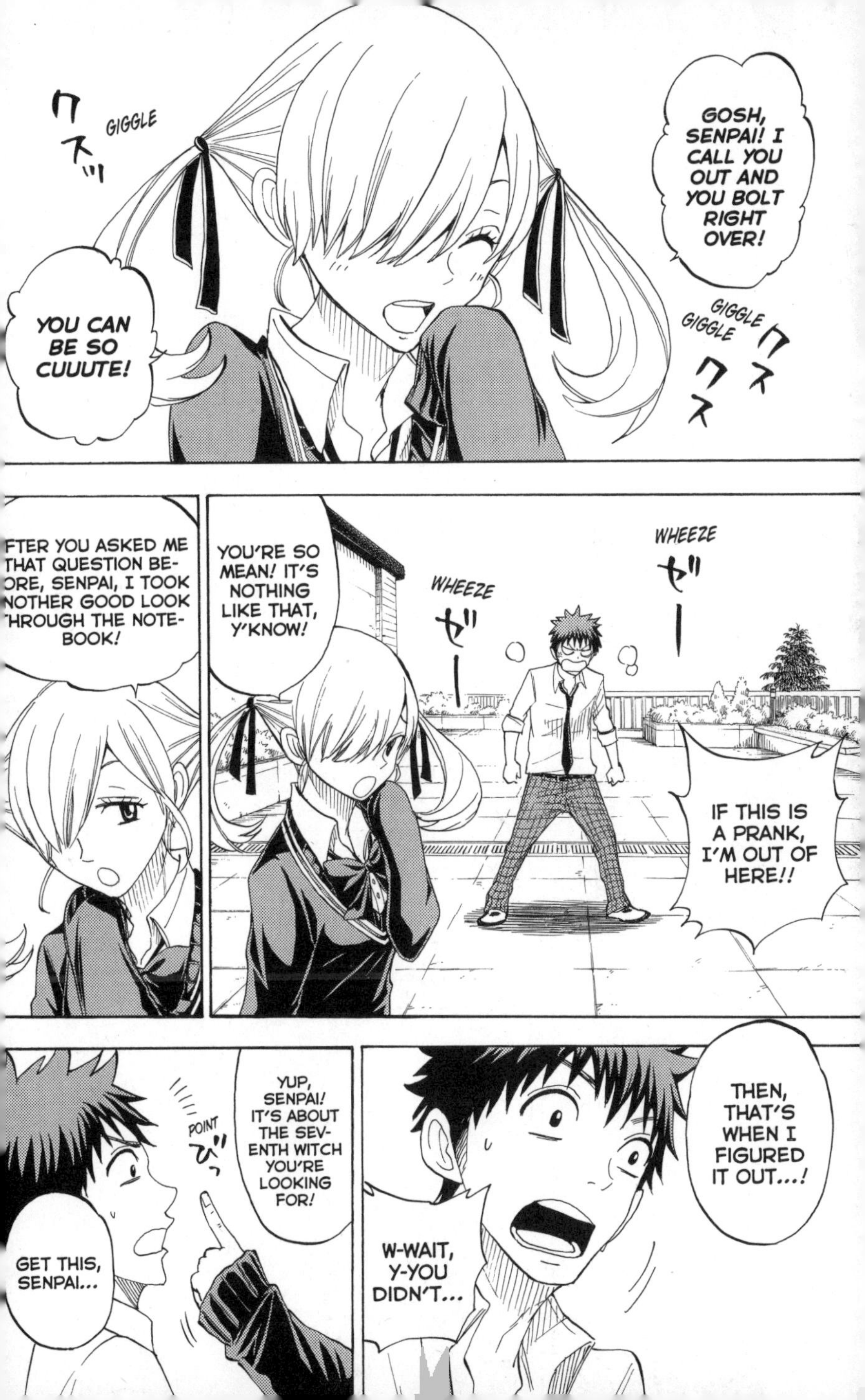
GOSH, SENPAI! I CALL YOU OUT AND YOU BOLT RIGHT OVER!
GIGGLE GIGGLE
クスクス
クスッ
GIGGLE
YOU CAN BE SO CUUUTE!
WHEEZE
ゼー
WHEEZE
ゼー
IF THIS IS A PRANK, I'M OUT OF HERE!!
YOU'RE SO MEAN! IT'S NOTHING LIKE THAT, Y'KNOW!
FTER YOU ASKED ME THAT QUESTION BE-ORE, SENPAI, I TOOK NOTHER GOOD LOOK THROUGH THE NOTEBOOK!
THEN, THAT'S WHEN I FIGURED IT OUT...!
W-WAIT, Y-YOU DIDN'T...
YUP, SENPAI! IT'S ABOUT THE SEVENTH WITCH YOU'RE LOOKING FOR!
POINT
ぴっ
GET THIS, SENPAI...

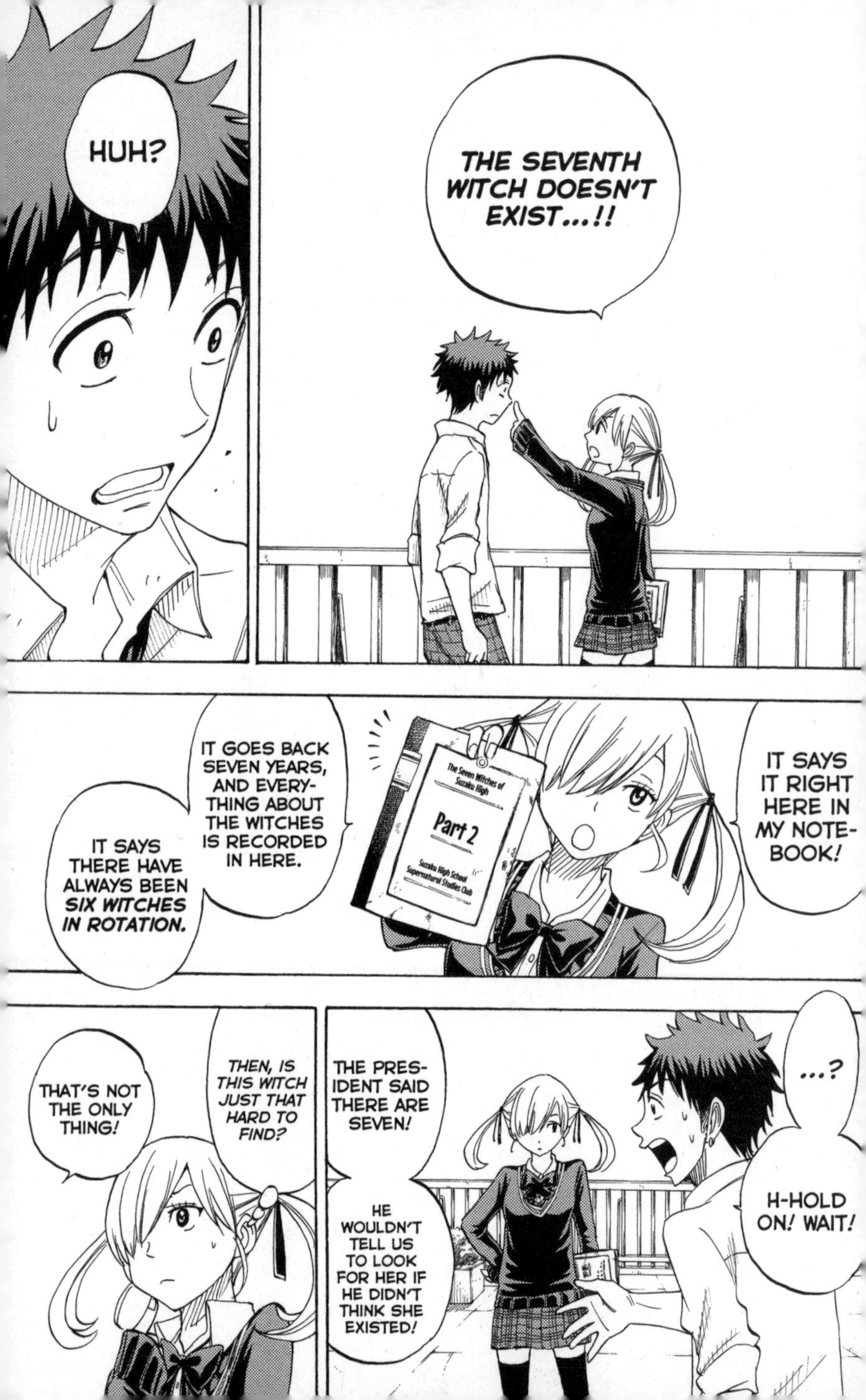
THE SEVENTH WITCH DOESN'T EXIST...!!
HUH?
IT SAYS IT RIGHT HERE IN MY NOTEBOOK!
The Seven Witches of Suzaku High
Part 2
Suzaku High School Supernatural Studies Club
IT GOES BACK SEVEN YEARS, AND EVERYTHING ABOUT THE WITCHES IS RECORDED IN HERE.
IT SAYS THERE HAVE ALWAYS BEEN SIX WITCHES IN ROTATION.
...?
H-HOLD ON! WAIT!
THE PRESIDENT SAID THERE ARE SEVEN!
HE WOULDN'T TELL US TO LOOK FOR HER IF HE DIDN'T THINK SHE EXISTED!
THEN, IS THIS WITCH JUST THAT HARD TO FIND?
THAT'S NOT THE ONLY THING!

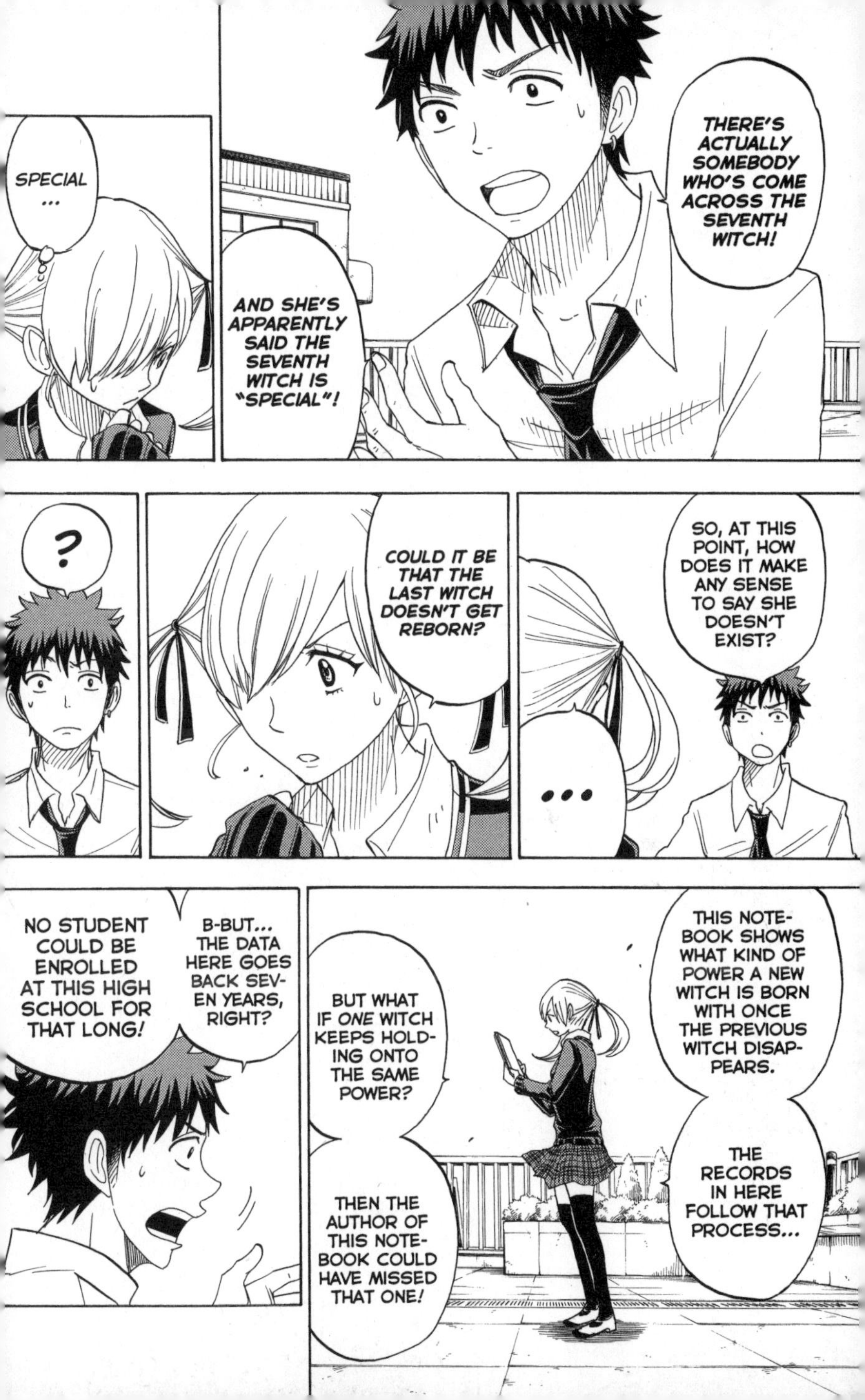
THERE'S ACTUALLY SOMEBODY WHO'S COME ACROSS THE SEVENTH WITCH!
AND SHE'S APPARENTLY SAID THE SEVENTH WITCH IS "SPECIAL"!
SPECIAL ...
SO, AT THIS POINT, HOW DOES IT MAKE ANY SENSE TO SAY SHE DOESN'T EXIST?
...
COULD IT BE THAT THE LAST WITCH DOESN'T GET REBORN?
?
THIS NOTEBOOK SHOWS WHAT KIND OF POWER A NEW WITCH IS BORN WITH ONCE THE PREVIOUS WITCH DISAPPEARS.
THE RECORDS IN HERE FOLLOW THAT PROCESS...
BUT WHAT IF *ONE* WITCH KEEPS HOLDING ONTO THE SAME POWER?
THEN THE AUTHOR OF THIS NOTEBOOK COULD HAVE MISSED THAT ONE!
B-BUT... THE DATA HERE GOES BACK SEVEN YEARS, RIGHT?
NO STUDENT COULD BE ENROLLED AT THIS HIGH SCHOOL FOR THAT LONG!

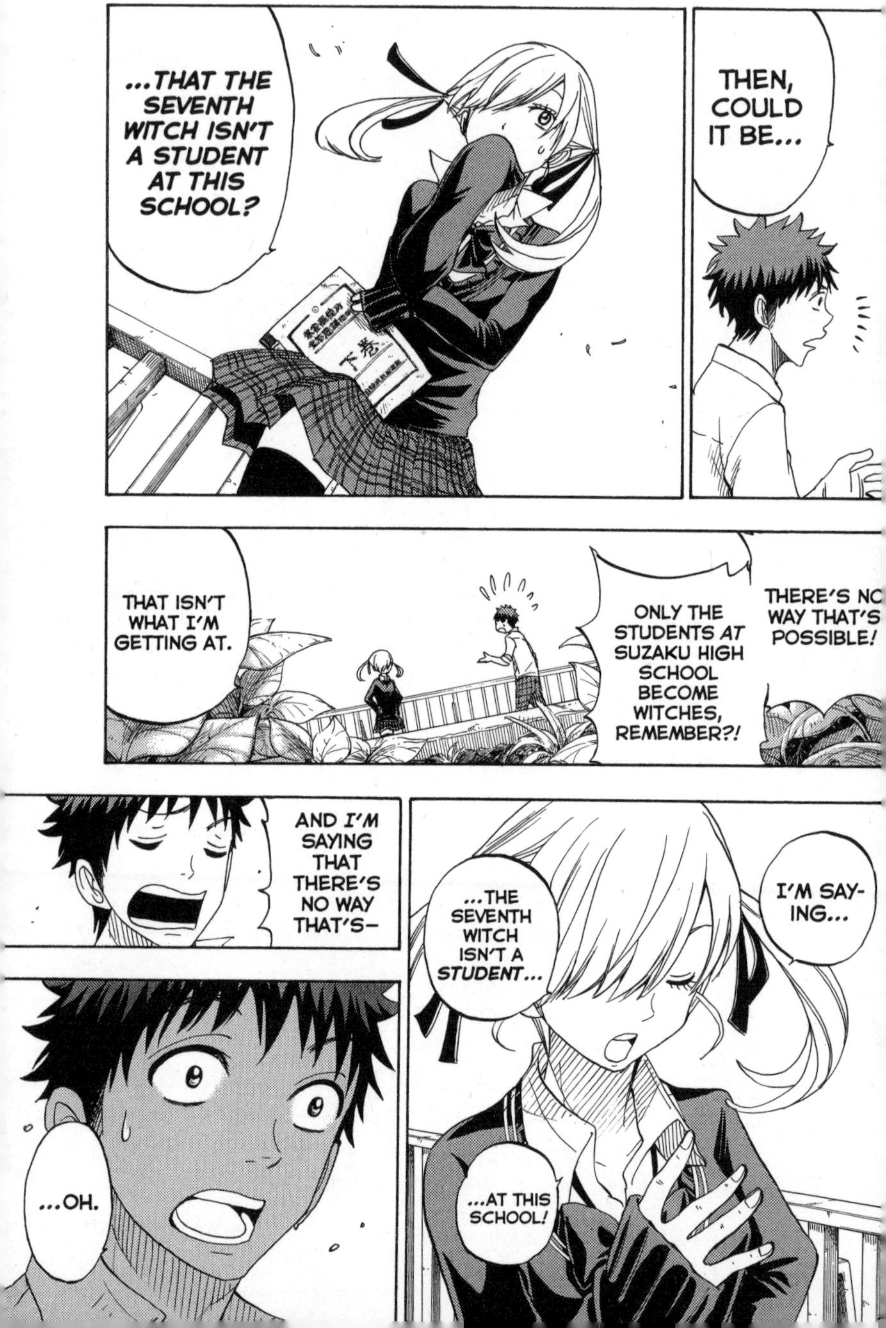
THEN, COULD IT BE...
...THAT THE SEVENTH WITCH ISN'T A STUDENT AT THIS SCHOOL?
THERE'S NO WAY THAT'S POSSIBLE!
ONLY THE STUDENTS AT SUZAKU HIGH SCHOOL BECOME WITCHES, REMEMBER?!
THAT ISN'T WHAT I'M GETTING AT.
I'M SAYING...
...THE SEVENTH WITCH ISN'T A STUDENT...
...AT THIS SCHOOL!
AND I'M SAYING THAT THERE'S NO WAY THAT'S—
...OH.

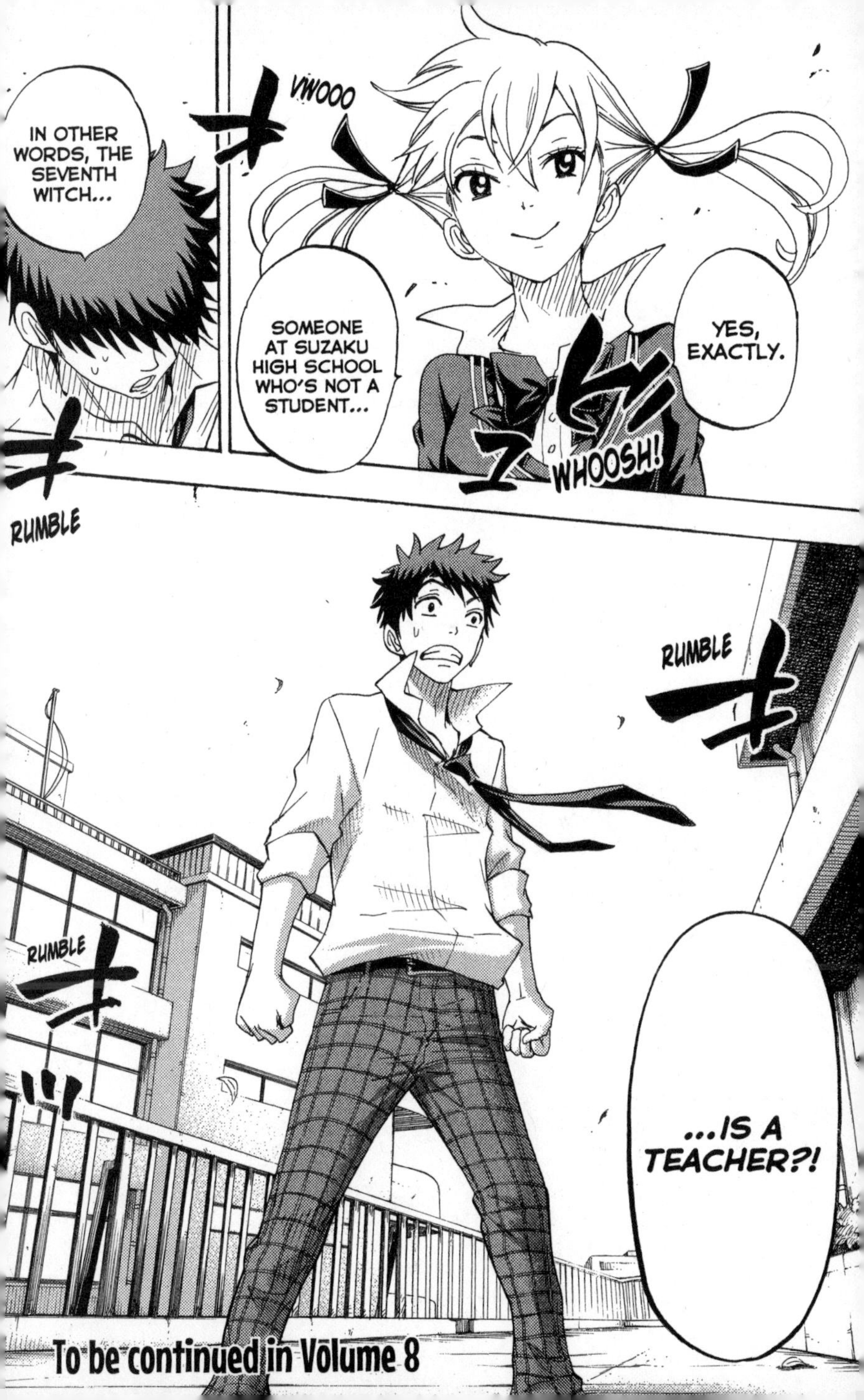
VWOOO
YES, EXACTLY.
SOMEONE AT SUZAKU HIGH SCHOOL WHO'S NOT A STUDENT...
WHOOSH!
IN OTHER WORDS, THE SEVENTH WITCH...
RUMBLE
RUMBLE
...IS A TEACHER?!
RUMBLE

To be continued in Volume 8

Miyabi Itou's Witch Research Notes File.3

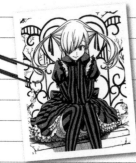

Noa Takigawa

The Retrocognition Witch
Power: Trauma

A despicable first-year! ← That's not true! She's cute.
(Miyamura)

She has the ability to see the past of whomever she kisses in her dreams.

The past that she sees is of something traumatic that happened. I wonder if she can see other types of pasts.

She's in possession of the second part of the notebook that contains information on the witches.

Why does she turn red when she sees Yamada lately?

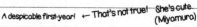

Shinichi Tamaki

"The Witch Killer" Power: Capture (Invisibility)

A special abilities user who's aiming to be the next president. When he kisses a witch, he can steal the power of that witch.

If he kisses another witch, he overwrites his current witch power with a new one.

He currently has the ability to turn invisible (invisibility).

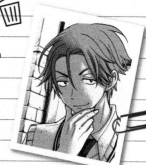

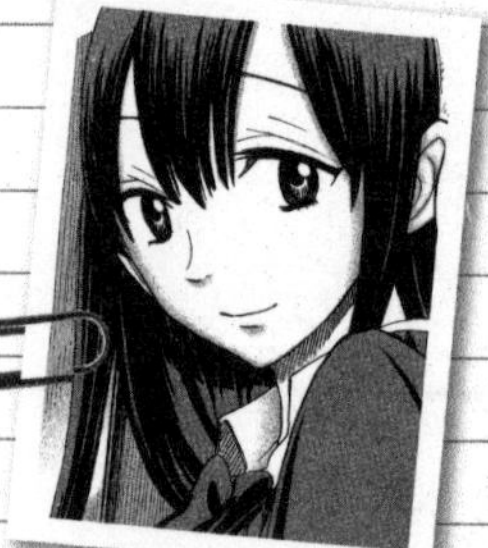

Mikoto Asuka

The former invisibility witch Power:
and current advisor to She used to have the power of invisibility
the student council president.

Her power was erased with Tamaki-kun's ability.

Why would she do that???

⭐ Common rules for the witch powers that I've figured out!

• One person, one power

• If a person under a witch's spell is kissed by another witch, the person being kissed will not be affected.

• A witch cannot put another witch under their spell with a kiss.

• Yamada and Tamaki are not witches.

• There are always six witches (or seven?).

When a witch leaves the school and loses her power, a new witch is born in her place.

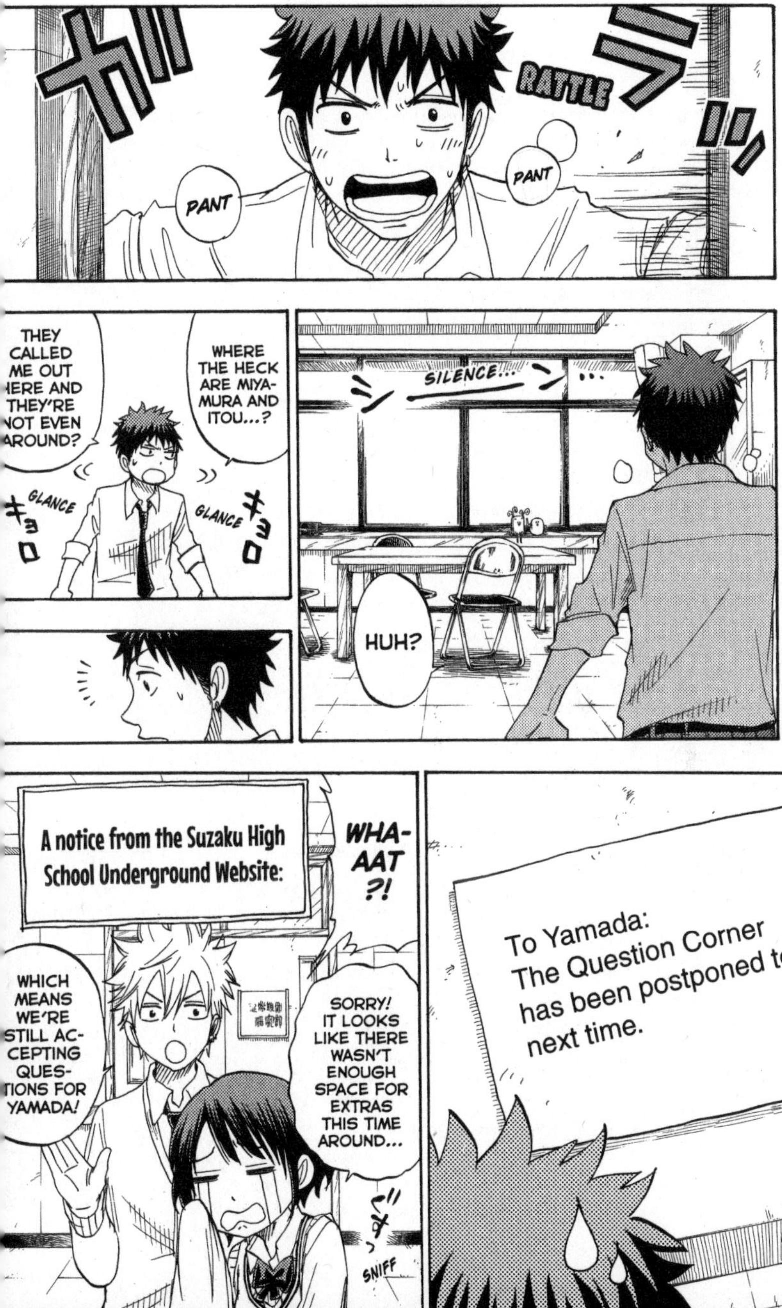
RATTLE
PANT
PANT
SILENCE...
HUH?
WHERE THE HECK ARE MIYAMURA AND ITOU...?
THEY CALLED ME OUT HERE AND THEY'RE NOT EVEN AROUND?
GLANCE
GLANCE
To Yamada:
The Question Corner has been postponed to next time.
WHA-AAT?!
A notice from the Suzaku High School Underground Website:
SORRY! IT LOOKS LIKE THERE WASN'T ENOUGH SPACE FOR EXTRAS THIS TIME AROUND...
WHICH MEANS WE'RE STILL ACCEPTING QUESTIONS FOR YAMADA!
SNIFF

Translation Notes

Karuta, page 7

Japanese playing cards that have proverbs or poems written on them. The name *karuta* originates from the Portuguese *carta*, which simply means "card." The game played with these cards typically involves two or more players who face off to be the quickest to identify and grab cards matching the proverb or excerpt of a poem read aloud by a third party.

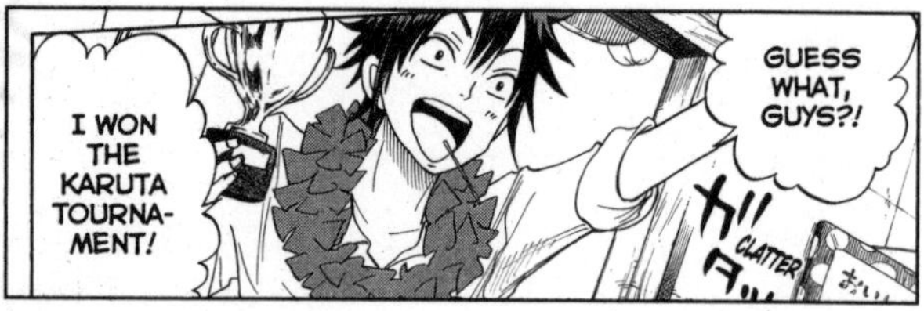
GUESS WHAT, GUYS?!
CLATTER
I WON THE KARUTA TOURNAMENT!

Dragon Daayama, page 11

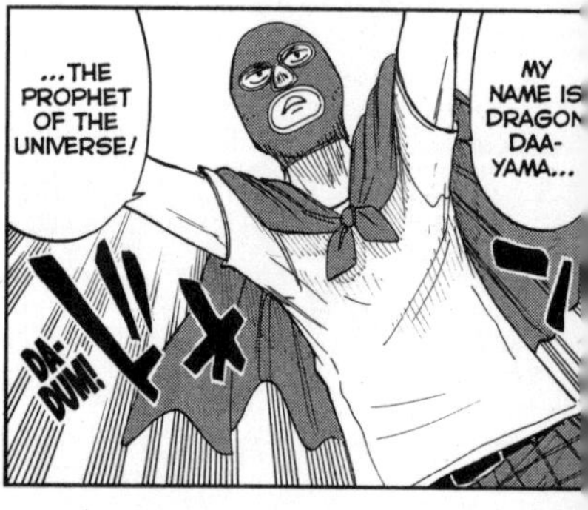
MY NAME IS DRAGON DAA-YAMA...
...THE PROPHET OF THE UNIVERSE!
DA-DUM!

The "prophet of the universe" is obviously Yamada and this is evident not only from his appearance but from his choice of name. "Daayama" is a rearranged version of Yamada where the last syllable has been moved to the front of his (Ya-ma-da to Daa-ya-ma). This is a similar construction to verlan (a French argot, or type of slang). In Japanese this construction is often used in the entertainment industry in words like *Giroppon* (*Roppongi*) or *Waiha* (*Hawaii*).

Sister complex, page 154

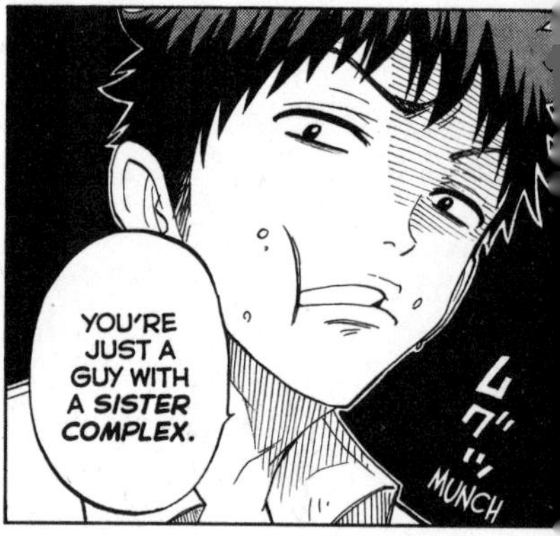
MUNCH
YOU'RE JUST A GUY WITH A *SISTER COMPLEX*.

In Japanese, complex can be attached to many phrases, more often than not to denote psychological dependence or obsession. In this case, a sister complex would be a deep, psychosexual attachment to one's sister. Other examples present in Japanese are father complex (En. = Electra complex, shortened to *fazakon* in Japanese), Mother complex (En. = Oedipus complex, shortened to *mazakon* in Japanese), and Lolita complex.

Yamada-kun and the Seven Witches volume 7 is a work of fiction. Names, characters, places, and incidents are the products of the author's imagination or are used fictitiously. Any resemblance to actual events, locales, or persons, living or dead, is entirely coincidental.

A Kodansha Comics Trade Paperback Original.

Published in the United States by Kodansha Comics, an imprint of Kodansha USA Publishing, LLC, New York.

Publication rights for this English edition arranged through Kodansha Ltd., Tokyo.

First published in Japan in 2013 by Kodansha Ltd., Tokyo, as *Yamada-kun to Nananin no Majo* volume 7.

ISBN 978-1-63236-136-3

Printed in the United States of America.

www.kodanshacomics.com

9 8 7 6 5 4 3 2 1

Translation: David Rhie
Lettering: Sara Linsley
Editing: Ajani Oloye
Kodansha Comics Edition Cover Design: Phil Balsman